The Deflationary Approach to Truth

The Deflationary Approach to Truth

A Guide

BRADLEY ARMOUR-GARB AND
JAMES A. WOODBRIDGE

OXFORD
UNIVERSITY PRESS

Oxford University Press is a department of the University of Oxford.
It furthers the University's objective of excellence in research, scholarship,
and education by publishing worldwide. Oxford is a registered trade mark of
Oxford University Press in the UK and in certain other countries.

Published in the United States of America by Oxford University Press
198 Madison Avenue, New York, NY 10016, United States of America.

© Oxford University Press 2025

All rights reserved. No part of this publication may be reproduced, stored in a retrieval system, transmitted, used for text and data mining, or used for training artificial intelligence, in any form or by any means, without the prior permission in writing of Oxford University Press, or as expressly permitted by law, by license or under terms agreed with the appropriate reprographics rights organization. Inquiries concerning reproduction outside the scope of the above should be sent to the Rights Department, Oxford University Press, at the address above.

You must not circulate this work in any other form
and you must impose this same condition on any acquirer

Library of Congress Cataloging-in-Publication Data
Names: Armour-Garb, Bradley P., 1968– author. |
Woodbridge, James A., author.
Title: The deflationary approach to truth : a guide /
Bradley Armour-Garb and James A. Woodbridge.
Description: New York, NY : Oxford University Press, [2025] |
Includes bibliographical references and index. |
Identifiers: LCCN 2024051287 (print) | LCCN 2024051288 (ebook) |
ISBN 9780197577400 (paperback) | ISBN 9780197577394 (hardback) |
ISBN 9780197577431 | ISBN 9780197577424 (epub)
Subjects: LCSH: Truth—Deflationary theory.
Classification: LCC BD171 .A74 2025 (print) | LCC BD171 (ebook) |
DDC 121—dc23/eng/20241229
LC record available at https://lccn.loc.gov/2024051287
LC ebook record available at https://lccn.loc.gov/2024051288

DOI: 10.1093/9780197577431.001.0001

Paperback printed by Integrated Books International, United States of America
Hardback printed by Lightning Source, Inc., United States of America

Contents

Preface   ix

PART 1. WHAT DEFLATIONISM IS

1. Framing the General Approach   3
   - 1.1 Deflationism vs. Inflationism   4
   - 1.2 The Dimensions of Deflationism   7
   - 1.3 On the Instability of "Partial Deflationism"   17
   - 1.4 Motivations and Methodological Disputes   24

2. Early and Proto-Deflationary Accounts   34
   - 2.1 Frege on Truth   34
   - 2.2 Ramsey and the Redundancy Theory   37
   - 2.3 Ayer on 'True'   44
   - 2.4 Wittgenstein on Truth-Talk   46
   - 2.5 Strawson on What We Do with Truth-Talk   48
   - 2.6 Tarski and the (T)-Schema   52

3. The Species of Deflationism   57
   - 3.1 Prosententialism   59
     - 3.1.1 Prior's Adverbial Prosententialism   61
     - 3.1.2 Williams's Substitutional Prosententialism   64
     - 3.1.3 Grover, Camp, and Belnap's Atomic Prosententialism   68
     - 3.1.4 Brandom's Operator Prosententialism   72
   - 3.2 Disquotationalism   76
     - 3.2.1 Quine's Disquotationalism   77
     - 3.2.2 Leeds's Recursive Disquotationalism   82
     - 3.2.3 Field's Pure Disquotational Truth   85
   - 3.3 Minimalism   93
     - 3.3.1 Horwich's Minimalism   94
     - 3.3.2 Hill's Substitutional Minimalism   102

PART 2. CHALLENGES TO DEFLATIONISM

4. Challenges to Linguistic Deflationism — 109
  4.1 Immanence and Limitations on Truth-Ascriptions — 109
    4.1.1 Immanence and Deflationism — 110
    4.1.2 Immanence, Foreign Sentences, Sentences Speakers Do Not Understand — 113
  4.2 The Formulation and Generalization Problems — 120
    4.2.1 The Formulation Problem — 120
    4.2.2 Understanding the Generalization Problem — 123
    4.2.3 Justifying Generalizations vs. Proving Generalizations — 126
    4.2.4 Field and Hill on Proving Generalizations — 131

5. Challenges to Metaphysical Deflationism — 135
  5.1 The Causal-Explanatory Role Challenge — 135
    5.1.1 Explaining the Success of Science — 137
    5.1.2 Explaining Behavioral Success — 140
  5.2 The Conservativeness Argument — 152
    5.2.1 Explaining the Conservativeness Argument — 153
    5.2.2 Responses to the Conservativeness Argument — 166
    5.2.3 Consequences of the Conservativeness Argument — 172
  5.3 The Correspondence Intuition, Truthmaking, and the Truth Property Thesis — 177
    5.3.1 From the Correspondence Intuition to Truth-Maker Theory — 179
    5.3.2 The Truth-Property Thesis — 196
  5.4 The Challenge from Normativity — 201

6. Challenges to Conceptual Deflationism — 207
  6.1 "Truth-Involving" Accounts That Deflationists Can Accept — 209
  6.2 "Truth-Involving" Accounts That Deflationists Must Replace — 214
  6.3 Deflationism and Theories of Meaning/Content — 219

7. Formal Challenges and Paradox Treatment
   Deflationism   224
   7.1 Constraints on an Adequate Resolution of the Liar
       Paradox   225
       7.1.1 General Constraints on Adequate
             Paradox Treatment   226
       7.1.2 Constraints for Paradox Treatment Deflationism   230
   7.2 Tarski's Replacement Theory and the Liar Paradox   238
   7.3 Kripke and Ungroundedness   245
   7.4 Field on the 'Determinately' Operator   253
   7.5 Grover and Semantic Inheritors   258
   7.6 Horwich's Semantic Epistemicism   262
   7.7 Deflationary Dialetheism   275
   7.8 Deflationism, the Paradoxes, and Concluding Remarks   283

Appendix: New Directions via Sentential-Variable
Deflationism and Alethic Fictionalism   287
   A.1 ASVD and the "How-Talk" NLI Approach   291
   A.2 The Merits of ASVD   296
       A.2.1 Avoiding the Formulation and Generalization
             Problems   296
       A.2.2 Emergence and Resolution of the Liar Paradox   299
       A.2.3 ASVD and the Conservativeness Argument   303
       A.2.4 Why Have a Truth Predicate?   306
   A.3 From ASVD to Alethic Fictionalism   308
   A.4 Conclusions: Accommodating Broad
       Four-Dimensional Deflationism   312
Bibliography   317
Index   333

Preface

Our philosophical friendship began twenty-five years ago, when we were introduced and discovered that we were both working on deflationism about truth—Armour-Garb investigating its fit with dialetheism and Woodbridge developing a fictionalist version. Amusingly, we also discovered that we had both spent summers working at a fishery in Kenai, Alaska, though that is a story for a very different occasion. As fast friends, we have spent thousands of hours discussing deflationism and philosophy more generally and thus have developed a wonderful, close, enduring philosophical collaboration that extends to the present.

One important element of our understanding of deflationism that emerged early on was the recognition that this approach to the topic of truth is actually best understood as one applied primarily as an analysis of language, that is, as more of an approach to truth-*talk* than to *truth*. We felt that the lack of clarity about this in the earlier literature—by both proponents and critics of the approach—resulted in an inaccurate understanding of what deflationism "about truth" really involves. This had clouded recognition of what the legitimate challenges to deflationism are, which has to some extent hampered progress on resolving them. This problem is illustrated in the inaccurate ways that the deflationary approach has been labeled—typically as "deflationism about truth" (and sometimes even as "the deflationary theory of truth"). This labeling suggests that there is some *thing* that is getting deflated. This suggestion is reinforced by the fact that deflationary accounts are usually developed negatively, by specifying features that something lacks. A first step in providing a clearer understanding of deflationism in general involves framing this mode of analysis as an approach to a *topic*, providing a distancing from an analysis of a *thing* (e.g., a property). The next step is to understand a deflationary analysis as a kind of meta-theorizing that involves the acceptance of some discourse or concept without granting the semantic, metaphysical, or epistemological presuppositions that are commonly associated with it. *Alethic* or, more broadly, *semantic* deflationism should be understood as theorizing primarily about *the topic of* truth and secondarily about *the topics of* reference and predicate-satisfaction. While it might be simpler to identify "the topic of truth" just as *truth*, thereby suggesting a metaphysical framing, we maintain that deflationists would be better served by adopting a "language-first" meta-theoretical approach. This involves starting one's theorizing by investigating how the relevant semantic notions operate in language and only later contemplating certain epistemological or metaphysical conclusions that arise from the results of that investigation. While a semantic deflationist might ultimately advocate a form of metaphysical anti-realism, it is important to note that, in contrast with eliminativists, semantic deflationists grant that there is still some role or function for the traditional semantic fragments of discourse. This is why we identify semantic deflationism with a language-first approach and emphasize that it is primarily a position on language and only secondarily on metaphysics or epistemology.

While our own adherence to semantic deflationism has largely been motivated by accepting the proposed merits of this approach to truth-talk, there is also a broader philosophical framework that makes semantic deflationism particularly attractive to us. This is the framework of a kind of naturalism that embraces physicalism and nominalism. That this framework is not a necessary condition for deflationism is shown by Paul Horwich's (1990/1998) influential deflationary account according to which the truth predicate functions to attribute a property determined by the concept that it expresses. And Michael Devitt's (1997, 2001) physicalist, inflationist correspondence theory of truth shows that our rejection of the sorts of abstracta that Horwich posits is also not a sufficient reason for adopting semantic deflationism. However, we take the deflationary approach—especially the particular kind of deflationary account that we favor—to be a good fit with the more general philosophical framework that we endorse. As we see it, the success of semantic deflationism keeps the door open for the broader framework that we both advocate.

When Armour-Garb was invited to revise the *Stanford Encyclopedia of Philosophy* entry now retitled "Deflationism About Truth", it made sense, in light of what we had written together, for the two of us to make the requisite revisions together. The result was published in 2021. While we were happy with the changes and additions that we incorporated into the entry, Ed Zalta, the editor of the *SEP*, had imposed a necessary word limitation on it. Unsurprisingly, in the process of researching and formulating our revisions, we realized that more needed to be said about the many versions of and challenges to deflationism. We would like to thank Peter Ohlin for providing us with the opportunity to develop this more complete guide to the deflationary approach to truth. In this guide, our primary goal is to clarify the myriad aspects of the different versions of deflationism about truth-talk, to highlight many of the virtues of these accounts, and to explore many of the potential challenges to them. We have written this guide with two sorts of readers in mind. The first includes graduate students, advanced undergraduates, and professional philosophers who are curious about deflationism and aim for a better understanding of the approach, including its historical development, how it fits into the broader philosophical landscape, and the challenges that it faces. The second group comprises philosophers who are already familiar with theories of truth and with deflationism but are interested in seeing how this guide maps the latter's extensive terrain and how it articulates the issues, challenges, and potential new directions pertaining to this approach to truth. This is made evident by the format of our guide.

This guide is divided into three parts. Part 1 explains what the deflationary approach to the topic of truth involves and both identifies and clarifies the four deflationary dimensions that theorizing via this approach must adhere to: Linguistic, Metaphysical, Conceptual, and Paradox Treatment Deflationism. In Chapter 1, we frame the general deflationary approach to the topic of truth by first distinguishing it from its rival, inflationism about truth. We then explore certain general themes associated with deflationism, framing it as a genus of different species of theories and highlighting the primary linguistic focus of those theories. In Chapter 2, we survey the early history of deflationism by identifying various precursors to contemporary deflationary accounts. Chapter 3 surveys the main species that fall under the genus of deflationism and explains in detail how they differ from inflationary views and from each other.

Part 2 of the guide addresses the many challenges to deflationism by honing in on each of the four dimensions common to deflationary views and discussing the history of certain important challenges to them, along with the main responses to those challenges. Chapter 4 addresses challenges to the linguistic dimension of deflationary views; Chapter 5 addresses challenges to the metaphysical dimension; Chapter 6 addresses challenges to the conceptual dimension; and Chapter 7 addresses formal challenges that emanate from the semantic paradoxes, most centrally the Liar Paradox.

"Part 3" is the appendix to the book, where we present new directions for deflationism based on our assessment of the best version of the approach for the purposes of meeting the challenges considered in Part 2 of the guide. It is in the appendix that we present, defend, and elaborate our particular version of deflationism.

Our hope in writing this guide is that readers will come away with a greater appreciation of both the various aspects of, and some of the evident challenges to, the deflationary approach to truth.

Armour-Garb: I would like to thank James Woodbridge for both his friendship and his intellectual partnership, the latter of which has been and I know will continue to be indescribably rewarding. I would also like to thank Allison Armour-Garb for her support and for convincing me that love is actually, rather than merely potentially, infinite. Lastly, I'd like to thank Isabel and Zev Armour-Garb, who remind him frequently that there is so much more to life than I could have ever imagined.

Woodbridge: I would like to thank Brad Armour-Garb for his abiding friendship and support, and for sharing his seemingly inexhaustible energy for doing philosophy with me. Our ongoing collaboration is both more fun and more productive than any solo project could be. I also want to thank my family—all of the Seeleys and, in particular, Kristin Johnson—for their continual love and encouragement. As always, thanks, Mom.

PART 1

WHAT DEFLATIONISM IS

To be a deflationist about truth is to focus on the role or function of semantic discourse (specifically, talk of what is true or false) without focusing on questions about the nature of truth. We therefore think of deflationism about truth as more of an approach to analyzing language than one for doing metaphysics or epistemology. As noted in the preface, the first part of this book explains the general deflationary approach to the topic of truth. Chapter 1 provides a framework for understanding this approach as it will be articulated in this book. It proceeds by first identifying deflationism as a genus of different species of views and explaining why these views have primarily a linguistic focus, specifically on the purpose and functioning of the fragment of discourse that involves the alethic notions of truth and falsity. Characterizing this genus requires distinguishing deflationism from its rival genus, inflationism. This is done, in part, by identifying a sequence of linguistic, conceptual, and metaphysical presuppositions that are made by the traditional inflationary theories of truth, presuppositions at least some of which all deflationary theories reject. The chapter then introduces what we call "broad four-dimensional deflationism", explores certain general themes associated with that approach, and examines some motivations for endorsing it. Chapter 2 discusses the early (or pre)history of deflationism, by identifying various precursors to contemporary deflationary accounts and explaining the extent to which they do or do not fall under the approach discussed in Chapter 1. Chapter 3 explains the principle deflationary accounts that belong to the three main species of the genus: prosententialism, disquotationalism, and minimalism. It proceeds by providing a guided historical survey of the development of each species, laying out the central details of the different members of each, and indicating both how they differ from traditional inflationary theories and from one another.

1
Framing the General Approach

Deflationism about truth, what we shall call simply "deflationism", is not actually a *theory of truth* because, first, it is not *a theory* at all. Rather, the term denotes a *genus* of which various theories are *species*. In this sense, the chief contrast with deflationism is an opposing genus, inflationism about truth, what we shall call simply "inflationism", which frames a project in metaphysics. The traditional species of inflationism include correspondence theories of truth, coherence theories of truth, pragmatist theories of truth, primitivist theories of truth, etc.[1] Second, the species of which deflationism is the genus are best understood not as theories *of truth* but, rather, as various theories of truth-*talk*, that is, as various accounts of how best to understand, and explain the operation of, this particular fragment of discourse. The fragment of discourse in question (truth-talk) can be circumscribed as the one that employs what we can call the "alethic locutions" (e.g., 'is true' and 'is false'). After all, many advocates of deflationism deny that there is any property of truth, and those deflationists who do grant that 'is true' attributes a property take this property to be a "thin" or insubstantial one. As Leon Horsten (2011, p. 557) notes, "Deflationism is a label for a loose connection of more precise views that share a family resemblance with each other." In this chapter, we elucidate a number of the various

---

[1] A newer type of inflationary view that has emerged over the past few decades is *pluralism* about truth. According to pluralism, different properties count as the truth property for different domains of discourse or subject matters. We will not address pluralist theories explicitly here, since we consider views of this kind to be versions of what is still a species of the genus *inflationism*, though it differs from other species of that genus in that pluralists maintain that there is more than one way for truth-bearers to be true. For more on pluralism about truth, see Wright (1992), Lynch (2009), and Pedersen and Wright (2018).

resemblances between the different, more precise views in order to shed light on the genus to which they belong.

1.1 Deflationism vs. Inflationism

Deflationism is a newish approach to the topic of truth developed in the 20th century as an alternative to inflationism. The inflationary approach covers all of the traditional theories of truth. What these theories have in common is a hierarchical series of assumptions about the most central alethic locutions, and the alethic concepts and alethic properties that they supposedly express and attribute. Paradigmatically, all traditional theories of truth presuppose or assume:

(i) The alethic locutions (centrally, 'true') function logically as predicates.
(ii) These predicates express "attributive" concepts and thereby serve to describe or characterize putative truth-bearers.
(iii) These attributive concepts determine alethic properties, the possession (or lack) of which is attributed in the descriptions that the uses of the alethic locutions provide.
(iv) The alethic properties attributed via the alethic locutions have robust (or substantive) natures.

What differentiates the various inflationary theories is the different accounts of the supposed alethic property of truth that the different theories provide. All of these theories also presuppose that the alethic locutions play the semantic role of attributing the possession (or lack) of the truth property (or the falsity property) to *truth-bearers*, which are usually taken to include such items as sentences, sentence tokens, utterances, propositions, assertions, beliefs, or judgments. One consequence of the assumption that 'is true' is a descriptive predicate is that there is no "meaning equivalence" between a sentence or proposition and an ascription of truth to that sentence or proposition. As a consequence, for inflationists about truth, a truth-attribution like "'Snow is white' is true" *says more* than the truth-bearing sentence, 'Snow is white', does. An inflationist will, of course, acknowledge some sort of equivalence between every truth-bearer and an ascription of truth to it, an equivalence expressed by the instances of the theorist's preferred version of the "neutral" truth schema,

(TS) [p] is true iff p.

To identify (TS) as a *schema* is to indicate that it consists of a sort of template that is composed of words and symbols, together with certain rules or conditions that serve to indicate what the "fillings" or "instances" of the template are. For (TS), those conditions specify that 'p' is a variable that gets filled in with (declarative) English sentences, that the square brackets stand for some unspecified nominalizing/naming device, and that 'iff' (i.e., 'if, and only if') indicates an unspecified *equivalence*, a combination of implication and reverse implication that is not necessarily material.[2] Understood in this way, a schema is really a sort of "system" that has the capacity to generate an infinite number of instances *of* that schema. In the case of (TS), it generates the "truth equivalences", sometimes called the "T-sentences" or "T-biconditionals". For inflationists, these equivalences are substantive and hold in virtue of the nature of the truth property attributed by the use of the truth predicate. Most inflationists thereby maintain that these equivalences require a robust explanation involving an analysis of

---

[2] We leave open the strength of the equivalence in the instances of (TS) and also the interpretation of the name-forming device encoded by the square brackets. The latter is left open in virtue of the different things that different inflationary theories take as the primary bearers of the truth property. The same sort of diversity holds among deflationary theories as well, but we maintain that, to keep the contrast with inflationism clear, this should not be described in terms of differences regarding 'bearers of the (or a) truth property', or even differences regarding 'truth-bearers', but instead in terms of differences regarding 'the targets of truth-ascriptions'. (Note: We use 'ascriptions' to keep it on the linguistic side, as opposed to the metaphysically loaded use of 'attributions'.) This is the practice we shall adopt in what follows. We discuss the diversity among deflationary views on this front further in Chapter 3.

that property in terms of more basic concepts, and certain substantive properties and relations that those concepts determine.

By contrast, a deflationist will take the instances of their preferred version of (TS) as "conceptually basic and explanatorily fundamental" (cf. Horwich (1990/1998, pp. 21, n. 4, 50)), or as simply trivial, immediate products of how the truth predicate operates,[3] logico-linguistically (cf. Quine (1970/1986), Field (1994a), Grover et al. (1975)). As a result, deflationists maintain that the 'iff' in the instances of (TS) indicates a very strong equivalence between the left- and right-hand sides of these biconditionals. They thus reject at least some of the standard assumptions and presuppositions that generate inflationary theories of truth, resisting their move to positing a substantive truth property. Instead, deflationists offer a new understanding of both the concept of truth and the functioning of the alethic locutions. For this reason, rather than offering a "theory of truth", which would amount to a characterization of a truth property, the various species of deflationism are best understood as *meta*-theories of truth, that is, as theories of truth-talk and of the concept of truth.[4] In this context, the notions of a truth property and of truth-bearers typically get replaced by the notions of ascribing the truth predicate to certain targets of application.

The most prominent species of deflationism are the redundancy theory, disquotationalism, minimalism, and prosententialism. The meta-theories that these different species of deflationism provide diverge from one another in virtue of the different alternatives they offer in place of the presuppositions that traditional

---

[3] While everyone recognizes that 'is true', etc. function *grammatically* as predicates, not all deflationists take the alethic locutions to function *logically* as predicates (e.g., prosententialists do not). We shall use the expression 'truth predicate' in a loose way that does not involve a commitment to the logical operation of the alethic locutions.

[4] Cf. Leeds (1978, p. 120), where a distinction is drawn between theories of truth and theories of the *concept* of truth, and see Brandom (1988, p. 77), where he identifies a project in which "[t]he central theoretical focus is on ... our use of 'true', the acts and practices of taking things to be true that collectively constitute the use we make of this expression."

inflationary theories of truth share. This has not always been clear in discussions of deflationism, especially in the earlier literature, where the differences were sometimes unrecognized.[5] As we discuss in Chapter 3, there are, moreover, different varieties or versions of each of these species, each offering different details within the kind of meta-theory it develops. But there are also common "deflating" themes, which unify the many versions as all falling under the genus of deflationism.

1.2 The Dimensions of Deflationism

The themes common to all deflationary views can be organized under four general headings that indicate four different dimensions of deflationary accounts: Linguistic Deflationism, Metaphysical Deflationism, Conceptual Deflationism, and Paradox Treatment Deflationism.[6] We shall use these labels in what follows always to indicate different dimensions of deflationary conceptions in general.

Linguistic Deflationism is focused explicitly on truth-*talk* and maintains that this fragment of discourse plays exclusively an "expressive" role, typically some *logically* expressive role. Since we have explained deflationism as first and foremost an approach to analyzing this fragment of discourse, Linguistic Deflationism is the primary dimension of all deflationary views. Being a deflationist requires endorsing Linguistic Deflationism. What this involves maintaining is that the real use of the alethic locutions is not to

---

[5] Alston (1996) confuses the redundancy theory for deflationism in general, and others (e.g., Putnam (1991)) have confused disquotationalism for deflationism.

[6] See Bar-On and Simmons (2007, pp. 61–62) for the introduction of the first three headings. Cf. O'Leary-Hawthorne and Oppy (1997, pp. 170–76) for similar distinctions. The distinguishing of these three dimensions of deflationism has also recently been endorsed and applied by several other theorists, typically as part of criticisms of deflationism (cf. Howat (2018), Simmons (2018), Asay (2021), Heck (2021)). It bears noting that, when identifying and applying the distinctions between these facets of deflationism, none of these theorists go on to consider what we postulate as a fourth dimension of a complete deflationary view: Paradox Treatment Deflationism.

describe certain truth-bearers as having (or lacking) certain substantive properties that are determined by attributive concepts that the locutions express, but to provide a broader logical (or "logico-linguistic") sort of addition to the expressive power of a language, by playing a special logical (or, again, "logico-linguistic") role that is typically said to be otherwise inexpressible in a natural language.[7] Part of the idea that the alethic locutions do not play a descriptive role of attributing substantive properties is that these expressions, centrally, the truth predicate, are *primitive terms*. As such, the truth predicate is governed by some form of equivalence in terms of the biconditional instances of some version of (TS) or in terms of related inference rules, between truth-ascriptions and the sentences or propositions that are their targets. This understanding of the truth predicate thus counsels against providing an explicit truth definition. In turn, this aspect of Linguistic Deflationism has consequences for Conceptual and Metaphysical Deflationism. If the truth predicate is a primitive term, this argues against providing a conceptual analysis according to which there is a nature of truth to uncover by means of an explicit definition, which thereby provides the basis for an argument against the need for taking there to be any substantive truth property.

To get a sense of the special logical role that truth-talk is said to implement in a language, consider a claim like

(1) If the Oracle says that birds are dinosaurs, then birds are dinosaurs.

Now imagine that we want to generalize the relationship indicated in (1), beyond just what the Oracle says about birds, to anything

---

[7] Horsten (2011, p. 65) describes the truth predicate as performing a *logico-linguistic* function. By contrast, Field (1994a, 1999) simply calls its function "logical". While Field is no doubt right that the truth predicate performs certain logical functions, we agree with Horsten that it also performs various linguistic functions, since it also operates in natural language and on linguistic entities, given certain conceptions of these entities.

they might say. What we want to do is generalize on the embedded sentence-in-use positions, so we need to replace both occurrences of 'birds are dinosaurs' with a sentential variable, 'p', to yield

(2) If the Oracle says that p, then p.

But, even after making this move, (2) is at most a schema, which, as with (TS), consists of a template plus rules or conditions that indicate what the instances are to be. For the schema captured by (2), the conditions would maintain that what goes in for 'p' are sentences of English, placing 'that' in front of a sentence creates a complex nominal expression, and that 'if . . . then . . .' operates as a conditional. Understood in this way, (2) generates the infinite number of instances *of* that schema.

What we want is a way of expressing something genuinely general, which we might represent quasi-formally with a string like

(3) For all p, if the Oracle says that p, then p.

The difficulty with (3) is that we cannot capture this kind of generalization in English (or in any other natural language) using standard first-order quantification, which generalizes over objects. This is because the 'p' in (3)'s consequent is in a sentence-in-use position, rather than a mentioned or nominalized sentence-position (as it is in its antecedent) that would be replaceable with an object-variable. That is, the familiar first-order quantifiers available in a natural language, for example, 'everything' and 'something' in English, do not enable us to quantify into sentence-in-use positions.[8] If we

---

[8] While almost all deflationists take the central purpose of truth-talk to provide a means of implementing a special logical role in a language, most deflationists (e.g., Quine (1970/1986), Leeds (1978), Field (1994a), Horwich (1990/1998)) also deny that natural languages have the resources for otherwise expressing that special logical role, making truth-talk *expressively indispensable*. We raise questions about this "expressive-indispensability" assumption in the appendix to this book, where we set out our own version of deflationism.

attempted to interpret (3) in terms of these first-order quantifiers, along with the English object-variable 'it', all we would get is the ungrammatical string

(4) Everything is such that if the Oracle says that it, then it.

This is where truth-talk comes in. According to Linguistic Deflationism, the primary reason for having a truth predicate in a language is because it enables us to achieve the effect of generalizing over sentence-positions by using first-order quantifiers, which, as (4) makes clear, are devices that cannot do this on their own. More specifically, Linguistic Deflationism maintains that the primary reason for having a truth predicate is that, in conjunction with ordinary first-order quantifiers, it enables users of English to achieve the effects of quantifying into sentence-positions.[9]

What we do, in order to capture generalizing into sentence-positions in the way illustrated in (1) through (3) above, is employ the truth predicate with an object-variable to produce the complete sentence,

(5) Everything is such that, if the Oracle says it, then it *is true*.[10]

This amounts to a way of capturing the kind of generalizing indicated in (3) because the truth predicate generates every instance of (some version of) the (neutral) truth schema, (TS). Since the form '[p]' nominalizes the sentential variable, 'p', it amounts to a nominal expression that functions, in effect, as an object-variable. So, 'the Oracle says it' (rather than the ungrammatical 'the Oracle says

---

[9] In addition, while first-order quantifiers do not enable us to generalize on the syntactic position of predicates, if we are armed with a truth predicate, we can achieve the effect of this indirectly. (For an explanation of how this works, see Picollo and Schindler (2018, pp. 333–34).)

[10] Relatedly, an instance of truth-talk like 'What the Oracle said is true', the logical expansion of which is 'Something is such that the Oracle said it, and it is true', captures the existential (or, less committing, "particular") sentential generalization, 'For some p, the Oracle said that p, and p'.

that it' from (4)) is the English rendering of 'the Oracle says [p]', where the latter is just a notational variant of 'the Oracle says *that p*'. More importantly, 'it is true' is the English rendering of '[p] is true', every instance of which is, as revealed in the relevant instance of (TS), equivalent to the matching filling of 'p' in a sentence-in-use position. In this way, the truth predicate generates something that functions like a sentential variable by using standard object-variables already familiar in ordinary language ('it') and the usual object quantifiers ('everything') that govern them.[11] This is standardly considered a significant logically expressive addition to the language, accomplished without going beyond the familiar first-order logical devices already available in it. Proponents of Linguistic Deflationism maintain that explaining this kind of expressive addition to a language exhausts what there is to say about the functioning of the truth predicate; its central purpose is to play this and other related sorts of logico-linguistic roles. We address some direct challenges to Linguistic Deflationism in Chapter 4.

A further, but infrequently addressed, issue that is related to some of the challenges to Linguistic Deflationism that we consider below in the appendix to this book pertains to its claim regarding the central purpose of the truth predicate. This issue is how exactly a would-be deflationist should understand the special logico-linguistic role that truth-talk is said to play in a language. We take this to amount to the question of how we should understand (3) and its ilk. We have seen that a reading of (3) that takes the quantifier as objectual is ill-formed, as illustrated by (4). It seems inadequate to leave the matter at an impressionistic state along the lines of Paul Horwich's (1990/1998, p. 4, n. 1) gloss on the function of truth-talk: "to achieve the effect of generalizing ... over sentences ... but

---

[11] Inflationary theories of truth also recognize that truth-talk accomplishes this. But inflationists maintain that truth-talk performs more than just this sort of expressive role. They take it that there is a substantive explanation for why the instances of (TS) hold, an explanation that proceeds in terms of the underlying nature(s) of the property (or properties) that the instances of truth-talk attribute. All deflationists reject these claims.

by means of ordinary [quantifiers and] variables (i.e., pronouns), which range over *objects*" (italics original). (Cf. Quine (1970/1986, pp. 11–12).) This seems more to identify what requires explanation than to explain it. What we still need, in order to understand what it is that Linguistic Deflationism identifies as the central purpose of truth-talk, is an account of what it is to "generalize over sentences", that is, to quantify into sentence-in-use positions.[12] Even saying, as in our sketch above of the deflationary understanding of the role of the truth predicate, that an alethic generalization like (5) should be understood as capturing the kind of generalization presented in (3) is not particularly informative if one has only an impressionistic sense of what (3) involves, that is, of how the devices 'For all p' and 'p' actually operate in it.

Many theorists have assumed that these formal devices should be interpreted as *substitutional* quantifiers and variables. But Horwich (1990/1998, pp. 25–26) does not think that we can make (independent) sense of this sort of formal device, and, famously, neither does Peter van Inwagen (1981). The original approach to defining substitutional quantification in terms of *truth* (cf. Parsons (1971), Kripke (1976), David (1994, pp. 85–90), Horwich (1990/1998)) yields circularity worries for Linguistic Deflationism. Attempts (e.g., in Hill (2002)) to explain substitutional quantifiers with introduction and elimination rules in the style of Gentzen (1935/1969) have also been assessed as problematic. (Cf. Horwich (1990/1998, p. 26), David (2006), Simmons (2006).) It might seem that employing alternative, "truth-free" accounts of substitutional quantifiers, in terms of "encoding" infinite conjunctions and infinite disjunctions of the substitution instances of the schemata they prefix (cf. David (1994, pp. 98–99) and potentially Field (1994a,

---

[12] In light of Quine's insistence that quantification is exclusively first-order quantification over objects, he would reject our claim that there is a further explanatory task for Linguistic Deflationism, since he would reject the ideas of "generalizing over sentences" or of sentential quantification as illegitimate. We say more about this when we discuss Quine's views in Section 3.2.1.

p. 264, n. 17), as discussed in Section 3.2.3, below), can avoid these problems. But, as we explain at several points in Part 2 of this book, they generate certain "fragmentation" concerns connected to the Formulation Problem and the Generalization Problem that we examine in Chapter 4.[13] We address this "further issue" for Linguistic Deflationism, regarding how deflationists should understand the special generalizing role that they maintain truth-talk implements in a language, in the appendix of this book.

Metaphysical Deflationism maintains that there is no substantive property of truth attributed by the alethic locutions or determined by the concepts of truth or falsity. As we have noted above some deflationary theories deny that there is any property of truth at all, while others still accept that there is some sort of "nonsubstantive" truth property. So, in general, according to deflationists, if there is a property of truth, it is a "metaphysically thin" property with no robust nature that could admit of a substantive analysis. If the truth predicate attributes a property at all, it is a disunified ("fragmented") one, as there is no shared underlying property that all of the true sentences, beliefs, propositions, etc. have in common, in virtue of which they all end up being true. We discuss challenges to deflationism that attack Metaphysical Deflationism in Chapter 5.

According to Conceptual Deflationism, the truth concept is "thin" in the sense that what it takes to grasp that concept—and thus to be competent with truth-talk—does not require much more than a disposition to accept all instances of some version of

---

[13] Partly in response to the problems confronting a substitutional interpretation of sentential quantifiers and variables, a number of recent truth theorists offer non-substitutional accounts of these devices. For example, Jody Azzouni (2001, 2006) attempts to explain the truth predicate's role in capturing generalizations beyond those of first-order logic by positing a special kind of quantifier that simultaneously binds sentential variables in nominal and sentence-in-use positions. Lavinia Picollo and Thomas Schindler (2018, 2022) take inspiration from Azzouni's proposal and introduce and advocate other notions of "higher-order" quantification to capture the special logical role that truth-talk implements. However, one might have worries about their shared strategy of introducing stipulated technical formalisms to explain the idea of "generalizing over sentences" as represented in (3). We address their "stipulated formalism" approach in the appendix to this book.

the truth schema, (TS). Horwich (1990/1998) maintains that our understanding of the truth concept consists in our disposition to accept all non-paradoxical instances of a propositional version of (TS). By contrast, Hartry Field (1994a) takes the centrality of the sentential version of (TS) to be a consequence of the fact that, for competent speakers who understand some utterance, u, there is a cognitive equivalence between u and an ascription of truth to it. Whether one prefers Horwich's view, Field's view, or some other deflationary account of truth-talk, what seems to be at the heart of the conceptual dimension of deflationism is that the meaning of (i.e., the concept expressed by) the truth predicate, as it is applied in instances of truth-talk, is exhausted by some form of equivalence between the truth-ascription and whatever the truth predicate is applied to. It would follow from Conceptual Deflationism that the truth concept does not play a fundamentally explanatory role in accounts of any other concepts. We discuss challenges to deflationism that attack Conceptual Deflationism in Chapter 6.

One general condition of adequacy on any approach to theorizing about the topic of truth, whether deflationary or inflationary, is that it provide a resolution of the semantic paradoxes, the most famous of which is the Liar Paradox. This paradox emerges from certain instances of truth-talk, such as a "simple" liar sentence,

(SL) Sentence (SL) is false,

which ascribes falsity to itself.

To explain the issue briefly, paradox appears to arise from sentence (SL) because if we assess the sentence as true, then, in virtue of the instance of (TS) for it, it follows that sentence (SL) is false. But if we assess this sentence as false, then it follows that it is true, in virtue of that same instance of (TS). So, this sentence appears to be false if it is true and true if it is false. Classically, every meaningful sentence is either true or false and no sentence is both true and false; hence, (SL) appears to yield a contradiction, which renders it paradoxical. As such, any approach to the topic of truth must address the problem that liar sentences like (SL) present.

Reflecting on the Liar Paradox, Alfred Tarski (1969, p. 66) notes that "[t]he appearance of an antinomy is for me a symptom of disease". According to Charles Chihara (1979, p. 590), identifying what seems to be deceiving us and, where possible, discovering what gives rise to the prima facie pathology of the Liar Paradox is the "diagnostic problem of the paradox". Chihara continues: "The related problem of devising languages or logical systems which capture certain essential or useful features of the relevant semantical concepts, but within which the paradox cannot arise, I shall call *'the preventative problem of the paradox'*" (1979, pp. 590–91, italics original). What Chihara (1979, p. 616) calls "the treatment problem of the paradox" involves altering natural language "in order to remove the causes of the paradox". All truth theorists, if they are going to resolve the Liar Paradox in an adequate fashion, are required to offer some form of "treatment", in the sense that they must provide a resolution of the alleged paradox presented.

In Chapter 7, we identify certain constraints that any proposed resolution of the Liar Paradox and of the other semantic paradoxes must satisfy in order to be considered adequate, whether one is an inflationist or a deflationist. We then discuss and motivate some additional "deflationism-specific" constraints that a proposed treatment of the semantic paradoxes must satisfy to count as deflationary. The satisfaction of these constraints amounts to a fourth dimension of any adequate deflationary account of truth-talk: Paradox Treatment Deflationism. We discuss various treatment proposals and the degree to which they adhere to Paradox Treatment Deflationism in Chapter 7 and return briefly to this in the appendix to this book.

We do not consider these four dimensions of deflationary accounts to be independent of one another, so it is important to clarify their dependencies. Contra Dorit Bar-On and Keith Simmons (2007), we take the linguistic thesis as the primary dimension of any deflationary view, having a priority over the other three dimensions, all of which should be seen as following from a deflationary understanding of truth-talk. On our view, Metaphysical Deflationism, Conceptual Deflationism, and Paradox Treatment Deflationism are each necessary for Linguistic Deflationism, which, in turn, is necessary for an account of truth-talk to be deflationary. A separation (and independence) thesis of the sort that Bar-On and Simmons endorse suggests the possibility of views that would amount to what one might call "partial deflationism", where, starting with an endorsement of Linguistic Deflationism, fewer than all four of the dimensions of deflationism are endorsed. We maintain that so-called "partial deflationism" is unstable. We take up this issue in the next section.

Before addressing the problem with partial deflationism, however, there is a further "breadth" aspect of deflationism that also needs highlighting. While 'deflationism' is primarily applied to accounts of truth-talk, this fragment of discourse is just one member of a larger family of discourses (traditional *semantic* discourse) that the deflationary approach would need to be applied to all together. In addition to deflationism about truth, there is what we might call "deflationism about reference" and "deflationism about predicate-satisfaction". This is because anyone who espouse a deflationary account of truth-talk will have to endorse a deflationary account of reference-talk, centered on a schema like

(R) For all x, a singular term 'n' refers to x iff n = x,

and a deflationary account of predicate-satisfaction-talk, which includes 'true of'-talk and is centered on a schema like

(S) For all x, 'F' is true of/satisfied by x iff Fx.

We are not alone in claiming this. Horwich (1990/1998, p. 130) notes that his preferred species of deflationism, "minimalism[,] is primarily the view that the equivalence schema is conceptually basic vis-à-vis the truth predicate—and, analogously, that parallel schemata are conceptually basic vis-à-vis 'is true of' and 'refers'". (Cf. Brandom (1994, pp. 322–36), Field (1994a, pp. 260–61).) So, what we are calling "deflationism" is really a broader package deal, which encompasses deflationary accounts of all three of these semantic concepts and their cognates.[14]

1.3 On the Instability of "Partial Deflationism"

As indicated above, in addition to the "broadness" of deflationism, we also maintain a "non-partiality" thesis with respect to the dimensions of deflationism identified in Bar-On and Simmons's (2007) distinction between Linguistic Deflationism, Metaphysical Deflationism, and Conceptual Deflationism and our addition of Paradox Treatment Deflationism. We call the endorsement of all of these factors "four-dimensional deflationism", making the full-package combination *broad four-dimensional deflationism*. This is in contrast with a putative partial deflationism that Bar-On and Simmons attribute to Gottlob Frege and Robert Brandom, claiming that these philosophers accept Linguistic Deflationism while rejecting Conceptual Deflationism (as well as Metaphysical Deflationism, in the case of Brandom).[15] However, Bar-On and Simmons's contentions regarding these philosophers involve mistakes, for example, with their reasons for characterizing Frege as violating Conceptual Deflationism, and by classifying Brandom

---

[14] We shall not discuss deflationary accounts of reference or predicate-satisfaction any further here. For discussions of these sorts of accounts, see Brandom (1984) and (1994, Ch. 5), Horwich (1990/1998, pp. 10–11, 115–16), Hill (2002, pp. 11, 29–31), Armour-Garb and Beall (2005a), Båve (2009a), and Armour-Garb and Woodbridge (2015, Ch. 6).

[15] Bar-On and Simmons do not consider the issue of the semantic paradoxes in their (2007), so they offer no take on whether Frege's or Brandom's views on truth would satisfy Paradox Treatment Deflationism.

as a partial deflationist, when he actually subscribes to broad four-dimensional deflationism.

Bar-On and Simmons argue for their attributions of partial deflationism on the basis of how Frege and Brandom appeal to the truth concept in their accounts of assertion. They claim that, by respectively identifying assertion with *presenting as true* and with *taking-true*, these philosophers make the truth concept ineliminable from their understandings of the concept of assertion. This is then supposed to show that the truth concept plays a genuinely explanatory role in their accounts of assertion, which is incompatible with Conceptual Deflationism. The problem with this strategy for attempting to identify cases of partial deflationism is that the line of reasoning just sketched is mistaken in the case of Frege's views and involves mistakenly presupposing a separability thesis in the case of Brandom's. But in neither case does the philosopher's understanding of assertion warrant an attribution of partial deflationism.

Even if one followed Bar-On and Simmons in attributing Linguistic Deflationism to Frege, his understanding of assertion would not yield a rejection of Conceptual Deflationism.[16] Although, in various places in his corpus (e.g., (1897/1997, 1915/1997, 1918)), Frege uses phrases like 'acknowledge to be true' when discussing judgment, and 'present as true' when discussing assertion, Bar-On and Simmons provide no textual evidence for the claim that Frege *identifies* asserting with presenting as true. This is for good reason since, as a number of philosophers (e.g., Mark Textor (2010), Nicholas Smith (2009), and William Taschek (2008)) have convincingly argued, Frege takes the concept of assertion to be sui generis and indefinable, that is, a primitive notion that is not to be explained in terms of any other concepts.

---

[16] In discussing Frege's views in Chapter 2, we explain how, ultimately, he does not accept any of the four dimensions of deflationism. So, while we agree with Bar-On and Simmons that Frege rejects Conceptual Deflationism, this is not for the reasons that they propose, and we reject their attribution of Linguistic Deflationism to him. Frege is thus no deflationist at all.

According to this view of assertion, it is prior to any cognitive kind or any other illocutionary act, both conceptually and metaphysically, and the assertion concept is a theoretical primitive. As a result, none of the proposed conditions for asserting, for example, that asserting involves presenting as true, serves to specify the nature of assertion. Since Frege does not identify assertion with presenting as true, his account of assertion does not constitute a violation of Conceptual Deflationism. After all, if the assertion concept is primitive and indefinable, then the truth concept cannot play an explanatory role in any account of it. That said, even granting that Frege would not identify asserting with presenting as true, he does subscribe to a weaker claim that when we assert, we present as true. But this still yields no violation of Conceptual Deflationism since, for Frege, 'presenting as true' just indicates a consequence of asserting and, thus, serves merely as a "distinguishing mark" of this illocutionary force. (Cf. Armour-Garb and Woodbridge (2023b).)

By contrast with Frege, Brandom does identify asserting with taking-true, which makes the truth concept, as expressed in the use of truth-talk, part of his overall account of assertion. (Cf. Brandom (1983) and (1994, Ch. 3).) But taking this to show that the truth concept plays a genuine explanatory role for Brandom ignores the consequences of his Linguistic Deflationism. For Brandom, the truth concept comes into his account of assertion only via the use of truth-talk in a linguistic formulation of the latter. But to reason from the supposed *expressive* ineliminability of truth-talk from that formulation to an ineliminable explanatory role for the truth concept confuses two different types of ineliminability. Moreover, to conclude that Brandom rejects Conceptual Deflationism misses his reliance on Linguistic Deflationism in his use of truth-talk to invoke the truth concept in his account of assertion.

Bar-On and Simmons (2007, pp. 82–83) contend that, although Brandom's anaphoric prosentential account for uses of 'is true' (see Chapter 3, below) adheres to Linguistic Deflationism, his account does not cover either his use of the phrase '*as* true' or the concept that the alethic locution expresses there in relating asserting to presenting as true. But their take on Brandom's account involves a misunderstanding of certain aspects of his project. Even though he identifies asserting with presenting as true, Brandom offers a separate account of assertion that avoids any appeal to the truth concept. He simply uses the expression 'true' as part of a convenient label for something substantive, but this does not render the concept of truth expressed by that use of 'true' incompatible with any aspect of deflationism. In a similar fashion, Brandom (1994, p. 329) allows the use of the locution 'truth' in the expression 'truth conditions', as a label for what one indicates in a specification of the content of a declarative utterance. But, as with assertion, he explains content via an independent account that makes no use of the truth concept.[17] So, with respect to his accounts of both assertion and content, there is no need to take any alethic locution used in convenient labels for these other concepts as expressing a separate, explanatory truth concept. Thus, contrary to what Bar-On and Simmons contend, neither Frege's view on assertion nor Brandom's views on assertion and content provide any reasons for rejecting Conceptual Deflationism.[18]

We maintain that any view that attempts to offer a case of partial deflationism would involve a kind of internal instability. An apparent example of this situation arises in a natural reading of Jody Azzouni's (2017, pp. 74–79) account of how different sorts of claims—those he calls "ontically saturated" and those he calls "ontically unsaturated"—get their truth-values on the basis of what he calls "truth-value inducers" (or *TVIs*). The main difference between ontically saturated claims and ontically unsaturated claims

---

[17] We discuss the challenge that truth-conditional theories of meaning and content pose for deflationism in Section 6.3.
[18] With respect to the fourth dimension of deflationism, Paradox Treatment Deflationism, Brandom (1994, pp. 321–32) defers to Grover's (1977) proposed prosentential diagnosis and treatment of the Liar Paradox. We examine and evaluate Grover's approach to the Liar in Chapter 7.

is that, while all the expressions employed in claims of the former type pick out elements of reality, ontically unsaturated claims involve some vacuous expressions (e.g., empty names).

Azzouni (2017, p. 78) is a self-proclaimed deflationist about truth-talk who endorses Linguistic Deflationism.[19] But his broader views—specifically, those that pertain to how both of these different sorts of claims can end up being *truths*—suggest a violation of Metaphysical Deflationism. (Azzouni's broader view also suggests a violation of Conceptual Deflationism, since understanding what it takes for a claim to be a truth involves more than just grasping the instances of (TS) on his view.) Azzouni's framing of the determination of truth-values in terms of TVIs (instead of the standard, inflationary-seeming talk of "truth-makers", which he himself employs in earlier work (cf. Azzouni (2010, pp. 25, 47))) at least initially seems compatible with deflationism. Something not obviously in keeping with a commitment to deflationism, however, is what Azzouni claims regarding the ways that the different kinds of statements get their truth-values.[20] As he (2017, p. 74) says, "Sometimes this is through a straightforward correspondence relation; more often, truth values are induced by coherence conditions." Azzouni (2017, pp. 77–79) claims that

---

[19] Azzouni (2006) maintains that the semantic paradoxes reveal that natural languages are inconsistent. Given his commitment to classical logic, he concludes that every sentence of a natural language is both true and false. He (2006) offers a regimentation of natural languages that imposes a hierarchy within which paradox-yielding sentences are excluded from semantic evaluation. While this approach might be modified to satisfy Paradox Treatment Deflationism, its ultimate fit with Linguistic Deflationism is unclear. We shall not discuss his response to the paradoxes here. However, as we discuss in this section, his overall approach to truth-talk already faces challenges with respect to its adherence to Linguistic Deflationism in virtue of apparent violations of Metaphysical and Conceptual Deflationism.

[20] Azzouni (2017, p. 75) uses the term 'statement' as a catchall for whatever ultimately is truth-apt. If we combine this stipulation with the intuitive schematic principle regarding sentences and statements, to the effect that an assertoric utterance of sentence 'p' makes the statement that p, Azzouni more or less collapses the difference between using quotation marks in the instances of (TS) and using 'that'-clauses in them. As he (2017, p. 75) puts it, "None of the issues I'm concerned with are affected by the cluster of issues about sentences, speech acts, propositions, and the like." Here, as is standard, we use 'that'-clauses to pick out statements.

his separate appeals to correspondence and coherence are part of what he calls "a theory of *truths*", which is a theory about how the statements in our discourse get *truth-valued*. This is supposed to be a supplement to his deflationary account of the operation of the truth predicate.

What does not seem clear, however, is how Azzouni can maintain the distinction he wants to draw between theories of *truths* and theories of the functioning of the truth predicate. He (2017) claims that all it takes for the truth predicate to serve as a logical device for "blind [or, as we prefer, *opaque*] truth-ascriptions" is that its operation yield the instances of (TS), but he correctly adds that this logical requirement is metaphysically neutral. As noted above, inflationists typically accept the instances of (TS) as well. The difference between an inflationist and a deflationist on this issue is that the latter will maintain that the holding of the instances of (TS) gets no substantive explanation. That means that the holding of the left-hand side of any instance involving the application of the truth predicate cannot have a substantively different explanation than the holding of the right-hand side. For deflationists, there are not two different answers to the following two questions, 'Why is it that snow is white?' and 'Why is it that it is true that snow is white?'. But on Azzouni's account, while 'Why is it that snow is white?' is answered in terms of the optics and the reflective properties of snow, the question, 'Why is it that it is true that snow is white?' is answered in terms of compositional principles and certain correspondence relations between the subsentential expressions in 'Snow is white' and various elements and features in the world. This yields a substantive explanation for why the equivalence 'It is true that snow is white iff snow is white' holds, contrary to a deflationary understanding.[21] There seems to be more required for and thus more indicated by the application of the truth predicate on

---

[21] Azzouni's view about how ontically unsaturated statements like 'Mickey Mouse has black ears' get truth-valued runs into a parallel sort of problem.

the left-hand side than just semantic descent or denominalization, which is in violation of Linguistic Deflationism.

Another way that Azzouni's account seems to end up violating Linguistic Deflationism is through his apparent embracing of substantive views about reference and predicate-satisfaction in his explanation of how ontically saturated statements get their truth-values (specifically, by way of correspondence relations that subsentential expressions bear to elements of the world (2017, pp. 77–79)). These views, in combination with a deflationary view about truth-talk, would violate the "broadness" aspect of broad four-dimensional deflationism. The problem with that sort of combination of views is that inflationary accounts of reference and predicate-satisfaction would yield a substantive property of truth (at least in a Tarskian way, à la Field (1972)). Compounding problems for Azzouni, his marking the difference between the inducing of truth-values in ontically saturated statements and in ontically unsaturated statements as a difference in kind, bolsters the idea that the true members of either kind possess a substantive property of truth. If there were such a property that served to induce the truth-value 'true' on a sentence, it would be implausible to claim that the truth predicate did not function to express the possession of that truth-value, and thus the possession of the truth-value-inducing property, when applied to ontically saturated statements. If it did not, it would make little sense to consider the locution to be a *truth* predicate.

Ultimately, Azzouni may have some way to avoid the internal tension that his views suggest. But doing so would require developing a suitably deflationary account of *getting truth-valued*, along with providing accounts of reference and predicate-satisfaction that are compatible with the "broad package" aspect of deflationism—perhaps by explaining them as "fragmented" in such a way that these "correspondence relations" do not underwrite a reductive account of a substantive truth property. In other words, Azzouni would have to explain how he does not, in fact, violate Metaphysical (or

Conceptual) Deflationism. We have explained the initial reading that his views suggest mainly to illustrate a general point: A violation of either Metaphysical or Conceptual Deflationism will yield a violation of Linguistic Deflationism,[22] meaning that attempts to maintain what we are calling "partial deflationism" are unstable.

1.4 Motivations and Methodological Disputes

Given the break from traditional theorizing that the deflationary approach to truth involves, specifically in making a linguistic focus primary, one question that can arise about deflationism is how an approach with this kind of reorientation enters into the debate regarding how one might pursue theorizing on the subject of truth. Sometimes this is attributed to the 20th century's "linguistic turn" in philosophy, with its focus on language, but that seems more of a labeling of the difference in the approach than a motive for endorsing specifically what deflationism claims about truth-talk. Clearly more is needed by way of a reason for adopting the deflationary approach to truth with the linguistic starting point we have identified.

A number of theorists have looked to Field's work for this motive because of his (1994a) articulation and defense of an approach to theorizing that he calls "methodological deflationism". While we will ultimately identify and endorse a kind of methodological deflationism here, it is important to recognize that Field is not labeling an approach for theorizing directly about *truth* when he first introduces this methodology. Rather, as the quotation below makes clear, he proposes a starting point for theorizing about meaning and content, which contrasts with an inflationary view that takes truth conditions to play the central explanatory role in accounts of

---

[22] As we explain in Chapter 7, the same holds for a violation of Paradox Treatment Deflationism.

these notions. Field (1994a, p. 263) describes his proposed stance on this particular inflationism/deflationism debate as follows:

> All I really hope to motivate here is that we should be "methodological deflationists": that is, we should start out assuming deflationism as a working hypothesis; we should adhere to it unless and until we find ourselves reconstructing what amounts to the inflationist's relation "S has the truth conditions p". So methodological deflationism is simply a methodological policy, which if pursued could lead to the discovery that deflationism in the original sense ("metaphysical deflationism") is workable or could lead to the discovery that inflationism is inevitable. It could also turn out that we end up constructing something that might or might not be regarded as the inflationist's relation "S has the truth conditions p"; in that case, the line between inflationism and metaphysical deflationism will turn out to have blurred.

According to Field's methodological deflationism, we should assume a starting point that does not give the notion of truth conditions a substantive explanatory role (that would require a metaphysically robust notion of truth), and we should adhere to it unless we find that it can no longer be sustained. In Field's view, deflationism about meaning and content would have to be abandoned if it were determined that truth conditions played an ineliminable explanatory role in theorizing about something non-alethic. If explanatory considerations, from philosophy, linguistics, or psychology, lead us to posit what amounts to an "inflationary" account of truth conditions, then so be it. But, as philosophers, we should be led to this conclusion by conceptual and empirical investigation, rather than taking it as our starting point.

Field's proposed methodology has frequently been misinterpreted as pertaining directly, and exclusively, to theorizing about truth. For example, Bradley Armour-Garb and JC Beall (2005a, p. 29) cite Field as the source of methodological deflationism before characterizing it as "a promising strategy for investigating the nature and structure of truth."[23] Douglas Edwards (2018, p. 58) describes methodological deflationism as the position that "deflationism should be considered the default view of truth." Adam Podlaskowski (2022, p. 1415) also misinterprets Field's methodological deflationism and takes it to constitute a policy about "how we should conduct ourselves when it comes to *theories of truth*" (emphasis added). In particular, he maintains that it advocates starting with a deflationary account of truth and inflating that notion only when necessary. He goes on to argue that truth is too entangled with semantic theories to motivate such a starting point for truth theorizing. Johannes Stern (2023, p. 6) also attributes to Field (1994a) the view that methodological deflationism constitutes an approach to theorizing about truth and goes on to advocate a similar starting point for theorizing about the nature of *grounding*. He proposes that we adopt a deflated account of grounding as a working hypothesis and then investigate whether more substantial metaphysical assumptions are required. On the hierarchy of the dimensions of deflationism that we endorse, these understandings of methodological deflationism all suffer from a metaphysical misdirection. Richard Kimberly Heck (2005) does a bit better with a more linguistic or logical orientation, but still cites Field's methodological deflationism as the target before proceeding to argue directly against the thesis that we need, and that ordinary language contains, a disquotational truth predicate. As a result of these misunderstandings, and of Field's actual focus, we still lack a direct motivation for adopting the deflationary approach to truth.

While Field's methodological deflationism does not provide this direct motivation, there is a connection between his proposed methodology and the primarily linguistic understanding of deflationism about truth that we have provided above. Field (1994a,

---

[23] See also Beall (2004, p. 207), which identifies methodological deflationism as an approach to truth-talk.

pp. 263–64) is aware that his suggested policy of refraining from a default assumption of an inflationary notion of truth conditions in our theorizing about meaning and content raises the question of why we would have a truth predicate, if not for that specific purpose. He (1994a) addresses this question by explaining many of the useful logical expressive functions that a "pure disquotational" truth predicate fulfills, and he goes on to suggest that there is no reason for thinking that truth-talk does anything more than that. The connection between this version of Linguistic Deflationism and Field's methodological deflationism, then, is that we should not assume that there is more to truth conditions than what deflationists about truth-talk would allow. This is the link to the different form of methodological deflationism that deflationists need, one that pertains directly to theorizing about truth-talk. This methodological proposal starts with Linguistic Deflationism about truth-talk, rather than proposing a policy for theorizing about a property of truth, and it further contends that we should not move beyond this understanding of truth-talk unless developments in our overall theorizing require us to do so. The task then is to provide motivations for this "directly alethic" methodological deflationism.

The most obvious motivation for adopting the methodological proposal that deflationists need involves a prior commitment to an "Ockham's razor" type of parsimony in theorizing, something often tied to a preference for a nominalistic metaphysics, viz., that it is better not to commit oneself to any substantive posits unless one must do so. But not everyone has such preferences or is willing to take on such commitments. Also, while the methodological deflationism that we have proposed has metaphysical consequences that fit with these commitments and preferences, the latter do seem to pertain most directly to a metaphysical position (something Field himself notes) rather than to a linguistic one. However, as mentioned above, while accepting Metaphysical Deflationism is necessary for taking the deflationary approach to truth, it is not sufficient. Hence, it seems that parsimony might not be enough of a motivation for endorsing the version of methodological deflationism that we are advocating, which starts with the assumption of Linguistic Deflationism about truth-talk. There are, moreover, competing methodological stances that run counter to the linguistically focused starting point we are proposing, and these stances reject the particular default position that we advocate, regarding how one should understand truth-talk.

Michael Devitt (2001) offers a contrasting methodology of this sort, one that begins by accepting the surface appearances of truth-talk and thus takes it to involve describing the targets of truth-ascriptions via the attribution of a truth property. This is to endorse the inflationary presuppositions about truth-talk highlighted above, and to do so mainly by relying on a grammatical analogy. Devitt maintains that one should adopt an alternative (what he would describe as "nonstandard") linguistic account of some fragment of discourse only if one is given reasons—in particular, anti-realist metaphysical reasons—for doing so. After all, as he notes, an inflationary theory of truth would also underwrite truth-talk playing the logically expressive roles that deflationists have highlighted. Furthermore, he objects to the order of theorizing that developing a deflationary account involves, since he sees deflationists as first positing an alternative semantics for truth-talk and then going on to draw metaphysical conclusions from that. As Devitt (2001, p. 588) notes, "[Deflationism] finds a defect in reality because of something special about language, whereas we need to find a defect in reality to motivate the view that the language is special." He (2001, p. 587) objects to deflationism's direction of theorizing and claims that "the metaphysical difference between deflationism and [an inflationary theory of truth] is explanatorily prior to the linguistic difference" because he maintains that the former is required to motivate the latter. This is a consequence of his recognition that deflationism is a kind of anti-realism and because of his general view that when it comes to disputes pertaining to realism about some topic, from a naturalistic perspective, we should *always* "put metaphysics first" by establishing a metaphysical base with near enough no appeal to semantics and by arguing from that base for a semantics. For we know far more about the world than we do about meanings (italics original). (2001, pp. 606–7, n. 13)

It is important to note that Devitt's "metaphysics first" methodology for engaging in the inflationism/deflationism debate is incompatible with the linguistic starting point that we (and he) have identified with the deflationary approach.[24] He (2001, pp. 603–5) extends his case against deflationism by attacking its postulation of a "nonstandard" account of truth-talk's operation in its core and primary linguistic dimension via a challenge to the ensuing Conceptual Deflationism that this requires. His challenge involves making a case for taking truth conditions as the central explanatory concept in an account of meaning and content.

While Devitt's claims about the explanatory role of truth conditions in semantic theory might pose a challenge to sustaining a deflationary theory of truth-talk, it does not necessarily counter a deflationary *methodological* proposal, whether it is Field's original "content" understanding of methodological deflationism or the "directly alethic" methodological deflationism that we are suggesting here. Field acknowledges that theoretical and explanatory considerations could lead us to accept an inflationary notion of truth conditions in explaining meaning, and, in explaining the hierarchical relation that we claim exists among the three per se

---

[24] Kirkham (1992, pp. 311–12, 314–15, 331–32) also recognizes that deflationism has a linguistic starting point and raises a similar objection to this aspect of the approach. He claims that deflationists need a positive argument for their first step, which he describes as not taking the truth predicate to be a "genuine predicate", but in fact they provide no such argument. Instead, the debate has proceeded "backward", by allowing deflationists to demand reasons for accepting that the truth predicate is a genuine predicate and to resist thinking that it is unless such reasons are provided. But Kirkham claims that if this methodology were implemented generally, then almost no predicate could be considered genuine, given the underdeveloped state of contemporary semantics.

dimensions of deflationism, we have acknowledged that one might challenge deflationism's core linguistic thesis indirectly by attacking its conceptual or metaphysical dimensions. (We examine the challenge to Conceptual Deflationism posed specifically by the putative role of truth (as it factors into truth conditions) in explanations of meaning and content in Section 6.3, below.)

The issue that emerges now is how one might adjudicate this debate regarding which methodology to endorse, Devitt's "metaphysics first" approach or the linguistically focused version of methodological deflationism that we have described above. While we cannot hope to resolve this debate completely here, we will note some considerations that favor opting for our version of methodological deflationism.

To begin, it is not at all clear how to apply Devitt's "metaphysics first" approach to theorizing about truth as opposed to starting with an examination of truth-talk. If we are supposed to gather up "samples of truth", the way we might gather up samples of gold or samples of personhood, to then investigate truth itself, it would seem that we could only do this by collecting some *truths*, for example, some statements or what have you that we take to be true, and then investigating what, if anything, they have in common. But consider the following representative examples of truths: a statement that the earth is roughly spherical, a statement that $2 + 3 = 5$, and a statement that Frege smells the scent of violets. While all of these statements are (or at least seem) unequivocally true, they also seem to be so for very different kinds of reasons. The first is true because of how the physical world is, the second is true as a result of the correctness of Peano Arithmetic (or, if one prefers, because of the result of applying the arithmetical function of addition to certain abstract objects), and the third is true because Frege is in a particular phenomenal mental state. It is difficult to identify something that these sentences have in common as *truths*, something they share *in virtue of which* each of them happens to be true. Also, while Devitt might be right that we know more about the world than we do about meanings, this is not necessarily an objection to the methodological deflationism that we are proposing here. The Linguistic Deflationism that this policy takes as its starting point is not really an account of the *meaning* of the truth predicate; it is an account of the operation and function of a particular fragment of discourse. This discourse is something that exists in the world, so its operation and function can be investigated directly. In fact, this seems like something that can be more easily investigated than what the true statements have in common as truths.

In support of the "directly alethic" methodological deflationism that we have described, we maintain that there are certain directly linguistic reasons for stepping back from and accessing the inflationary assumptions about truth-talk identified above, reasons that stem from certain unusual (and, to those who advocate consistency, undesirable) features that this fragment of discourse appears to exhibit. One such feature is the possibility of generating the Liar Paradox via a sentence like 'This sentence is not true'. Like the "Simple Liar" explained above, the instance of (TS) generated from the present liar sentence yields that the sentence is true iff it is not true. But this suggests that any truth property attributed by the truth predicate is one that this sentence has iff it does not have that property, which is incompatible with classical metaphysical assumptions. This seems to result in an inconsistent truth property and thus provides us with a reason for being wary of Devitt's "metaphysics first" approach, which assumes that truth-talk operates in the same "property attributing" way that other fragments of discourse do. (We discuss the Liar Paradox in detail in Chapter 7 and return to it in the appendix.) These considerations put pressure on the inflationary assumption that the truth predicate attributes a property.

Another unusual feature of truth-talk is captured by Tarski's (1935b/1983) Undefinability Theorem to the effect that no language of sufficient complexity can define its own truth predicate, on pain of inconsistency. This strongly suggests that there is something different about truth-talk compared with other fragments of discourse. (Tarski's theorem is also connected to truth-talk's apparent capacity to generate paradoxes.) This difference suggests that the inflationary presupposition that truth-talk expresses a thick or substantial concept is questionable. Another challenge to this inflationary presupposition arises from the seeming unequivocal acceptability of the instances of (TS). Language users competent with truth-talk accept them, and they do so before theorizing about either the nature of meaning or the nature of truth. They take the correctness of these equivalences to be a more fundamental or conceptual matter. This observation could motivate starting one's theorizing on the topic of truth by taking the instances of (TS) as basic and moving to an inflationary view of those instances only if one is given reason for doing so. In other words, rather than finding "a defect in reality because of something special about language", theorizing could start with an unequivocal datum, the correctness of the instances of (TS), and could move beyond that to a substantive underlying explanation of these equivalences only if there emerged reason for doing so.

The evident correctness of the instances of (TS) leads to a related unusual feature of truth-talk, something first noted by Frege (whom we discuss in the next chapter) and now sometimes called its "transparency" (cf. Blackburn (1984, pp. 226–29) and Kalderon (1997)). This is the observation that an utterance of a truth-ascription like 'It is true that birds are dinosaurs' does not seem to say more than what an utterance of 'Birds are dinosaurs' says. There is another related unusual feature of truth-talk that is encapsulated in the instances of (TS). These equivalences can be read as stating necessary and sufficient conditions for the application of the truth predicate made on the left-hand side. An interesting aspect of those necessary and sufficient conditions is that they require nothing of the putative target of the truth-ascription made (the sentence, proposition, etc. named). For example, the necessary and sufficient conditions for the application of 'is true' to the statement that birds are dinosaurs is birds being dinosaurs, which requires something of *birds*, but not anything of the target statement. (Cf. Armour-Garb and Woodbridge (2015, pp. 65–66, 133).) These considerations motivate questioning, if not challenging, the inflationary assumption that truth-talk functions descriptively.

Contra Devitt, the unusual features of truth-talk provide a reason for questioning the inflationary assumptions about this fragment of discourse and initially postulating a "nonstandard" linguistic account for it, without any need to discover any prior metaphysical justification for doing so. At the very least, they could motivate questioning the assumption that the truth predicate serves to make descriptions of the targets of its application (and therefore could motivate questioning the assumptions that it expresses a substantial concept and attributes a robust property).[25] In addition, stepping back from the inflationary presuppositions about truth-talk and investigating which, if any, of them we need to accept as part of our overall theorizing amounts to resisting the grammatical analogy that is at the basis of a Devitt-style objection. That objection turns on the fact that the starting point of any species of deflationism will involve postulating some alternative account of how truth-talk operates. But, in light of our considerations above, this is as it should be. The methodology that we recommend here thus amounts to a kind of methodological deflationism motivated by an examination of truth-talk itself and by questioning, rather than just defaulting to, the presuppositions or assumptions about truth-talk that a theorist must make in order to take up the traditional inflationary metaphysical project of developing a theory of truth.

---

[25] It thus also seems to address Kirkham's (1992) demand for a justification for deflationism's linguistic starting point.

2
Early and Proto-Deflationary Accounts

There have been a number of philosophers who have espoused theses that are in some ways compatible with, if not suggestive of, deflationism, in virtue of comporting with some of the dimensions of deflationism described in Chapter 1.[1] While W. V. O. Quine (1970/1986) is generally taken to be the first full-fledged deflationist in the contemporary understanding of that approach to truth-talk,[2] it is useful to identify the insights of various early and proto-deflationists.

2.1 Frege on Truth

Gottlob Frege is not a deflationist, nor does he even endorse a "partial deflationism", for he holds that truth is the most fundamental notion for both logic and semantics, in a way that seems to violate Conceptual Deflationism. As he (1918/1977, p. 58) puts it,

---

[1] Other than Alfred Tarski, the early truth theorists that we consider here mostly set the Liar Paradox aside, so consideration of Paradox Treatment Deflationism is not really applicable to their views, but we can assess their degree of fit with the other three dimensions.

[2] We think that this is probably inaccurate. Hartry Field (1994a) discounts Frank Ramsey as one of the first deflationists on grounds that the latter offers what amounts to a substantive account of meaning, but we think this may be too quick, as we briefly discuss in Section 2.2. We also maintain that A. N. Prior's Ramsey-inspired views in his (1956, 1971) are fully deflationary. See our discussion in Section 3.1.

> Just as "beautiful" points the way for aesthetics and "good" for ethics, so does the word "true" for logic. All sciences have truth as their goal; but logic is also concerned with it in a quite different way: logic has much the same relation to truth as physics has to weight or heat. To discover truths is the task of all sciences; it falls to logic to discern the laws of truth.

Even so, there are other points that Frege makes that suggest that he is friendly to some deflationary themes. Consider, for example, Frege's (1918/1977, p. 36) famous statement on truth-ascriptions, noting their aforementioned "transparency":

> It may ... be thought that we cannot recognize a property of a thing without at the same time realizing the thought that this thing has the property to be true. So with every property of a thing is joined a property of a thought, namely, that of truth. It is also worthy of notice that the sentence 'I smell the scent of violets' has just the same content as 'it is true that I smell the scent of violets'. So it seems, then, that nothing is added to the thought by my ascribing to it the property of truth. And yet is it not a great result when a scientist after much hesitation and laborious research can finally say 'My conjecture is true'? The meaning of the word 'true' seems to be altogether *sui generis*. (Italics original)

On Frege's view, the truth operator adds no new content to those sentences to which it is prefixed, so 'It is true that I smell the scent of violets' and 'I smell the scent of violets' seem to express the same proposition.[3] But Frege does not endorse a general version of Linguistic Deflationism, since there are occurrences of 'true' where its content cannot be so easily explained away. As Scott

---

[3] Frege's views on this are complicated. For an interesting discussion, see Heck and May (2020).

Soames (1998, p. 22) notes, Frege wishes to distinguish "opaque" truth-ascriptions, like 'My conjecture is true', from standard truth-operator-containing sentences because, in the former case, there is no sentence that lacks the truth predicate, which can be seen as trivially equivalent to it. So, Frege distinguishes cases in which adding the truth operator is redundant from those in which the truth predicate seems far from redundant, though it is worth noting that he does not go on to say how we should understand the content of the latter sorts of cases.

Furthermore, Frege holds that the reference of a sentence is a truth-value. According to him, sentences function as proper names and have the semantic role of referring, and what they refer to are the truth-values, the True and the False. (For more on this, see Heck and May (2020).) So, although adding 'it is true that' does not alter what an assertoric utterance of 'I smell the scent of violets' expresses, for Frege, both sentences refer to the same object, the True. This certainly seems incompatible with Metaphysical Deflationism, even if it appeals to a Truth *object* rather than a truth property.[4]

Be that as it may, some (e.g., Horwich (1990/1998, pp. 5, n. 2, 38, 122)) label Frege a deflationist because of his claim that the sentence 'The thought that five is prime is true' has the same sense as 'Five is prime' itself (Frege (1892/1997, pp. 157–71)). But others (e.g., Heck and May (2020) and Bar-On and Simmons (2007)) argue that Frege is not a (four-dimensional) deflationist. While, as we have seen, Frege thinks that in some contexts both the truth predicate and the truth operator are redundant for a natural language, there are reasons for thinking that Frege

---

[4] Frege's argument for why truth-values are "thing-like" is a consequence of some of his most central theses and discoveries. If, as he holds, concepts are functions from objects to truth-values, and if sentential connectives are to be truth-functional, then truth-values must be able to occur as arguments and as values of functions. As a result, they must be objects—"thing-like". For an elaboration of this point, see Heck and May (2020, p. 11).

would not have agreed with any of the first three dimensions of deflationism.[5]

2.2 Ramsey and the Redundancy Theory

The received view on Frank Ramsey is that he is the first philosopher to have defended a thoroughgoing version of the redundancy theory of truth, which is considered an early version of deflationism. Indeed, A. J. Ayer (1936/1952, p. 89) cites Ramsey's (1927/1990) article with approval when Ayer offers an account of truth-talk according to which saying *p is true* is just a way of asserting *p*. (We discuss Ayer's view in the next section.) But whether Ramsey genuinely endorses deflationism has been contentious. For example, Hartry Field (1987, p. 60) argues that, given Ramsey's views on the role of truth conditions in both a theory of meaning and a theory of the content of intentional states, he should not be considered a deflationist. Others, such as Michael Lynch (2001), disagree and do classify Ramsey as a deflationist. We will try to shed some light on Ramsey's overall theory and provide some reason for thinking that Field's (1987) contention, that Ramsey is not a deflationist, might be too quick.

Ramsey maintains that if we separate theories of truth from theories of judgment, then we will be able to see that, once we provide a theory of judgment, "there is really no separate problem of truth but merely a linguistic muddle" (Ramsey (1927/1990, p. 38)). In particular, Ramsey (1927/1990, p. 39) announces that there is no problem about what it is for a judgment to be true that is separable from the question of what it is for a judgment to have the content that it possesses. Thus, Ramsey seems to hold the view that what

---

[5] Evidently, Frege did not explicitly discuss the Liar and other semantic paradoxes, so we cannot determine whether he would endorse Paradox Treatment Deflationism. Thanks to Robert May for discussion.

can be said about truth is exhausted by a particular theory of judgment.[6] (In this, he seems to go against G. E. Moore's (1953, p. 251) views on the nature of truth, where he contends that truth is an unanalyzable property.)[7]

What seems to be at the heart of the redundancy theory is that truth-ascriptions are *superfluous* in the sense that what is said with a use of a truth-ascription can be said equally well without the use of truth-talk. But, as Peter Sullivan and Colin Johnston (2018) contend, the redundancy theory is distinguished not just by advocating this eliminability claim, but also by the explanation such a theorist offers for it. In particular, redundancy theorists hold that 'true' is eliminable without loss because there is no substantial property for it to attribute. Understood in this way, the redundancy theory of truth-talk satisfies Metaphysical Deflationism, in addition to Linguistic Deflationism.

Ramsey accepts this sort of redundancy for the truth operator, for he (1927/1990, p. 38), like Frege, holds that 'It is true that Caesar was murdered' means no more than 'Caesar was murdered' does. So, for biconditionals of the form,

(RTS) It is true that p iff p,

Ramsey would hold that the right- and left-hand sides are *meaning-equivalent*.[8] In addition, all evidence suggests that Ramsey's redundancy theory of truth is even more thoroughgoing, for he also

---

[6] As Rumfitt (2014, p. 28, n. 9) notes, "Ramsey aims to define the condition for [the truth] predicate to be correctly applicable to beliefs."

[7] Moore's view is sometimes called an "identity theory of truth" because it takes true propositions to be identical to facts. This might seem like an analysis of *truth*, which would be incompatible with his view that *truth* is a simple, unanalyzable property. But the identity theory does not really attempt to define *truth*, at least in the way that a correspondence theory does, because, first, it holds that the true propositions and the facts are the same things and, second, it does not try to explain what differentiates truths from falsehoods. For more on the identity theory of truth, see Dodd (2008).

[8] Because 'It is true that...' functions here as a sentential operator, (RTS) is not really a version of (TS), but the similarity is clear.

holds that the truth predicate is, in principle, eliminable even in cases of opaque truth-ascriptions, like 'What he believes is true' and 'Everything Einstein said is true'. We return to this point below.

While Ramsey follows Frege in thinking that for any filling of the sentential variable, 'it is true that p' and 'p' have the same content or meaning, he also recognizes certain pragmatic differences between them, along with certain other, non-assertoric uses of 'true'. As he (1929/1991, p. 12) puts it,

> "It is true that" . . . is generally added not to alter the meaning but for what in a wide sense are reasons of style [and does not affect the meaning of the statements]. Thus we can use it rather like "although" in conceding a point but denying a supposed consequence, "It is true that the earth is round, but still . . . ," or again we often use it when what we say has been questioned: "Is that true?" "Yes, it is perfectly true".[9]

Ramsey (1929/1991, p. 9) thinks that the meaning of 'true' is entirely obvious and that "the only difficulty is to formulate this explanation strictly as a definition". As he (1929/1991, p. 9) says, "Suppose a man believes that the earth is round; then his belief is true because the earth is round; or generalising this, if he believes that A is B, his belief will be true if A is B and false otherwise". This captures the meaning of 'true', according to Ramsey, but, as he notes (1929/1991, p. 9), we cannot describe *all* beliefs as a belief that A is B, since the 'that'-clause (what he calls the "propositional reference") of a belief may have many different and more complicated forms. In order to avoid cataloging the huge number of complicated forms a propositional reference might take, Ramsey notes a general point about propositional reference and offers a sufficient

---

[9] See also Carnap (1942, p. 26), who contends that even though S and 'S is true' have the same logical or semantical sense, they "have different features and different conditions of application; from this point of view we might e.g. point to the difference between these two statements in emphasis and emotional function".

condition for an application of the truth predicate to a belief. As he (1929/1991, p. 9) puts it,

> any belief whatever we may symbolise as a belief that p, where 'p' is a variable sentence just as 'A' and 'B' are variable words or phrases (or terms as they are called in logic). We can then say that a belief is true if it is a belief that p, and p.

As this claim shows, to get a handle on Ramsey's broader theory of truth-talk, we need to understand the role of sentential variables, like 'p' as used in the quotation. He (1929/1991, p. 11) claims that an opaque ascription like 'What he believed is true' can be analyzed as 'if p was what he believed, p'. As mentioned in Chapter 1, if we want an analysis that is more complete than just a sentential schema, we must explicitly include a quantifier binding the sentential variable, as in 'For some p, he believed that p, and p' (and for 'What he believed is false' we have 'For some p, he believed that p, and ~p').[10]

Ramsey extends his appeal to sentential variables and quantifiers to cover quantificational opaque ascription cases, like 'Everything Einstein said is true', a standard logical expansion of which is 'Everything is such that, if Einstein said it, then it is true'. As a redundancy theorist, one might initially be tempted to simply eliminate the truth predicate from this, but as also noted in Chapter 1, the result, 'Everything is such that, if Einstein said it, then it', is ungrammatical. Recognizing this fact, Ramsey argues that, in the case of opaque ascriptions, we often cannot eliminate the truth predicate. However, he (1927/1990, p. 39) is the first person to notice that if we restrict ourselves to propositions of the relational form

---

[10] Ramsey (1929/1991, p. 15, n. 7) attempts to explain sentential variables and quantifiers via an analogy with Bertrand Russell's account of objectual quantification, analyzing (or defining) an opaque instance of truth-talk like 'B is true' as '∃p(p ∧ B is a belief that p)'. (We have here reordered the conjuncts, updated the operator symbols, and changed the Russellian dot-notation to parentheses.) However, as we explain in the appendix to this book, the analogy with Russellian quantification results in an inadequate account of sentential variables and quantifiers.

'aRb', then 'They are right' could be expressed by 'For all a, R, b, if they assert aRb, then aRb', to which, as he said, "'is true' would be an obviously superfluous addition". In this case, no truth predicate is required because the sentence allows us to use the verb already within the embedded sentence, meaning that the consequent of the conditional is already a sentence, rather than a pronoun (e.g., 'it') that is linked to some putative name of a sentence (or proposition).

Perhaps encouraged by the success of eliminating the truth predicate in the above case, Ramsey contends that what is then needed is to uncover all of the different forms that propositions can take, so that for each we can come up with something similar to the example just considered, rendering the truth predicate fully redundant. But, again, he later (1929/1991, p. 9) notes that this would involve cataloging an infinite variety of possible forms, and the only way to avoid the infinity is to resort to a general sentential variable, 'p'. Then the general claim above could be re-rendered along the lines of his earlier (1927/1990, p. 39) suggestion, viz., 'For all p, if Einstein said that p, then that p is true', from which (since 'p' is a sentential variable) 'is true' (along with the 'that' nominalizing 'p') could be removed per the redundancy theory to yield 'For all p, if Einstein said that p, then p'. As he notes, "We have in English to add 'is true' to give the sentence a verb, forgetting that 'p' already contains a (variable) verb" (1927/1990, p. 39).

What we can see here is that Ramsey is one of the first truth theorists to recognize the truth predicate's logical role of expressing something equivalent to quantification into sentence-in-use positions. In fact, what emerges is that Ramsey actually *explains* the operation of truth-talk and what its quantificational instances express *in terms of* sentential variables and quantifiers. His view thus amounts to the earliest case of what we call "sentential-variable deflationism" (henceforth, *SVD*).[11] This deflationary

---

[11] For a more recent account that takes a similar approach, see Künne (2003). Künne there defines truth by using sentential variables and quantifiers. However, as we discuss in the appendix below, his interpretation of that logical machinery in 2003 renders his

approach relies on an antecedent account of sentential variables and quantifiers that is independent of our understanding of truth-talk. SVD is contentious because some philosophers maintain that no adequate independent account of this sort is available. (Cf. Horwich (1990/1998, pp. 25–26), but see Armour-Garb and Woodbridge (2023a and forthcoming) and the appendix to this book for further development of SVD.)

Something else that Ramsey notices is that, given his strategy of analyzing the truth of a belief (or judgment) in terms of its content, one cannot explain a belief having the content that it does in terms of the truth conditions for that belief. Thus, predating Michael Dummett (1959/1978) on this topic, and in keeping with certain other contemporary deflationists (as we discuss in Section 6.3), Ramsey holds that what is needed is a *non-truth-conditional* account of meaning and content, which makes him a deflationist about these notions in the sense of Field (1994a) discussed in Section 1.4. To this end, Ramsey offers a *pragmatist* account of how to understand the meaning of a sentence or content of a belief. (Cf. Rumfitt (2014, p. 23).) As he (1927/1990, p. 51) says, "the meaning of a sentence is to be defined by reference to the actions to which asserting it would lead, or more vaguely still, by its possible causes and effects". On Ramsey's view, a belief has the propositional content that it does iff that propositional content obtaining would result in the success of the action performed on the basis of that belief. (See Whyte (1990) for more on "success semantics" and on Ramsey.) Ramsey also holds that his theory of the content of beliefs explains why we want our beliefs to be true, viz., because true beliefs lead to the satisfaction of our desires. (We discuss the significance for deflationism of this kind of "success" claim about true beliefs in Section 5.1.2.)

---

account non-deflationary. But see Künne (forthcoming) for a version of his approach that aligns more closely with SVD.

One of the notable aspects of Ramsey's understanding of truth-talk that is in line with Linguistic Deflationism is his explanation of the role of the truth predicate as just filling a grammatical need, one that keeps us from eliminating it altogether. As he (1929/1991, p. 10) explains,

> the difficulty we have mentioned renders this [the elimination of the truth predicate] impossible in ordinary language which treats what really should be called *pro-sentences* as if they were *pronouns*. The only pro-sentences admitted by ordinary language are 'yes' and 'no', which are regarded as by themselves expressing a complete sense, whereas 'that' and 'what' even when functioning as short for sentences always require to be supplied with a verb: this verb is often 'is true' and this peculiarity of language gives rise to artificial problems as to the nature of truth, which disappear at once when they are expressed in logical symbolism.

Here, Ramsey introduces the term 'pro-sentence', anticipating an aspect of *prosententialism* about truth-talk, and contending that the reason that we cannot eliminate the truth predicate in all places is because English fails to contain the right sort of prosentences. (We discuss prosententialism in Section 3.1.)

While it is clear that Ramsey endorses versions of Linguistic and Metaphysical Deflationism, it bears noting that he still has some allegiance to a traditional conception of truth. He (1929/1991, p. 10) takes his characterization of 'true' to capture Aristotle's conception of truth as what has come to be known as the paradigm of a "correspondence theory of truth". Ramsey holds that his theory is more than just compatible with a correspondence theory of truth, but that the former captures a central aspect of the latter. As he (1929/1991, p. 11) says,

> Although we have not yet used the word 'correspondence' ours will probably be called a Correspondence Theory of Truth. For

if A is B we can speak according to common usage of the fact that A is B and say that it corresponds to the belief that A is B in a way in which if A is not B there is no such fact corresponding to it.

However, given the "thinness" of Ramsey's understanding of the correspondence that he takes to be part of his conception of truth, it is clear that his view also satisfies Conceptual Deflationism.

2.3 Ayer on 'True'

A. J. Ayer (1936/1952) is widely credited with introducing logical positivism or logical empiricism, the philosophical program of the Vienna Circle, to the English-speaking world. In embracing that philosophical perspective, he advances the logical empiricist account of meaningfulness in terms of verification conditions. In light of this view, logical empiricists reject many standard "metaphysical" philosophical questions as meaningless, making them skeptical of semantic questions insofar as they appear to ask after metaphysical relations between natural language and an extra-linguistic reality. Following Rudolf Carnap (1934/1937), they at one point maintain that semantic questions must be formulated and addressed in purely syntactic terms. Carnap himself, for example, denies that we need a truth predicate in logic and proposes a quasi-redundancy view about how to treat at least some 'true'-employing claims in logic. For example, he proposes that 'S is true' could be translated as just S and that 'If S_1 is true, then S_2 is true' could be translated as 'S_2 is a consequence of S_1.'

While Carnap (1934/1937) contends that we do not need a truth predicate in, or for, *logic*, Ayer (1936/1952) espouses a thoroughgoing, Ramsey-inspired redundancy theory of truth-talk. He was an early advocate of the method of approaching the topic of truth from a meta-theoretical perspective and of embracing a form of Linguistic Deflationism, rejecting the traditional issue of giving a theory of truth as a pseudo-problem. He (1936/1952, p. 87) argues that "to ask 'What is truth?' is to ask for . . . a translation of '(the proposition) p is true.'" The "translation" or analysis that he (p. 88) provides of the latter involves the idea that

> in all sentences of the form 'p is true', the phrase 'is true' is logically superfluous. When, for example, one says that the proposition 'Queen Anne is dead' is true, all that one is saying is that Queen Anne is dead. And similarly, when one says that the proposition 'Oxford is the capital of England' is false, all that one is saying is that Oxford is not the capital of England. Thus, to say that a proposition is true is just to assert it, and to say that a proposition is false is just to assert its contradictory.

Here Ayer describes uses of a truth predicate as redundant, embracing a meaning equivalence between the two sides of the relevant instances of (TS). There are, however, at least two concerns to note about Ayer's analysis. The first is that Ayer is rather imprecise and cavalier about his use of sentential variables like 'p', letting them work both nominally (as in 'p is true') and sententially (via his claim that 'is true' is superfluous), that is, as standing in for both a mention and a use of a sentence. He also seems to have offered an account of 'true' that ties its use specifically to assertion. But this is to neglect the role that 'true' can play in other, non-assertoric sorts of speech acts, such as in the question, 'Is that true?' or in the command, 'Make that true!' (or, more colloquially, 'Make it so!'). (Cf. Brandom (1988).) In addition, in contrast with Ramsey, Ayer does not explain how to analyze cases of truth-talk that are not "transparent", such as 'What they said is true' or 'Everything Einstein said is true'. Ayer does, however, consider the issue of certain sentences that employ the notion of truth in a nominal form, noting (1936/1952, p. 89),

> There are sentences . . . in which the word 'truth' seems to stand for something real; and this leads the speculative philosopher

to enquire what this "something" is. Naturally he fails to obtain a satisfactory answer, since his question is illegitimate. For our analysis has shown that the word 'truth' does not stand for anything in the way which such a question requires.

Here Ayer seems to extend his redundancy theory to involve an explicit endorsement of Metaphysical Deflationism via a denial that there is any truth property, making any question as to what 'truth' stands for illegitimate. As we will see in Section 3.3, not all deflationists go as far as Ayer and deny that there is any truth property. For example, Paul Horwich (1990/1998) claims that 'is true' does attribute a property, endorsing a suggestion by Field (1992) and classifying it as a "logical property". In some ways, this may be compatible with Ayer's view, since Horwich seems mostly to be arguing against any view that purports to reveal a substantive *nature* for truth. Like Ayer, in this respect, and in line with Metaphysical Deflationism, Horwich and Field both deny that there is any such nature to truth, a nature of the sort that inflationary theorists aim to discover or reveal.

2.4 Wittgenstein on Truth-Talk

Ludwig Wittgenstein's (1953) insight, that not every predicative expression plays the same role, viz., attributing a property, is one of the ideas that paved the way (independently) for the present authors' work on deflationism. Horwich has also referenced Wittgenstein, in introducing his version of the approach. As Horwich (1990/1998, p. 2) says,

> Unlike most other predicates, 'is true' is not used to attribute to certain entities (i.e. statements, beliefs, etc.) an ordinary sort of property—a characteristic whose underlying nature will account for its relations to other ingredients of reality. Therefore, unlike

most other predicates, 'is true' should not be expected to participate in some deep theory of that to which it refers—a theory that articulates general conditions for its application. Thus its assimilation to superficially similar expressions is misleading. The role of truth is not what it seems.

Moreover, as John Searle (2006, p. 545) notes, discussing later Wittgenstein's work,

On his account, we should not think of the philosophically troubling words, such as "meaning," "truth," "causation," and "intention," as representing phenomena in the world. We should think of them rather as pieces in language games, where we understand the piece when we understand the sort of moves it can be used to make.

Many philosophers take early Wittgenstein (1921/1961) to advocate a correspondence theory of truth. (See Horwich (2016), for more on this reading.) Whether it is correct to do so is irrelevant for present purposes, for there are several reasons for thinking that later Wittgenstein's (1953) views on truth-talk have a strong deflationary flavor (cf. Horwich (2016, pp. 99–100)). For a start, Wittgenstein (1953, §136) notes that "p is true = p" and "p is false = not-p", so that ascribing truth and falsity to a statement is equivalent to asserting that very proposition (or the negation of that proposition, if one were to ascribe falsity to it). On the basis of this, a number of philosophers, for example, G. P. Baker and P. M. S. Hacker (1980, p. 317), Michael Dummett (1978, pp. xxxiv, 317), Michael Forster (2004, pp. 60–64), Saul Kripke (1982, p. 86), Rupert Read (2000, p. 75), Graham Priest (2004, p. 210), and Michael Williams (2004, p. 268) and (2009, pp. 64, 144), all take Wittgenstein's observation to amount to a redundancy theory of truth-talk. Second, Wittgenstein is aware of Ramsey's views on a number of matters, as is evident from the fact that he credits Ramsey in the preface to his (1953) for greatly influencing his thinking. Moreover, in manuscripts from the 1930s, Wittgenstein also says the following: "What he says is true = Things are as he says" (Wittgenstein (1934/1974), §79, p. 123) and "The word 'true' is used in contexts such as 'What he says is true', but that says the same thing as 'He says "p", and p is the case'" (Wittgenstein (1937/2005), p. 61). Both of these claims also have something of a Ramseyan flavor to them.

Given all of this, Wittgenstein's views seem to be in line with both Linguistic and Metaphysical Deflationism. Moreover, for later Wittgenstein, the truth concept is given no important role in accounts of anything else. This is in line with the Conceptual Deflationism that deflationary views endorse and the resulting thesis that competence with other concepts does not require a prior possession of the truth concept. So it seems that later Wittgenstein's views on truth-talk comport with many of the dimensions of deflationism, which, according to later Wittgenstein (and many contemporary deflationists), go hand in hand with a use-based understanding of meaning. (We discuss the connection between deflationary views and use-based theories of meaning in Section 6.3.) Despite the significant amount of evidence suggesting that later Wittgenstein adopts an early (proto-)version of deflationism, Nicolleta Bartunek (2019) argues that in his (1953) Wittgenstein returns to his "pre-Tractarian" view and, hence, that later Wittgenstein does not endorse a form of deflationism. We leave it to the (interested) reader to decide who is right.

2.5 Strawson on What We Do with Truth-Talk

P. F. Strawson's views on truth-talk emerge most fully in his debate about truth with J. L. Austin. The Austin-Strawson debate appeared as a pair of talks, one for and one against Austin's correspondence theory of truth. We shall focus on Strawson's positive proposal for what appears to be a Ramsey-style approach to truth-talk, viz., a proto-deflationary account. Indeed, in an earlier paper, Strawson (1949, p. 83) notes that his positive thesis about truth-talk is an elaboration of Ramsey's view.

Like Austin, Strawson (1950) focuses on how we use the truth predicate, and, akin to some of Ramsey's work, he maintains that the statement made by an assertoric utterance of 'p' is the very same one that is made by an utterance of "'p' is true". But Strawson goes further than Ramsey's recognition of differences of style and emphasis between 'p' and 'it is true that p' and maintains that we use the two sentences for very different purposes. Strawson (1949) and (1950) both endorse a *performative* view of truth-talk, so that a use of a 'true'-employing sentence has important non-assertoric functions. On Strawson's view, to the extent that one makes a statement when one utters 'S is true', the only statement made is the same one that would be made by uttering the sentence, S, on its own. However, when we utter the former 'true'-employing sentence, we also perform other speech acts beyond just (re-)asserting what an assertoric utterance of S would state.

Following Ramsey, Strawson (1949) maintains that utterances of the following sentences make the same statement,

(A) Snow is white.
(B) 'Snow is white' is true. (or: That is true.)

Strawson's (1949) claim, that an utterance of (B) does more than simply reassert the statement that an utterance of (A) makes, does not amount to an endorsement of the kind of naive reading of the surface grammar of sentences employing 'is true' that underwrites the inflationary presuppositions about truth-talk. In criticizing the recently emerged "semantic conception of truth", Strawson denies that an utterance of (B) makes a "meta-statement" about (A) or even about what (A) says. On his view, (B) does not make any statement "in itself"; the truth predicate plays no descriptive role. What an utterance of (B) accomplishes, beyond making the same statement that an utterance of (A) would make, is an endorsement or confirmation of that statement.

Strawson (1949, p. 91) compares 'That is true' with 'Ditto', stating,

> When somebody has made an assertion previously, my saying 'Ditto' acquires a point, has an occasion: and, if you like, you may say that I am now making a statement, repeating in a manner, what the speaker said. But I am not making an additional statement.... It would perhaps be better to say that my utterance is not a statement at all, but a linguistic performance.

He (p. 93) continues: "In using such expressions we are confirming, underwriting, admitting, agreeing with, what someone has said". So, for Strawson (1949), if someone were to assert something that you agreed with, and you wished to express your confirmation of, or agreement with, the statement that was made, your utterance of 'That is true' or 'What you said is true' would accomplish this. It would not constitute a statement about the statement you agreed with, nor would it amount to a description of yourself as agreeing. What such an instance of truth-talk would constitute is a non-assertoric linguistic performance of confirming, etc. without saying that you are doing so. Strawson (1950), while responding to Austin, reiterates his claim that the main point of uttering (B) is to perform a speech act of confirming or agreeing with (A), but he also states that when we make a truth-ascription, we are not *just* confirming; we are also reasserting what we are confirming, which suggests that part of what we are doing when we utter a declarative 'truth'-employing sentence is asserting.

In order for Strawson (1949) to hold that when we utter 'S is true' with the right force, we perform the speech act of endorsing a statement that was made, he needs it to be the case that a prior agent assertorically uttered the sentence, S, to which the truth predicate is now being applied, so that we have something there to agree with or confirm. He takes this purported fact to explain why some are incorrectly tempted to conclude that, in a truth-ascription, we attribute a property to what was said (or worse, to the sentence uttered). Strawson (1949) denies that we actually attribute any such property in those circumstances. Rather than using 'is true' to say something about the statement made by the sentence to which truth appears to be attributed, we are signaling our endorsement of the statement made by a previous (or even just a possible) assertoric utterance of that very sentence. In this way, Strawson (1949) endorses a version of Metaphysical Deflationism. Moreover, by focusing on the role of the truth predicate in standard direct truth-ascriptions, he makes the point, as against correspondence theories (e.g., like the sort that Austin advocates), that we ought not to theorize about a property of truth by comparing language to the world. Instead, we ought to try to understand truth-talk by considering how the truth predicate is used within a given discourse. Strawson (1949) thus rejects the idea of trying to understand a property of truth by focusing on some form of representation, and he (1949, p. 84) explicitly denies that there is any property of truth. As he says (p. 84), "Truth is not a property of symbols; for it is not a property".

As noted above, Strawson rejects any descriptive role for the truth predicate and offers a performative view of truth-talk according to which the adjective 'true' functions as an illocutionary device. Thus, for Strawson, the truth predicate functions merely as an expressive device, rather than as a descriptive one, which seems to be in line with Linguistic Deflationism. Moreover, like Ramsey, Strawson is committed to the view that any statement made with an utterance that includes the truth predicate can be made with an utterance that does not. So, for example, were one to utter a sentence like 'Everything Einstein said is true', the utterance would get paraphrased by Strawson as something like 'Einstein has made some statements. I affirm them all'. (Cf. Strawson

(1949, p. 93).) What is central to Strawson's performative view is that when one utters such a sentence token, one does not *say* that one affirms Einstein's statements; rather, one performs the act of affirming Einstein's statements. That is, one conveys the "implicit meta-statement" that Einstein has made some statements, and one performs the speech act of affirming the statements that he made. As Strawson (1949, p. 93) says, an opaque truth-ascription is a device for affirming a story (or some statements) that someone has told (made) without explicitly retelling the story (or repeating the statements).

Soames (1998, pp. 236–37) argues that this has the unfortunate consequence that even if some of what Einstein said is false, Strawson's analysis of 'Everything Einstein said is true' would still come out as true, since Einstein has, indeed, made some statements. We understand Soames's criticism here, but it seems that there is a response available to Strawson: 'Everything Einstein said is true' would come out as true, on Strawson's analysis, only if truth-ascriptions like this made no statement beyond the implicit meta-statement that Einstein made some statements (and then performed the speech act of affirming them). While Strawson (1949) does claim that no other *meta*-statement gets made via an utterance of the 'true'-employing generalization, his (1949) and (1950) general view includes the thesis that truth-ascriptions also reassert what they confirm. Thus, the falsity of any of Einstein's statements would make the 'true'-employing generalization false as well on Strawson's analysis; hence, Soames's criticism fails.

2.6 Tarski and the (T)-Schema

Although we, along with many other theorists (e.g., Douglas Patterson (2012), Jeffrey Ketland (1999), Donald Davidson (1999, 1990), Hilary Putnam (1983, 1978)), would balk at the claim that Alfred Tarski should be considered a deflationist, or that his formal work on truth (cf. Tarski (1935a/1983) and (1944)) yields deflationary theories, there is no denying the influence his work has had on deflationism. Some early deflationists, such as Quine (1970/1986) and Stephen Leeds (1978), whose "disquotational" accounts we discuss in Section 3.2, are quite explicit about taking inspiration from Tarski's work in developing their views. Horwich (1982, p. 182) introduces the term 'deflationist' as a label for a kind of "redundancy theory which ... contends that Tarski's schema [given as "('p' is true iff p)"] is quite sufficient to capture the concept [of truth]." Leon Horsten (2011, p. 1) describes early deflationism as being associated with a theory ("disquotationalism") that has "its origins in Tarski's work". Even certain critics of deflationism have linked it with Tarski. For example, Putnam (1983/1994, 1985), identifies deflationists as theorists who "refer to the work of Alfred Tarski and to the semantical conception of truth" and who take Tarski's work "as a solution to the philosophical problem of truth".

As a sketch of the part of Tarski's work that has influenced deflationism, we can say that his project is to provide a means of defining truth predicates for formalized languages, where the definition produced satisfies both the criterion of material adequacy and the conditions of formal correctness that he specifies. The latter conditions have to do with exactly specifying the structure of the formal language to which the truth predicate is to apply, and defining the semantic terms (such as 'true') that apply to items from that object-language in an essentially (logically) richer metalanguage that contains it, in a way that blocks the inconsistency that natural languages appear to manifest in the Liar Paradox.[12]

Tarski is able to develop a method for defining a truth predicate that not only satisfies the conditions of formal correctness but also turn out to satisfy the criterion of material adequacy he identifies (Tarski (1944, pp. 347–53)). This criterion is intended to ensure that the definition captures the central meaning of the conception

---

[12] We discuss some of the main elements of Tarski's approach to the Liar Paradox in Chapter 7.

of truth that we actually have, rather than defining some new notion (1944, p. 341). The criterion he offers (what has come to be called "Convention (T)") is that of implying all "equivalences of the form (T)".

(T) X is true iff p,

where 'X' gets replaced by a name of a sentence from the object-language *for* which the truth predicate is being defined, and 'p' gets replaced by a sentence that is a translation of that sentence in the metalanguage *in* which the truth predicate is being defined (1944, p. 344). Using the unformalized English sentence 'Birds are dinosaurs' for illustration, the instance of Tarski's (T)-schema for this case (what has come to be called the "(T)-sentence" or "(T)-biconditional" for it) is

'Birds are dinosaurs' is true iff birds are dinosaurs.

As should be obvious, the (T)-schema is the original version of the neutral schema, (TS), mentioned in Chapter 1.

A standard way of understanding what Tarski accomplishes on this front is due to Field (1972). Field claims that Tarski shows how the notion of truth can be reduced formally to more basic semantic notions, which Field lumps together under the label "primitive denotation". He then provides accounts of primitive denotation without employing any semantic terms. (Simplified examples of Tarskian definitions are given in Putnam (1978, pp. 10–13); Soames (1984, pp. 416–17); David (1994, pp. 110–15).) The simplicity of the (T)-sentences and the "non-metaphysical" requirements of Tarski's machinery for defining them have made his work attractive to some logical empiricists (e.g., Carnap, after 1935), as well as to theorists developing deflationary views.

Seeing Tarski's work as even more closely connected with deflationism arguably traces back to Field's (1972) critique of Tarski's work on defining truth. There Field claims that while Tarski shows how to reduce truth to primitive denotation, he does not give an account of primitive denotation that meets physicalist theorizing standards. Field notes that what Tarski provides on this front are just "list-like" accounts that state for each name or predicate (from the language for which the truth predicate is being defined) what object or set of objects it denotes. Field (1972, pp. 370–73) explains that this sort of account would not underwrite a reductive naturalistic/physicalist analysis, but such an account could be attained by supplementing the Tarskian machinery with causal accounts of reference and satisfaction (i.e., of primitive denotation). In an early deflationist response to Field, Leeds (1978), elaborating on a point from Quine (1970/1986), claims that the utility of the truth predicate is exhausted by its logically expressive role, meaning no physicalist analysis of it is required, since an account of it with "Tarskian" list-like definitions at its base was sufficient for it to perform its logical functions. Leeds thus comes close to claiming that Field's reading of Tarski makes the latter out as a deflationist, but that the sort of account that he provides is exactly what we should endorse. Soames (1984, p. 429) suggests this even more strongly by responding to Field's critique of Tarski with the counter, "What does seem right about Tarski's approach is its deflationist character."

More recently, Horwich (2003, p. 3) argues that his own brand of deflationism is "very close to the account offered by Alfred Tarski" in (1935a/1983). Horwich attributes to Tarski the view that one's truth theory should amount to nothing more than a generalization of the equivalence instances. He further claims that, like Tarski, his minimalist theory of truth-talk captures the correspondence intuition without relying on questionable notions like *correspondence* or *reality* or *facts*. (For more on Horwich's response to the correspondence intuition, see Section 5.2.1.) But there are also differences between the two theories. One difference between them involves their choices of the primary targets of truth-ascriptions: sentences, for Tarski, and propositions, for Horwich. Another primary difference between the two theories turns on the status they afford to the instances of their respective equivalence schemata. For Tarski (1944, p. 344), his (T)-schema provides a criterion of adequacy for a formal theory of truth. For Horwich (1990/1998, p. 10), the instances of the propositional version of (TS) he prefers, the equivalence schema

(E) <p> is true iff p,

where '<p>' symbolizes 'the proposition that p' (making this just a notational variant, in Horwich's (1990/1998, p. 6) view, of the schema 'It is true *that p* iff *p*'), exhaust what can be said about the concept of *truth* and about the role of the truth predicate. Thus, while the instances of (T) amount to *theorems* for Tarski, for Horwich, the propositional instances of (E) are the *axioms* in his theory of truth. Hence, whereas Tarski offers a definition of truth-in-L, for some language, L, Horwich chooses to axiomatize the notion of truth using the instances of (E).

Deflationists and inflationists alike recognize the legitimacy and importance of Tarski's (T)-schema and the various versions of (TS) that are its descendants, such as (E) (or, as we will call it later, "(ES)") and the "disquotational schema",

(DS) 'p' is true iff p.

Without taking Tarski himself as a deflationist, it seems fair to say that his work provides a basis for distinguishing between deflationary and inflationary views as done in Chapter 1, viz., in terms of what status they assign to the instances of their preferred version of (TS). We return to Tarski's work in Chapter 7, where we discuss deflationism and the Liar Paradox, and we discuss Horwich's views further in Chapters 3 and 7.

3
The Species of Deflationism

Recall the collection of assumptions or presuppositions shared by most traditional inflationary theories (e.g., correspondence theories, coherence theories, pragmatist theories, and primitivist theories) noted in Chapter 1. These assumptions or presuppositions can be ordered in an expanding sequence as follows:

(i) The alethic locutions (centrally, 'true') function logically as predicates.
(ii) These predicates express "attributive" concepts and thereby serve to describe or characterize putative truth-bearers.
(iii) These attributive concepts determine alethic properties the possession (or lack) of which is attributed in the descriptions that the uses of the alethic locutions provide.
(iv) The alethic properties attributed via the alethic locutions have robust (or substantive) natures.

The traditional, inflationary theories of truth differ from one another mainly in the different accounts they gave of the substantive properties that they assume the alethic locutions function to attribute. The various species of deflationism take a different approach to the topic of truth that involves rejecting, at different stages in the above sequence, the presuppositions made by traditional (inflationary) theories. What is not in question for inflationary theories becomes specific points of contention for the various species of deflationism. Locating these contentions relative to the expanding sequence of (i)–(iv) provides a useful way of organizing discussion of the various species of deflationism, namely, in terms of where a given species dissents (in most cases, thereby also rejecting the presuppositions that follow as well) from the inflationary assumptions. Placing the different deflationary theories along this sort of "axis" sheds light on how each contrasts with various forms of inflationism (including how most of the former are primarily accounts of truth-*talk*, rather than theories of *truth*), as well as how the different deflationary accounts relate to one another.

To elaborate on the relation between rejections of the inflationary presuppositions and the dimensions of deflationism, note that anyone rejecting (i) is committed to rejecting (ii)–(iv) as well. Such a theorist would thereby accept Conceptual and Metaphysical Deflationism, which are necessary for Linguistic Deflationism.[1] A theorist who accepts (i) but rejects (ii) must also reject (iii) and (iv), since, if one maintains that the truth predicate is not in the business of performing a descriptive role, one could not endorse (iii) or (iv). Thus, while this stance would require more explanation for the rejection of (ii) given the acceptance of (i), such a position would also satisfy Conceptual and Metaphysical Deflationism and comport with Linguistic Deflationism. On the other hand, if deflationists accept (i) and (ii), it is hard to see how they could reject (iii) entirely, so the deflationary move would be to maintain that the truth predicate expresses a "thin" concept that cannot support (iv). Such a deflationist would thus accept (i)–(iii) without accepting (iv). Rejection of (iv) satisfies Metaphysical Deflationism, but, given the acceptance of (i)–(iii), deflationists taking this position must substantiate their satisfaction of Linguistic and Conceptual Deflationism.

---

[1] Since the Liar Paradox and its kin pose a problem for all truth theorists, deflationary or inflationary, and, as we discuss in Chapter 7, there is substantial overlap on what conditions must be met for an adequate resolution of the semantic paradoxes, satisfying this dimension is not a matter of diverging from the inflationary presuppositions.

3.1 Prosententialism

Prosententialism is the species of deflationism that diverges from inflationism at the latter genus's first presupposition, viz., (i) The alethic locutions (centrally, 'true') function logically as predicates. Prosententialists consequently also reject assumptions (ii)–(iv) (although, as we discuss in Section 5.3.2, the rejection of assumption (iii) does not have to involve a full rejection of the existence of any sort of truth property). The leading idea behind prosententialism is that the alethic locutions instead occur in what are called "prosentences", where a prosentence is the sentence-level analog of the more familiar category of pronoun. In the most basic use of a pronoun, it inherits its content anaphorically from some other noun, typically called the pronoun's "anaphoric antecedent" (although it need not actually occur before the pronoun). For example, the pronoun 'he' in the sentence 'Bob went out, but now he is back' inherits its content from the occurrence of 'Bob' in the sentence. This is sometimes called the "lazy" use of pronouns, since grammatically the pronoun could be replaced with a repetition of the noun, even though the result of doing so is stylistically awkward and less clearly about the same person. Pronouns also have a quantificational use, where they function as bound variables, as 'she' does in 'If any woman is elected president, she will make history'. Here, the pronoun 'she' cannot be replaced by its antecedent, 'any woman'; the antecedent functions as a quantifier, and 'she' ranges over its whole domain. At the sentential level, the words 'yes' and 'no' function as one-word "lazy" prosentences in ordinary language, when used to answer questions. Prosententialists extend this idea and view truth-talk as just involving the use of prosentences, in both the "lazy" and the quantificational ways.

As an example of the former, consider the following conversation.

MARIA: The average global temperature is rising.
TONY: That's true.

According to prosententialists, the sentence Tony assertorically utters is a prosentence, one that inherits its content as a whole anaphorically from the sentence that Maria assertorically utters. Thus, the content of Tony's assertoric utterance of 'That's true' is just the same as that of Maria's assertoric utterance, viz., that the average global temperature is rising. Sometimes the sentential antecedent is even more closely connected to the relevant instance of truth-talk, for example, by being embedded in it. Thus, 'It is true that the average global temperature is rising' has for its content just that the average global temperature is rising. The whole sentence is understood in terms of a prosentence that inherits its content from the sentence that it contains.

Prosententialism invokes a quantificational use of prosentences to explain quantificational instances of truth-talk, such as 'Something Faiz believes is true' and 'Everything the pope asserts is true'. The former gets re-rendered as 'Something is such that Faiz believes that it is true, and it is true'; the latter gets expanded into 'Everything is such that if the pope asserts that it is true, then it is true'. In both cases, 'it is true' is taken to serve as a quantificational prosentence.

As should be clear, in particular from the "lazy" prosentence cases, this species of deflationism descends principally from Ramsey's theory. In fact, as noted in Section 2.2, Frank Ramsey introduces what is probably the earliest use of the term 'prosentence'.[2] In the development of prosententialism, we can also see the effects of P. F. Strawson's (1949, 1950) push for a reorientation of investigation into the topic of truth—that of moving away from attempts to *define* truth (or better, 'true') over to considering what 'true' *does* in the instances of truth-talk. Ramsey's work includes this shift in a subtle way, but with Strawson it is both overt and emphasized. As

---

[2] Ramsey actually uses the expression `pro-sentence`, but the hyphen has been dropped by later philosophers. Künne (2003, p. 68, n. 104) points out that Brentano (1904/1966) employs 'Fürsatz' in an equivalent way, explaining that 'ja'—as Ramsey also notes about 'yes' and 'no'—can function prosententially. Grover et al. (1975, p. 88) also note this (albeit with a botched translation), while indicating an ordinary-language prosentential role for 'so' as well.

a result, it seems that, like Ramsey and Strawson, prosententialists satisfy Linguistic Deflationism.

3.1.1 Prior's Adverbial Prosententialism

A. N. Prior picks up the change in focus that interested Strawson (though not the particulars of Strawson's view), along with Ramsey's claim that truth-talk can be thought of as providing a surrogate for prosentences, understood in terms of sentential variables and quantifiers (Prior (1971, p. 24)). Thus, Prior also satisfies Linguistic Deflationism and endorses what we call "sentential-variable deflationism" (SVD), an approach that relies on an independent understanding of sentential variables and quantifiers, in order to explain truth-talk in terms of these logical devices. A new detail Prior adds is explaining the function of sentential quantifiers and variables both *non-nominally* and *adverbially*.[3]

Following Wittgenstein (1953, §134), Prior (1971, p. 38) takes 'This is *how* things are' to be a "propositional variable" (i.e., a sentence-in-use variable), quoting an example Ludwig Wittgenstein provides where a use of the phrase gets its content "by a previous whole sentence". In this vein, as a means for "improving standard English" with respect to its "paucity of quantifiers", Prior introduces a kind of adverbial quantification to govern variables for presentations of "how things are". He coins the informal adverbial quantifier expressions 'anywhether', 'everywhether', and 'somewhether', derived from the question-word 'whether', along with a corresponding 'th-' answer-word, 'thether', to serve as the variable they govern (Prior (1956, p. 201) and (1971, pp. 37)). On this approach, we can understand

---

[3] While Prior is the first to develop an adverbial analysis of truth-talk in natural language, there is an earlier suggestion in Strawson (1949) of this kind of analysis via his gloss on a sentence like 'What she said is true' in terms of the sentence 'Things are as she said they are'.

a sentence like 'Everything Jamal believes is true' in terms of 'For all p, if Jamal believes that p, then p' (Prior (1971, p. 24)), which can be rendered informally using Prior's neologisms as 'For anywhether, if Jamal believes that thether, then thether'. A sentence like 'What they believe is true' becomes 'They believe that somewhether, and thether'. Like Frege (1918) and Ramsey (1929/1991, p. 12), Prior (1971, p. 12) holds that a transparent instance of truth-talk, such as 'It is true that the earth is round', is basically just a stylistic variant of, and means no more than, its embedded sentence. So, Prior, like Ramsey, provides two separate theories for these different forms of truth-talk: a simple content-redundancy view for "transparent" instances, plus an account in term of sentential variables and quantifiers (SVD) for opaque and quantificational instances.[4] In virtue of taking truth-talk just to play these logico-linguistic expressive roles, Prior's account satisfies Linguistic Deflationism and, insofar as his view reflects the "thinness" of a truth concept, his account would also satisfy Conceptual Deflationism.

While Prior also maintains generally that no instance of truth-talk is really about any proposition (being instead "about whatever the proposition is about") (1971, p. 21), he allows that one might still talk about propositions (as the quotation just given illustrates), including about them being true or false. But he (1971, pp. 29–30) considers any case of this just to involve a figure of speech about a logical construct, rather than some genuinely ontologically committing form of discourse, which indicates that he satisfies Metaphysical Deflationism as well.

---

[4] Prior (1967, p. 229 and 1971, p. 38) also briefly notes a way of understanding sentential variables and quantifiers adverbially in natural language without his neologisms, in terms of what we call "how-talk". He claims that one can understand 'For some p, p' in terms of 'Things are somehow' and 'For all p, if she says that p, then p' in terms of 'However she says things are, thus they are (or, that's how they are)'. We pursue and develop this "how-talk" approach in Armour-Garb and Woodbridge (2023a, 2023b, and forthcoming) and in the appendix to this book.

When it comes to the semantic paradoxes, such as the Liar Paradox, Prior (1958, 1960b) seems focused on "contingent" liar sentences, viz., sentences that may become paradoxical given certain contingent facts, such as the paradoxical case introduced in Chapter 1, viz., (SL). (SL)'s apparent paradoxicality depends on the contingent fact that the sentence has the name that it has. If that sentence had a different name, for example, '(A)', and the name '(SL)' was applied to the sentence, 'Snow is purple', then (A), the sentence 'Sentence (SL) is false' would be true, rather than paradoxical. Prior seems to be one of the first philosophers to distinguish this sort of case from the "Eubulidean Paradox" exemplified by an assertoric utterance of "What I am now saying is false" (Prior (1960b, p. 16)). Prior (1958, 1960b) offers a diagnosis of contingent liar sentences, pointing out that in some circumstances they resolve unproblematically, but that in other circumstances they appear to lead to contradiction. His diagnosis of these cases when unfavorable circumstances obtain is that the relevant utterances do not say anything (and that nothing is thought in cases involving mental states). Prior (1971, p. 91) also seems to apply this diagnosis to Eubulidean cases.

Given the anaphoric element of his prosentential account of truth-talk, one might presume that his diagnosis of "meaninglessness" is a consequence of a failure of anaphoric content inheritance in the relevant cases. However, that is not how he seems to argue. Rather, he shows that a contradiction results if one assumes that the relevant utterances say something (or that something is thought via the relevant mental activity), and, via reductio ad absurdum, concludes that such an assumption is false, and hence that nothing is said (or thought). He seems to think that this diagnosis is sufficient, or at least all that can be said on the matter (Prior (1960b, p. 32)), even though he does note some reservations about it. Prior therefore appears to take his diagnosis as also amounting to a kind of treatment of the semantic paradoxes, but, pertaining to treatment, it does not go far enough. If one focuses on the anaphoric aspect of his account of truth-talk, it might seem that his view could satisfy Paradox Treatment Deflationism. This is because the strong equivalence that a prosentential account generates between any sentence, S, and a truth-ascription to it, 'S is true', would underwrite satisfaction of the "deflationism-specific" conditions on a solution to the Liar Paradox that we explain in Chapter 7. However, since Prior does not rely on the anaphoric aspect of his account in his diagnosis of the problematic cases, he misses out on a better approach to treating the semantic paradoxes. So while his view goes some way toward satisfying Paradox Treatment Deflationism, we think it does not go far enough.

3.1.2 Williams's Substitutional Prosententialism

C. J. F. Williams develops Prior's ideas further in his own prosentential account of truth-talk, first explaining the alethic locutions as devices for expressing what would be expressed via sentential variables and quantifiers, giving these logical devices an explicitly *substitutional* reading.[5] (Cf. Williams (1976, pp. 1–2, 10–15).) This raises an immediate concern about his view, given the question noted in Chapter 1, regarding how a deflationist can understand substitutional quantification. His strategy on this front seems to involve assuming that the prosentential element of Prior's view takes care of this. Similar to Prior (and Ramsey), Williams maintains that the sentence 'Percy's statement is true' is to be re-rendered as 'For some p, both Percy's statement states that p and p'. This, Williams claims, shows us "what it is that 'x is true' says about x. 'Percy's statement is true' says about Percy's statement that, for some p, [both] it states that p and p" (1976, p. 28). Thus, like Prior, Williams holds that an

---

[5] Williams's understanding of truth-talk thus seems to make his view a version of SVD as well, albeit less explicitly so.

account of truth-talk in terms of sentential variables and quantifiers still allows one to think of the instances of truth-talk as "about" someone's statement, etc., so long as one does not read too much into that, which seems in line with Linguistic Deflationism.

Williams acknowledges that the expression '__ is true' is a grammatical predicate, and he allows that by replacing the 'it' (or 'Percy's statement') with a slot, even his analysis could yield an expression that generates a sentence when completed with the right sort of denoting phrase. But Williams continues to reject the assumption that '__ is true' functions as a predicate logically (as opposed to just grammatically). If taking 'is true' to function predicatively is necessary for one to maintain that it expresses a property, then his approach is in line with Metaphysical Deflationism. This also seems to make his account satisfy Conceptual Deflationism, since the non-predicative aspect of the alethic locutions means that they do not function to describe anything, which they must do if they are to express an attributive concept.

Williams's reasons for rejecting this first inflationary presupposition involve denying that the expressions that form sentences with 'is true' are genuine logical subjects. An expression like 'What Jana says', or any other putative designation of a proposition (replaceable by a 'that'-clause), is really, Williams says, itself a kind of second-level function, similar in form to a Russellian analysis of definite descriptions, but involving sentential variables bound by sentential quantifiers. What Williams (1976, p. 45) suggests as the general form of these expressions was (translating from the Polish notation Williams adopts from Prior) 'For some unique p, Jp and __p' (where 'J' symbolizes an operator involving 'that', e.g., 'Jana says that'). But while this seems to need completion via a predicate going into the slot, Williams holds that actually there is no slot here, in contrast with the analysis of definite descriptions. A slot "opens up" for formal renderings of expressions like 'is believed by Ray' or 'is surprising', when one appends those to expressions like 'What Jana says', but since the completing expressions would slot in as prefixes to a sentential variable in Williams's (1976, pp. 47–48) analysis, they would be operators in this context ('Ray believes that' and 'it is surprising that'). By contrast, in the case of the expression 'is true', in a sentence like 'What Jana says is true', no slot ever opens up for any filling expression, leaving the basic, but complete, formula 'For some unique p, Jp and p' unaltered (1976, pp. 41–42). Thus, Williams (1976, pp. 52–53) maintains, there is no predication of anything to anything in the instances of truth-talk.

Williams carries this analysis over to a later presentation of his view, where he highlights the *adverbial* aspect of Prior's account, making extended use of the latter's adverbial neologisms (previously mentioned only in passing (1976, p. 49)). Williams (1992, pp. 86, 92) claims that rendering 'What she said is true' as 'She said that somewhether, and thether' offers a more precise presentation of Strawson's (1949) gloss, 'Things are as she said they are'. He maintains that truth-talk could be replaced without loss (and perhaps even made more perspicuous) by Prior's informal adverbial sentential quantifier and variable neologisms, which clearly do not involve any form of predication. However, since English does not actually contain 'somewhether' or 'thether', or, it is widely maintained, any other general-purpose prosentential expressions, Williams (1992, pp. 91–96) claims that the alethic locutions function to convert object pronouns, such as 'it' or 'that', into prosentences, which aligns with what others who advocate Linguistic Deflationism have said. In an attempt to avoid offering a separate account of transparent instances of truth-talk, as Ramsey and Prior do, Williams (1992, p. 99) also analyzes explicit 'that'-clauses, such as 'that birds are dinosaurs', as definite descriptions, along the lines of 'What someone who says that birds are dinosaurs thereby says'.

It is not clear, however, that the merits of adopting a univocal account of truth-talk can bear the costs of the means that Williams offers for attaining it. He analyzes a claim like 'That birds are dinosaurs is true' as 'What someone who says that birds are dinosaurs thereby says is true', or, equivalently, 'Someone who says that birds are dinosaurs thereby says that somewhether, and thether'. But this, in turn, according to Williams, is logically equivalent to 'Someone who says that birds are dinosaurs thereby says that birds are dinosaurs, and birds are dinosaurs'. Moreover, since the first conjunct is a tautology, he (1992, pp. 100–101) concludes that "the informational content of [this] is indistinguishable from that of ['Birds are dinosaurs']." However, his approach turns all transparent cases of truth-talk into implicitly quantificational claims (with regard to hypothetical speakers, not just via implementing quantification into sentence-positions). He also attempts a parallel analysis of quotational cases, for example, "'Birds are dinosaurs' is true". A sentence like this he renders as "Someone who says 'Birds are dinosaurs' thereby says that somewhether, and thether", which he (1992, pp. 104–5) instantiates as "Someone who says 'Birds are dinosaurs' thereby says that birds are dinosaurs, and birds are dinosaurs". This not only has the counterintuitive implicit quantification concerns of his 'that'-clause analysis, but, unlike in the former case, the first conjunct here is not obviously tautologous. Thus, Williams's (1992, p. 106) claim, that appending 'is true' just reverses the effect of putting quotation marks around a sentence, seems even less plausible.

Williams does not address the semantic paradoxes, so it remains an open question as to whether his view could satisfy Paradox Treatment Deflationism. Given that his view is based on Prior's, Williams might just endorse Prior's approach to the Liar Paradox and its kin. Alternatively, one might be able to extend Williams's account to address the paradoxes, and, as mentioned regarding Prior's view, given the anaphoric aspect of any prosentential account of truth-talk, the result could satisfy the "deflationism-specific" conditions on a proposed resolution that underwrite Paradox Treatment Deflationism. However, Williams's official view does not take on this dimension of deflationism.

3.1.3 Grover, Camp, and Belnap's Atomic Prosententialism

Dorothy Grover, Joseph Camp, and Nuel Belnap (1975) introduce a more sophisticated version of the prosententialism originally developed by Ramsey and Prior. Their account explains the idea of a prosentence in rich detail and, in fact, was the first to call itself a "prosentential theory". The paper's title specifies prosententialism as a "theory of truth", but, as with the account presented by Ramsey (in 1929/1991, under the chapter title "The Nature of Truth"), the inflationary project that this suggests is quickly dispelled. Their actual project is to develop the theory "that 'true' can be thought of always as part of a prosentence" (Grover et al. (1975, p. 83)). They (p. 73) explicitly reject the inflationary assumption that the alethic locutions function as predicates logically, with their stated goal being "to offer a coherent alternative to this subject-predicate analysis [of 'x is true']". As they (p. 92) say, "In the spirit of Ramsey, our claim is that all truth talk can be viewed as involving only prosentential uses of 'that is true' [and 'it is true']". They (p. 91) explain that 'it is true' and 'that is true' as generally available atomic or "fused" prosentences that can go into any sentence-position, where these expressions are not to be given a subject-predicate analysis with the 'that' and the 'it' having separate references. Both of these prosentences can function in the "lazy" way, as in the following conversation:

DAVID: There is life on Mars.
MARC: That is true.
LOU: David claims that there is life on Mars, but I don't believe that it is true.

Moreover, Grover et al. (1975, pp. 91–92) claim that 'it is true' can also operate as a quantificational prosentence, in the ways explained above, for example, in a sentence like 'For every proposition, if the pope asserts that it is true, then it is true'. This latter role, they (1975, p. 101) claim, shows that 'true' is not a redundant expression, at least in its occurrence in a prosentence. It is needed for expressive purposes, such as the example's generalizing on sentence-positions. This understanding involves endorsing Linguistic Deflationism and, by denying any directly descriptive function, it seems that, akin to Prior's and Williams's views, it also adheres to Conceptual Deflationism.

An interesting element of Grover et al.'s prosentential approach (cf. 1975, p. 114) is that its appeal to quantificational anaphora keeps the generalization at the object-language level, instead of invoking Quinean semantic ascent (see the next section on disquotationalism) to make the quantification one over sentences taken as objects.

Grover et al. (1975, p. 87) define a prosentence in terms of four conditions:

(i) It can occupy the position of a declarative sentence.
(ii) It can be used anaphorically in either the lazy way or the quantificational way.
(iii) Consequently, in each such use it has an antecedent from which one may derive an anaphoric substituend (in the laziness cases) or a family of anaphoric substituends (in the quantificational cases)—in either case, the substituends are sentential, matching the position of the anaphor.
(iv) It is 'generic' in the sense that, in one way or another, any declarative sentence might turn up as an anaphoric substituend.

Grover et al. (1975, p. 80) also stress the merits of prosentialism as a way of accounting for the pragmatics of truth-talk, in the spirit of Strawson's performative/pragmatic point. Even in "lazy" anaphora cases, one is not just issuing a repetition of the prior utterance in applying truth-talk to it. Saying 'That's true' indicates "prior authorship" and shows that one is just saying the same thing as was already said (1975, p. 101). To illustrate how anaphora does this, Grover et al. (1975, pp. 84–85) draw attention to the fact that, in a sentence like 'If Mary is invited, she will bring snacks', the use of 'she', as opposed to a second occurrence of 'Mary', makes it clear that only one person is the subject of discussion.

To support their thesis that we can understand all truth-talk as involving only prosentential uses of the alethic locutions, Grover et al. take a different tack than the one that Ramsey, Prior, and Williams take. They avoid concerns one might have about analyzing truth-talk by considering what would be expressible if English were supplemented with new logical devices or terminology, by instead examining what could be expressed within a fragment of English they call "English*". In this fragment, 'that is true' and 'it is true' are treated as atomic expressions (like Prior's 'thether'), so that 'true' is not an isolable expression, and the expression 'is' cannot be modified. For greater scope, they also allow English* to include various modifying "connectives" (operators) from English, to cover tense, modality, negation, and falsity, where these can be prefixed to the basic prosentences. Some of these modifying connectives employ alethic locutions themselves (for example, 'it-was-true-that' and 'it-might-be-true-that', along with 'it-is-false-that'), but even here they still are not separable, as Grover et al. indicate with hyphens (1975, p. 93). So, in addition to paraphrasing an English sentence like 'Everything the pope asserts is true' into English* as 'For every proposition, if the pope asserts that it is true, then it is true', they also claim that modified instances of English truth-talk get the following sorts of paraphrases into English*.

(a) That might be true.   (a*) It-might-be-true-that that is true.
(b) That's not true.   (b*) It-is-not-true-that that is true.
(c) That used to be true.   (c*) It-used-to-be-true-that that is true.
(d) That's false.   (d*) It-is-false-that that is true.

The authors' position, then, is that English can be translated without semantic loss into its fragment, English*. Since this involves a restriction on English, rather than adding any non-standard terminology or logical devices to it, they claim that the "mere surface grammar" of English's separable alethic locutions with modifiable copulas should not lead anyone to think that truth-talk is anything more than prosentential, in terms of its underlying logic. They (1975, p. 96) note that "[t]he upshot is that English truth talk can be thought of as prosentential precisely as English* truth talk is prosentential". Their (1975, p. 99) stronger thesis is revealed in their claim that "English* can do everything English can, and more perspicuously at that". Moreover, Grover et al. are clear that a rejection of the further presuppositions of inflationism follows from this rejection of inflationary assumption (i). As they (1975, p. 118) note, "if the prosentential account is right, a philosophical theory cannot have as its purpose characterizing a predicate that expresses an ordinary property of truth—a property we ascribe to things in the course of ordinary truth talk—because there is no such property". This contention about the prosentential account clearly indicates an adherence to Metaphysical Deflationism. (Whether the view adheres to Paradox Treatment Deflationism depends on the details of the approach to the semantic paradoxes that Grover (1977) develops from within this framework, something we assess as doubtful in Chapter 7.)

One immediate concern that Grover et al.'s version of prosententialism faces pertains to the operators that they claim need to be included in English*. Many of them, for example, (a*)–(d*) above, involve alethic locutions in non-prosentential uses. While this might not conflict with a rejection of the alethic locutions functioning predicatively, it does seem to conflict with the thesis that all truth-talk involves prosentential uses of 'true'. It also seems to be a return to a two-part view of truth-talk, albeit of a slightly different sort from what Ramsey and Prior offer, where some contexts of alethic locution use are explained in terms of sentential variables, while others are analyzed in terms of simple redundancy. Finally, it strains against intuition that cases (b) and (d) in particular have, as their underlying logical forms, the complicated forms of (b*) and (d*).

This last point extends to other examples of what one might call "paraphrastic gymnastics" that Grover et al.'s account requires. As they see it, a sentence like 'It is true that humans are causing climate change' has the underlying logical form (via paraphrase into English*) of 'Humans are causing climate change. That is true' (1975, p. 94). This avoids the problem that Williams's attempt at a univocal view creates, viz., making transparent cases of truth-talk all implicitly quantificational. But the alternative offered here is that when one utters an instance of truth-talk of the form 'It is true that p', one states the content of 'p' *twice*. In cases of quotation, such as "'Birds are dinosaurs' is true", Grover et al. (1975, p. 103) offer the following rendering in English*, 'Consider: Birds are dinosaurs. That is true'. Taking this as the underlying logic of the quotational instance of truth-talk does not have speakers asserting the content of the quoted sentence twice, but it rejects the standard idea that quotation marks around linguistic items form names of those items. An interrogative instance of truth-talk, such as 'Is that true?' poses an even more serious difficulty, if English* is said to provide a perspicuous rendering of every form of truth-talk. The question "would have to be rendered as the composition of a [declarative] prosentence plus a functor which takes as input a declarative sentence and yields as output a yes-no question" (1975, p. 99). These issues pose serious concerns regarding the adequacy of Grover et al.'s version of prosententialism.

3.1.4 Brandom's Operator Prosententialism

Partly in response to the issues that Grover et al.'s account faces, Robert Brandom (1988 and 1994) has developed a variation on their view with an important modification. In place of taking the underlying logic of 'true' to involve the expression occurring as a non-separable component in a semantically atomic prosentential expression, 'that is true' or 'it is true', Brandom treats 'is true' as a separable *prosentence-forming operator*, which "applies to a term that is a sentence nominalization or that refers to or picks out a sentence tokening. It yields a prosentence that has that tokening as its anaphoric antecedent" (Brandom (1994, p. 305)). In this way, Brandom's account avoids much of the paraphrase concerns that Grover et al.'s prosententialism faces, while still explicitly maintaining prosententialism's rejection of inflationism's first presupposition, namely, that the alethic locutions function (logically) as predicates. As he (1994, 305) notes, "To take such a line is not to fall back into a subject-predicate picture, for there is all the difference in the world between a prosentence-forming operator and the predicates that form ordinary sentences". As a consequence of his operator approach, Brandom also provides a slightly different analysis of quantificational uses of prosentences. He (1994, p. 302) expands an instance of truth-talk like 'Everything [or Something] the policeman said is true' into 'For anything one can say, if the policeman said it, then it is true' (or 'For something one can say, the policeman said it, and it is true'). Here only the second 'it' is converted into a prosentence. The first 'it' still functions as a pronoun, anaphorically linked to a set of noun phrases (sentence nominalizations) supplying objects (sentence tokenings) as a domain being quantified over with standard (as opposed to sentential or "propositional") quantifiers.

While Brandom does not discuss Williams's account, his approach is in some ways closer to Williams's view that the alethic locutions convert pronouns to prosentences, than it is to Grover et al.'s view, that the underlying logic of truth-talk involves only non-separable uses of alethic locutions. Still, Brandom presents an even more general and flexible view than Williams does. Brandom proposes treating 'is true' as a denominalizing device that applies to singular terms formed from the nominalization of sentences broadly, not just to pronouns that indicate them. On his view, a sentence such as 'It is true that humans are causing climate change', considered via a re-rendering as 'That humans are causing climate change is true', is itself already a prosentence as is a quotation-name case like "'Birds are dinosaurs' is true", and an opaque instance of truth-talk like 'Goldbach's Conjecture is true'. In the case of a quantificational instance of truth-talk, "Each quantificational instance of this quantificational claim can be understood in terms of the lazy functioning of prosentences, and the quantificational claim is related to those instances in the usual conjunctive [disjunctive] way" (1994, p. 302).[6] Thus, Brandom endorses Linguistic Deflationism by offering a univocal prosentential account, according to which "[i]n each use, a prosentence will have an anaphoric antecedent that determines a class of admissible substituends for the prosentence (in the lazy case, a singleton). This class of substituends determines the significance of the prosentence associated with it" (1994, 302). He does this while avoiding Williams's controversial tactics of making transparent and quotational instances of truth-talk all implicitly quantificational claims, as well as the latter's analysis of any subject-expression occurring in instances of truth-talk in terms of sentential quantifiers and variables. Brandom's account also avoids some of the "paraphrastic gymnastics" of Grover et al.'s approach, at least regarding transparent and quotational instances of truth-talk, and perhaps even their proposed sentence-modification operators and their suggested treatment of questions involving alethic locutions.

As explained in Section 1.3, given Brandom's denial that the truth concept plays any genuine explanatory role and his rejection of any truth property, his view satisfies Conceptual and Metaphysical

---

[6] As we note in Chapter 4, this appears to saddle him with what we call the "Formulation Problem", which was originally broached in Gupta (1993b) in terms of the "Infinite Conjunction Thesis".

Deflationism along with Linguistic Deflationism. This is shown again by his prosententialist rejection of inflationary presupposition (i) and the rejection of (ii)–(iv) that this entails. Since Brandom (1994, pp. 321–22) explicitly defers to Grover's (1977) approach to the Liar Paradox and its kin, whether his view satisfies Paradox Treatment Deflationism depends on the deflationary status of Grover's proposed resolution of the semantic paradoxes. In Section 7.5, we discuss in detail why it is doubtful that Grover's approach satisfies Paradox Treatment Deflationism. As a result, it is likewise doubtful that Brandom's view satisfies this dimension of deflationism.

While Brandom's modification of prosententialism, to viewing 'is true' as a general prosentence-forming operator, presents an advance over earlier versions (and ties in with a parallel "pronoun-forming" operator account of reference-talk (1994, pp. 306–21)), the main worry for Brandom's account is the same one that threatens any prosentential account, viz., that truth-talk really does seem predicative, and not just in surface grammatical form, but in our inferential practices with it. We accept as valid, for instance, inferences employing alethic locutions like the following.

'Birds are dinosaurs' is true.
So, something is true.

Everything Zev asserts is true.
Isabel believes some things that Zev has asserted.
So, something Isabel believes is true.

The validity of seemingly straightforward inferences like these is not at all straightforward on any prosentential view, Brandom's included. In arguing for the superiority of his view over that of Grover et al., Brandom (1994, p. 304) states that "[t]he account of truth talk should bear the weight of such divergence of logical from grammatical form only if no similarly adequate account can be constructed that lacks this feature". One might find it plausible to extend this principle beyond grammatical form, to behavior in inferences as well. This is an abiding concern for attempts to resist inflationism by rejecting its first presupposition, namely, that the alethic locutions function as predicates.

3.2 Disquotationalism

Disquotationalism avoids the concerns that come with rejecting the first assumption of inflationism. Disquotational accounts of truth-talk accept that the central alethic locutions function predicatively, at least logically speaking. Where the versions of this species diverge from inflationism is at assumption (ii), namely, that these alethic predicates serve to describe or characterize putative truth-bearers by expressing attributive concepts.[7] According to disquotational views, the truth predicate really just plays a kind of logically expressive role, by performing a particular syntactic function, namely the one the view's name indicates: mutually canceling out with the quotation marks involved in forming the quotation-name of a sentence. The instances of truth-talk that involve applying the truth predicate to a given quotation-named sentence are the basic cases, but also the least interesting ones. Disquotational views treat these instances, for example, "'Birds are dinosaurs' is true" in a manner similar to A. J. Ayer's analysis of truth-talk, discussed in Section 2.3: Applying the truth predicate to the quoted sentence is equivalent to asserting the sentence on its own, unquoted (Ayer (1936/1952, pp. 88–89)). So, in

---

[7] By contrast with our claim above, that deflationists deny that the alethic predicates describe the entities picked out by the expressions with which they are combined, Stephen Gross (2015, pp. 51–52) argues that, on Quine's view, truth-ascriptions are still about the sentences. (Cf. Simpson (2021, pp. 3173–75).) This seems to run counter to our contention, since it appears to result in the claim that truth-ascriptions are descriptive. However, Gross's argument fails because it assumes that mentioning a sentence in a claim is sufficient for making the claim be about that sentence. As we discuss below, Quine's point is that this is not the case with claims employing the truth predicate, even when they do mention or otherwise "pick out" sentences.

this case, the instance of truth-talk just mentioned means nothing more than what 'Birds are dinosaurs' means. This view provides a "non-metaphysical" account of truth-talk that fits with the anti-metaphysical sentiments of the logical empiricists, including suspicion about semantic notions like truth.

3.2.1 Quine's Disquotationalism

The first account of truth-talk to be called a "disquotational" view, and the one often considered to be the earliest full-fledged deflationary view, is the one that W. V. O. Quine (1970/1986, pp. 10–12) presents. In general, Quine, like the logical empiricists, is skeptical about a number of semantic assumptions, regarding the reification of meanings and certain meaning features (including, contra the logical empiricists, the analytic-synthetic distinction). Additionally, Quine (1960) famously denies the existence of either objective translations or synonymies. For Quine, a given translation may be better or worse than another translation, largely on pragmatic grounds, but there is no sense in asking whether a given translation is objectively correct.

Given Quine's skepticism about the existence of meaning entities of the sort that propositions are supposed to be, he takes sentences to be the only targets of the applications of 'is true' and 'is false'. Indeed, Quine contends that truth (or, more accurately, "truth-talk") is "immanent", which is to say that the truth predicate can only meaningfully be applied to sentences of one's idiolect—that is, to sentences that one understands. Quine allows that we can apply the truth predicate to sentences of foreign languages, but he claims that what we are actually ascribing truth to are sentences of our own idiolect that we consider to be translations of the foreign sentences via some translation scheme. (We discuss the consequences of immanence and the question as to how we can apply the truth predicate to sentences of foreign languages in Section 4.1.1.) To avoid the problems concerning context-dependence (indexicals, demonstratives, etc.), Quine defines a category of sentence that he dubs "eternal", viz., sentence types, the tokens of which always have the same truth-values. It is for these sentences that Quine offers his disquotational view of truth-talk. As he (1970/1986, p. 12) says,

> This cancellatory force of the truth predicate is explicit in Tarski's paradigm:
> 'Snow is white' is true iff snow is white.
> Quotation marks make all the difference between talking about words and talking about snow. The quotation is a name of a sentence that contains the name, namely 'snow', of snow. By calling the sentence true, we call snow white. The truth predicate is a device of disquotation.

To unpack Quine's contention that the truth predicate is a "device of disquotation", note that, instead of assertorically uttering a sentence, a speaker can always transform the sentence that would be used in performing that speech act into an object of sorts—a mentioned, rather than used, sentence—and instead assert that this object is true. Quine's point about the truth predicate being a device of disquotation is that the latter simply amounts to a syntactically different means of doing the former—hence, calling the sentence true is just calling snow white.

In addition, as the quote noted above suggests, and as mentioned in Section 2.6, Quine takes Alfred Tarski's formal work on defining truth predicates for formalized languages as potentially underwriting a disquotational analysis of truth-talk for natural languages, or at least regimented fragments of them.[8] The fact that

---

[8] For Quine, a *regimentation* involves paraphrasing a fragment of ordinary discourse into an acceptable logical notation—for Quine, first-order classical logic (cf. Quine (1960, pp. 159–60))—with the goal of clarifying or simplifying that fragment of

Tarski's method for defining a consistent truth predicate for a language also implies all of the equivalences of the form

(T) X is true iff p

(where 'X' gets replaced by a name of a sentence from the (object-)language *for* which the truth predicate is being defined, and 'p' gets replaced by a sentence that is a translation of that sentence in the (meta)language *in* which the truth predicate is being defined), motivates Quine to take Tarski's work as the logical basis of his own account of truth-talk. One difference is that, in place of Tarski's (T)-schema, Quine's view lines up with a sentential version of the neutral equivalence schema, (TS), that is often called the "disquotational schema",

(DS) 'p' is true iff p,

which demands that the sentence used on the right side of the biconditional be explicitly mentioned via use of its quotation-name on the left side of the biconditional.[9] More importantly, Quine reads the equivalence in the instances of (DS) not just (as Tarski does with the instances of (T)) as a material biconditional, but as

---

discourse so as to reveal certain inferences that might be hidden from that fragment. Azzouni (2006, Ch. 4) builds on Quine's notion of regimentation and describes that practice as employing an artificial language as a means for replacing a fragment of discourse with the aim of providing normative constraints on inferences to which speakers who employ that fragment seem to be committed.

[9] Quine (1970/1986, p. 13) is, however, cautious about claiming that one could use (DS) directly to provide an account of the truth predicate, since technically "quoting the schematic sentence letter 'p' produces a name only of the sixteenth letter of the alphabet, and no generality over sentences." Given Quine's refusal to take on the commitments that he thinks the idea of "generalizing over sentences" would require—in this case, to propositions—and his resulting commitment to the exclusivity of first-order objectual quantification, he would not take that idea to indicate the role that the truth predicate implements in a language. What it implements is simply disquotation. For a complete account or definition of the truth predicate, Quine defers to Tarski's work.

a kind of cognitive equivalence, due to the logical functioning of the truth predicate. This is the sense in which Quine still rejects the second inflationary presupposition, viz., that the alethic locutions, such as 'is true', function to describe what they are applied to via the expression of an attributive concept (which Quine would reject in any case), even though, unlike the prosententialists, he accepts the first inflationary presupposition, that these expressions function logically as predicates. This indicates Quine's endorsement of Conceptual Deflationism.

As a result of his understanding the truth predicate as serving simply as a device of disquotation, Quine (1992, p. 80), echoing Ramsey (discussed in Section 2.2), notes,

> So the truth predicate is superfluous when ascribed to a given sentence; you could just utter the sentence. But it is needed for sentences that are not given. Thus we may want to say that everything someone said on some occasion was true, or that all consequences of true theories are true.

This is an explicit statement of Quine's endorsement of Linguistic Deflationism. In fact, he is often credited with having been the first philosopher to emphasize the importance of the truth predicate's special logical role of implementing a kind of generalization that it seems we could not otherwise express. As he (1992, pp. 80–81) explains it,

> The truth predicate proves invaluable when we want to generalize along a dimension that cannot be swept out by a general term.... The harder sort of generalization is illustrated by generalization on the clause 'time flies' in 'If time flies then time flies'.... We could not generalize as in 'All men are mortal' because 'time flies' is not, like 'Socrates', a name of one of a range of objects (men) over which to generalize. We cleared this obstacle by *semantic ascent*: by

ascending to a level where there were indeed objects over which to generalize, namely linguistic objects, sentences.

Since, via the instances of (DS), every sentence, S, is equivalent to 'S is true', 'If time flies then time flies' is equivalent to "'If time flies then time flies' is true". We therefore can automatically make the *semantic ascent* from the first to the second, and, having done so, we can now abstract the form ('if p then p') out of the named sentence and use this to formulate a generalization, viz., "All sentences of the form 'If p then p' are true".

The idea of using semantic ascent to make the relevant generalization about sentences connects with Quine's rejection of propositions in favor of eternal sentences. He holds that any utterance could be paraphrased into an eternal sentence. Having done the requisite paraphrase, if we want to generalize on embedded sentence-positions within sentences—that is, along a dimension where there are no objects over which to generalize—"we ascend to talk of truth and sentences" (Quine (1970/1986, p. 11)). This maneuver allows us to "affirm some infinite lot of sentences that we can demarcate only by talking about the sentences" (1970/1986, p. 12). In setting out his disquotational account of truth-talk, Quine sees the role of the truth predicate as simply canceling out the semantic ascent achieved by forming the quotation-name of a sentence. Thus, even in nontransparent ascriptions, the use of the truth predicate shows that "[t]his ascent to a linguistic plane of reference is only a momentary retreat from the world, for the utility of the truth predicate is precisely the cancellation of linguistic reference. The truth predicate is a reminder that, despite a technical ascent to talk of sentences, our eye is on the world" (1970/1986, p. 12). This again makes evident Quine's endorsement of Linguistic Deflationism and, given his attitude toward concepts and (against) properties, indicates an endorsement of both Conceptual and Metaphysical Deflationism.

While Quine's point above, about "affirming some infinite lot of sentences", does attribute a special *expressive* role to the truth predicate, contrary to what it might seem to accomplish, it does not actually characterize this role as a different kind of *generalizing*. It also leaves the larger purpose of the truth predicate at a fairly impressionistic level. Moreover, Quine's characterization of what truth-talk allows speakers to do seems to indicate something more like enabling them to assert a finite sentence that is equivalent to an infinite conjunction of the instances of a schema. To see this, note that in a 'true'-employing generalization like "All sentences of the form 'if p then p' are true", which gives us each of its instances (where the truth predicate is applied transparently to a particular sentence), we just have the semantic ascent and the truth predicate canceling each other out. But this simply leaves us with each of the instances, rather than a genuine generalization over them. We discuss this issue further below, in particular in Section 4.2.

It is important to note that, with respect to dealing with the semantic paradoxes, Quine (1966/1976, pp. 7–8) simply defers to Tarski's proposed resolution of the Liar Paradox. Hence, whether Quine's disquotationalism satisfies the fourth dimension of deflationism comes down to the status of Tarski's approach. As we discuss in Section 7.2, this revisionary proposal does not satisfy Paradox Treatment Deflationism; hence it would seem that Quine's view fails to satisfy this dimension.

3.2.2 Leeds's Recursive Disquotationalism

Extending Quine's project, Stephen Leeds (1978, pp. 111–12, 115–16, 120–22) is even more explicit about tracing the disquotational account of truth-talk that he endorses back to Tarski and the recursive method employed in his definition of truth. Hilary Putnam (1978, pp. 15–17) explains how one could understand Leeds's point as highlighting the fact that a list-like (or "Tarskian") definition of reference is all that one requires to produce a disquotational truth predicate given Tarski's (1935a/1983) procedure. As noted above, Putnam (1978, pp. 10–13) provides a simplified version of the Tarskian procedure, illustrating how this works, and how Tarski's compositional principles account for quantificational and opaque instances of truth-talk, along with the transparent cases that appear in the instances of (DS). (Soames (1984, pp. 416–17) also offers a clear, simplified example.) Marian David (1994, pp. 110–15) provides a slightly more detailed account of the procedure, labeling disquotational views based on it "recursive disquotationalism".

Despite the triviality that disquotationalism suggests for transparent instances of truth-talk, Leeds is quite clear about the importance of other uses of the truth predicate in extending the expressive power of a language. He attempts to explain the special logical role of a disquotational truth predicate explicitly in terms of providing a means for expressing what would otherwise require an infinitely long sentence. As Leeds (1978, p. 121) notes,

> It is not surprising that we should have use for a predicate P with the property that "'___' is P" and "___" are always interdeducible. For we frequently find ourselves in a position to assert each sentence in a certain infinite set z (e.g., when all the members of z share a common form); lacking the means to formulate infinite conjunctions, we find it convenient to have a single sentence which is warranted precisely when each member of z is warranted. A predicate P with the property described allows us to construct such a sentence.... Truth is thus a notion we might reasonably want to have on hand, for expressing semantic ascent and descent, infinite conjunction and disjunction.

So, like Quine, Leeds notes that a central utility of the truth predicate, one provided essentially by its yielding the instances of (DS) via its disquotational operation, is the satisfaction of a certain logical need. In addition to thus endorsing Linguistic Deflationism, Leeds also explicitly identifies this logical role as a matter of expressing what would be covered by potentially infinite conjunctions or potentially infinite disjunctions. Since natural languages do not seem to have the means for capturing infinite conjunctions or infinite disjunctions, the truth predicate allows us to use the ordinary devices of first-order logic in ways that provide surrogates for these logical devices. As a result, in place of an infinite conjunction of conditionals (e.g., all of the fillings of the form "If the Oracle says 'p', then p"), we can assert the finite sentence, 'Everything the Oracle says is true' (expanded as 'For all x, if the Oracle says x, then x is true'), and, in place of an infinite disjunction of conjunctions (all of the fillings of the form "Percy said 'p', and p"), we can assert the finite sentence 'What Percy said is true' (expanded as 'For some x, Percy said x, and x is true').[10] Leeds is also clear about accepting the consequences of his Linguistic Deflationism, that is, of taking the logically expressive role of the truth predicate to exhaust its linguistic function. In particular, he points out that there is no need to think that truth-talk plays any sort of explanatory role, thereby making his Conceptual and Metaphysical Deflationism explicit as well. Indeed, he seems to be one of the first deflationists—if not the first—to embrace a form of Conceptual Deflationism explicitly.[11] (Hartry Field (1987) seemed to be against Conceptual Deflationism and (in his (1994a)) credits Leeds with convincing him to adopt what amounts to a form of Conceptual Deflationism. We discuss Field's version of deflationism in the next subsection.)

---

[10] As a result, Leeds's disquotationalism faces the same challenges regarding generalizations noted for Quine's view in Section 3.2.1.

[11] Leeds does not discuss the semantic paradoxes, so it remains an open question as to whether he can or would satisfy Paradox Treatment Deflationism. His reliance on Quine's and Tarski's views in general suggests that he would not.

3.2.3 Field's Pure Disquotational Truth

An alternative disquotational approach looks not to the recursive method of defining a truth predicate that Tarski provides but instead directly to the instances of the (T)-schema at the center of his criterion of material adequacy. Tarski himself (1944, pp. 344–45) raises the possibility that each (T)-sentence could be considered a "partial definition" of truth, and that a logical conjunction of all of these partial definitions amounted to a general definition of truth (for the language the sentences belonged to).[12] Generalizing slightly from Tarski, we can call this alternative approach "(TS)-schema disquotationalism". Field (1987, 1994a) develops a version of this approach that he calls "pure disquotational truth", focusing specifically on the instances of his preferred version of (TS), the disquotational schema (Field (1994a, p. 258)),

(T[/DS]) "p" is true iff p.

In setting out his version of (TS)-schema disquotationalism, however, Field does not take the (T/DS)-biconditionals as fundamental. Like Quine, Field takes the truth predicate to apply to all and only the utterances that a speaker understands, and he explains the (T/DS)-sentences as following from its functioning in this way. As he notes: "As a rough heuristic, we could say that for a person to call an utterance true in this pure disquotational sense is to say that it is true-as-he-understands-it ... and for such an utterance u, the claim that u is true (true-as-he-understands-it) is cognitively equivalent (for the person) to u itself (as he understands it)" (1994a, p. 250). The use of the truth predicate on the left-hand side of an instance of (T/DS) does not add any cognitive content to the mentioned utterance (aside from presupposing the existence of the utterance) beyond the content the quoted sentence has on

---

[12] Tarski ultimately rejects this thesis. We explain why in Section 4.2.2.

its own when used. So, Field's version of deflationism also rejects the second assumption of inflationism, by taking the truth predicate as not really functioning to describe an utterance in any substantive sense, that is, by expressing an attributive concept. This reveals his commitment to Conceptual Deflationism. As a result, each instance of (T/DS) "holds of conceptual necessity, that is, by virtue of the cognitive equivalence of the left and right hand sides" (1994a, p. 258).

Field characterizes his preferred understanding of two sentences being cognitively equivalent for a person in terms of the person's inferential procedures licensing intersubstitution of the sentences in any context that is not within quotation marks or in an intentional attitude ascription (1994a, p. 251, n. 2). This is both broader and more direct than the interdeducibility mentioned in the Leeds quotation above. It also suggests a connection to a broad version of what has been called "inference-rule deflationism" (Gauker (1999)), according to which the operation of the truth predicate is determined by introduction and elimination rules, "True-in" and "True-out", respectively, such as the following:

'True'-In	'True'-Out
ϕ	$\ulcorner\phi\urcorner$ is true
---	---
$\ulcorner\phi\urcorner$ is true[13]	ϕ

One of Field's motives for explicitly eschewing recursive disquotationalism and favoring (TS)-schema disquotationalism (at least in (1994a)) is the goal of keeping the scope of the intersubstitutability between a sentence and the instance of truth-talk involving its quotation-name as broad as possible (within

---

[13] '⌜' and '⌝' function as corner quotes. Corner quotes allow the variable expressions within them to get filled in in various ways, while keeping the rest of the quoted formula fixed. They are also called "Quine quotes", since they were introduced in Quine (1940/2003).

the class of utterances a speaker understands). Tarskian truth-definitions provided by recursive accounts apply only to a fragment of one's language (viz., not to any utterances that employ semantic expressions), and some of the recursive clauses that give a Tarskian truth-definition its compositional structure cannot be applied to certain forms of sentences (e.g., those with unrestricted quantifiers). (Cf. Field (1994a, p. 268).) Sentences that attribute intentional attitudes (or involve other intensional contexts or indexicals) pose additional problems for Tarski's procedure. These restrictions limit a Tarskian truth predicate's usefulness "as a device of infinite conjunction and infinite disjunction" (Field (1994a, p. 268). Instead of a Tarskian definition, or even a variant of Tarski's approach that treats the compositional clauses as axioms, Field (1994a, p. 267) proposes treating some generalized version of the (T/DS)-schema (restricted to the utterances that a speaker understands, as this speaker understands them) as axiomatic, where this can be formulated by prefixing the schema with a universal substitutional quantifier, 'Πp'.[14] A weaker proposal (Field (1994a, p. 259)) involves "incorporat[ing] schematic letters for sentences into the language, reasoning with them as with variables" with two rules of inference governing them:

(i) a rule that allows replacement of all instances of a schematic letter by a sentence;
(ii) a rule that allows inference of $\forall x(\text{Sentence}(x) \to A(x))$ from the schema $A(\text{"}p\text{"})$ ... in which all occurrences of the schematic letter p are surrounded by quotes.

---

[14] It bears noting that, in the course of dealing with the challenges to deflationism that we discuss in Part 2 of this book, Field (1999, 2001d, 2006, 2008) modifies his view in ways that end up involving the inclusion of certain compositional principles, ultimately bringing it closer to recursive disquotationalism than to (TS)-schema disquotationalism. For more details, see our discussions of Field's responses to the Generalization Problem (Chapter 4), the Conservativeness Argument (Chapter 5), and the Liar Paradox (Chapter 7), below.

Both of these proposals downplay the compositionality that recursive disquotationalism tends to emphasize, but Field (2001d, p. 142) sees this as an advantage, claiming that his view allows us to see that "[t]he fact that truth is compositional in some cases but not others isn't fundamentally a fact about truth, but rather about the underlying logic of the domains [of discourse] to which it is applied".

Field (1994a, p. 264) presents his understanding of the important logical role that the truth predicate plays in terms similar to those of Leeds and, seemingly, Quine: "It allows us to formulate certain infinite conjunctions and disjunctions that can't be formulated otherwise [n. 17: at least in a language that does not contain substitutional quantifiers]". He (1994a, pp. 264–68, 283) emphasizes this by repeatedly calling a disquotational truth predicate a "device of infinite conjunction and disjunction".[15] Field also stresses the importance of this logical role in the alethic locutions' utility in expressing rejection or denial, or in claims of contingency. As he (1994a, p. 265) notes, "Suppose that one rejects [some not finitely axiomatizable] theory without knowing which specific part of it to

---

[15] While Field also describes the substitutional quantifiers as devices of this sort, he seems to recognize the point indicated above, that ultimately this is inadequate for taking these quantifiers or truth-talk to provide a means for expressing what he later (Field (1999, p. 533)) comes to call "fertile generalizations". For example, he remarks in his (1994a, n. 17) that his understanding of the substitutional quantifiers (as well as his strategy for incorporating free schematic variables into a language) "allows statements that are really a bit stronger than infinite conjunctions, in the same way that first order quantifiers are stronger than the totality of their instances". However, he (1994a, p. 266) also claims that in order for 'All sentences of type Q are true' to serve "as an infinite conjunction of all sentences of type Q, then we want it to entail each such sentence, *and be entailed by all of them together*" (emphasis added). Unless this last claim involves an implicit assumption in keeping with his remarks in n. 17, it would mean that his understanding of alethic "generalizations" makes them out as not genuine generalizations, which would saddle his view with both the Formulation Problem and the Generalization Problem discussed in Section 4.2. However, in Field (1994a), it is just not obvious how either the truth predicate or substitutional quantifiers perform the "stronger" role that he suggests; it seems to be something that he simply assumes about them. Field (2006) goes further in explaining how the free schematic variable strategy is supposed to get around this issue, in his attempt to resolve the Generalization Problem. See Section 4.2.4, below.

reject; or alternatively, suppose that one accepts it but regards it as contingent. In the first case one will put the rejection by saying 'Not every axiom of this theory is true'; in the second case, by saying 'It might have been the case that not every axiom of the theory was true'". All of this demonstrates Field's endorsement of Linguistic Deflationism. It also indicates his commitment to Metaphysical Deflationism.

Among contemporary deflationists, Field is one of the most attentive with regard to the satisfaction of Paradox Treatment Deflationism. He (2008) self-consciously develops a detailed proposal for resolving the semantic paradoxes specifically within the context of a deflationary account of truth-talk. We discuss his approach in Section 7.4.

Field claims that a crucial feature for the pure disquotational truth predicate's role as a device of infinite conjunction is the predicate's "use-independence", a feature it has, essentially, by antecedently fixing all issues of use or interpretation to the actual understanding a speaker has of sentences. This, he thinks, is what makes a rejection of a theory, or a claim of its contingency, that employs the truth predicate turn out to be about how the world is, or about how it might have been, rather than about how language is being used, or might have been used, in the sentences that constitute the axioms of the theory (1994a, p. 266). However, Field also acknowledges that this feature of a pure disquotational truth predicate has some seemingly counterintuitive consequences. For example, he initially acknowledges that, on his view, a speaker cannot understand an application of this truth predicate to utterances that they do not understand (1994a, pp. 265–66). So, on Field's account, if Kurt is a monolingual German speaker, then a monolingual English speaker would not understand the claim 'Something Kurt said is true'. (It is worth noting that, so as to avoid this consequence, Field (2001d, pp. 147–48) modifies his view in a way that brings it closer to prosententialism.) In addition, the use-independence of the pure disquotational truth predicate has notable consequences for truth-talk's modal features. Since 'snow is white' is true iff snow is white, it follows on Field's pure disquotational theory of truth-talk that, even in certain counterfactual circumstances, for example, those in which 'Snow is white' is used in English in the way that 'Grass is red' is actually used, 'snow is white' would still have been true in the purely disquotational sense. (Cf. Field (1994a, p. 275), for discussion.)

Since it seems that ordinary speakers would likely wish to resist the last results of these counterfactual circumstances for pure disquotational truth and would accept that if 'Snow is white' had been used in very different ways, it would have had the truth conditions that grass is green, this suggests that such speakers are not using 'true' in Field's pure disquotational sense. While this might seem to create a problem for Field's approach to truth-talk, he claims it does not. He (1994a, p. 277) professes a lack of interest as to whether his account ends up being a revisionary replacement proposal, rather than an explanation of the "ordinary" use of truth-talk. He takes the question of whether any "ordinary" uses of 'true' deviate from "the pure disquotational mold" as being a boring issue that is "of only sociological interest" (1994a, p. 277), and he is suspicious of claims about what ordinary speakers mean when they make 'true'-employing assertions. Since he dismisses such possible concerns, we should take Field to maintain simply that a pure disquotational truth predicate captures the important logical function of truth-talk, and that it must be use-independent to do so.

Field's acceptance of pure disquotational truth notwithstanding, he does consider various maneuvers one might make to go beyond that view of truth-talk. With regard to applying the truth predicate to utterances that people make in other languages, Field considers what he calls "extended disquotational truth". This involves adding a notion of "interlinguistic synonymy" to the operation of a pure disquotational truth predicate, so that 'Foreign sentence S is true' is understood as equivalent to 'S is synonymous with a sentence of mine that is true in the purely disquotational sense' (1994a, p. 272).

Since Field (following Quine) finds the notion of synonymy to be problematic, he (1994a, p. 273) prefers a weaker notion of truth-relative-to-a-correlation, which only involves correlating a foreign sentence with one of our own sentences, where these correlations are decided not on the basis of right or wrong translations but on the basis of better or worse translations. This enables Field to avoid being committed to objective correctness conditions for translations.

As a means for capturing the intuitive modal features of truth-talk discussed above, Field considers what he calls "quasi-disquotational truth", which involves "a prior notion of meaning such that two sentences are synonymous if they have the same meaning; but meaning is to be defined independently of truth conditions" (1994a, p. 275). This would allow us to characterize a truth predicate that would "mimic an inflationary truth predicate in making the truth of sentences use-dependent" (1994a, p. 276). But Field is suspicious of this notion of meanings as entities, which the approach seems to need to quantify over, and, so, he prefers to treat sentences considered in such counterfactual situations as more like foreign sentences, and to analyze their "cash value" in terms of "reasonable translations" of them into sentences as one actually understands them (1994a, p. 277). Defining a truth predicate in these terms, whether "quasi-disquotational" or not, would not require taking the acceptance of such a locution as a move toward inflationism. (Cf. Field (2001d, pp. 151–52).)

Given that Field's account of truth-talk potentially extends beyond applying the truth predicate to utterances-as-the-speaker-actually-understands-them via the idea of existing standards of translation, this addresses some of the worries that arise for earlier versions of disquotationalism in light of their connections with Tarski's method of defining truth predicates. Field (1994a, pp. 278–81) also explains how to apply a pure disquotational truth predicate to ambiguous utterances and to indexical utterances. As a result, his view addresses many of the concerns that David (1994, pp. 130–66) raises for disquotationalism. However, an abiding central concern about every version of this species of deflationism is one that stems from its inspiration in Tarski's work on formalized languages: Disquotationalism is an account of truth-talk as applied specifically to sentences. Tarski takes the relevant target to be sentence types, understood orthographically, and Quine refines this focus to types of eternal sentences. Field switches the focus to sentence tokens, or utterances, with attached interpretations that get explained in terms of computational roles. (Cf. Field (2001d, p. 151).) However, this still takes truth-talk to apply to linguistic items, which opens the door to the sort of complaint that Strawson (1950) makes against Austin's view, viz., that it is not one's *act of stating* (or, similarly, the linguistic item uttered) but what thereby *gets stated* that is the target of truth-talk. (Cf. Alston (1996, p. 14).)[16]

While disquotationalists do not seem to worry much about this issue, the scope restriction that is imposed on the application of truth-talk might strike others as problematic. For example, it raises questions about how we are to understand truth-talk as applied to beliefs or judgments. Field (1978) develops a detailed view that treats beliefs as mental states that relate thinkers to sentences of a language of thought, in contrast with the quicker claims that Quine (1992, pp. 68–69) and Leeds (1978, p. 127 and 1995, pp. 10–11) make about "believing sentences". But David (1994, pp. 172–77) raises some worries for applying disquotationalism to beliefs taken to be a relation to sentences of a person's language of thought, even for a developed account like Field's. The thesis that we believe sentences remains highly controversial, but it seems to be one that disquotationalists must endorse. Similarly, it seems that they must take on the view that

---

[16] For another concern about Field-style disquotationalism that also stems from its taking linguistic items as the targets of truth-ascriptions, see Heck (2023). Heck's objection is that it is not clear how this type of view can account for applications of the truth predicate to sentences that involve context-sensitive expressions, for example, indexicals.

scientific theories are to be understood as sets of sentences, in order for truth-talk to be applicable to them, but even if this is not limited to a purely syntactic understanding, it still requires that we identify a scientific theory like Darwin's theory of evolution with a particular collection of sentences. This identification suggests that one could not state the same theory in a different language, which echoes the Strawsonian complaint against taking truth-talk to apply to sentences. These sorts of concerns continue to press for disquotational versions of deflationism.

3.3 Minimalism

Minimalism, initially developed by Paul Horwich (1990/1998), is the species of deflationism that diverges the least from inflationism, by accepting the first three inflationary contentions:

(i) The alethic locutions (centrally, 'true') function logically as predicates.
(ii) These predicates express "attributive" concepts and thereby serve to describe or characterize putative truth-bearers.
(iii) These attributive concepts determine alethic properties the possession (or lack) of which is attributed in the descriptions that the uses of the alethic locutions provide.

Horwich does this on the basis of their accommodation of the surface grammar and inferential behavior of truth-talk, as well as certain linguistic intuitions about what predication or description involves (1990/1998, pp. 37–40, 125). What makes minimalism a species of deflationism is its denial of assumption (iv): The alethic properties attributed via the alethic locutions have robust (or substantive) natures. While Horwich grants minimalism a kind of neutrality on the metaphysics of properties, so that its rejection of assumption (iv) might lead one to conclude that the view requires rejecting assumption (iii) as well (1990/1998, 141), he accepts that there is a truth property, and seems amenable to Field's (1992) suggestion of the label 'logical property' (1990/1998 pp. 37, 125, 142). Horwich's distinguishing claim is that there is no substantive or naturalistic property of truth with an underlying nature that requires analysis (1990/1998, pp. 2, 38, 120–21). This reveals his endorsement of Metaphysical Deflationism. One consequence of accepting inflationary assumptions (i)–(iii) is that minimalism has a broader focus than the other species of deflationism. It not only purports to explain the functioning and role of truth-talk; it also offers a theory of "truth itself", as well as a theory of the concept of truth and of our grasp of it (1990/1998, pp. 36–37). In light of this, and because minimalism accepts more of inflationism's assumptions, minimalists have more work to do to show that their views satisfy Linguistic and Conceptual Deflationism.

3.3.1 Horwich's Minimalism

Horwich's first examination of deflationism focuses on a version of (TS)-schema disquotationalism connected with Tarski's work (Horwich (1982, pp. 182, 192–94)). However, further consideration of the use of truth-talk in natural language (Horwich (1990/1998, pp. 16, 129–30)), especially its surface grammar and role in inference (1990/1998, pp. 2–3, 39–40), leads him to conclude that propositions are what the alethic locutions describe most fundamentally (the falsity predicate just being a means for describing propositions as not true (1990/1998, pp. 71–72)). At the same time, Horwich (1990/1998, pp. 2–3) attempts to substantiate a commitment to Linguistic Deflationism by endorsing a propositional version of disquotationalism's thesis about the utility of the truth predicate (and, he adds, the concept it expresses), namely, that it "exists solely for the sake of a certain logical need". As he goes on to say,

On occasion we wish to adopt some attitude towards a proposition—for example, believing it, assuming it for the sake of argument, or desiring it be the case—but find ourselves thwarted by ignorance of what exactly the proposition is. We might know it only as 'what Oscar thinks' or 'Einstein's principle'; perhaps it was expressed, but not clearly or loudly enough, or in a language we don't understand; or—and this is especially common in logical or philosophical contexts—we may wish to cover infinitely many propositions (in the course of generalizing) and simply can't have all of them in mind. In such situations the concept of truth is invaluable. For it enables the construction of another proposition, intimately related to the one we can't identify, which is perfectly appropriate as the alternative object of our attitude.

Because he sees the utility of the concept of truth in this way, Horwich (1990/1998 pp. 138–39) goes so far as to claim that the concept has a "non-descriptive" function. But in doing so, his aim is not to follow disquotationalism all the way to its repudiation of the inflationary assumption that truth-talk describes or characterizes truth-bearers by attributing a property to them. Rather, his point is just to adopt the disquotationalist's thesis, that the utility of the truth predicate is mainly a matter of its role in providing a means for formulating claims that generalize on embedded sentence-positions (1990/1998, pp. 31–33, 37), instead of some role in the indication of specifically truth-involving states of affairs. This is supposed to amount to an endorsement of Linguistic Deflationism, but it weakens the claim that truth-talk performs *exclusively* an expressive role to just the claim that playing a logically expressive role is truth-talk's *main* or *important* function, or its raison d'être. Horwich still maintains that, even when playing this expressive role, the instances of truth-talk describe propositions, in the sense that they make statements *about* the propositions to which the truth predicate is applied, and they do so by expressing a concept (1990/1998, pp. 38–40). But he takes 'is true' to express a "thin" concept that determines a "thin" (or "logical") property, which is supposed to satisfy Conceptual Deflationism, along with Metaphysical Deflationism.

Since he takes propositions as the primary targets of truth-ascriptions, as what truth-talk describes as having or lacking the property of truth, Horwich proposes a propositional version of the sort of (TS)-schema disquotational view that he (1982) first took to be definitive of deflationism. The schema that Horwich makes the basis of his theory is the one mentioned in Section 2.6, what he (1990/1998, p. 6) calls "the equivalence schema",

(E) It is true that p iff p.

Taking truth-talk to involve describing propositions with a predicate, Horwich (1990/1998, p. 136) considers 'It is true that p' to be just a trivial variant of 'The proposition that p is true', making (E) equivalently expressible as 'The proposition that p is true iff p'. He (1990/1998, p. 10) also employs the notation '<p>' as capturing *the proposition that p*, generating a further rendering of the equivalence schema that we can clearly recognize as a version of (TS), namely,

(E) <p> is true iff p.

As this is Horwich's favored equivalence *schema*, we shall henceforth use the label '(ES)' for it, in parallel with the neutral schema's label '(TS)' and the label for the disquotational schema, '(DS)'. Since Horwich (1990/1998, p. 28) takes minimalism to be an infinitely axiomatized theory of truth in general, and not just for current English, the axioms of the theory really have to be propositions themselves, viz., the propositions expressed by the instances of (ES), along with any other propositions with the same form (*modulo* some restriction to exclude the instances that give rise to the semantic paradoxes (1990/1998, p. 40)). To specify all such propositions implicitly, even those not currently expressible in a natural language like English, Horwich (1990/1998, pp. 17–20) identifies the axioms of his theory as the instances of the schema

(E*) <<p> is true iff p>,

which stands for a function that yields an axiom of minimalism—a proposition of a particular form—when applied to any (non-paradoxical) proposition.

However, it seems clear that Horwich cannot express his theory in terms of (E*) because this is a *schema* in which we replace the variable 'p' with an English-language sentence, which results in an expression that denotes a proposition. The problem is that the collection of instances that the schema (E*) generates is inadequate as a characterization of his theory of truth since it would be incomplete.[17] This incompleteness results from the fact that Horwich's theory should apply to *all* propositions. But, assuming propositions, there are uncountably many of them and only countably many sentences of English. To see this, note that, for any real number n, there is a proposition that n is a real number. Hence, assuming Georg Cantor's conclusions about the reals, there are uncountably many propositions of this form. Since there are at most only countably many sentences of English, there are propositions for which there are no English sentences that can be substituted in for 'p' in (E*) to yield an axiom that states what it takes for that proposition to be true. Thus, Horwich's minimalism qua theory of truth cannot be stated by defining its axioms in terms of a schema on sentences, since it would follow that the theory is incomplete. Horwich (1990/1998, 17–20) attempts to evade this problem by characterizing the axioms of his theory (MT) in terms of

(E**) $\forall x(x$ is an axiom of MT iff $\exists y(x = E^*(y)))$.

---

[17] For discussion of this, see Schindler and Schlöder (2022, p. 699).

Unfortunately, as Timothy Button (2014) and Thomas Schindler and Julian J. Schlöder (2022) note, (E**) is confused. The variable 'y' must be a singular term, since it is bound by an objectual quantifier. But (E*) within (E**) cannot be applied to a singular term for a proposition because if 'y' were a singular term, then '<<y> is true iff y>' would be ill-formed.[18] As a result, the theory remains inexpressible for Horwich, which is a serious concern for any truth theorist.

Setting the problem with expressibility aside, we note that Horwich (1990/1998, p. 136) considers the instances of (E*) to constitute the axioms of both an account of the property of truth and an account of the concept of truth. He identifies the concept of truth with what is meant by the word 'true', and, in accordance with the use-theory of meaning that he (1998) advocates, Horwich (1990/1998, pp. 35–36, 126) maintains that 'true' gets the meaning it has from the fact that the behavioral regularity that explains all our ways of using the truth predicate, and thus our understanding of it or knowledge of its meaning, is our disposition to accept all of the instances of (ES) (which express instances of (E*)). According to Horwichian minimalism, then, the instances of (ES) are explanatorily fundamental, which Horwich suggests is a reason to consider them all necessary.[19] In contrast with other species of deflationism, minimalism takes these equivalences to be the basis of the functioning of the truth predicate (of its role as a de-nominalizer of 'that'-clauses (1990/1998, p. 5)), rather than as being explained by that functioning (as the analogous equivalences

---

[18] Schindler and Schlöder (2022, p. 698) explain the ill-formedness by noting that if we replace 'y' with a term that denotes a proposition, such as '<snow is white>', then the result is '<<<snow is white> is true iff <snow is white>>'. While, on the left-hand side of the biconditional, angle brackets surround a name for a proposition, they were originally explained as surrounding sentences; and, on the right-hand side, the singular term '<snow is white>' occurs in sentence-position. Both cases result in ill-formedness.

[19] Horwich (1990/1998, p. 21, n. 4) notes that this thought must be finessed in response to the Liar Paradox, since the instances of (ES) for liar sentences are, he claims, false. For more on this see Section 7.8.

are for both disquotationalism and prosententialism). Horwich (1990/1998, pp. 50, 138) also contends that the (true) instances of (ES) are conceptually basic and a priori. He (1990/1998, pp. 27–30, 33, 112) denies that truth admits of any sort of explicit definition or reductive analysis in terms of other concepts, such as reference or predicate-satisfaction. In fact, Horwich (1990/1998, pp. 10–11, 111–12, 115–16) holds that reference and predicate satisfaction should both be given their own, infinitely axiomatized, minimalist accounts, which would then clarify the non-reductive nature of the intuitive connections between these notions and truth.

Horwich claims that the infinite axiomatic nature of minimalism is unavoidable. According to him (1990/1998, 11–12), traditional inflationary attempts to explain the instances of (ES), or any other version of (TS), in terms of some unified account of the essence or underlying nature of truth, have all proven to be inadequate. He (1990/1998, pp. 27–30) argues that other proposed, finite analyses of truth, such as those that apply Tarski's method to the notion as it is employed in natural language, or in terms of Russellian propositions or propositions taken as sets of possible worlds, also all turn out to require their own infinite schemata. He also rejects the possibility of finding a finite formulation of minimalism via the use of sentential quantifiers, which he takes to implement substitutional quantification, as in the principle

$\forall x(x \text{ is true iff } \Sigma p(x = \text{<p>} \wedge p))$,

where 'Σ' is an existential substitutional quantifier. This principle is formally equivalent to what David (1994, p. 100) presents as disquotationalism's definition of 'true sentence', and it is somewhat similar to Field's (1994a, p. 259) proposal to treat a generalized version of the (T/DS)-schema, prefixed with a universal substitutional quantifier, as a finitely formulated axiom for his disquotational account of the truth predicate. Horwich's (1990/1998, pp. 25–26) main reason for rejecting this proposed finite formulation of minimalism is that an account of substitutional quantifiers seems to require an appeal to truth, generating circularity concerns. These concerns arise from a standard way of understanding the existential substitutional quantifier:

(SQ) A sentence of the form $\Sigma p(\ldots p \ldots)$ is true iff there is a sentence, S, from the class of substituends for 'p', such that the sentence that results from replacing occurrences of the sentential variable in the matrix $(\ldots p \ldots)$ by S is true.[20]

Moreover, on Horwich's (1990/1998, p. 4, n. 1; cf. pp. 25, 32–33) understanding, the whole point of the truth predicate is to provide a surrogate for substitutional quantification and sentential variables in natural language. Horwich maintains that the infinite "list-like" nature of minimalism poses no problem for the view's adequacy with respect to explaining all of our uses of the truth predicate, and the bulk of his (1990/1998) book attempts to establish that. However, Anil Gupta (1993a, p. 365) points out that minimalism's infinite axiomatization, in terms of every (non-paradox-inducing) proposition, makes it maximally ideologically complex in virtue of involving every other concept. Moreover, the overtly "fragmented" nature of the theory makes it particularly vulnerable to the Formulation and Generalization Problems, which Gupta also raises and which we discuss in Section 4.2.

By taking truth to apply primarily to propositions, Horwich positions himself well with respect to explaining the instances of truth-talk that is directed at beliefs and theories. This is because, on his view, the former are just mental acts or states directed at propositions and the latter are just collections of propositions. He explains the

---

[20] David's (1994, pp. 98–99) alternative, "truth-free" account of the substitutional quantifiers, in terms of encoding infinite disjunctions (existential) and infinite conjunctions (universal), avoids these circularity concerns, but, using substitutional quantifiers as he understands them, in a finite formulation of a theory of truth, would not avoid certain logical problems discussed in Chapter 4 that the infinitely axiomatic nature of Horwich's account generates for the latter.

application of truth-talk to utterances by proposing a way of picking them out in terms of their meaning (for the speaker) as well as their syntax, and then extending application beyond the speaker's home language via translation. (Cf. Horwich (1990/1998, pp. 100–101).) The end result is thus somewhat similar to the view of utterance truth found in Field's pure disquotationalism, but the basis and paths of the two are very different. Horwich connects utterance truth with minimalism by relating the meaning of an utterance with its expression of a proposition, but not in a way that explains the former in terms of the latter. According to Horwich (1998, pp. 82–85), the explanation runs in the other direction, so that utterance-meaning factors into both a schematic account of utterance truth and a schematic account of expressing a proposition. In general, the two schemata can be combined to yield (ES), just as (ES), combined with the proposition-expression schema, will yield the schema for utterance truth (mutatis mutandis for belief-truth). (Cf. Horwich (1990/1998, pp. 133–35).)

On Horwich's minimalist theory, the meaning of 'true' is given by specifying a fundamental regularity of use—what Horwich (1998) calls "a basic acceptance property"—through which our overall use of truth-talk is best explained. He (1998, p. 104) notes that the sum of everything we do with the truth predicate is best explained by taking as the fundamental fact about its use our underived disposition to accept all instances of (ES), and the same applies for the meaning of 'false', given our underived disposition to accept all instances of the falsity schema,

(FS) <p> is false iff ~p,

where

(i) Each 'p' is replaced with a token of an English sentence;
(ii) Those tokens are given the same interpretation as one another;
(iii) Under that interpretation, they express the same proposition; and

(iv) The terms 'that' and 'proposition' are given their standard English meaning.

While Horwich is usually taken to endorse a use-theory of meaning, it is important to understand what this theory amounts to. His contention is not that meanings are uses, nor is it that meanings are to be correlated with uses. Rather, he (1998, 25) contends that meaning properties are constituted by use properties. His account of meaning comprises three central theses:

> Thesis I: Meanings are concepts, so that linguistic expressions mean concepts.
>
> Thesis II: The overall use of a word derives from its possession of a basic acceptance property, which is a basic regularity of use from which all other facts about its use are to be explained.
>
> Thesis III: Two expressions, for example, 'true' and 'verdad', express the same concept in virtue of possessing the same basic acceptance property.

In his (1990/1998), Horwich briefly discusses the problem that the Liar Paradox presents and sketches a proposal for how his account can resolve it. He has developed that sketch substantially in more recent work (cf. Horwich (2005, 2010b)). We consider his approach's adequacy and satisfaction of Paradox Treatment Deflationism in Section 7.6, where we conclude that it fails on both fronts.

3.3.2 Hill's Substitutional Minimalism

Christopher Hill (2002) presents a view that he takes to be a newer version of minimalism, one intended to avoid certain problems that Horwich's version faces. Hill appeals to a kind of substitutional quantification to provide a finite definition of 'true thought (proposition)'. Hill's (2002, p. 22) formulation of his account,

(S) For any object x, x is true if and only if $\Sigma p((x = \text{the thought that } p) \text{ and } p)$,

is formally similar to the "single principle" version of minimalism that Horwich (1990/1998, p. 25) rejects, and thus is also similar in form to the disquotational definition of 'true sentence' that David (1994, p. 100) presents. To avoid the circularity concerns that lead Horwich to reject substitutional quantifiers (and a finite formulation of minimalism), Hill's (2002, pp. 18–22) idea is to offer rules of inference—introduction and elimination rules—as a means for defining the substitutional quantifiers. The central difference with Hill's view is that his substitutional quantifiers are intended to apply to thoughts (propositions) instead of to sentences, thereby ruling out David's (1994, pp. 98–99) account of them in terms of encoding certain infinite sentences.

Horwich (1990/1998, p. 26) rejects an inference-rule sort of approach, but he directs his critique against defining linguistic substitutional quantification. Hill (2002, pp. 25–26) claims that his understanding of substitutional quantification is motivated, since certain English sentences employing the expression 'so-and-so' express open thoughts bound by quantifiers. His aim in using substitutional quantifiers for thoughts is to achieve both the kind of finite formulation in an explicit definition that Horwich's view lacks (Hill (2002, p. 134, n. 11)) and to provide a version of minimalism that accounts more adequately for generalizations involving the notion of truth (2002, pp. 16–17). One notable aspect of Hill's account is that he is more explicit about attempting to satisfy the "broadness" aspect of broad four-dimensional deflationism than most deflationary theorists. This is shown in his (2006a, p. 174) attempt to provide a framework for deflationary accounts of relational semantic concepts in general, as well as explaining the correspondence intuitions we have about them (see Section 5.3.1). Regarding the four dimensions of deflationism, since Hill intends his account to piggyback on Horwich's, we can allow that the extent to which Horwich's view satisfies Linguistic, Metaphysical, and Conceptual Deflationism will carry over to Hill's proposed "improvement" of minimalism. Regarding Paradox Treatment Deflationism, it is an open question whether Hill's account satisfies this dimension. This is because, in the first instance, he (2002, pp. 119–20) acknowledges that the portion of our conceptual scheme that involves truth (or rather the substitutional machinery that he employs to explain truth) is "incoherent" in the sense that it yields contradictions. But, noting that the task of his project is to describe our conceptual scheme rather than to reform it, he (2002, p. 120) looks to other theorists to take on the task of offering a proposal regarding dealing with the Liar Paradox and its kin. He claims that this would involve revising the substitutional machinery that he has identified in his analysis of truth in a way that blocks the generation of the semantic paradoxes, but he also states that he is hopefully optimistic regarding the future success of this venture. Of course, it might turn out to be impossible to revise his machinery in a way that adequately resolves the paradoxes. And, even if that does turn out to be possible, it might turn out that this sort of resolution requires violating the conditions for Paradox Treatment Deflationism that we explain in Chapter 7.

There is a sense in which Hill's account looks like an attempt to pursue something like what we call "sentential-variable deflationism" (SVD), since the general formulation of his account via (S), which is intended as an analysis of truth, employs variables in sentence-positions with quantifiers binding them. The difference is that Hill maintains that this "higher-order" logical machinery applies to propositions (or, what he calls "thoughts") rather than to sentences. However, there are genuine concerns about the logical machinery that he postulates, since there are genuine concerns about the coherence of a non-linguistic account of substitutional quantification. (Cf. David (2006), Gupta (2006), and Simmons (2006).[21]) As a result, it is unclear whether Hill's account makes sense, let alone whether it amounts to an improvement on Horwich's version of minimalism.

---

[21] It is worth noting that the ordinary English term 'so-and-so' that Hill uses as a means for expressing "open thoughts" is adverbial. It is essentially a variant of the phrase 'thus-and-so', which is perhaps more clearly adverbial than the expression that Hill employs. In reading 'so-and-so' as a variable expression, Hill proposes binding it with a substitutional quantifier, since that is a fairly standard alternative to a first-order nominal quantifier. But this approach is challenged by these critics' concerns about the coherence of a kind of substitutional quantification that is supposed to fill in the variable with thoughts, i.e., propositions. By contrast, if Hill had instead followed Prior's lead, taking the adverbial nature of the variable to suggest binding it with a sui generis *adverbial* quantifier, he would have avoided this problem, and, in that case, his approach would have been closer to the adverbial version of SVD that we develop in the appendix to this book.

PART 2

CHALLENGES TO DEFLATIONISM

As explained in Part 1 of this book, deflationism, as an approach to the topic of truth, is primarily focused on a linguistic thesis about the role and functioning of the alethic locutions, which then has certain consequences that go beyond the linguistic. Whichever species of deflationism one considers, its commitments are determined by its readings of the four deflationary dimensions of Linguistic Deflationism, Metaphysical Deflationism, Conceptual Deflationism, and Paradox Treatment Deflationism. These dimensions are ordered hierarchically, with the first taken as primary, that is, as a necessary condition for a view to be deflationary, and the other three dimensions serving as necessary conditions for it. Challenges to deflationism (often made through objections to particular versions or species of it), then, might target Linguistic Deflationism directly, or they might target deflationism's central linguistic thesis indirectly, by raising objections either to Metaphysical Deflationism or to Conceptual Deflationism. While discovery of a violation of Paradox Treatment Deflationism does not explicitly target Linguistic Deflationism, such a violation can also undermine deflationism's primary linguistic thesis. Chapter 4 discusses some direct challenges to Linguistic Deflationism, specifically those pertaining to the scope it determines for truth-talk's applicability and to deflationism's ability to account fully for generalizations that employ the truth predicate. Chapter 5 examines some of the indirect challenges that target Metaphysical Deflationism, namely those based on identifying different sorts of putative explanatory roles that have been attributed to truth. Chapter 6 assesses some indirect challenges that target Conceptual Deflationism, challenges arising from the apparent role that truth plays in accounts of various other philosophically interesting concepts. Chapter 7 discusses certain formal challenges that the Liar Paradox and related phenomena present for any approach to theorizing about truth and isolates the requirements for a proposed resolution to satisfy Paradox Treatment Deflationism. The discussion explains how these formal challenges bear specifically on deflationism and considers responses that have been made on behalf of certain central deflationary accounts of truth-talk.

4

Challenges to Linguistic Deflationism

Instances of the more direct sort of challenge to deflationism, which target its linguistic thesis, typically proceed by claiming that that the theory of the functioning of the alethic locutions offered by some specific species of deflationism fails to account for all of the uses of truth-talk that are taken to be legitimate. An early example of this sort of challenge is the one launched against the classical redundancy theory, claiming that it could only account for instances of "transparent" truth-talk of the form 'It is true that p', leaving out the more interesting opaque ascription cases with forms like 'What they said is true' and 'Everything Einstein said is true'. Contemporary versions of deflationism have been developed largely to address that limitation, but newer challenges to the adequacy of their accounts of the functioning of the alethic locutions have emerged: Immanence, the Formulation Problem, and the Generalization Problem.

4.1 Immanence and Limitations on Truth-Ascriptions

Recall W. V. O. Quine's (1981, p. 21) contention that truth-talk is *immanent*, that a speaker can meaningfully apply the truth (and the falsity) predicate only to a sentence or an utterance that they understand. Most deflationists subscribe to a version of the immanence of truth-talk. In particular, according to Hartry Field (1994a), advocates of deflationism who adopt a "pure" version of disquotationalism will endorse a form of immanence. But there are questions about how 'immanence' is to be understood, including questions about the connection between immanence and deflationism and questions about how deflationists who endorse some form of immanence can allow for truth-ascriptions to sentences of foreign languages and to those sentences that a speaker does not (or even cannot) understand.

4.1.1 Immanence and Deflationism

As noted in Section 3.2.2, Field (1994a, p. 250) contends that "a person can meaningfully apply 'true' in the disquotational sense only to utterances he has some understanding of; and, for such an utterance u, the claim that u is true (true-as-he-understands-it) is cognitively equivalent (for the person) to u itself as he understands it" (italics original). Stewart Shapiro (2005, p. 155) explains how this form of immanence emerges from Field's brand of deflationism, roughly as follows.

Recall Field's disquotational schema,

(T/DS) 'p' is true iff p.

In each instance of the schema, the item that goes in for 'p' is mentioned on the left-hand side and is used on the right-hand side. In virtue of the latter, an instance of the disquotational schema is in a person's idiolect only if the item that goes in for 'p' is also in that person's idiolect. As a result, speakers can understand an instance of (T/DS) only if they understand the item that goes in for 'p'.

To see another way in which Field's brand of disquotationalism leads to the Quinean conception of *immanence*, consider Field's (1994a, p. 250) contention that "for ... an utterance u, the claim that u is true (true-as-he-understands-it) is cognitively equivalent (for the person) to u itself (as he understands it)". Given his claims about cognitive equivalence, together with his endorsement of conceptual-role semantics, if there are no conceptual roles associated with our thinking about some utterance *u*, or about a sentence that goes in for 'p' in the (T/DS), then, in a certain sense, that sentence is "meaningless" for us, and we cannot be said to understand it. On the assumption, which all truth theorists seem to accept, that we are only sanctioned to ascribe the truth (and the falsity) predicate to meaningful expressions, it follows that if there are no conceptual roles associated with what goes in for 'p' for a given thinker, then they do not understand what goes in for 'p', and, for that thinker, what goes in for 'p' is not meaningful, in which case they cannot meaningfully apply the truth predicate to it. Hence, the truth (and the falsity) predicate should be applied to some 'p' by a given speaker only if they understand 'p'.

We have thus far followed the Quine-Field conception of *immanence*. But theirs is not the only characterization of that notion. Michael Resnik (1997, pp. 25–26) explains *immanence* for truth theories as follows:

> Conceptions of truth that lead one to build truth-theories covering no sentences beyond one's home language are *immanent*. Conceptions of truth which require one to develop a truth-theory applying beyond one's language are *transcendent*... [A] truth-theory is *transcendent* if it applies to sentences of at least one other language (and strongly transcendent if it applies to sentences in arbitrary languages). (Italics original)

The difference between the Quine-Field understanding of *immanence* and Resnik's understanding of that notion amounts to this: For Quine and Field, the truth predicate is restricted to one's idiolect, to the sentences that a thinker understands; by contrast, for Resnik, the truth predicate for a given speaker is restricted to the entirety of a single public language. (Cf. Shapiro (2005) for more on this.) As we will see below, Resnik's characterizations of *immanence* and *transcendence* make it difficult to see how a speaker who subscribes to immanence can apply the truth predicate to sentences of a foreign language.

We have seen how disquotationalism leads to a form of immanence, where the relevant targets of truth-ascriptions are utterances, but there is a question as to whether immanence extends to Paul Horwich's propositional variant of deflationism. For Horwichian minimalism, since the individual instances of the propositional equivalence schema,

(ES) <p> is true iff p,

are axioms, they are brute in the sense that Horwich does not try to explain or justify them on the basis of anything else. As Shapiro (2005, pp. 155–56) notes, an advocate of Horwichian minimalism does not embrace (ES) and then derive its instances; rather, for such an advocate, accepting the instances of (ES) a priori is the source of everything they do with the truth predicate. It is surprising that, although (ES) is propositional in nature, if we restrict our understanding of 'immanence' to the Quine-Field conception, Horwichian minimalism also ends up as immanent.

To see how Horwichian minimalism ends up as immanent under the Quine-Field conception, consider the fact that, while (ES) is intended to have propositions as the primary targets of truth-ascriptions, since the item that goes in for 'p' in an instance of (ES) is used, rather than mentioned, a speaker can understand the relevant instances of (ES) only if they understand the item that goes in for 'p'. Hence, as Field (1992, p. 325) notes, it seems that Horwichian minimalism will also take truth-talk to be immanent in the Quine-Field conception of that notion.[1]

---

[1] As we note below, Field (2008) argues that one can understand a biconditional without understanding the left- or the right-hand side of that biconditional. If he is correct, then his (1992) contention that Horwichian minimalism takes truth-talk to be immanent must be rethought.

4.1.2 Immanence, Foreign Sentences, Sentences Speakers Do Not Understand

As we have seen, a number of deflationists endorse some form of immanence.[2] Since speakers regularly apply the truth predicate to sentences of foreign languages and to sentences they do not understand, this raises the question of how deflationists can explain ascriptions of truth to such sentences.

Field (1994a) considers three options for addressing the question of how deflationists can apply the truth predicate to sentences of a foreign language. His first proposed option, which he (1994a, p. 272) calls "*extended* disquotational truth" (italics original), makes use of a notion of "interlinguistic synonymy". According to this option, we treat "'p' is true" as equivalent to "'p' is synonymous with a sentence of my home language that is true in the purely disquotational sense" (where 'p' within the quotation marks is filled in by a name of some foreign-language sentence, providing a mention of that sentence). What is needed for extended disquotational truth to work is a notion of "interlinguistic synonymy" that does not rely on a prior notion of truth conditions. Field sees this as a challenge, rather than as an objection, to extended disquotational truth, and considers some ways of making out "interlinguistic synonymy" that deflationists could find acceptable. Even so, ultimately he (1994a, p. 274) contends that, for three reasons, extended disquotational truth should be avoided if possible: (1) It is not obvious that a deflationist can really make sense of the required notion of interlinguistic synonymy; (2) It is not obvious that a deflationist needs a notion of interlinguistic synonymy; and, (3) It

---

[2] There is a question about how or whether Quine-Field immanence bears on prosententialist accounts. According to Båve (2009b), neither Brandom (1994) nor either Grover et al. (1975) or Grover (1992) has explicitly considered whether truth-talk is immanent. Båve (2009b) states some alleged reasons for thinking that immanence is a worry for their views, but it is not clear that immanence even arises for prosentential views.

seems to be good practice to separate cleanly the logical aspects of truth-talk from any semantic or quasi-semantic elements. As a result, Field focuses on the other two options that he has adduced in order to answer the question of how deflationists who subscribe to a form of *immanence* can apply the truth predicate to sentences of a foreign language.

Field's second option, which eschews synonymy, is to "define what it is for a foreign language sentence to be true relative to a correlation of it to one of our sentences" (1994a, pp. 272–73). On this option, we let a foreign sentence be true relative to the correlation if the sentence of our idiolect correlated with it is true in a purely disquotational sense. Stephen Schiffer (2017, p. 470) summarizes this second option as follows: On this view, for a foreign language, L, and some correlation, C, of the sentences of L with the sentences of my idiolect, some sentence 'q' of L is true relative to C provided there is a sentence 'p' of my idiolect such that C correlates 'q' with 'p', and 'p' is true-as-I-understand-it. Schiffer (2017) goes on to highlight Field's (1994a, p. 273) claim that, for deflationists, there is no such thing as a sentence I do not understand being true or false per se. Rather, ways of correlating sentences of a foreign language with my sentences are in effect ways of translating the sentences of that language into my own idiolect. On this approach, there is no question as to whether a translation is objectively right or wrong. We thus cannot say that a given translation is correct or incorrect; we can only say that it is better or worse in a way that is highly context-dependent, since the purposes for which translations are better or worse might well vary from one context to the next.

Schiffer (2017, pp. 470–71) is skeptical about Field's second option because he maintains that there are many sentences from a foreign language that he does not understand that are true or false irrespective of his ways of correlating them with sentences of his home language (i.e., his idiolect). Moreover, as against Field's (and Quine's) denial of objective correctness conditions for translations, Schiffer contends that if a sentence in French, for example, 'La neige est blanche', is translated into any sentence other than 'Snow is white', then the translator has obviously mistranslated this French sentence. Schiffer makes an intuitive point here, but Field (1994a) acknowledges that translating this sentence as something other than 'Snow is white' could be a worse translation than one that translates it as 'Snow is white'. So, Field can challenge Schiffer to say *why* translating it in a nonstandard way, viz., as something other than 'Snow is white', is *objectively* (or at least *obviously*) wrong in a way that does not straightforwardly beg the question against a Field-style deflationist. If Schiffer cannot answer this challenge, then it seems that Field's second option is viable after all.

In any case, in addition to extended disquotational truth and truth relative to a correlation, Field considers a third option for a deflationist who wants to apply the truth predicate to foreign utterances. This is to employ the concept of pure disquotational truth, as originally understood, directly in connection with utterances of sentences from a foreign language, without any relativization at all. As Field (1994a, p. 274) notes, this may seem incompatible with things that he has said previously, since he has previously gone on record as saying that the truth predicate can only be applied to sentences of his idiolect or home language. But actually this move is not incompatible with his prior claims, since the Quine-Field notion of immanence is one of his most central commitments. Thus, even though the following instance of the disquotational schema,

(DS*) 'Der Schnee ist weiss' is true iff der Schnee ist weiss,

is incompatible with the grammatical rules of either English or German, it should be fine according to Field (1994a), since he claims to understand (DS*) perfectly well.[3]

---

[3] Field (2001d, p. 147) endorses a fairly permissive view according to which once a speaker understands that a given expression 'p' is an acceptable, declarative sentence, then, even if they do not (or even cannot), understand 'p' itself, they should still accept

116   THE DEFLATIONARY APPROACH TO TRUTH

Field does not see any reason for favoring the second option over the third, nor does he think that a deflationist must adopt one or the other option exclusively. In fact, Field endorses what seems to be an innocuous form of *pluralism* for strategies in support of how deflationists can apply the truth predicate to sentences from a foreign language, contending that the second option may be appropriate for some circumstances, while the third option might be appropriate for others.

If any of Field's options work, then deflationists who embrace immanence can ascribe truth to sentences of foreign languages. But now the question arises as to whether they can ascribe truth to sentences that one does not, or perhaps even cannot, understand. This question is relevant to an important objection to deflationism raised by Shapiro (2005).[4]

Shapiro's argument proceeds from an assumption that there is a guru, a disciple, and a logician. The guru knows everything about set theory (specifically, ZF) and Peano Arithmetic (PA) and can often be found making statements couched in the language of ZF and in the language of PA. The disciple understands the language of PA but is so constituted that he is incapable of understanding statements made in the language of ZF. The logician, well versed in both ZF and PA, can reliably draw the PA consequences of the

---

its corresponding instance of (T/DS). Of course, as Field is well aware, given the cognitive equivalence of a sentence to an ascription of truth to it, if someone does not or cannot understand 'p', then to the same extent they will not understand "'p' is true". But Field (2001d, p. 147) contends that this has no impact on one's acceptance of the instance of the (T)-schema for it. To explain why, he appeals to a form of *indeterminacy*. An utterance that one does not understand may be maximally indeterminate in its content for that person, and ditto for an ascription of truth to that utterance, but, as Field (2001d, p. 147) notes, the two are "tied together" via the (T)-schema, so that the relevant instance of the (T)-schema is still something the speaker can accept and employ in inference. (That said, Field (1994a) applies immanence as a means for imposing a stronger view according to which the truth schema applies only to utterances that a given speaker understands.)

---

[4] Shapiro (2005) is an extension from an earlier unpublished version that Field (2001d) references.

guru's ZF statements, and the disciple trusts the logician in this respect. Suppose that the disciple maintains that everything the guru says is true, and suppose that the guru has assertorically uttered a ZF sentence, 'q', which the disciple cannot understand. Now, the logician sees that 'p', which is in the language of PA, is a logical consequence of 'q', and the logician says as much to the disciple. If the disciple trusts the logician's acumen about logic (and we assume that he does), then the disciple ought to be able to reason as follows: Because I accept that everything the guru says is true, and because logical consequence is truth preserving, and because the guru, whom I trust implicitly, has assertorically uttered 'q', it follows that 'q' is true, and, since I've been assured by the logician that 'p' is a logical consequence of 'q', it follows that I should accept, and, so, should be prepared to assertorically utter, that 'p' is true. Now, while the disciple can understand 'p' and can ascribe truth to 'p', since it is in the language of PA, which he understands, his reasoning to the conclusion that 'p' is true seems to be blocked for a deflationist, since the disciple cannot apply the truth predicate to 'q', since he does not understand it. By contrast, an inflationist seems able to recreate this reasoning and to explain how the disciple is entitled to arrive at his conclusion, that 'p' is true, without a problem, since the inflationist is not restricted by any notion of immanence. This reasoning seems fairly run-of-the-mill, so if a deflationist cannot capture it, this seems to be a problem for deflationism.

Field (2001d, pp. 147–48) replies to Shapiro as follows. Our disciple regards the guru's sentence, 'q', as part of a potential expansion of the disciple's own language, which thereby enables the disciple to carry out his reasoning. This may seem somewhat mysterious, since, from the disciple's perspective, the guru's utterance of 'q' and the resultant truth-ascription for this utterance appears to have an indeterminate content. But recall that, for Field, even if an utterance is indeterminate, as is an ascription of truth to it, it does not follow that the truth schema for that instance is indeterminate. In light of that point, Field maintains that there is "just enough determinacy to enable the reasoning to be carried out", given acceptance of the following: (i) that the guru's utterances are true, (ii) that one of them, 'q', logically implies the number-theoretic claim 'p', (iii) that logical consequence preserves truth, and (iv) the truth schema for 'q'. We leave it to the (interested) reader to determine whether or not Field's reply is adequate.

We have thus far considered two notions of *immanence* and have explained how, for certain disquotationalists, truth-talk can be extended to apply to foreign languages and even to sentences a given thinker does not (or perhaps even cannot) understand. But now contrast how a Horwichian minimalist deals with the challenges that immanence appears to present. Since Horwich (1990/1998, 1998) takes propositions to be the primary targets of truth-ascriptions, he can existentially quantify over them. As a result, for Horwich, one's application of the truth predicate to a foreign sentence amounts to the claim that there is some true proposition that the foreign-language sentence expresses, where "proposition expression" gets explained in terms of Horwich's (1998) use-theory of meaning. Hence, it seems that Horwich can quite easily make sense of truth-ascriptions to sentences of a foreign language.

Field (2001d, p. 148) contends that the guru problem presents a special challenge for a propositional deflationist like Horwich. According to Field, a propositionalist has the task of explaining what it is for a sentence to express the proposition *that p* in terms of an equivalence of content with a sentence, 'p', which is in the propositionalist's idiolect. But this explanation seems unavailable to Shapiro's disciple for the guru's sentence, 'q', since the disciple cannot understand 'q', since it is not in his idiolect. Hence, it seems that the disciple cannot identify the proposition expressed by the guru's assertoric utterance of 'q' and, so, is unable to reason with a propositional variant of Shapiro's guru problem.

We agree that 'q' is not in the disciple's idiolect, and we even grant, with Field, that a propositional deflationist must acknowledge that the guru's disciple will not be able to understand or identify the proposition that 'q' expresses. But this has no bearing on a propositional deflationist's ability to account for the disciple's reasoning in Shapiro's guru problem. According to a propositional deflationist, the disciple should, and presumably will, reason as follows: The guru has said 'q'. I do not understand 'q' and do not know which proposition it expresses, but I recognize that 'q' expresses some proposition, so let's assume that it expresses a proposition that I shall call "β". Since everything the guru says is true, it follows that β is true. Now the logician has stated that a proposition <p> that I do understand is a logical consequence of β, where I understand "logical consequence" as follows: Whenever a proposition is true, any proposition that is a logical consequence of it must also be true. Since we have seen that β is true, and since the logician, whose reasoning I trust implicitly, has stated that <p> is a logical consequence of β, it follows that <p> is true. Since 'p' is in my idiolect, I know what proposition <p> is and can use the truth schema to reason from '<p> is true' to 'p' and thus to assertorically utter 'p'. In this way, a propositional deflationist can capture reasoning the disciple could employ, reasoning that Field contends they cannot capture.

Even if Horwich can adequately answer Field's proposed challenge, there is a more limited challenge from immanence that confronts Horwich's view. It has to do with special cases of situations where Horwich would want to rely on a specific instance of (ES), as in his (1990/1998, pp. 22–23) strategy for explaining the role of truth-talk in an account of someone's behavioral success in terms of their having a true belief. In the relevant special cases, the content of the successful agent's belief is a proposition that the person giving the account cannot understand. The person giving the account can then only claim that the agent believes some true proposition, but they cannot give the deflationary explanation of the behavioral success Horwich claims is available. In response, Horwich might accept this, but he could go on to say that, while the person cannot express (or understand) the deflationary explanation, thereby making it unavailable *to her*, given the propositional nature of Horwich's view, the relevant deflationary explanation still *exists* and is available to anyone who does understand the relevant proposition (e.g., the aforementioned successful agent). We take up the issue of deflationary explanations of behavioral success in detail in Chapter 5.

4.2 The Formulation and Generalization Problems

One of the strongest challenges to the adequacy of Linguistic Deflationism is what has become known as the "Generalization Problem" (henceforth, *GP*), the issue of how a deflationary account of truth-talk can underwrite proofs of certain 'true'-employing generalizations, such as "All sentences of the form 'If p then p' are true". There is also a related challenge that arises from what we will call "the Formulation Problem" (henceforth, *FP*), an issue initially broached in Gupta (1993b) and discussed briefly in Armour-Garb and Woodbridge (2015, pp. 139–43), and in Woodbridge (2003) and (2005, pp. 154–61). The FP has garnered considerably less notice among deflationists than the GP has. Horwich and Field, for example, gloss over the FP and focus on addressing the GP. However, since the FP raises an important challenge to Linguistic Deflationism that is in a sense prior to the GP, we consider it first.

4.2.1 The Formulation Problem

The FP involves the question of how deflationary accounts of truth-talk can explain the formulation of genuine generalizations employing the truth predicate, given the seemingly meager resources that are available to them. The FP purports to threaten the Linguistic Deflationism that all species of deflationism must endorse, by arguing that deflationary accounts of the functioning of the alethic locutions are inadequate for underwriting the very expressive role that deflationists have emphasized as the central purpose of the truth predicate: the role of implementing something equivalent to generalizing over sentence-positions. Deflationists, like Field (1999, 2008), Horwich (1990/1998, 2001), Robert Brandom (1994), and others note that having a truth predicate allows for the formulation of this kind of generalization, using just ordinary objectual quantifiers and pronominal variables to do so. However, Anil Gupta (1993b, pp. 60–63) points out a problem with a common deflationary understanding of what the truth predicate accomplishes—one presented in, for example, Leeds (1978), Field (1994a), and possibly Quine (1970/1986)—that is encapsulated in the claim that "the truth predicate is a device for expressing certain infinite conjunctions and disjunctions". Gupta calls this "The Infinite Conjunction Thesis". When combined with the Connection Thesis that he (1993b, p. 60) also attributes to deflationists, viz., the claim that "[t]he truth predicate serves its expressive functions in virtue of its disquotation feature" (p. 60), this requires a very strong reading of the former according to which a 'true'-employing generalization of the form

(Q) All sentences of type Q are true

must have the same sense as the (potentially) infinite conjunction of its instances. They at least must be mutually entailing. As Field (1994a, p. 266) puts it, "For if [Q] is to serve as an infinite conjunction of all sentences of type Q, then we want it to entail each such instances, and be entailed by all of them together." But the problem Gupta (1993b, p. 63) notes is that

> A universal statement (e.g., [Q]) does not have the same sense as the conjunction of its instances.... The two do not even imply the same things.... I think that proponents of the disquotational

theory have gone astray because they have ignored the difference between wanting to affirm a generalization and wanting to affirm each of its instances.

Field's (1994a) claim that we want a sentence of form (Q) to "be entailed by all of [its instances] together" appears to ignore this difference, as do Stephen Leeds's (1978) understanding of the truth predicate as a means for formulating infinite conjunctions and disjunctions and Quine's (1970/1986) explanation of how truth-talk lets us affirm some infinite lot of sentences. Thus, they all appear to make (Q) a "fragmented" ersatz generalization, rather than a genuine generalization, from which we get the FP.

Extending his point beyond just disquotationalists, Gupta (1993b, p. 67) notes that Horwich (1990/1998) too presupposes "that a generalization is equivalent to the conjunction of its instances in a sense strong enough to guarantee that an explanation of one is an explanation of the other", which, Gupta points out, requires something beyond even necessary equivalence—something like sameness of sense. But, he explains, the two do not have the same sense. There is a logical gap between them in that the generalization entails each (and so a conjunction of all) of the instances, but the conjunction of all of the latter does not entail the generalization. The same challenge extends to Brandom's (1994) prosententialism, in virtue of his interpretation of (Q) (and all universal generalizations) as involving substitutional quantification governing sentential variables, in the form of variable prosentences formed from the application of 'true'. He, along with anyone who attempts to make (Q) a genuine generalization by appealing to substitutional quantification, must address the issue noted above: It is not clear how to understand substitutional quantifiers without either presupposing a notion of truth (cf. Horwich (1990/1998, p. 25, n. 10)) or taking them (cf. David (1994, pp. 99–100) and potentially Field (1994a, p. 264, n. 17)) as devices for encoding infinite conjunctions (and disjunctions). As explained in Chapter 1, the former strategy is unavailable to a deflationist on pain of an unacceptable circularity. But the latter simply returns one to the FP, in virtue of the "fragmentation" of universal substitutional generalizations into conjunctions of their instances that it yields.[5]

Since sentences of form (Q) look like universal generalizations that Linguistic Deflationism understands as implementing generalizing of a "logically special" kind (viz., on embedded sentence-positions), the FP challenges deflationists to explain how those 'true'-employing sentences turn out to be actual generalizations, rather than just conjunctions of their instances. (Cf. Woodbridge (2003).) In general, if a deflationary account is going to make good on its claim to offer an adequate account of truth-talk, it needs to answer the challenge posed by the FP without violating Linguistic Deflationism. This challenge then extends to the issue introduced in Chapter 1, regarding Linguistic Deflationism's thesis about the purpose of the truth predicate.

4.2.2 Understanding the Generalization Problem

Setting the FP aside, the GP raises an important connected challenge to Linguistic Deflationism. It is now common to expect one's theory of truth-talk to allow one to prove the sorts of generalizations that Quine (1970/1986) notes, for example, "All sentences of the form 'If p then p' are true", at least where 'p' is a 'true'-free sentence. The GP suggests that deflationists whose accounts of truth-talk

---

[5] In our (2015), we develop a strategy that we there maintain avoids this result and addresses the FP, while employing substitutional quantifiers on the "encoding" interpretation of them. We claim there that this is accomplished in virtue of the semantic-pretense framework we employ. This is in contrast with the approach we now take in Armour-Garb and Woodbridge (2023a, 2023b, and forthcoming) and in the appendix, below.

rely only on their favored version of the "neutral truth schema" mentioned in Chapter 1,

(TS) [p] is true iff p,

will have difficulties proving such generalizations without additional resources.[6] Thus, the GP presents the worry that deflationary accounts are inadequate to explain our commitments to certain facts typically expressed by generalizations that employ the truth predicate. This raises the question of whether and, if so, how these accounts earn the right to endorse such generalizations.

In an important sense, the GP should not be seen as a "new" problem. Indeed, while it appears to challenge deflationary theories, the problem is clearly flagged by Alfred Tarski (1935a/1983) in developing his non-deflationary theory. Although Tarski assigns primacy of place to the instances of (TS), in the form of the instance of his schema,

(T) X is true-in-L iff p,

where the 'X' is replaced with the name of a sentence from a given language, L, and 'p' is replaced by a translation of that sentence into the (meta)language in which one is theorizing, he does not see the totality of the schema's instances as the axioms of a theory of truth-in-L.[7] Moreover, even when such instances are taken as theorems, Tarski (1935a/1983) points out that they are insufficient for proving a generalization like

(i) All sentences of the form 'If p then p' are true,

---

[6] For details, see Gupta (1993a, 1993b), Horwich (1990/1998, pp. 137–38, 2001), Field (1994a, 2006, 2008), Armour-Garb (2010), and Halbach (2011, pp. 57–59).

[7] What Tarski (1935a/1983, p. 187) holds is that an adequate definition of truth would be one that implies an attribution of truth conditions to all sentences of a given language, L, where each such attribution satisfies his (T)-schema.

since the collection of the instances of (TS) is ω-incomplete.[8]

We arrive at a related problem when we combine a reliance on the instances of (TS) with Quine's discussion of the utility of the truth predicate. As we have seen, he (1992, p. 80–81) considers the purpose of (i) to be to "generalize along a dimension that cannot be swept out by a general term", that is, something like generalizing over sentences like

(ii) If it is raining, then it is raining,

and

(iii) If snow is white, then snow is white.

As explained in Section 3.2.1, in addition to instantiating and semantically descending from (i), to get (ii) and (iii), Quine also points out that we want to be able to generalize on the embedded sentences in those particular conditionals, by semantically ascending, abstracting logical form, and deriving (i). But, as Tarski (1935a/1983) also notes, this feat may not be achieved, given only a commitment to (the instances of) (TS). To be sure, from (TS) and (i), we can prove (ii) and (iii) but, given the finitude of deduction, when equipped only with the instances of (TS), we cannot prove the generalization from the instances. As Tarski explains, since, as a consequence of the Compactness Theorem of first-order logic, anything provable from the totality of instances of (TS) is provable from just finitely many of them, any theory that takes the totality of instances of (TS) to characterize truth will be unable to prove any of the generalizations like (i).[9] Any such view would have to be able to prove (i) from only finitely many instances of (TS) (and the finitely many conditionals they are

---

[8] A theory, understood as a collection of sentences, is ω-incomplete if it can prove every instance of an open formula 'F(x)' but cannot prove the generalization '$\forall x F(x)$'.

[9] As Tarski (1935a/1983, p. 257) notes, in reference to the instances of his schema, (T): "A theory of truth founded on them would be a highly incomplete system, which would lack the most important and most fruitful general theorems".

the instances of (TS) for), but (i) does not follow from any finite set of instances of (TS). Hence, without further refinements, deflationists seem stuck with ω-incompleteness.

This strongly suggests that just a commitment to the truth schema (or to an account of truth-talk that takes generating them "directly" or as immediate consequences of the functioning of the truth predicate as sufficient) is not enough—that something more is needed if deflationary theories are going to prove such generalizations. The question this raises is why deflationists must be able to prove these 'true'-employing generalizations.

4.2.3 Justifying Generalizations vs. Proving Generalizations

While we have discussed why a would-be deflationist needs to be able to explain how 'true'-employing "generalizations" amount to genuine generalizations, and we have noted the difference between that problem (the FP) and the GP, we still need to distinguish addressing the need to justify 'true'-employing generalizations from addressing the need to prove them. This distinction is important since, while it is uniformly recognized that if we wish to be entitled to accept a generalization, we must be in a position to provide warrant for it, there really is no need to prove all of the 'true'-employing generalizations that people want to accept.[10]

For example, we need not—indeed, we most likely cannot—*prove* the likes of

(M) Everything G. E. Moore said about goodness is true,

---

[10] Since the issue at hand does not specifically trade on a particular conception of *proof*, for this section we shall assume a rather generic reading of that notion, viz., one that involves derivations and deductions.

in order to be justified in accepting it. Rather, like anyone who seeks warrant for accepting something contingent, one would presumably attain warrant for accepting (M) via consideration of the meaning of 'true', together with induction on the basis of a (large) class of (M)'s instances. For this reason, the GP's requirement that deflationists be able to *prove* 'true'-employing generalizations is restricted to a particular class of them, namely, those, like (i), the acceptance of which seems to require a proof. Here, an appeal to simple induction and evidence regarding previous cases will not help us. Nevertheless, one might still wonder why it seems that deflationists must be able to prove (i) and its ilk in order to establish their acceptability.

Horwich (2001) provides a reason for maintaining this by imposing the following condition on the acceptability of an account of the meaning of 'true'. Say that we accept at least some truth-involving propositions, including a proposition like <Every proposition of the form <if p then p> is true>, which we shall call "β".[11] Call the set of these propositions "A". According to Horwich (2001), an account of the meaning of 'true' will be adequate only if it aids in explaining why we accept the members of A, where such explanations must amount to proofs of those propositions by, among other things, employing an explanatory premise that does not explicitly employ the truth predicate. So, one reason why it is important to be able to prove a truth-involving generalization like β is because doing so satisfies a condition of adequacy for an account of the meaning of that term.

To focus on a specific example, assuming that the truth-involving generalization β is correct, one might argue that a given account of truth-talk, along with one of the relevant conditional, together, perhaps, with other logical notions, should be able to yield β as a consequence.[12] But if an account of truth-talk, together with an

---

[11] For present purposes, we shall assume that we are dealing with propositions, rather than with sentences, though this assumption is dispensable (and is only in place so as to comport with Horwichian minimalism).

[12] Assuming, of course, that β is correct. If you do not take it to be correct, then substitute a β-style generalization that you do take to be correct.

account of the conditional (and other logical notions), does not yield β as a consequence, then it does not amount to an acceptable account of truth-talk (assuming that the accounts of the relevant logical notions is acceptable). Hence, an account of truth-talk, together with an account of other logical notions, must yield—that is, must "prove", in some sense of that notion—the truth-involving generalization, β.

Another reason for thinking that generalizations like β, etc. must be proved is that a theory of the meaning of 'true' should explain our acceptance of propositions like β. As Gupta (1993a) and Christopher Hill (2002) emphasize, this generalization should be taken as being knowable a priori by anyone who possesses the concept of truth (and who grasps the relevant logical concepts). But if such a proposition can be known a priori on the basis of a grasp of the concept of truth (and of the relevant logical concepts), then a theory that purports to specify the meaning of 'true' should explain our acceptance of that proposition. However, if an account of the meaning of 'true' is to explain our acceptance of a proposition such as β, then it must be possible to prove the proposition from one or more of the clauses of which our grasp of the concept of truth is constituted.

This creates a problem for a Horwichian minimalist. If, as we have noted, a theory of truth-talk will be adequate only if it explains our acceptance of such truth-involving propositions, then it must prove such propositions from one or more clauses that the characterization of 'true' comprises. Let us suppose that β is one such proposition. Restricted to the resources available through Horwich's minimalism, we can show that β cannot be proved. Here is how. If β could be proved then it would have to be proved from instances of (TS) for propositions, viz., for a Horwichian minimalist, the instances of

(ES) <p> is true iff p.

But this is problematic. In general there cannot be a valid derivation of a universal generalization from a set of particular propositions unless that set is inconsistent. Now, since, according to Horwich (1990/1998), every instance of (ES) that is part of his theory of truth is consistent, it follows that there cannot be a proof of β from its instances along with the instances of (ES). This is a purely logical point. As such, considerations of pure logic dictate that our acceptance of β cannot be explained by the characterization of truth-talk that is provided by Horwich's minimalism. This is a serious problem for Horwichian minimalism, but it is not necessarily a problem for deflationism. What would be a problem for deflationism is if the Linguistic Deflationism endorsed by each species of deflationism made all of them incapable of proving such generalizations.

We have thus far considered some adequacy-conditions for an account of the meaning of 'true' as a means for explaining why some truth-involving, or at least 'true'-employing, generalizations must be proved. One might also contend that a good account of truth-talk must be able to explain all of the facts that are in some sense "about truth". (Cf. Horwich (1990/1998, pp. 21, 24–25).) Since the acceptability of certain truth-involving generalizations seem to be among those facts, it follows that a good account of truth-talk must establish those generalizations, where to establish those generalizations just is to be able to prove them.

This last point is worth emphasizing. Truth-involving generalizations, like β and its ilk, must follow, at least in part, from one's overall theory of truth-talk. As such, it seems that they ought to be provable from a deflationist's theory of truth-talk, if that theory is to be deemed acceptable. If they are not provable (alternatively: not derivable, in some sense of "derive") from a given theory of truth-talk, then it would seem that that theory would be too weak to meet our needs. So, any theory of truth-talk that does not deliver such truth-involving or 'true'-employing generalizations would be too weak to meet (at least some of) our needs for having the truth predicate in the first place.

The jury is still out on whether Horwichian minimalists will be able to resolve the GP. Since Horwich takes all instances of (ES), the propositional version of (TS), as axioms, for any of what Tarski (1935a/1983, p. 257) calls "the most fruitful theorems", Horwich can prove each of their instances. Thus, he can prove, for any proposition, that either it or its negation is true, but, as we have seen, restricted to the instances of (ES), he cannot prove the generalization 'For every proposition, either it or its negation is true'. (For suggestions as to how the needed refinements might go, see Horwich (1990/1998, 2001). For challenges to Horwich, see Armour-Garb (2004, 2010, 2011a), Gupta (1993a, 1993b), and Soames (1998). For responses to Armour-Garb's attack on Horwich's (2001) attempt at establishing the most fruitful theorems, see Oms (2019) and Cieśliński (2018).)

For the reasons we have provided, it seems unacceptable for deflationists to deny that such generalizations need to be proved. After all, they presumably accept such generalizations and wish to be justified in doing so. Perhaps they will deny that it is the job of a theory of truth-talk to prove such generalizations. But this seems also to be unacceptable; nothing else seems suited to the task. In the case of something like (i), the sentence seems to be "about" the conditional; hence, it would seem, at least prima facie, that nothing aside from a theory of truth-talk (and logic) will do the trick. If that is insufficient to facilitate the proof of that sentence, then, one might think, so much the worse for deflationism. Thus, the challenge remains, at least for some deflationists. For other deflationists' attempts to prove at least some such truth-involving or 'true'-employing generalizations, see Field (1994a, 2006, 2008) and Hill (2002), whose positions we consider below.

4.2.4 Field and Hill on Proving Generalizations

As we have said, Field takes competence with truth-talk to consist in grasping the *cognitive equivalence* between an utterance, u, as a speaker understands it, and an ascription of truth to that utterance, where "cognitive equivalence" is cashed out in computational terms. Field (1994a, 2006) offers a solution to the GP by going beyond a mere acceptance of a sentential version of (TS), for example,

(T/DS) 'p' is true iff p.

As noted in the discussion of Field's pure disquotational account of truth-talk, in Section 3.2.3, Field endorses working directly with a schema like (T/DS), by allowing for a kind of reasoning with the schematic sentential variables it employs. As Field explains this sort of reasoning, it is governed by two rules of inference, one that allows for the replacement of all instances of a schematic variable by a sentence, and one that allows us to infer '$\forall x(\text{Sentence}(x) \to \phi(x))$' from a schema, '$\phi(\text{"p"})$', in which all occurrences of the schematic sentential variable are inside quotation marks. This, he claims, allows one to derive generalizations from (T/DS).

Field (2006) clarifies the inference rules he proposes for governing reasoning with schematic variables, explaining the first as stipulating that if one has inferred $\phi(p_1, p_2, \ldots, p_n)$, for all schematic letters 'p_i', then one can infer $\phi(A_1, A_2, \ldots, A_n)$, where the A_i's are sentences of the metalanguage (subject to certain qualifications, which we do not need to worry about here). The second rule he names '*Rule Gen*', stipulating that if one has inferred

$\phi(\text{'}p_1\text{'}, \text{'}p_2\text{'}, \text{'}p_3\text{'}, \ldots, \text{'}p_n\text{'})$, then one is licensed to conclude

$$\text{For any sentence, } x_1, x_2, \ldots, x_n, \phi(x_1, x_2, \ldots, x_n).$$[13]

To illustrate how this works, given (T/DS) and *Rule Gen*, suppose that we want to prove

(NC) There is no sentence such that both it and its negation are true.

According to Field, we can prove (NC), by reasoning as follows:

Step 1: If 'p' is true then p; if 'not-p' is true then not-p; so if both 'p' and 'not-p' are true then p and not-p, which is a contradiction. Therefore, it is not the case that both 'p' is true and 'not-p' is true.
Step 2: 'not-p' is the negation of 'p'; so, by the result of step 1, it is not the case that both 'p' is true and the negation of 'p' is true.
Step 3: By the result of step 2 and *Rule Gen*, (NC) follows.

If Field can extend schematic reasoning to account generally for all of the 'true'-employing generalizations that one might want to prove, then the schema (T/DS) becomes a powerful theory in the context of schematic reasoning, taken to include *Rule Gen*.

In his (1994a, p. 259), Field sees his method of incorporating reasoning with schematic sentence letters into the language as corresponding to "a very weak fragment of a substitutional quantificational language", which would seem to saddle him with the concerns we have noted regarding appeals to substitutional quantification. By contrast, Field's (2006) understanding of schemata and reasoning with schematic variables seems to go in a different direction, potentially avoiding those concerns.

---

[13] Given Field's (2006) more sophisticated understanding of schematic reasoning, *Rule Gen* does not fall victim to Gupta's point about generalizations not following from the collections of their instances. Rather, this rule is related to a form of universal generalization found in the proof theory for first-order logic.

However, Even granting that last point, a concern that Field's approach still faces pertains to disquotationalism's restriction of the applicability of truth-talk to sentences. Picking up on this, Hill (2002, p. 133) notes, "Field's proposal encounters grave difficulties when it is reformulated as a theory of the semantic concepts we apply to thought". To address this, Hill (2002, p. 133) proposes making use of a different understanding of substitutional quantification as an alternative to Field's approach. As mentioned in Section 3.3.2, Hill (2002, p. 22) offers a finitely axiomatized version of minimalism, which he takes to have all of the virtues of a fully deflationary account of truth-talk. The central, general axiom of his account is

(S) For any object x, x is true iff $\Sigma p((x = $ the thought that p) and p).

Hill's proposal bears some similarity to what Tarski offers. Tarski (1935a/1983) shows how to take a finitely axiomatized first-order theory, implicitly define satisfaction, and convert it to an explicit second-order definition of satisfaction from which he obtains an explicit second-order definition of truth. Hill's idea is to convert an implicit definition provided by the instances of (TS) for thoughts (propositions) into an explicit definition, by deploying a particular version of substitutional quantification. Because his account is formulated as a general claim, if otherwise adequate, it would provide the basis for deriving the desired 'true'-employing generalizations.

But Hill's approach re-raises a question of adequacy that we have considered before: How is one supposed to understand the substitutional quantification here? As discussed in Section 3.3.2, Hill claims that his general axiom employs substitutional quantification for "thought" instead of linguistic substitutional quantification, but others find this proposal, together with Hill's attempt to define his quantifiers with introduction and elimination rules, to be incoherent or confused. Moreover, as discussed at several points above, many theorists have expressed serious reservations about linguistic substitutional quantification, as well as about its employment specifically in giving an account of truth-talk. Some, for example Marian David (1994), find it congenial, but we have also noted problems with his understanding of these logical devices, especially in Section 4.2.1. It seems unlikely that substitutional quantifiers can be used to resolve challenges to deflationism, such as the FP and the GP. It thus appears that deflationists require a different, non-substitutional understanding of sentential variables and quantifiers if they are to employ these "higher-level" logical devices in addressing challenges to deflationism.[14]

---

[14] In Armour-Garb and Woodbridge (2015, Ch. 4.3), we take the way of employing standard linguistic substitutional quantification developed there, and mentioned in a footnote above as a means for resolving the FP, to extend to resolving the GP as well. In our (2023a, 2023b, and forthcoming) we apply a different, non-substitutional understanding of sentential quantification to these issues. We explain an updated version of this alternative approach in the appendix to this book.

5

Challenges to Metaphysical Deflationism

As mentioned in Chapter 4, attacks on Metaphysical Deflationism seem to yield indirect challenges to Linguistic Deflationism, which, as noted in Chapter 1, is at the center of any deflationary account. These attacks are intended to establish the need for a substantive property of truth. There are four main types of attempts to put this kind of pressure on Metaphysical Deflationism that we discuss in this chapter:

(i) Those that try to establish that there is some causal-explanatory role that requires a substantive property of truth for its implementation
(ii) Those that try to establish that certain mathematico-logical results require a substantive property of truth
(iii) Those that try to adhere to a particular correspondence intuition that supposedly can only be satisfied by a more-than-deflationary account of the property of truth, and
(iv) Those that try to establish that there is some sort of normative role that can only be filled by a substantive property of truth

5.1 The Causal-Explanatory Role Challenge

This first type of challenge to Metaphysical Deflationism emerges out of the argument from Hartry Field (1972) noted in Section 2.6, which is against accepting what amounts to a Tarskian version of recursive disquotationalism that possesses list-like definitions of reference and satisfaction at its base. Field (1972, pp. 370–73) claims that this sort of account would not underwrite attributing truth any causal-explanatory role of the sort suggested by the notion's utility and importance; such a role requires that truth admit of a reductive naturalistic/physicalist analysis, which could be attained by supplementing the Tarskian machinery with causal accounts of reference and satisfaction. Extending a point made by W. V. O. Quine (1970/1986), Stephen Leeds's (1978) early defense of recursive disquotationalism involves claiming that the utility of the truth predicate is exhausted by its logically expressive role, which implies that there are no causal-explanatory uses of truth-talk. The controversial natures of both causation and explanation suggest that this question about truth-talk might be hostage to one's views about these other notions. For example, Nic Damnjanovic (2005) claims that, on the account of explanation from Frank Jackson and Philip Pettit (1990), even a deflationist account of the truth predicate would count as giving truth a causal-explanatory role. Other accounts of explanation (e.g., those presented in van Fraassen (1980), Railton (1981), and Kitcher (1989)) might also see deflationist accounts of truth-talk as sufficient for making truth an explanatory (even causal-explanatory) notion without seeming to violate Metaphysical Deflationism. Despite these complexities, the dispute about whether the truth predicate ever appears in any fundamental causal-explanatory context is one of the central focuses of challenges to Metaphysical Deflationism, with the relevant phenomenon that is the target of explanation typically being some sort of success.

There are two kinds of success phenomena that have been the main focuses of this kind of challenge to deflationism—successful scientific theorizing and successful behavior—and each of these has been examined at two different levels—the particular level and a more general level. Hilary Putnam (1978) presents the first challenges to deflationism based on both of these kinds of success phenomena. He does so specifically in response to Leeds's early contention that the concept of truth does not play any causal-explanatory role, claiming, first, that (accepting Richard Boyd's view of the convergence of scientific knowledge) "the notions of 'truth' and 'reference' have a causal-explanatory role in ... an *explanation* of the behavior of scientists and the success of science" (Putnam (1978, pp. 20–21)), and, second, that "the notion of truth can be used in causal explanations—the success of a man's behavior may, after all, depend on the fact that certain of his beliefs are *true*—and the formal logic of 'true' [its *disquotation property*] is not all there is to the notion of *truth*" (Putnam (1978, p. 38)).

5.1.1 Explaining the Success of Science

In considering the success of scientific theorizing at the particular level, Putnam (1978, p. 19) notes that "a natural explanation of the success of [electron theory or DNA theory] is that they are *partially true accounts* of how [electrons or DNA molecules] behave", where "success" involves "making many true predictions, devising better ways of controlling nature, etc." (italics original). So, in summary we seem to have many explanations of the form

(ST) Theory θ is successful (predictively and instrumentally) *because* it is (approximately) true.

However, many putative explanations of this form have been unacceptable, since historically there are many successful theories that we now think are not true, as Larry Laudan (1981) contends. Moreover, even for theories that we do consider to be true, the use of the truth predicate in instances of (ST) does not seem to require this predicate to do anything more than what deflationists claim it does linguistically. Consider, for example, the specific case of electron theory. The relevant instance of (ST) for it is

(ST_E) Electron theory is (predictively and instrumentally) successful because it is (approximately) true.

However, rather than this explanation, one might instead offer

(ST_E') Electron theory is (predictively and instrumentally) successful because it claims (among other things) that there are (more or less) fundamental particles with unit negative charge, rest mass m_e, and spin ½, and there are (more or less) fundamental particles with unit negative charge, rest mass m_e, and spin ½.

Or, if one does not know the details of electron theory, one might use (ST_E) to express what would otherwise require an infinite disjunction of conjunctions, each of which is an instance of the form 'electron theory claims (among other things) that p, and p'. So, in the acceptable explanations of the success of particular scientific theories that employ the truth predicate, truth-talk appears to play just the kind of expressive role that deflationists claim it plays in other opaque ascriptions. (Cf. Horwich (1982, p. 193) and (1990/1998, p. 49).)

A putatively more challenging argument for a causal-explanatory role for truth considers the scientific success phenomenon at the more general level of scientific methods. Boyd (1983, p. 65) presents the most sophisticated version of this argument, centered on the following explanation.

(SM) Scientific method is (increasingly) instrumentally reliable (successful) because the theories that inform it (in a dialectically improving way) are (increasingly approximately) true.

Here the use of the truth predicate cannot be replaced, as it is above, with a mention and a use of the specific content of a particular theory, since (SM) makes a general (and diachronic) claim about scientific theories and methods. Nevertheless, even granting that (SM) offers an acceptable explanation, a deflationist will still hold that there is no reason to attribute to the truth predicate a fundamentally explanatory—as opposed to an expressive—role there. Michael Williams (1986, pp. 230–31) makes this point, claiming that "in Boyd's argument the use of 'true' is an expressive convenience but adds nothing to scientific realism's explanatory force". He maintains that the truth predicate just allows for the expression of what would otherwise require a long conjunction of all the theories we currently accept from the "mature" sciences, with conjuncts like, "that the methods we use to investigate elementary particles work as well as they do because the world is made of such particles behaving more or less the way we think they do". According to Williams (1986, p. 230), the central idea behind Boyd's scientific realism is just "that certain empirical claims (those made by theories belonging to mature sciences) explain others (having to do with the fruitfulness of methods informed by those theories)".

Philip Kitcher (2002) presents a putative counterexample to the sort of deflationist understanding of the truth predicate's role in general explanations of success that Williams (1986) offers. Kitcher's move is to highlight a systematicity that needs explaining. He (2002, pp. 360–64) examines patterns of success involving the use of map-like devices in bioengineering procedures, but, applying his point to (SM) and assuming it offers an acceptable explanation, his thought is that there is a pattern of methodologies being successful when informed by theories from mature sciences. In addition to the success of each such methodology, this pattern itself also seems in need of an explanation in terms of something in common across all of its instances. A conjunction of statements of each separate theory, along with a note in each case that some theory says that is how things are and this is why the particular methodology that the theory informs is successful, would not indicate anything common and so would not express any systematicity.[1] Kitcher's point is that a deflationary understanding of (SM) does not seem to capture the full explanation of the success phenomenon that scientific realism purports to explain with a claim like (SM). A deflationist must either deny the systematicity (perhaps by rejecting any connection between truth and success) or reconstruct it in terms that maintain Metaphysical Deflationism. Various opponents of scientific realism (e.g., Laudan (1981)) have pursued the former tactic independently of deflationism.

5.1.2 Explaining Behavioral Success

The role of the truth predicate in explanations of behavioral success appears to parallel its role in explanations of scientific success. However, as we will see, certain additional complexities emerge, due to the involvement of intentional cognitive or psychological states, such as beliefs and desires, in the generation of the sort of behavior that is eligible for success. Even before the complexities emerge, one common type of behavioral success involves agents fulfilling certain desires or goals by acting on their beliefs about how to fulfill those desires/goals. 'True'-employing explanations of particular instances of this sort of success will typically fit into the following form. (Cf. Horwich (1990/1998, pp. 44–45).)

  (i) Agent A wants X to be the case.
 (ii) A believes that if A does Y, then X will come to be the case.
(iii) Because of (i) and (ii), A does Y (ceteris paribus).
(iv) Because A's belief in (ii) was true, X comes to be in virtue of (iii).
 (v) So, A succeeds in fulfilling A's desire/goal.

---

[1] This is related to the Formulation Problem discussed in Section 4.2.1.

As Putnam (1978, p. 38) suggests, in any specific explanation of this form, the truth of the agent's belief will seem to explain their success, viz., their fulfilling their desire or goal. However, as in the case of an explanation of a particular scientific theory's success, the truth predicate's use in any instance of (iv) appears to require nothing beyond what deflationists claim the truth predicate does linguistically. One could replace (iv) with (iv'):

(iv') Because if A does Y, X will come to be the case, X comes to be in virtue of (iii).

A deflationist would claim that (iv') functions equally well in any explanation of a particular instance of an agent's behavioral success. Since (iv') does not involve any truth-talk, the use of the truth predicate in (iv) is just an expressive convenience (including, perhaps, the convenience of expressing what would otherwise require an infinite disjunction, if one did not know on which belief the agent acted). Paul Horwich (1990/1998, pp. 22–23) presents a slightly more detailed way of analyzing the role of the truth predicate in the instance of (iv) employed in an explanation of a particular case of behavioral success. Following his analysis, we first note that A's belief is that if A does Y, then X will come to be the case. As a result of this identity, the claim that A's belief is true is equivalent to the claim that (the proposition that) if A does Y, then X will come to be the case is true. The role of the truth predicate in (iv), then, is only to establish an equivalence between this last claim and the claim that if A does Y, then X will come to be the case. The latter is what replaces the instance of truth-talk embedded in (iv) to produce (iv'). So, a deflationary account of the operation of the truth predicate (any species of which will provide the final equivalence at no metaphysical expense) would suffice for this sort of explanation.

The role of the truth predicate in explanations of behavioral success beyond just particular instances has become the main focus of the challenge to Metaphysical Deflationism based on claiming that some causal-explanatory role requires there be a substantive property of truth. Putnam (1978, pp. 101–2) initiates this strategy with his claim that any account of the contribution of our linguistic behavior to the success of our total behavior will include recognizing the following:

(1) People act (in general) in such a way that their goals will be obtained (as well as possible in the given situation), or in such a way that their expectations will not be frustrated, ... if their beliefs are *true*.
(2) Many beliefs [people have about how to attain their goals] *are* true.
(3) So, as a consequence of (1) and (2), people have a tendency to attain certain kinds of goals.

His point is that one explains (3) via (1) and (2), thereby using the truth predicate in what appears to be a causal-explanatory context. Moreover, to the extent that one considers this an acceptable explanation of (3), it appears to treat (1) as a kind of covering law, and thus to employ the truth predicate in the statement of a law-like generalization. This is different from the role the truth predicate plays in general-level explanations of scientific success, since even there (in (MS) above) it simply applied to theories of mature science, which could, in principle, all be stated directly. (Cf. Williams (1986, p. 232).) But the generality of (1) seems to cover more cases than any definite list of beliefs could include, including a list of everything actually believed by anyone. The fact that (1) supports counterfactuals by applying to whatever one might possibly believe (about attaining goals) suggests that it is a law-like generalization. If the truth predicate played a fundamental role in the expression of an explanatory law, then Metaphysical Deflationism, and deflationism along with it, would be undermined. Providing a deflationary response to this line of thought, Williams (1986, p. 232) rejects the thesis that the general claim about true belief is a law.

He sees it as just a more indefinite principle than the one regarding true scientific theories involved in Boyd's argument, in the sense that we cannot actually list all the beliefs in the way that we could with the current scientific theories. But, Williams claims, the function of the truth predicate in (1) is still just to express a kind of infinite generalizing from ordinary cases. As he (1986, p. 232) puts it,

> If I want a cold drink and believe that the refrigerator, rather than the oven, is the place to look, I will increase the likelihood of getting what I want. This is because cold drinks are more likely found in the refrigerator than the oven. To say that my having true beliefs makes it more likely that I will attain my goals is just a compact way of pointing to the indefinite number of mundane facts of this sort.

Anil Gupta (1993b) argues that his points about the GP have particular relevance in challenging the sort of deflationary response that Williams provides. After all, the latter is claiming that (1) just expresses an infinite conjunction of its instances (as in Leeds (1978)), which involves no unity. Gupta argues that a claim of this sort cannot provide an explanation, meaning that deflationists would have to deny that (1)–(3) offer any explanation. In response to Gupta's claim, Darren Bradley (2023) argues that even a disunified infinite conjunction or disjunction can play an explanatory role, similar to the way that claims about averages can be explanatory, concluding that a Williams-style deflationary reading of (1) *can* play an explanatory role in Putnam's example, without violating deflationary principles.

According to Field (1994a, p. 271), "the most serious worry about deflationism is that it can't make sense of the explanatory role of truth conditions: e.g., their role in explaining behaviour, or their role in explaining the extent to which behaviour is successful". In a pre-deflationary paper, Field (1987) examines challenges to deflationism based on precisely these purported explanatory roles of truth conditions. The first, explaining intentional behavior, is related to the debate among theories of psychological explanation about wide versus narrow content.[2] It has seemed to some (e.g., Michael Devitt (1997, pp. 325–30)) that explaining behavior must appeal to truth-conditional and/or referential (wide) content, given that one's behavior might arise, e.g., from one's desire for *water*. But, due to certain semantic externalist considerations (e.g., Putnam (1973)), this desire specifically for water seems to get its identifying content by referring to something outside of the agent's head. Field, however, concludes that explaining behavior in general does not require any appeal to truth conditions. He (1987, p. 82) notes that one might agree with Quine (1960, p. 219) that psychological explanation is "projectivist", perhaps in the way developed by simulation theorists as opposed to 'theory'-theorists (familiar from theories of mind), which would not require anything more than a deflationist account of truth-talk. Alternatively, if one thinks, as Field himself does in this article, that an explanation of someone else's behavior should be given only in terms of that person's thought-states, with no mention of the person giving the explanation, then there are several approaches to theorizing about cognition that provide "truth-conditionless" accounts of mental states and their generation of behavior (1987, pp. 84–85). Devitt (1997, pp. 91–97) initially agrees that psychological explanations of behavior only need to invoke narrow content, so that truth plays no substantive role in these explanations. But, as noted above, he later recants this position and embraces the appeal to wide content, in the afterword to Devitt (1997).

Where Field (1987, p. 93) thinks that truth conditions do play an explanatory role is in an appeal to a kind of reliability, what he calls "T-reliability", that is made in explanations of behavioral success.

---

[2] This issue also connects with the challenge to Conceptual Deflationism involving the putative role of truth in explaining what meaning or content is, which we discuss in Section 6.3.

He recognizes that taking success, that is, satisfaction of desires, as the explanandum relies on truth conditions from the start, so, to avoid begging the question on this, Field reframes success explanations as explanations of the particular behaviors that constitute success in specific contexts. What gets added is a T-reliability assumption about the agent's beliefs that are involved in generating the relevant behavior (1987, pp. 94–95). As with explanations of behavior in general, Field (1987, p. 96) sees recasting the explanatory specifications of the agent's thought-states in computational ("language of thought") terms as an option for a deflationist, but only "in situations where we have detailed knowledge of people's psychologies and of what sort of behavior tends towards the kinds of success in question" (1987, p. 99). In explanations of behavior in general, Field (1987, pp. 86–87) permits recourse to "second-class" projectivist explanations in situations where we are ignorant of such factors. But the T-reliability assumptions included in explanations of successful behavior require that they be non-projective (1987, p. 93). So, the challenge Field sees for deflationism is that "we give 'success explanations' in the absence of such knowledge, and in doing so we apparently rely on a body of theory in which the notion of truth-conditions plays a role" (1987, p. 99).

In response to Field's (1987) arguments, Leeds (1995, p. 17) addresses Field's contention that "in such cases of ignorance, although the truth-conditions explanation continues to go through, the deflationist's counterpart cannot be formulated". Leeds (1995) acknowledges that conditions of ignorance prevent the formulation of an explanation free of truth-talk. This is because we do not know the full details of the "language of thought" sentences to which the agent bears the computational analog of belief (belief*), so we cannot correlate all of them plus when the agent believes* them with specified situations. Instead, we must resort to a T-reliability claim for some of them, e.g., W, and say that the agent "tends to believe* W when it's true" (1995, p. 18). But this, Leeds (1995, p. 19) claims, is not to use the truth predicate in an explanatory fashion: "Rather, the use is disquotational: instead of presenting the explanation in terms of the truth-conditions of the [agent's] beliefs, we offer a disjunction of possible explanations—truth here is playing its familiar role as a device for expressing the disjunction".

We can see that the standard deflationist reply to challenges claiming that truth plays a substantive role in explanations of behavioral success is to claim that the truth predicate just plays an expressive generalizing role in these explanations. This response has come under certain criticisms that look at factors that arise at certain "higher-level" perspectives. Before drawing his conclusions about scientific realism discussed above, Kitcher (2002, pp. 355–59) examines Horwich's (1990/1998, pp. 22–23) account of how the truth predicate functions in explanations of behavioral success and concludes that the latter operates at too shallow a level. He claims that Horwich's account misses the more systematic role that truth plays in explaining patterns of successful behavior, such as when means-ends beliefs flow from a representational device, as might be found in a map. The accuracy of a map and the beliefs it generates are part of an explanation of someone's using the map to navigate to several different places successfully. As Kitcher (2002, p. 360) notes, "Horwich-style explanations, even if they turned out to be psychologically plausible in their invocation of beliefs about means-ends relations, wouldn't yield any insight into the pattern of success". The accounts that Williams and Leeds offer of the truth predicate's role in such explanations, in terms of potentially infinite conjunctions and disjunctions, also do not seem to capture the systematicity that Kitcher emphasizes, since there is no unity across the conjuncts or disjuncts the deflationist's truth predicate expresses. Chase Wrenn (2011) agrees that deflationists need to explain systematic as opposed to just singular success, but, against Kitcher, he argues that they are actually better off than inflationists on this front. According to Wrenn (2011, pp. 460–62), there are no explanatory links between the sort of causation some inflationists believe truth involves and successful behavior; the real issue is why psychologically pertinent actions (those agents take as relevant to achieving their goals, given their beliefs) are ever effectively pertinent actions (those that would lead to them achieving their goals). But this, he maintains, is an issue for philosophy of mind that has nothing to do with a notion of truth. A deflationist can accept whatever theory in philosophy of mind explains this, while maintaining a logically (and ontologically) weaker approach to truth than an inflationist who accepts the relevant philosophy of mind (Wrenn (2011), p. 469).

Michael Lynch (2009, pp. 124–26) offers another sort of "higher-level-factor" behavioral success argument against deflationism, one that considers the putative modal information provided by a 'true'-employing explanation. He maintains that an explanation "in terms of the truth of her belief tells us that *in any relevantly similar situation, as in the actual situation,* [an agent's] having a true belief about how to get what she wants will be a good explanation for why she gets what she wants" (2009, p. 125; italics original). Lynch (2009, 126) also claims that a deflationist's particularized explanation, in terms of the specific content of the belief and a specific situation in the world (as per Horwich (1990/1998, pp. 22–23)), or even an account of the role of the truth predicate as a generalizing device that avoids having to state a long conjunction of conditionals (as per Williams (1986, p. 232)), could not express the same information. Lynch (2009, p. 126) argues the point as follows.

> But again, by explaining the success of my actions in terms of the *truth* of my belief, I implicitly convey new modal information: I convey the information that *other* true beliefs would also have brought about success had the world been different than it is—even if, in fact, it had been very different, different in ways I cannot even imagine. In making claims about truth's link to success, I am ranging over worlds and situations that I might not even understand, and hence would not recognize were one to include them in some long list of conditionals. (italics original)

To see how a deflationist might resist Lynch's challenge, notice that, in claiming that a long, potentially infinite list or conjunction of conditionals could not capture the relevant range of alternative situations, Lynch seems to be assuming that such a conjunction of conditionals is somehow constrained by what a speaker can imagine or understand. But that assumption needs some support. Lynch might attempt to provide this by appealing to immanence and by claiming that any such (potentially infinite) conjunction of conditionals that is expressed by a 'true'-employing generalization will be restricted to conditionals that the speaker understands. However, as discussed in Section 4.1, while immanence is a feature of certain deflationary theories, it is not a feature of all of them (e.g., prosentential views do not appear to be restricted in this way, and neither does Horwichian minimalism). Moreover, a deflationist need not (and, as noted above, actually should not) understand the logical role of 'true'-employing generalizations in terms of the expression of potentially infinite conjunctions (as suggested in Williams's (1986) account of 'true'-employing explanations of behavioral success), since these conjunctions do not amount to, and are not logically equivalent to, genuine generalizations. Instead, deflationists should take truth-talk to implement the effect of quantifying into sentence-positions, expressing in a first-order framework what sentential quantifiers would express in genuine "higher-level" generalizations.[3] Qua genuine generalizations, what they express would not be restricted to what speakers understand or even to what is expressible in a given language. Thus, while Lynch's challenge might threaten certain deflationary accounts, viz., those that understand the truth predicate as a device of infinite conjunction and disjunction, and that maintain that truth-talk is restricted by immanence, his "higher-level-factor" objection to deflationary views does not threaten all versions of deflationism.

---

[3] We expand on this point at the end of this subsection. We discuss this sort of approach in the appendix to this book.

Will Gamester (2018, pp. 1252–55) presents yet another "higher-level-factor" challenge to deflationism. It is also directed at the kind of deflationist understanding that Williams (1986) presents of the role of the truth predicate in explanations of behavioral success, and it turns on deflationism's supposed inability to distinguish between coincidental and non-coincidental success. In Gamester's examples of these different kinds of success, two agents perform the same psychologically pertinent action-type, which turns out to be effectively pertinent for both agents as well. As a result, there is success in both cases. The difference between them is that the action being pertinent in both ways is surprising in the coincidental case, while it is unsurprising in the non-coincidental case. The problem is that a Horwich-style deflationist's explanations of the two cases run in parallel, thereby missing the explanatory contrast between them and showing that these explanations are incomplete. Gamester (2018, pp. 1256–57) argues that an inflationist's explanation can mark and account for the different statuses of the two instances of success. He (2018, pp. 1256–57) notes that, in the non-coincidental case, the belief that factors into the psychological pertinence of the agent's action is the product of valid reasoning from true prior beliefs, while, in the coincidental case, the belief that factors into the psychological pertinence of the agent's action, while true, is true only coincidentally, being the product of reasoning from at least one false prior belief. He further contends that this account of the difference is of no use to the deflationist, since it proceeds in terms of the truth and falsity of the two agents' prior beliefs. While the inflationist can appeal to something like Putnam's principle (1) (above) as an explanatory generalization, "The deflationist is thus stuck with the unenviable task of trying to explain [the non-coincidentally successful agent's] success *in particular*, by reference to something that is true of [that agent] but not true of [the coincidentally successful agent] *other than* the truth of [the former's] beliefs" (2018, p. 1255; italics original).

It is not clear, however, that the deflationist cannot avail herself of a version of the explanation of the difference that Gamester provides. They could understand the explanation as a way of expressing, in natural language, not the sort of infinite conjunction that Williams (1986) contends, but rather what would otherwise be expressed using sentential variables and quantifiers. So, for the coincidentally successful agent, for some p and for some q, the agent believes that p, and their belief that p factors into their (valid) reasoning to their action-generating belief that q. It is surprising and coincidental, then, that q, since ~p. By contrast, the non-coincidentally successful agent's reasoning from some p to their belief that q is sound, so it is unsurprising that q. This rendering appeals to sentential variables and quantifiers, but the deflationist can claim that the point of truth-talk is to implement the logical role of such devices in a natural language. An even stronger response that is available to deflationists is to uphold SVD and claim that the 'true'-employing account of the difference gets explained in terms of the generalizations employing sentential variables and quantifiers, along the lines that Frank Ramsey (1927/1990, 1929/1991) and A. N. Prior (1971) spell out, where these devices get a prior, independent account.[4]

Wrenn (2021) provides a similar sort of deflationary response to the "higher-level-factor" challenges lodged by Kitcher, Lynch, and Gamester, by drawing a distinction between *content-truth* and *vehicle-truth*, along with an appeal to sentential variables and quantifiers. Wrenn claims that, on a deflationary view, content-truth is thin and fragmented, which makes it incapable of expressing systematic success or modal characteristics or capturing the difference between non-coincidental success and coincidental

---

[4] To completely avoid any appeal to truth, in explaining the coincidental/non-coincidental difference, the notions of valid and sound reasoning would also have to be explained in "truth-free" terms. SVD can do this by employing sentential variables and quantifiers, where, again, these devices would get a prior, independent account. We address this issue in Section 6.1.

success. By contrast, vehicle-truth is more substantive in the sense of being the property of having a true content. This is something that different content-vehicles can have in common but only in the sense of all of them being such that there is some p, where p and the content-vehicle (belief, utterance) has the content that p. All of the true truth-vehicles have this same non-truth-involving, metaphysically deflationary feature in common, and the truth predicate is just a natural-language way of expressing it, as most deflationists maintain. Wrenn (2021, p. 109) points out that Gamester (2018, p. 1260) considers but rejects a "truth-talk as just a generalizing device" type of response to the "higher-level factor" challenges to deflationism. Gamester's rejection involves assuming a rather strict constraint on deflationary accounts, viz., that they must "*earn the right* to the claim that true beliefs facilitate practical success by *first* explaining (or providing a recipe for explaining) each individual instance of practical success; and *then* generalizing over them" (2018, p. 1260; italics original). However, as Wrenn notes, it is not clear that deflationists must endorse this constraint, as it assumes that 'true'-employing generalizations just express the collections of their instances, rather than genuine generalizations.

Wrenn's proposal for dealing with certain "higher-level-factor" challenges to deflationism is another instance of a response that we call "sentential-variable deflationism" (Cf. Sections 2.2, 3.1, and the appendix). SVD appeals to some sort of sentential quantification to explain the logical function of truth-talk as well as what its instances express. As with all versions of SVD, the effectiveness of Wrenn's proposal turns on whether he has an account of the higher-order quantification that his notion of vehicle-truth involves which yields real generalizations. This is because an account of these quantifiers that yields only fragmented, ersatz generalizations will not render vehicle-truth a unified and thus shared property of the true truth-vehicles, one that is thereby capable of explaining the "higher-level" factors that are specified in the challenges involving them. It is worth highlighting that, while the other deflationary responses to the sorts of challenges considered in this section do not involve attempts to provide any unified, shared property as part of their replies, they too make an appeal to sentential variables and quantifiers and thus also need some account of them. As mentioned above, it has seemed to many that the only way to interpret these formal devices is as implementing *substitutional* quantification. However, as noted in Sections 1.2, 3.3, 4.2.4, and elsewhere, there are problems with employing that form of quantification in response to challenges to deflationary accounts.[5] As a result, and similar to what emerged in assessing deflationary responses to the FP and GP in Section 4.2.4, if deflationists are going to appeal to sentential variables and quantifiers in response to "higher-level-factor" challenges of the sort considered here as well, they again will need to provide some understanding of these devices in a way that explains them non-substitutionally.[6]

5.2 The Conservativeness Argument

A separate challenge to Metaphysical Deflationism comes from what is now called the "Conservativeness Argument". The issue is that certain mathematico-logical results appear to conflict with a "conservativeness constraint" that some theorists claim deflationary views must satisfy, in virtue of their acceptance of both

---

[5] Wrenn (2021, pp. 107–9) recognizes this and proposes a non-substitutional reading of sentential variables and quantifiers. However, rather than providing an account of these logical devices, he follows Williamson (2013) and takes this "higher-order" machinery to be primitive. We explain our concerns about this sort of approach in the appendix.

[6] As noted in Chapter 1, Azzouni (2001, 2006) also provides a different non-substitutional account of these sentential devices, as do Picollo and Schindler (2018, 2022), but, as we discuss in the appendix below, we also have concerns about their approaches in virtue of the purely formal stipulations of logical machinery that they employ. By contrast, in Armour-Garb and Woodbridge (2023a, 2023b, and forthcoming) and in the appendix, we develop a different non-substitutional and non-nominal approach to explaining sentential variables and quantifiers in natural language, based on suggestions from Yablo (1996) and Rayo and Yablo (2001) that are inspired by Prior's work.

Metaphysical and Linguistic Deflationism. The constraint these theorists suggest is that a deflationary theory of truth-talk must be conservative in the sense that adding it to a theory, θ, couched in a "truth-free" language, L, does not make it possible to prove sentences of L that are not already provable by θ. So, on a deflationary understanding, truth-talk ought not to allow us to establish any new claims that do not involve the notion of truth (e.g., nothing beyond the trivial sort of addition involved in now being able to prove that a theorem is true in addition to proving the theorem). But some critics of deflationism (notably, Stewart Shapiro (1998) and Jeffrey Ketland (1999), as well as Leon Horsten (1995)) have argued that the imposition of such a conservativeness constraint on deflationary views leads to trouble for deflationists. The challenge takes note of the fact that adding a truth predicate to certain formal systems makes it possible to prove more about truth-free matters than the system could prove before. Since the system can prove more with a truth predicate than it could without one, this supposedly shows that the truth predicate attributes a substantive property and plays more than a merely expressive role. This would violate Metaphysical Deflationism and thereby threaten the Linguistic Deflationism of any deflationary theory.

Prior to addressing the Conservativeness Argument and considering responses, some preliminaries are necessary.

5.2.1 Explaining the Conservativeness Argument

Certain deflationists adopt *axiomatic* theories of truth, which is to say that they treat truth as a primitive notion and provide axioms, such as the instances of (TS) or something analogous.[7] In such a theory, "'true' or 'T'" is taken to be a predicate that applies to

---

[7] For discussion of such theories for deflationists, see Halbach (2015) and Horsten (2011).

certain *truth-bearers*, e.g., propositions, sentence types, sentence tokens, etc. A theory that describes the features of the objects to which truth can be predicated is called the "base theory". The base theory might be an arithmetical theory, in which case truth may be ascribed to mathematical sentences by applying the truth predicate to the Gödel numbers of these sentences. What is crucial is that the base theory neither involves the truth predicate nor makes any assumptions that might be thought of as "truth-theoretic". Adding the axioms of a truth theory to a base theory results in an *extension* of the base theory. According to advocates of the Conservativeness Argument (e.g., Horsten (1995), Shapiro (1998), and Ketland (1999)), for deflationists, such an extension of the base theory must be *conservative*, that is, the axioms of their theory should not allow the theorist to prove any theorems that do not include the truth predicate. As Ketland (2005, p. 77) notes, "a deflationary conception of truth should be committed to some sort of conservation constraint for its favoured truth axioms".

We shall take Peano Arithmetic (henceforth, *PA*) as the base theory that describes the features of the things, e.g., the sentence tokens, to which the truth predicate is applied.[8] For any language, L, L^T is that language with a truth predicate, 'T', added. L^T allows for the formulation of infinitely many instances of a formalized version of (TS), viz., all biconditional statements of the form

(TS_F) $T([\phi]) \leftrightarrow \phi$,

---

[8] There is nothing particularly special about taking PA as the base theory. It seems that in many cases it is chosen because, when one adds the truth axioms to it, the results are interesting and because it can be shown that PA is equivalent to certain theories of propositions and to those of syntax. Mount and Waxman (2021, p. 440) contend that "PA plays a "double role": as a mathematical theory (about the natural numbers) and, by way of a Gödel coding, as a theory of syntax".

where 'φ' covers the sentences of L, and the nominalizing device '[ ]' takes a formula to its Gödel number.[9] Call the language of PA "L_{PA}". L_{PA}^T is then the language of PA with 'T' added. As Alfred Tarski (1935b/1983) notes, if (TS_F) is completely unrestricted, so that the schema applies to *any* sentence of a language like L_{PA}^T, one that contains a truth predicate and negation and that has the capacity for self-reference, so that sentences of that language can talk about themselves, then a version of the Liar Paradox results.[10] Indeed, as discussed in Sections 1.4 and 7.2, Tarski's Undefinability Theorem establishes that no language of sufficient complexity can consistently contain its own truth predicate. In light of the potential emergence of the Liar Paradox, some truth theorists have attempted to impose restrictions on what can constitute an instance of (TS_F). These considerations have led to a distinction between two kinds of approaches in developing formal theories of truth-talk, namely, that between *typed* and *type-free* (or "*untyped*") theories of truth. Typed theories have been motivated by an interest in avoiding the Liar Paradox along the lines of Tarski's solution by disallowing any application of the truth predicate to any sentence that contains that truth predicate. However, there are problems with the typed approach, some of which are akin to Saul Kripke's objection to Tarski's solution to the Liar Paradox (cf. our discussion in Chapter 7). In light of these problems, many contemporary truth theorists have moved away from typed theories and endorsed untyped theories, which do not impose the former's restriction on applications of the truth predicate. Since the issue of deciding between a typed and untyped

---

[9] Horsten (2011, p. 38) explicitly ignores the "Gödelizing" detail that we have included here, and he notes that this essentially results in treating 'T' as a sentential operator rather than as a predicate. As a consequence, many of his examples of sentences that contain 'T' are not altogether well-formed. He trusts that this will not lead to any misunderstandings by readers. By including the nominalizing device '[ ]' explicitly as a means of "Gödelizing" in the instances of (TS_F), we avoid these issues.

[10] For more on the Liar Paradox and semantic pathology more generally, see Chapter 7 and the appendix to this book.

approach seems orthogonal to our discussion of conservativeness, we set it aside in this subsection.

It is common, when discussing the Conservativeness Argument, both to focus on *axiomatic* theories of truth that are compatible with deflationism, specifically those with PA as the base theory, and to separate those axiomatic theories into a *disquotational* theory (henceforth, *DT*) and a *compositional* theory (henceforth, *TC*).[11] DT is the theory that encompasses the following axioms:

DT1 PA^T
DT2 $\Pi\varphi \in L_{PA}: T([\varphi]) \leftrightarrow \varphi$[12]

DT1 adds the one-place predicate, 'T', to the language L_{PA}, thereby extending it to L_{PA}^T. It then involves using L_{PA}^T to formulate PA^T, where PA^T is a formal system[13] that contains both the axioms of PA and the induction axiom schema[14] (henceforth, *(IS)*),

(IS) $\Omega(0) \wedge \forall x(\Omega(x) \rightarrow \Omega(S(x))) \rightarrow \forall x(\Omega(x))$.

While '$S(x)$' of (IS) captures the successor function, which maps any representative of an integer n onto that of its successor, $n + 1$, it is important to note that, as an axiom *schema*, (IS) yields

---

[11] As Horsten (1995, p. 171) notes, "It would be more felicitous to abbreviate it as *CT* were it not for the fact that the latter is the canonical abbreviation of *Church's Thesis*. In the literature, the theory *TC* is often referred to as *T(PA)*".

[12] As is standard in the literature, to allow for the formulation of DT2 as an axiom (rather than as a schema), it is given in a metalanguage stronger than L_{PA}^T, viz., one that includes variables for uses of the sentences of the language of the base theory, along with a quantifier 'Π', which functions to encode an infinite conjunction of the instances of the metalanguage formula that it prefixes. This allows for a finite formulation of an axiom that would otherwise require an infinitely long sentence. (Cf. Field (1994a, p. 267) on treating a "suitably generalized version" of (T/DS) as axiomatic.)

[13] To clarify terminology, "formal systems" consist of axioms and rules that prove theorems; "theories" consist of sets of formulae that are closed under some consequence relation. Given these characterizations, it follows that formal systems can generate theories.

[14] An *axiom schema* provides, or is short for its instances, of which there can be infinitely many, each of which counts as an axiom of some relevant theory.

infinitely many axioms of PA^T,[15] one for each predicate or open formula '$\Omega(x)$' of $L_{PA}{}^T$.[16]

By contrast to DT1, DT2 is specifically a *truth-theoretic* axiom, and the "fillings" of 'ϕ' that yield the instances of DT2 include all and only the sentences drawn either from L_{PA}, if the theory is typed, or from $L_{PA}{}^T$, if the theory is type-free. In the former case, the instances of DT2 are sometimes called "restricted biconditionals". The conjunction of DT1 and DT2 yields a set of closed formulae that is closed under first-order logical consequence, the axiomatic theory DT.

In light of the GP, as discussed in Section 4.2, while DT is able to prove all of the instances of a number of logical principles, including ones that involve the truth predicate, it can be shown that DT cannot prove the logical principles formulated as generalizations. Thus, for example, DT is unable to prove the following intuitively correct logical principle,

(CONJ) For all $\phi, \psi \in L_{PA}$: $(T([\phi]) \wedge T([\psi])) \leftrightarrow T([\phi \wedge \psi])$,

which a number of philosophers think should be proved, since it seems that truth should distribute over the logical connectives.[17] Since DT cannot prove (CONJ) and other principles like it, many of these philosophers take this as a reason for preferring the compositional truth theory, TC, over DT, where TC is taken to capture

---

[15] While PA, as understood here, is a first-order formulation of arithmetic, in light of the nature of (IS) as a schema, together with the fact that the only logic made use of is first-order, there is a second-order formulation of arithmetic, which results from replacing (IS) with a single axiom that makes use of second-order universal quantification over what 'Ω' stands in for (e.g., predicates). While second-order logic is standardly taken to be more powerful than first-order logic, it is notable that, unlike the latter, the former cannot be axiomatized, and, given any proof system, in contrast with first-order PA, second-order PA has consequences that cannot be deduced from its proof system its proof system.

[16] Although (IS) is formulated in L_{PA}, the schema need not include 'T' in its instances. That said, for what follows, we shall assume that (IS) does include at least some instances that contain 'T' except where we explicitly note that it does not.

[17] We note that since (CONJ) is understood to be a "logical law", the metalanguage generalizing device that it employs, 'For all $\phi, \psi \in L_{PA}$', is understood to express a genuine generalization. Thus, DT's inability to prove (CONJ) is an instance of the *Generalization Problem* (GP) discussed above in Section 4.2. We also note that DT's inability to prove

"compositional truth" because, within the axioms of TC, the truth-value of a sentence depends on those of its constituents.[18] While DT and TC, as truth theories for PA, are similar in certain respects, e.g., they both start by taking PA^T as an axiom, with both allowing 'T' to occur in some of the instances of (IS), there is an important difference between them: Instead of DT2, TC includes compositional truth-theoretic axioms that are formulated as *universally quantified* principles that generalize over the sentences of PA.[19] As a result, TC can prove the "most fruitful theorems", such as (CONJ), that every sentence or its negation is true, etc., thereby allowing for proofs of the attractive logical principles that DT is unable to prove.[20]

A theory, θ, is *arithmetically conservative* over PA provided that, for every sentence $\phi \in L_{PA}$, if PA + θ ⊢ φ, then already PA ⊢ φ. DT is arithmetically conservative over PA.[21] (Cf. Halbach (2011, pp. 55–56) and Horsten (2011, p. 75), for the proof of this.) Since TC is arithmetically stronger than DT, in the sense that the arithmetical theorems of PA^T with DT as the theory of 'T' are a proper subset of the set of theorems of PA^T with TC as the theory of 'T', it is not surprising that TC can be non-conservative over PA.[22]

---

logical principles like (CONJ) does not in any way depend on PA as the base theory. Halbach (2011, pp. 57–58) proves that this weakness of DT can be established for arbitrary base theories, not just for PA.

[18] For details on the compositional axiomatic theory of truth, see Halbach (2011), Horsten (1995), and Halbach and Leigh (2022).

[19] A standard means of generating these includes turning the clauses of Tarski's semantic definition of truth into axioms and adding them, sometimes supplemented with additional axioms, along with the truth predicate.

[20] It bears noting that *typed* axiomatic theories of truth limit their axioms only to ones that enable proofs of the truth of sentences that do not include that very truth predicate. For more of the details surrounding these issues, see Field (1994a, 2008), Halbach (2015), Horsten (2011), Waxman (2017, p. 438), and Murzi and Rossi (2018, p. 358, n. 7).

[21] It is important to qualify attributions of "conservativeness" to axiomatic truth theories. While DT is conservative "over PA", in the sense that everything that can be proved in DT, formulated from within L_{PA}^T, can already be proved in PA, also formulated from within L_{PA}^T, DT is not conservative *tout court*. This is because, as we show below (and see also Halbach (2001, pp. 178–80) and Horsten (2011, p. 81)), DT is not conservative "over logic", since adding DT to the system of first-order logic plus identity allows for proofs of truth-free sentences that the system of first-order logic with identity cannot prove on its own.

[22] We should note, however, that there are versions of TC that are arithmetically conservative, one of which we discuss below.

Given this background information, we can turn to the Conservativeness Argument.

As is familiar, by Gödel's second incompleteness theorem, a Gödel sentence, G, formulated within L_{PA},[23] is not a theorem of PA if PA is consistent. But G becomes a theorem when PA is expanded to PA^T by adding a truth predicate governed by certain plausible principles. Since the resultant theory of arithmetical truth is strong enough to allow for a proof of G, it appears to be non-conservative over PA. Hence, if, as has been argued by a number of theorists, any adequate account of truth-talk that includes arithmetical truth will be non-conservative over arithmetic itself, then deflationary accounts of truth-talk are in trouble if they cannot accommodate this non-conservativeness. Understood in this way, the Conservativeness Argument is a variant of the argument against deflationism to the effect that truth-talk plays an explanatory role in our understanding of the world, a role that requires a substantive property of truth and shows that the truth predicate plays a role that goes beyond the merely expressive ones sanctioned by deflationary accounts.

There are three steps to the Conservativeness Argument. Step 1: Argue that deflationary accounts of truth-talk are constrained by a conservativeness requirement, that is, that they must be conservative, either semantically or proof-theoretically, over any base theory to which they are added. Step 2: Establish that any adequate theory of arithmetical truth will be (at least) proof-theoretically non-conservative. Step 3: Explain why deflationists must maintain that the notion of consequence that figures in the conservativeness constraint is proof-theoretic and provide reasons for thinking that deflationists cannot employ, or make use of, a stronger, semantic notion of consequence.

---

[23] Since the standard Gödel sentence is formulated in L_{PA}, some theorists (e.g., Tennant (2002) and Waxman (2017)) designate this sentence as 'G_{PA}.' However, for what follows, we shall call it simply "G".

As Daniel Waxman (2017) categorizes potential responses from deflationists to the Conservativeness Argument, those who resist step one might be labeled "rejectionists"; those who resist step 2, while accepting the first step, might be labeled "proof-theoretic compatibilists"; and those who resist step 3, while accepting the first two steps, might be labeled "semantic compatibilists".

In support of the first step of the Conservativeness Argument, Shapiro and Ketland offer "step 1" arguments in favor of upholding a conservativeness constraint.

Shapiro (1998, pp. 497–98) argues as follows:

> I submit that in one form or other, conservativeness is essential to deflationism. Suppose, for instance, that Karl correctly holds a theory [θ] in a language that cannot express truth. He adds a truth predicate to the language and extends [θ] to a theory [θ^T] using only axioms essential to truth. Assume that [θ^T] is not conservative over [θ]. Then there is a sentence in the original language φ so that φ is a consequence of [θ^T] but not a consequence of [θ]. That is, it is logically possible for the axioms of [θ] to be true yet φ false, but it is not logically possible for the axioms of [θ^T] to be true and φ false. This undermines the central deflationist theme that truth is insubstantial. Before Karl moved to [θ^T], ∼φ was possible. The move from [θ] to [θ^T] *added* semantic content sufficient to rule out the falsity of φ. But by hypothesis, all that was added in [θ^T] were principles essential to truth. Thus, those principles have substantial semantic content.

Ketland (1999, p. 79) raises the following considerations.

> One might suggest that these [conservativeness results] illustrate a kind of 'analyticity' or 'contentlessness' that deflationary theories of truth exhibit. Adding them 'adds nothing'. Indeed, it is these metalogical properties that are closely connected to the idea that the deflationary truth theories illustrate the 'redundancy'

or 'non-substantiality' of truth. Indeed, one might go further: if truth is non-substantial as deflationists claim then the theory of truth should be conservative. Roughly: non-substantiality ≡ conservativeness.

Regarding Shapiro's and Ketland's arguments for a conservativeness constraint on deflationary theories, Volker Halbach (2001, pp. 178–80) offers an immediate challenge to any truth theorist who endorses the constraint, while also abiding by classical first-order logic and accepting Tarski's criterion of adequacy. (Cf. Horsten (2011, p. 81).) Consider the following instances of (TS_F).

(1) $T([\forall x(x = x)]) \leftrightarrow \forall x(x = x)$
(2) $T([\forall x(x \neq x)]) \leftrightarrow \forall x(x \neq x)$

Within first-order logic with identity, the right-hand side of (1) is a theorem, and, as a result, the right-hand side of (2) is disprovable (so its negation is provable). As a result, adding a truth theory that includes the instances of (TS_F) to classical first-order logic allows one to derive '$T([\forall x(x = x)])$' and '$\sim T([\forall x(x \neq x)])$'. Thus, given the uncontroversial consequence of Leibniz's Law, that if x and y are identical then they will not differ in any way, it follows that one can derive '$[\forall x(x = x)] \neq [\forall x(x \neq x)]$'. Existentially generalizing from this yields '$\exists x \exists y(x \neq y)$', which is something that classical first-order logic with identity cannot prove on its own. So, even if we were to restrict (TS_F), so that its fillings did not contain the truth predicate, it would still follow that it is not conservative over first-order logic with identity, since, as we have seen, in conjunction with that logic, it facilitates the proof of a formula not containing the truth predicate that first-order logic with identity cannot prove.[24] The lesson

---

[24] It is worth noting that the phenomenon of non-conservativeness arises even for versions of propositional logic. Following Prior's (1960a) introduction of the made-up connective "tonk", Nuel Belnap (1962) noted that the standard introduction- and elimination-rules for the connectives of classical propositional logic are conservative,

here seems clear: Since the instances of (TS_F) highlighted above enable us to prove certain truth-free sentences of classical first-order logic with identity that could not be proved given just that logic, theorists should acknowledge that any truth theory that affirms Tarski's criterion of adequacy, even one limited more or less to just these minimal principles, e.g., DT, conflicts with the conservativeness constraint.[25]

If the conservativeness constraint is upheld, then there are some evident difficulties for a number of formal theories of truth, which do not appear to be conservative over their base theories. This includes TC, as discussed by Halbach (2011) and Horsten (2011). Many philosophers judge TC to be an attractive philosophical theory of truth. The reason for this is that, given the truth predicate, an advocate of TC can prove that all axioms of PA are true and that the notion of logical inference at work in PA is truth-preserving. As a result, the TC advocate can establish that all of the theorems of the base theory are true, which implies that the theory is consistent. This statement of its consistency can be expressed

---

which Michael Dummett (1991) calls "harmony". But Dummett (1991, p. 290) has shown that non-conservativeness results in certain circumstances. The standard introduction- and elimination-rules for conjunction, ∧, and for disjunction, ∨, allow for the proof of "the distributive law", viz., the distributivity of conjunctions over disjunctions. However, if one were to sanction ∧ but introduce a deviant version of disjunction, ∨*, which includes the standard introduction-rule for ∨, which entitles one to infer 'p ∨* q' from either of its disjuncts, but which limits disjunction-elimination for ∨*, so that it is sanction only if there are no collateral assumptions in the minor premises, then the distributive law for ∧ and ∨* cannot be proved. That said, if one were to expand the logical language to include conjunction and both forms of disjunction, ∨ and ∨*, then the distributivity of ∧ over ∨* can be proved. As Dummett (1991, p. 290) notes, "the expanded language is not a conservative extension of the original one, despite the harmony between the introduction and elimination rules for the added connective [∨]."

[25] Halbach's intended lesson here applies more generally and, upon reflection, it is something that no one should find surprising: Adding expressive resources to a system often enables you to prove more than what you could have proved prior to including the addition. In particular, if you extend the logical expressive capacity of a system, e.g., by adding first-order quantifiers to a predicate logic that lacks quantifiers, then you can often prove more from within the extended system than you could have proved from within the original system. Cf. Picollo and Schindler (2018, pp. 346–47; 2021, pp. 61–62).

in the language of PA. But, as we also know by Gödel's second incompleteness theorem, provided that PA is consistent, it cannot prove its own consistency, that is, it cannot prove the L_{PA} sentence, CON_{PA}, that expresses this.

So, Halbach (2001, 2011) and Horsten (2011) argue that non-conservativeness seems inevitable for a large variety of formal theories of truth, including, as indicated above, certain deflationary theories of truth. Returning to the question of why Ketland and Shapiro are convinced that *any* adequate theory of truth (or of truth-talk) will be (proof-theoretically) non-conservative, the answer emerges from considerations that Michael Dummett raises regarding our ability to recognize the truth of the Gödel sentence for arithmetic. Dummett (1963/1978, p. 186) claims that

> [b]y Gödel's theorem there exists, for any intuitively correct formal system for elementary arithmetic, a statement [G] expressible in the system but not provable in it, *which not only is true but can be recognised by us to be true*. (Emphasis added)

He (1963/1978, p. 195) explains how we can recognize the truth of this sentence as follows.

> By hypothesis the axioms of the system are intuitively recognized as being true, and the rules of inference of the system as being correct. . . . Hence we may establish by an inductive argument on the lengths of formal proofs that each proof in the system has a true conclusion, and by another inductive argument on the number of logical constants in a statement that no statement is both true and false; concluding from this that the system is consistent [a statement which is provably equivalent in the system to G].

Dummett here elucidates a version of (what is known as) the *semantic argument*, one that can also be found in Shapiro (1998, p. 499) (cf. Ketland (1999, p. 91)):

> Once our subject has taken on the truth predicate, and he notices that all the axioms of [PA] are true and that the rules of inference preserve truth, he concludes that every theorem of [PA] is true. He also knows (from [the instances of (TS_F)]) that ⌈0 = 1⌉ is not true, and so ⌈0 = 1⌉ is not a theorem of [PA]. So our subject concludes that [PA] is consistent ([Con_{PA}]) and that [G] is true. The defect of [any weaker theory] as a theory of arithmetic truth is that it cannot reproduce this simple, informal reasoning.[26]

Ketland and Shapiro turn the semantic argument into the Conservativeness Argument in the following way: A theory of truth for first-order PA must enable one to prove G, the Gödel sentence for PA, and Con_{PA}, the sentence expressing PA's consistency.[27] But neither sentence is entailed by PA alone if PA is consistent. Hence, the notion of truth at play in the envisaged circumstances cannot be deflationary, since it enables one to prove these arithmetical truths, which could not be proved from PA alone. This is the basis of the Conservativeness Argument against deflationism.

To evaluate the effectiveness of the Conservativeness Argument, first consider the distinction between the following two notions of conservativeness for a theory S+ with language L_{S+} over a theory S with language L_S, where $L_S \subseteq L_{S+}$:

Syntactic Conservativeness: S+ is a syntactic conservative extension of S if, for every $\phi \in L_S$, if S+ ⊢ ϕ then S ⊢ ϕ, where '⊢' captures *syntactic (proof-theoretic) consequence*.

---

[26] Shapiro here uses '⌈' and '⌉' as a "Gödelizing" device. To avoid confusion with "corner quotes" (about which, see below), we employ our neutral "nominalizing brackets" for this purpose.

[27] For background on PA, G, and Con_{PA}, see Smorynski (1977) and Kaye (1991).

Semantic Conservativeness: S+ is a semantic conservative extension of S if, for every φ ∈ L_s, if S+ ⊨ φ then S ⊨ φ, where '⊨' captures *semantic consequence*.

As before, take PA as the base theory and extend it by adding a truth predicate, 'T', along with principles governing it, to produce PA^T. Following Waxman (2017) and Julien Murzi and Lorenzo Rossi (2018), we can distinguish two versions of PA^T: one that is given by PA plus TC's compositional axioms for 'T' and all of the infinitely many instances of (IS), including those in which the truth predicate occurs, and another, call it "PA^T-", that also includes all of the infinitely many instances of (IS) covering all of the formulae of L_PA but where the instances of (IS) do *not* include formulae that contain 'T'. This second theory, PA^T-, is conservative over PA, while PA^T is not. In particular, since, in PA^T, (IS) includes formulae that contain the truth predicate, a version of the semantic argument can be carried out in that theory, which establishes the consistency of PA. Additionally, since the Gödel sentence for PA, G, is provably equivalent to Con_PA, which states the consistency of PA in PA itself, this version of the Conservativeness Argument establishes that PA^T proves G, which is not provable in either PA^T- or any consistent arithmetical theory that lacks a truth predicate.

We have said that the Conservativeness Argument bears a relationship to other challenges to Metaphysical Deflationism that are based on claiming that truth plays some sort of explanatory role. Reading 'explains' as including *proof*, one might worry (i) that PA^T explains the Gödel sentence, G, (ii) that PA itself fails to explain G, but (iii) that deflationists are committed to a form of "explanatory conservativeness" according to which, for any sentence, S, in the base language, L, if S is explained by L^T, then S can be explained by L alone. (Cf. Waxman (2017, p. 446) for a discussion of "explanatory conservativeness".) If deflationists accept (i)–(iii) and do not subscribe to a form of "quietism", according to which (i) is true but we cannot say that it is true, then it seems that deflationists are in violation of explanatory conservativeness, which appears to spell trouble for them by indicating a violation of Metaphysical Deflationism. Recognizing this potential worry, several deflationists have offered responses.

5.2.2 Responses to the Conservativeness Argument

Field (1999) does not reject the conservativeness constraint but maintains that his deflationary version of TC ends up being conservative. Field formulates his version of TC in L_{PA}^{T}, that is, the language, L_{PA}, of PA extended with a truth predicate, 'T'. Field (1999, p. 537) also appeals to the expressive role of the truth predicate and maintains that deflationists are committed to a form of explanatory conservativeness only insofar as there are no explanations in which the truth predicate is not simply playing its generalizing role, viz., as a device for making opaque endorsements or affirmations. As a result, Field (1999) notes that "any use of 'true' in explanations which derives solely from its role as a device of generalization should be perfectly acceptable". He further contends that the relevant instances of (IS) that do contain the truth predicate are not purely truth-theoretic; they amount to "mathematical principles". As a result, he argues that the worry that arises from the claim that deflationists are in violation of explanatory conservativeness is unfounded.

More specifically, Field (1999) argues as follows. PA includes (IS). The evident violation of conservativeness for TC arises because the truth predicate occurs in certain instances of (IS). Field (1999) contends that those instances are not "genuine" truth principles. As a result, the fact that TC is not conservative over PA does not entail that Field's truth-theory is not arithmetically conservative. To determine whether his truth-theory is conservative, we must add the compositional truth axioms to PA. Evidently, doing so yields a truth theory that is arithmetically conservative over PA.

Horsten (2011, p. 61) expresses skepticism about Field's line of argument. He notes that it is not easy to see why the instances of (IS) that include the truth predicate count less as truth principles than do the compositional principles. This is not the only response to the Conservativeness Argument that is available to Field, however. An alternative response, alluded to above, to which Field (1999, p. 538) seemed sympathetic, is to take the 'T'-involving instances of (IS) to count as mathematical principles. As Field (1999, p. 538) says,

> [It] just seems false [that the truth of the induction axioms containing the truth predicate depend only on the nature of truth]: the corresponding axioms would hold for any other predicate, and what they depend on is a fact about the natural numbers, namely, that they are linearly ordered with each element having only finitely many predecessors.

Some philosophers (e.g., Horsten (2011) and Halbach (2011, pp. 315–16)) are critical of this alternative response. They note that it might be difficult to demarcate *truth-theoretic* content from *mathematical* content. But suppose that this distinction could be made, so that the relevant instances of (IS) are taken to be mathematical, rather than truth-theoretic. In that case, they should be taken to be part of the base theory, in which case adding the compositional truth principles that Field (1999) advocates yields a nonconservative extension of the base theory.

Another response to the Conservativeness Argument, by Waxman (2017), highlights that there are two readings of 'conservativeness', one semantic and the other syntactic, which correspond to two conceptions of arithmetic. On the first conception, arithmetic is understood *categorically* as given by the standard model, usually denoted by 'N'. On the second conception, arithmetic is understood *axiomatically*, which is captured by the acceptance of some first-order theory, such as PA. Waxman argues that deflationism can be conservative given either conception, so that the Conservativeness Argument does not go through. Waxman's main idea is that, on the categorical conception, consistent truth theories are semantically conservative over their arithmetical base theory, whereas, on the syntactic (axiomatic) conception, sentences like G and Con_{PA} are absent from one's conception of arithmetic, so one ought not to be able to prove them under that conception.

Murzi and Rossi (2018) argue that Waxman's attempt at marrying deflationism with conservativeness fails—that Waxman's "conservative deflationism" is unsuccessful. They argue, more specifically, that Waxman's account of "categorical deflationism" employs a notion of truth-in-a-higher-order-structure that seems to be incompatible with certain aspects of deflationism. They also argue that Waxman's axiomatic conception of arithmetic is unduly restrictive and ultimately self-undermining. While Murzi and Rossi (2018) are not attempting to argue against deflationism, they are arguing against the adoption of conservative deflationism, on the assumption that one's conception of arithmetic is axiomatic, claiming, in effect, that a deflationist's commitment to a conservative conception of truth-talk is misguided. (Cf. Halbach (2011), Horsten (2011, Sec. 7.5), Cieśliński (2015), and Galinon (2015) on why deflationists ought to reject the conservativeness constraint.) In particular, while they find appealing the idea that our grasp of mathematical notions is provided by our acceptance of axiomatic theories, they take their arguments to show that, on such a conception, one cannot reject non-conservative theories of truth because those theories are not conservative.

In addition, Murzi and Rossi (2018) critically assess Neil Tennant's (2002) strategy for escaping conservativeness while retaining our knowledge of G and Con_{PA}. Tennant (2002) argues against the idea that the grounds for accepting G must be truth-theoretic. He argues that a deflationist can adopt a syntactically conservative theory of truth-talk while proving sentences like G via non-truth-theoretic principles, such as a reflection principle for primitive-recursive formulae,

$R_{PA}: \forall x Bew_{PA}(\ulcorner \Phi(x) \urcorner) \to \forall x \Phi(x),$

where, '⌐' and '¬' function as corner quotes, rather than as a "Gödelizing" device, and where what goes in for 'Φ' is primitively recursive and '*Bew*' is a provability predicate (from the German, 'beweisen'). R_{PA} is, provably within PA, equivalent to G and Con_{PA}. According to Tennant (2002, p. 573), this is "just what we need in order to formalize faithfully the reasoning in the [semantic argument]". He maintains that this strategy, of providing a justification for recognizing the truth of G via R_{PA}, enables him, in effect, to accept a conservative truth theory while locating non-conservativeness on the reflection principle. And this principle, he holds, can be motivated without appealing to any truth-involving considerations at all.

Ketland contends that Tennant is unsuccessful in his attempt to provide a proof-theoretic compatibilist view. Tennant accepts that deflationism is committed to the proof-theoretic conservativeness of an arithmetical truth theory over PA, but he takes this to pose no threat whatsoever to deflationism. But according Ketland (2005, p. 83):

> *If* Tarski's theory of truth provides at least *one* way of 'recognizing the truth of Gödel sentences' then this fact alone contradicts deflationism (for a deflationary theory of truth should be conservative). The entirely different assumption, which I did not make, that this is 'the only way' is irrelevant. (Italics original)

Ketland's point is that the fact that there is a non-conservative theory of arithmetical truth that proves the Gödel sentence, G, creates a problem for deflationists. But, as Waxman (2017, p. 450) emphasizes, Ketland's line of argument only goes through on the premise, which is the crux of the current debate, and which Tennant would no doubt deny, that the relevant theory of arithmetical truth is properly taken to be deflationary. Because Tennant's reflection principle, R_{PA}, is employed as an attempt to undermine the aforenoted premise, Ketland's response to Tennant appears to beg the question and, as a result, seems to pose no actual threat.

Jody Azzouni (1999) replies to Shapiro's (1998) presentation of the Conservativeness Argument by defending what he calls the "first-order deflationist", viz., a deflationist who endorses what Waxman (2017, p. 450) calls "the axiomatic conception of arithmetic" and whose subsequent understanding cannot rule out the eligibility of nonstandard models. Azzouni gives two responses to Shapiro's arguments, which, as we have seen, are aimed at putting pressure on deflationism. First, Azzouni does not include sentences containing the truth predicate in the instance of (IS) but instead affirms proof-theoretic conservativeness. In fact, one of Azzouni's insights is that including formulae that contain the truth predicate in the instances of (IS) implicitly relies on considerations that seem motivated only by the standard model. Given Azzouni's truth theory, he accepts the need to prove certain 'true'-employing generalizations (Azzouni's example (1999, p. 542) is the compositional axiom for conjunction presented above as (CONJ)), but he maintains that there are some generalizations that are *about* truths, which a first-order deflationist need not prove. As Azzouni (1999, p. 542) says, "What *is* true (and how) is not, properly speaking, part of the *theory* of truth" (italics original). While Azzouni's first-order deflationists accept, for example,

(A) $0 \neq 1$, and
(B) $\forall x(\exists y PRF(x,y) \rightarrow T(x))$

(see 1999, p. 342), where 'PRF' represents a two-place proof predicate, they do not regard them as part of their theory of truth. Moreover, if one does extend their theory of truth so as to be able to establish these statements from it, they should not expect their theory to be conservative, nor should they continue describing it as a *deflationary* theory of truth, according to Azzouni.

CHALLENGES TO METAPHYSICAL DEFLATIONISM 171

As a first response to the criticism that a first-order deflationist of this sort cannot prove an important generalization like (B), Azzouni contends that (B), and other statements like it, are not part of the first-order deflationist's theory of truth. There seems to be a problem, however, with his claim (i) that certain 'true'-employing generalizations, like (CONJ), are "essential to a theory of truth" but (ii) that other 'true'-employing generalizations, like (B), are "not essential to a theory of truth". The reason for this is that if being "essential to a theory of truth" just means that a statement must be proved by one's theory of truth, then Azzouni's reason for claiming that (B) is not essential to a theory of truth seems to be circular. Moreover, if there is a different reading of what makes some statement essential to one's theory of truth, it is difficult to see what that could be. Azzouni (1999) does not shed any light on this.

Azzouni's second response emerges as a specific reaction to Shapiro's (1998, p. 501) argument, that if one admits that a predicate "has a determinate extension over the natural numbers (or whatever the numerals denote)", then they must allow that predicate to appear in instances of the induction schema. Azzouni notes that Shapiro's considerations in favor of extending the induction schema only apply to the standard model. The problem that Azzouni raises here is that Shapiro's considerations do not apply to those theorists, of which Azzouni is one, who are proponents of the axiomatic view. For those theorists, Azzouni contends that it is simply not true that any predicate with a determinate extension over the numbers of that model belongs to the induction schema. Azzouni seems to think that first-order deflationists—perhaps only first-order deflationists, provided they affirm the axiomatic conception of arithmetic—can thus avoid Shapiro's demand, as noted at the start of this paragraph.

Waxman (2017, p. 453) notes a limitation with respect to Azzouni's second response, viz., that it seems to commit the first-order deflationist to the axiomatic conception of arithmetic, whereas not all theorists will want to be so committed. It follows from Azzouni's view, for example, that the Gödel sentence, G, is not always an arithmetical truth, since even if PA is consistent, there are nonstandard models in which G ends up being false. Moreover, if deflationism demands this axiomatic conception, then an Azzouni-style first-order deflationist must provide what we, in Armour-Garb and Woodbridge (2010b), call a "plausibility argument" to the effect that it is more plausible that deflationism is correct than that we are able to grasp the standard model of arithmetic. Waxman (2017, p. 453) concludes that "[a]t best, deflationism is on highly controversial ground, and at worst it is landed with an impoverished and inadequate understanding of arithmetic."

5.2.3 Consequences of the Conservativeness Argument

The conclusions that Horsten, Ketland, and Shapiro draw from the Conservativeness Argument are very different. Shapiro (1998) concludes that deflationists need a strong and non-effective notion of logical consequence; Ketland (1999) seems to take the Conservativeness Argument to result in a reductio ad absurdum of deflationism itself; and Horsten (2011) takes the Conservativeness Argument to result in a reductio ad absurdum of the assumption that deflationary theories must be conservative over a base theory.[28]

Shapiro (1998) is the only theorist (one, nota bene, who does not subscribe to deflationism) who raises the Conservativeness Argument as a potential problem for deflationism but proposes a means whereby deflationists might be able to avoid being committed to a violation of conservativeness. His proposal is that deflationists take the notion of consequence that figures in the definition of 'conservativeness' as "second-order logical consequence"

---

[28] As we explain below, Picollo and Schindler (2018, 2021), in addition to raising worries for Shapiro's (1998) conclusion regarding the Conservativeness Argument, side with Horsten (2011) and argue that deflationists should not insist on conservativeness.

with what he calls "standard semantics". The reason for this is that, in a given model, second-order quantifiers are taken to range over the full power set of the domain.[29] If the base theory is second-order arithmetic, then, since that theory is categorical and, thus, has only one model up to isomorphism,[30] every true arithmetical sentence ends up as a second-order consequence of the base theory. As a result, the relevant truth theory cannot prove any arithmetical sentence that is not already a second-order consequence of the base theory, which yields the result that conservativeness appears to be maintained, as any new semantic consequence of the truth theory is already a consequence of the base theory. The question that presses, then, is whether this is an acceptable strategy for deflationists.

There are a number of reasons for being reluctant to take up what Shapiro is offering. For one thing, there is a sort of tension, which is not missed by Shapiro: His proposal appears to avoid aspects that would render the resultant non-deflationary, but it does so by bringing in a substantive, "robust" second-order logic consequence relation. As Shapiro (1998, p. 510) notes,

> The point here is that no matter what one's views are on the status of second-order logic, a critic of deflationism might respond to the second-order manoeuvre by arguing that the deflationist is hiding the robustness of truth in the second-order consequence relation. If the consequence relation is itself robust, then the contemplated manoeuvre fails to show that truth is thin and has no nature.

Shapiro concludes that a deflationist might take his move to be suspicious since the price of upholding deflationism about truth-talk is by introducing a substantive notion, viz., that of a second-order

---

[29] As a reminder, a power set is the set of all of the subsets of a set.
[30] A theory is *categorical* provided each of its models are isomorphic, which is to say that there is a one-to-one function, f, that preserves the structure of the models. For more on this, see Shapiro (1991, pp. 80–88).

consequence relation. Whether deflationists can be happy with this tension or not, there are other concerns about Shapiro's proposal.

As Lavinia Picollo and Thomas Schindler (2018) note, one may be uneasy employing the notion of second-order logical consequence for Quinean reasons, viz., because second-order logic comes with "staggering existence assumptions". Moreover, one may worry about the relation of second-order consequence, since it is not effective, and the validities of second-order logic are not recursively enumerable. Finally, as Murzi and Rossi (2018) contend, Shapiro's suggestion may ultimately not be compatible with deflationism.

Picollo and Schindler (2018, 2021) investigate this last issue, and draw conclusions that seem to be in line with Field's response to the Conservativeness Argument. They argue that the conservativeness constraint imposed by Horsten (1995), Shapiro (1998), Ketland (1999), and others is not a reasonable requirement to impose on deflationary accounts. Picollo and Schindler (2021) contend that the insistence on conservativeness for a deflationary understanding of truth-talk is a consequence of making too much of the metaphor of "insubstantiality" and that it fails to identify what the function of the truth predicate really amounts to. Their leading idea is that the disquotational truth predicate is a tool for simulating, in a first-order framework, the operation of higher-order quantification.[31] They (2018, p. 345) reason as follows: The adoption of higher-order logical resources (including those of second-order quantification into predicate position) occasionally results in non-conservative extensions of first-order theories.[32]

---

[31] See Nicolai (2021) for an argument that challenges Picollo and Schindler's contention that a disquotational truth predicate is a device for mimicking higher-order quantification. For a possible response, see Picollo and Schindler (2022).

[32] The example they employ, in order to make this point (Picollo and Schindler (2018, p. 344)), involves generalizing into predicate-position in the context of PA by employing second-order logic. Since second-order quantifiers are now available, one can transform the *induction schema* for PA, which, as we saw in Section 5.3.1, includes only first-order quantifiers, into the *induction axiom* for PA, which includes a second-order quantifier. Doing so results in a theory that is a non-conservative extension of PA, since the theory proves PA's consistency, which, as we know, PA itself cannot do.

If, as they maintain, a disquotational truth predicate, in conjunction with first-order quantifiers, mimics the operation of higher-order quantification (including both sentential quantification and second-order quantification), then, as with the higher-order resources, adding a disquotational truth theory to a first-order theory will occasionally result in a non-conservative extensions of that first-order theory. As a result, they conclude that we should not expect the deflationist's truth theory to extend its base theory conservatively. As they (2021, p. 68) put it, "non-conservativeness is just a feature of the truth predicate fulfilling its role". Since they maintain that the conservativeness requirement cannot stem from deflationists' restriction of the role of truth-talk to certain logico-linguistic functions, the truth predicate having a merely logically expressive role is compatible with a violation of conservativeness. (Cf. Azzouni (2018, pp. 499–500) on the truth predicate not having to be proof-theoretically conservative because that does not follow from its being a device of semantic descent: Even if that is all it is, it need not be expressively conservative.)

In response to Picollo and Schindler's reasoning on the conservativeness issue, consider the following line of reasoning that someone committed to the conservativeness (what they call "conservativity") of a deflationary understanding of truth-talk might pursue as a means for resisting their conclusion. First, acknowledging that the addition of second-order resources occasionally results in non-conservative extensions of first-order theories, it is worth pointing out that, even if one were to grant that the role of a disquotational truth predicate is to mimic higher-order quantification from within a first-order framework, one might still deny that adding a disquotational truth predicate to a first-order language will occasionally result in a non-conservative extension of that language. One might argue, for example, that the cases or circumstances under which second-order resources result in non-conservative extensions are separate or distinct from the cases or circumstances in which the role of the disquotational truth predicate mimics higher-order quantification. This provides a burden of proof argument to Picollo and Schindler: Demonstrate or establish that the circumstances under which the addition of higher-order resources results in a non-conservative extension are the very same circumstances in which the role of the disquotational truth predicate mimics higher-order quantification.

It is also worth noting that Picollo and Schindler (2021, p. 68) contend that their analysis of the function of a disquotational truth predicate accounts for a type of mathematical explanatory role that truth-talk appears to have, along with the deflationary contention that truth-talk attributes an insubstantial property, if it attributes a property at all. They do this by maintaining that the best way to understand the insubstantiality metaphor is as a rejection of the claim that the truth predicate plays any descriptive role in our language, which amounts to a rejection of inflationary presupposition (ii), viz. that the truth predicate serves to describe or characterize putative truth-bearers. While this runs counter to Horwich's (1990/1998) claim (as discussed in Section 3.3) that the truth predicate serves to make descriptions, their view does seem to line up with most species of deflationism and with our claim in Section 5.3.2, below, that, in line with the Lewisian distinction between sparse and abundant properties, if deflationists maintain that the truth predicate attributes a property, then they must maintain that it attributes an abundant, rather than a sparse, property. As a result, for most deflationists, the truth predicate does not play the standard explanatory role that many predicates play, namely that of shedding light on certain aspects of the things to which they apply.

However, if proofs have some explanatory value, and the truth predicate figures into those sorts of proofs, then the truth predicate, even as understood by deflationists, does have some sort of explanatory role. Picollo and Schindler (2021) maintain that adding higher-order quantifiers to a language can lead to new knowledge, thereby revealing that these devices have explanatory value without their use amounting in any way to the application of a descriptive predicate. The explanatory role of higher-order quantifiers derives solely, and exclusively, from their logico-linguistic role. Since, Picollo and Schindler maintain, the truth predicate essentially performs the same role as higher-order quantifiers, it, too, has this kind of explanatory role. Their point is related to the one that Field (1999, p. 537) makes, that "any use of 'true' in explanations which derive solely from its role as a device of generalization should be perfectly acceptable". If what Picollo and Schindler claim is right, then the question as to whether deflationists can allow that the truth predicate has an explanatory role needs to be rethought, along with whether it would violate Metaphysical Deflationism if the truth predicate did have certain explanatory roles.[33]

5.3 The Correspondence Intuition, Truthmaking, and the Truth Property Thesis

Pre-theoretically, when most people reflect on how they understand truth, they seem to accept that a sentence or thought is true only if it bears some sort of "correspondence" to the world. Hence, if truth theorists must account for certain prima facie intuitions, then it seems that they should explain, or at least explain away, this "correspondence intuition". In contemporary analytic philosophy, one way that this intuition is expressed is with the slogan 'Truth depends on being', which frequently figures into what is called "truth-maker theory" and its notion of truthmaking.[34]

---

[33] We return to Picollo and Schindler's (2018, 2021, 2022) response to the Conservativeness Argument in the appendix to this book.

[34] Contemporary truth-maker theory was introduced by Mulligan et al. (1984), Bigelow (1988), and Armstrong (1989). For an overview on the theory, see MacBride (2022).

In this way, the correspondence intuition is clarified in terms of the thesis that what is true depends on how reality is (but not vice versa). For example, if it is true that snow is white, this is *because* or *in virtue* of how the world is, specifically, with respect to snow. As David Armstrong (2004, p. 7) contends, "any truth should depend for its truth on something 'outside' it, in virtue of which it is true". Similarly, David Lewis (2001, p. 603) maintains that we should require "what's true to depend upon the way the world of existing things is". These claims are intended to elucidate the slogan that truth depends on reality. The issue for deflationism is whether these intuitions can be accommodated without endorsing an inflationary theory of truth involving a substantive correspondence relation.

Relatedly, both proto-deflationists, like Ramsey, A. J. Ayer, and P. F. Strawson, and contemporary deflationists (*pace* Horwich) have typically been reluctant to posit a truth property. Even so, if 'is true' functions as a predicate/predicatively, then it has an extension, and, thus, would seem, at least prima facie, to express a truth property. Moreover, as Stephen Schiffer (2003, p. 67) notes, there seems to be a generally available, direct inference from 'x is F' to 'x has the property of being F'.[35] Applying that to truth-talk, we get that there is a direct (and, to Schiffer, innocuous) inference (what he (2003, p. 67) calls a "trivial transformation") from '<p> is true' to '<p> has the property of being true', which, given an acceptance of the former sentence, seems to commit the speaker to a truth property. Both the correspondence intuition, along with its elaboration in terms of truth-maker theory, and the truth property thesis pose challenges to Metaphysical Deflationism, which, again, threatens deflationary views in toto. Thus, deflationists must address these challenges.

---

[35] See also Thomasson (2015), for a related approach.

5.3.1 From the Correspondence Intuition to Truth-Maker Theory

Deflationism is often thought to be incompatible with the platitude that being true is a matter of corresponding to *the facts*, which is identified with the correspondence intuition.[36] As the charge is sometimes mounted, deflationism, in virtue of its commitment to Metaphysical Deflationism, is thought to be incompatible with an understanding of correspondence that figures into paradigmatic versions of a correspondence theory of truth, viz., what Richard Kirkham (1992, p. 119) calls "congruence theories", according to which a truth-bearer—a sentence or a proposition—has the property of truth exactly when it mirrors, pictures, or is in some sense structurally isomorphic to certain facts or (obtaining) states of affairs in the world. The kind of theory that Kirkham outlines clearly violates Metaphysical Deflationism, so connecting the correspondence intuition with the features he describes conflicts with deflationism. But there are versions of the correspondence intuition and species of deflationism that appear to render the two compatible.

Christopher Hill (2002) attempts to accommodate the correspondence intuition from within a deflationary framework by identifying a correspondence relation that is suitably deflated. Letting 'R' stand for a correspondence relation, and taking the relevant target of truth-ascriptions to be thoughts, Hill (2002, p. 49) proposes the following:

(SC) For any thought x and any state of affair y, x bears R to y iff
$\Sigma p((x = \text{the thought that } p) \wedge (y = \text{the state of affairs that } p))$,

---

[36] Horwich (1990/1998, p. 105) argues for this reading of the correspondence intuition. Wright (1992, p. 34) lists this platitude among a collection of platitudes he claims any account of truth must accommodate.

where the existential quantifier 'Σ' in (SC) operates as some higher-order (for Hill, a substitutional) quantifier that governs quantification into sentence-positions, and the quantifier 'For any' operates as an objectual quantifier, ranging first over thoughts and then over states of affairs. According to Hill (2002), (SC) is the source of our intuitive notion of semantic correspondence, so (SC) (or something very much like it) is definitional with respect to our intuitive relational notion of that property. Hill also maintains that, by accepting (SC), deflationists can accommodate the correspondence intuition without violating Metaphysical Deflationism by having embraced a correspondence theory of truth that identifies correspondence with some part of an underlying nature that truth possesses. If Hill is right about this, then deflationism is compatible with the correspondence intuition after all.[37]

Of course, for Hill's proposal to succeed in accommodating the correspondence intuition, it must capture a relation that is plausibly construed as a genuine kind of correspondence, and this requires that the notion of states of affairs that it employs is sufficient for this task. However, if deflationists countenance states of affairs, they tend to endorse notions of them (or, more typically, of facts), that seem unsuitable for such work, and many deflationists deny their existence altogether. For example, Horwich (2008, pp. 268–70, echoing his 1990/1998, p. 106) argues that there are good reasons for identifying facts with true propositions. But, on that understanding of facts, Hill's (SC), at least for any x that is a *true* thought (i.e., proposition), would make its self-identity qualify as the R-relation he defines. But self-identity is not plausibly construed as a *correspondence* relation. Prior (1971, p. 5) also acknowledges an identification of facts with true propositions, but he couples this with a kind of rejection of both, maintaining that "facts and true

---

[37] We note, however, that there remain concerns, viz., those raised in Sections 3.3 and 4.2.4, about Hill's particular understanding of the higher-order quantification employed in (SC).

propositions alike are mere 'logical constructions'... and... they are the *same* 'logical constructions' (to have 'true propositions' and 'facts' is to have *too many* logical constructions)" (italics original). Quine (1992, p. 80) flatly rejects facts, claiming that positing "*facts*, as correspondents of true sentences as wholes ... is still a put-up job ... facts contribute nothing [to an account of the world] beyond their specious support of a correspondence theory" (italics original). Strawson (1950, pp. 141–43) similarly claims that so-called facts and states of affairs are pseudo-entities rather than anything to be found in the world that "make statements [or thoughts, etc.] true". Rather, he claims that these expressions serve merely to indicate a particular type of language use (viz., informative, as opposed to commanding). Finally, Ramsey (1927/1990, p. 39) notes that "[w]e can, if we like, say that [a judgment that *a* has *R* to *b*] is true if there exists a corresponding fact that *a* has *R* to *b*, but this is essentially not an analysis but periphrasis, for 'The fact that *a* has *R* to *b* exists' is no different from '*a* has *R* to *b*'", and he (1927/1990, p. 37) claims that "a phrase beginning 'the fact that' is not a name, and also not a description" of any kind of worldly item. So, while it might be possible for a deflationist to accept the sort of ontologically robust and independent notion of states of affairs that Hill's (SC) assumes in order to address the correspondence intuition, many deflationists would consider this a price not worth paying, especially if an alternative deflationary approach to the correspondence intuition were available.

Horwich (1990/1998, pp. 104–6) aims to provide just such an alternative approach, one that accommodates the correspondence intuition from within a deflationary framework without any appeal to facts or states of affairs and without identifying, or relying on, any correspondence relation. His proposal is to recast the correspondence intuition in terms of the claim that a proposition is true *because* or *in virtue of* how the world is and show that his deflationary view can justify this claim. In other words, he aims to accommodate the correspondence intuition by capturing the central slogan of truth-maker theory. As he (1990/1998, p. 104) notes, "It is indeed undeniable that whenever a proposition or an utterance is true, it is true *because* something in the world is a certain way—something typically external to the proposition or utterance" (italics original). While this echoes one of the most general aspects of truth-maker theory—the thesis that truth depends on being—and while truth-maker theory strikes many as an element of a correspondence theory of truth, and thus as incompatible with deflationism, Horwich argues that these intuitions are perfectly compatible with his species of deflationism.

Truth-maker theory is a popular approach to theorizing in contemporary analytic metaphysics. It is also applied to debates about realism in philosophy of mathematics and metaethics, and it has figured into certain critiques of presentism, phenomenalism, and behaviorism. (Cf. Asay (2022, pp. 116–17).) Again, the intuition behind the theoretical posits of *truthmaking* and *truthmakers* is that truth depends on being, that is, that the truth of something is not primitive but rather that the world or reality is what makes truths true. A common reading of this thesis has obvious inflationary overtones, including the seemingly substantive assumptions that truth is something *made* by certain truthmaking entities and that truth is something *borne* by truth-bearers. Applying the truth-maker framework to accommodate the intuition that truth involves "correspondence to the facts" would seem to involve viewing truthmaking as a correspondence relation and taking truth-makers to be complex entities like facts or states of affairs. Armstrong (1997, p. 14) claims that there is a natural affinity between truth-maker theory and a correspondence theory of truth because "[c]orrespondence demands a correspondent, and a correspondent for a truth is a truth-maker". This thought also leads him, and many other adherents of truth-maker theory following him, to endorse the truth-maker principle, also called "truth-maker maximalism", that, for each truth, there must be something, and, more specifically, some *entity*,[38] in the world that makes it true.[39] Given Armstrong's quote and the gloss of truth-maker theory presented above, all of this seems highly antithetical to Metaphysical Deflationism. So, on an initial reading of truth-maker theory and truthmaking, this framework seems to conflict with certain central themes of deflationism. One question for deflationists, then, is whether they can embrace this framework. Horwich (2008) argues that they can accept a suitably "sanitized" version of truth-maker theory, and Matthew Simpson (2021) and Jamin Asay (2022) agree.[40] In fact, one way of understanding the approach that Horwich relies on, in his original attempt to accommodate the correspondence intuition, is as a kind of deflated version of truth-maker theory, even if he does not use that terminology.

To show how his deflationary view can accommodate the intuition that whenever something is true, it is true *because* or *in virtue* of how the world is, Horwich shifts the focus of the issue to whether

---

[38] According to Armstrong (1997, pp. 115–16), these entities must typically be complex ones like states of affairs instead of just ordinary things, since truthmaking is thought to involve necessitation and the existence of, e.g., snow is not enough to necessitate the truth of <snow is white>, even if we add in the existence of the property of being white as well. What is required is that these are tied together in such a way as to yield the state of affairs of snow's being white. (Cf. Simpson (2021, p. 3170) and Asay (2022, p. 111).)

[39] This is not to say that every truth has its own *unique* truth-maker, in a one-one correspondence, what is sometimes called the "correspondence truth-maker principle". Most adherents of truth-maker maximalism, Armstrong included, take the mapping between truths and truth-makers to be a many-many relation. Note also that Armstrong (1997) and many other truth-maker theorists maintain that atomic/fundamental truths are made true by atomic/fundamental states of affairs, while the truth of other truths, e.g., disjunctions, then follows from those. It is also worth noting that Asay (2022, p. 121) maintains that, unlike correspondence theorists and other "substantivists", i.e., inflationists, deflationists need not and should not endorse truth-maker maximalism. He sees this as a virtue of deflationism as it yields the result that they do not have to find truth-makers for the truth of negative existential claims, and also notes (Asay (2022, p. 121)) that this makes evident that deflationists can employ truthmaking in more flexible and thus potentially theoretically advantageous ways in comparison to how it must be employed by "substantivists", who do abide by truth-maker maximalism.

[40] Asay (2022) claims that the kind of "explanation-based" approach to truth-maker theory pursued by Horwich and Simpson is problematic, but he still maintains that deflationists can and should embrace truth-maker theory understood in the traditional ontological way. We return to this distinction below.

his view can accommodate certain intuitive explanatory claims, specifically claims like the following:

(A) <Snow is white> is true *because* snow is white.
(B) <Snow is white>'s being true *is explained by* snow's being white.

As a means for mapping out the relations of explanatory dependence between phenomena, Horwich grants ultimate explanatory priority to things like the basic laws of nature and the initial conditions of the universe. From these conditions and laws, he contends that one can deduce, and thereby explain, why it is the case that (e.g.)

(C) Snow is white.

Having deduced (C) from the basic laws of nature, etc., one can then enlist an instance of (ES), the propositional version of (TS), and, so, can deduce, and, Horwich (2008) maintains, thereby explain why

(D) <Snow is white> is true.

Horwich argues that, because (C) is explanatorily prior to (D), it follows that both (A) and (B) are perfectly acceptable. If all of this is correct, then Horwich's brand of deflationism seems compatible with the thesis that various truths are "made true" by elements of reality, which is in keeping with truth-maker theory. Horwich further maintains that, since this thesis follows from his minimalist theory, together with the other non-alethic facts noted above, it accords with his overall minimalist account, thereby accommodating the correspondence intuition.

Crispin Wright (1992, pp. 26–27) sanctions Horwich's attempt at capturing the correspondence intuition but considers a potential concern that one might have about Horwich's attempt at this. He acknowledges that Horwich's argument in support of the acceptability of (A) is entirely compatible with deflationism, since the account amounts to a mere "trivial explanation". But Wright (1992, p. 27) notes that some might think that more is needed than what Horwich offers, because Horwich fails to "provide an account of the explanatory relationship adverted to by [(A)]". As presented, this concern is rather underdeveloped, and Wright (1992) all but concedes as much. In response, Horwich could simply point to his account of (A) and ask Wright what it is missing. Since Wright (1992) does not have anything more to offer regarding the (potential) concern, he concludes that Horwich has no problem accommodating the correspondence intuition.

David Liggins (2016), by contrast, argues that there is more to the kind of concern Wright raises and provides an objection to Horwich's proposal that can be seen as elaborating on that (potential) worry. Horwich's proposal involves recasting the correspondence intuition in terms of truth-maker theory, capturing that framework's central slogan via the explanatory claims (A) and (B), and then accounting for those claims from within the framework of his minimalism. Liggins argues that Horwich cannot adequately account for claims like (A) (and, presumably, by extension, claims like (B)) because he cannot explain the *asymmetry* of the explanatory direction that such claims involve.[41] This is because Horwich attempts to account for claims like (A) via inferences that invoke instances of (ES), and the symmetrical nature of these instances would also seem potentially to underwrite the intuitively unacceptable converses of (A) and (B). Liggins considers an approach involving an appeal to a kind of explanation based on "conceptual connections" to be a response to his challenge, but he argues that

---

[41] The asymmetry found in (A) and its ilk is to be expected, since explanation is asymmetric and since 'because' is usually taken to provide explanations as it occurs in claims like (A). (For more on this, see Schnieder (2010, pp. 321–22)).

neither Horwich nor deflationists of any other stripe can provide an adequate response via this approach. Liggins (2016, p. 100) concludes that, by contrast with inflationists, no deflationist can account for the explanatory asymmetry displayed in claims like (A) and (B), and, thus, no deflationist can accommodate the correspondence intuition by recasting it in terms of the aspects of truthmaker theory invoked in such claims.

Contrary to Liggins's conclusions, however, Horwich (1990/1998 and 2008) provides the materials for an adequate response to the explanatory asymmetry challenge, albeit via a different kind of response than the one Liggins (2016) considers and argues against. In fact, Horwich's (1990/1998, p. 105) original claim about the explanatory priority of (C) over (D) already accounts for the asymmetry exhibited by cases like (A) and (B). Recall Liggins's (2016) claim that, since the last step in Horwich's argument showing how he can justify claims like (A) just involves the application of the relevant instance of (ES), and since the instances of (ES) are all symmetrical, Horwich's view would seem to allow us equally to derive (C) from (D). This seems to yield the unfortunate result that Horwich's account also allows for the justification of the counterintuitive converse of (A). But Liggins's argument misses the point that, in Horwich's justification of (A), he explains how to derive (C) without first establishing (D), and then he derives (D) from the already secured (C). Liggins's charge of symmetry seems to involve imagining circumstances in which we have established (D) prior to and independently of establishing (C). If that were possible, then Horwich might well have a problem accounting for the asymmetry of claims like (A), but this is a highly implausible scenario for most claims of this sort. This shows the aforementioned explanatory priority of (C) over (D), which allows Horwich to draw (A), understood as exhibiting the requisite explanatory asymmetry, as a conclusion. Thus, it seems that Liggins's argument for his charge that Horwich is saddled with an unwanted symmetry should be resisted.

While Liggins (2016) directs his challenge at Horwich's minimalism, it turns out to be more of a threat to certain other species of deflationism. Consider deflationary views that maintain a stronger equivalence than Horwich does between the two sides of the instances of the truth schema, (TS). For views that consider the equivalence to result in the two sides amounting to more or less the same claim (e.g., Grover et al. (1975), Brandom (1988, 1994), Field (1994a), and plausibly even Quine (1970/1986)—see Section 3.2.1, above), it is far less clear that they have an adequate response to Liggins's challenge. To reformulate the challenge as it confronts these deflationary views, it is the matter of accounting for the intuitive asymmetry exhibited by certain seemingly explanatory claims like,

(A′) [Snow is white] is true because snow is white.
(B′) [Snow is white]'s being true is explained by snow's being white.

In these neutral versions, Horwich's assumed reference to propositions is replaced with the unspecified nominalizing device employed in (TS). On deflationary views that endorse the aforementioned stronger equivalence in the instances of (TS), it seems to follow that (A′) just amounts to the claim that snow is white because snow is white. That is clearly an improper use of 'because', and it appears to block accounting for the intuitive explanatory asymmetries exhibited in claims like (A′) and (B′). So, the question is whether these other deflationary views can deal with Liggins's challenge and accommodate the correspondence intuition by accounting for certain explanations of truth-ascriptions.

One possible response to this situation is to follow Douven and Hindriks (2005, p. 320) and claim that none of these tasks is necessary, that is, to deny that (A′) and (B′) make explanatory claims at all, and even to reject the correspondence intuition altogether. They claim that this intuition emerges from the thought that, whenever a sentence or a proposition is true, it is true *because* something in the world is a certain way—something typically external to that sentence or proposition. The problem for deflationists, and especially for adherents of the species of deflationism currently under consideration, is how they could accommodate these intuitions, including that (A') and (B') make explanatory claims that exhibit the requisite asymmetry. As a defense of deflationism, the strategy that Douven and Hindriks pursue is to consider various theories of explanation and argue that none of them can make sense of their proposed reading of the correspondence intuition, viz., that a given utterance is true because of the way the world is. If they are correct, this would strongly suggest that there is no sort of explanatory relationship between (e.g.) the whiteness of snow and the truth of an assertoric utterance of 'Snow is white', in which case not accommodating the alleged correspondence intuition would not create a problem for any species of deflationism. They (2005, p. 320) argue that the claim that [Snow is white] is true because of the whiteness of snow has the same explanatory force as the claim that [Snow is white] is true because [Snow is white] is true, which is to say, none. The same holds for the claim that snow is white because snow is white, which, as noted above, the deflationary views under consideration seem saddled with.

Rather than attempting to accommodate the correspondence intuition or the explanatory status of claims like (A') and (B'), Douven and Hindriks attempt to explain such intuitions away, claiming that even if thinkers possess something like the correspondence intuition, it cannot cut much philosophical ice and, so, is of little significance to deflationists. Their chief aim is to show that the leading accounts or theories of explanation cannot do justice to the claim that the target of a truth-ascription is true because of the way the world is. To this end, they consider three conceptions of explanation, viz., (i) causal explanation, (ii) mathematical explanation (as developed by Steiner (1978), Hersch (1997), and Mancosu (2001)), and (iii) the unification and pragmatic theories of explanation

(Friedman (1974) and Kitcher (1989), for the former view, and van Fraassen (1980), for the latter). They conclude that none of these is adequate to the task. As Douven and Hindriks are well aware, there could be other accounts of explanation that fit the bill, but they offer a burden-shifting argument. Since they have gone through the most standard accounts of explanation and have, in each case, shown that it cannot support the correspondence intuition, the burden is on anyone who wants to use this intuition in a challenge to deflationism to offer a notion of explanation that does support the claim that there is an explanatory connection between (e.g.) the whiteness of snow and the truth of an utterance of 'Snow is white'. Absent such an argument, we have no reason for thinking that the correspondence intuition indicates something (e.g., a genuine correspondence relation) that can threaten deflationism.

Douven and Hindriks's strategy might, however, strike one as too extreme. That is, one might not want to reject the thesis that claims like (A') and (B') offer explanations that accommodate the correspondence intuition by capturing the intuition expressed in the slogan that truth depends on reality. Fortunately, it seems possible for deflationists, at least those who endorse the kind of stronger reading mentioned above of the equivalence in the instances of (TS), to accept all of this by appealing to a notion of explanation that Douven and Hindriks do not consider. A notion of this sort figures into an approach that Liggins (2016) considers and rejects for responding to his explanatory asymmetry challenge. On this approach, which Liggins claims is suggested by Wolfgang Künne (2003, pp. 154–55), developed by Benjamin Schnieder (2006), and hinted at by Horwich (2008, p. 266, n. 13), the 'because' of (A') (and, by extension, of the 'is explained by' of (B')) is understood in a special way, involving matters of asymmetrical conceptual connections. (Cf. Schnieder (2010, p. 323).) Specifically, the right-hand side is said to explain the left-hand side by providing a reduction of conceptual complexity, which involves a use of more basic and better understood concepts. On this understanding of claims like (A′) and (B′), they do provide a kind of explanation and even exhibit the requisite asymmetry, but this is all accomplished in a way that is in no way inflationary.[42]

Liggins (2016, pp. 91–93) claims that this approach fails, since this sort of understanding of 'because' and 'is explained by' can only account for statements regarding the applicability of the truth concept on the left-hand side or, to put matters in linguistic terms, claims about the applicability of the truth predicate there. But, he claims, providing explanations of these matters and accounting for the asymmetry of these explanations is not the same thing as accounting for the asymmetry exhibited by claims like (A), and, by extension, claims like (B), and like (A′) and (B′). Liggins (2016, p. 93) argues that anyone who takes this sort of account to explain the asymmetries of (A′) and (B′) (e.g., Künne (2003, pp. 155, 165)) conflates an explanation of why something is true, the matter of its *being true*, with the explanation of why the truth concept or why the predicate 'true' applies to it. Because Horwich accepts a distinction between being true and these matters of concept or predicate applicability, Liggins is right to think that his "conflation objection" blocks Horwich from explaining the asymmetry of (A) and (B) in the proposed terms. But we have already discussed a different way that Horwich can respond to Liggins's challenge. So the question now is whether Liggins's objection also blocks other species of deflationism from appealing to something along the lines of Künne's and Schnieder's ideas.

Liggins's conflation objection does not seem to block other deflationists from explaining the asymmetry exhibited by claims like (A′) and (B′) by making this sort of appeal. Focusing on the matter of the applicability of the truth predicate, deflationists who are more explicitly concerned with giving an account of truth-*talk*,

---

[42] Although Douven and Hindriks do not consider Schnieder's notion of "conceptual explanation", as will emerge, if the correspondence intuition arises from this kind of account, then it does so in a way that is perfectly compatible with a deflationary accommodation of that intuition.

as opposed to an account of a deflated truth *property*, can understand the 'because' in a claim like (A') as pertaining to the appropriateness of the application of truth predicate on the left-hand side, that is, to just the appropriateness of the instance of truth-talk there, rather than as pertaining to why some entity (a proposition) has some property (truth). The latter framing of the matter, they might maintain, is a misleading holdover from inflationism. If all that is to be explained is the appropriateness of an instance of truth-talk, then it seems clear that this does depend on how the world is, and in the same way that the appropriateness of *any* statement does. Thus, if the 'because' in claims like (A') is understood in the proposed fashion, then the asymmetry of (A') and its ilk is accounted for, since their converses do not hold. After all, how the world is does not depend on the appropriateness of any statement. For species of deflationism other than minimalism, this does not amount to the kind of conflation that Liggins claims. Explaining the applicability of the truth predicate is all that there is to explaining "why something is true" for views of this sort. Similarly, since "something's being true" also just amounts to the appropriateness of some instance of truth-talk, the asymmetry of the 'is explained by' that claims like (B') contain is, again, a matter of this appropriateness of language use being explained by how the world is, but not vice versa. But this too is just a particular instance of the more general fact that the appropriateness of language use typically depends on how the world is, while how the world is almost never depends on, or gets explained by, the appropriateness of any language use.[43] Moreover, the appropriateness of different applications of the truth predicate is a fragmented matter, so any deflationist who understands "being true" in these linguistic terms is not sneaking in anything unified and thus potentially inflationary. Hence, an approach involving

---

[43] Any potential exceptions to this direction of dependency would likely involve explanations of certain *linguistic* facts in terms of the appropriateness of certain uses of language.

an appeal to notions of explanation like those that Künne and Schnieder offer will allow non-minimalist deflationists to account for the explanatory asymmetries in claims like (A') and (B') and to use them to account for the correspondence intuition.

It thus appears that adherents of many different species of deflationism can accommodate the correspondence intuition by reformulating it in terms of truth-maker theory and, within that framework, understanding the issue as a matter of accounting for certain intuitively explanatory claims. For Horwich, the dependence of truth on reality is captured by claims like (A) and (B) and the explanatory asymmetry they exhibit. On his (2008, p. 273) understanding, this dependency ends up being a matter of the explanatory priority expressed by instances of the truth-free schema 'p because $q_1, q_2, \ldots, q_n$.' An investigation of the dependency thus amounts to one that is "concerned simply with the ways in which various kinds of phenomena are to be explained (i.e., constitutively grounded), and with which of them must (or may, or may not) be regarded as explanatorily basic" (2008, p. 271). In more linguistic terms, on this take, truth-maker theory involves an investigation of what types of sentences may or must occur in the q-positions for given types of sentences that occur in the p-position, and Horwich (2008, p. 273) claims that it is a mistake to presuppose that only existential claims (he says "propositions") can be given "fundamental status". Similarly, Simpson (2021, p. 3179) maintains that "deflationists can accept truthmaking claims as explanations of (bearerless) truths, whether or not those explanations ultimately specify objects."[44] This understanding of truth-maker theory makes it very close to investigating the metaphysical issue of *grounding* (cf. Simpson (2021, p. 3165)), which is often taken to be the basis

---

[44] Simpson (2021, pp. 3160–61) explains his notion of "bearerless truths" as amounting to "ways the world is" or, better, since a truth of this sort is not supposed to be any kind of object but instead a capturing the sentential quantification in 'For some p, p', as amounting to "things being somehow".

of *constitutive* (as opposed to causal or probabilistic) explanation.[45] Indeed, a theory of grounding can be taken to be a general theory of the "in virtue of" relation, which Horwich (2008, p. 262) takes to be part of "the real content of a truthmaker theory." As he (2008, p. 263) sees matters, truth-maker theory is not really about truth, that is, explaining why propositions are true by determining what goes in for 'x' in the instances of '<p> is true in virtue of x'. Where truth-talk does figure into truth-maker theory, it just plays its usual generalizing role with respect to the sentential variables in the schema 'p in virtue of x'. (Cf. Lewis (2001, p. 604).) This "semantically descended" orientation toward truth-maker theory, and the expressive role that truth-talk plays in it, can be endorsed by any deflationist, not only Horwichian minimalists but also those who do not acknowledge any truth property and who endorse the aforementioned stronger equivalence in the instances of (TS).

While Asay ultimately concludes that deflationists can and, indeed, must embrace truth-maker theory, he (2022) raises a concern about the path to the compatibility of deflationism and truth-maker theory proposed by Horwich and Simpson. He claims that their "explanation-based" approach to truth-maker theory is on the wrong track. Asay (2022, pp. 122–23) points out that traditional truth-maker theory is not about explanation, that is, not about *explaining* why true propositions are true; it is about ontology, and he claims that "[t]ruthmaker theory's true utility consists in its ability to guide ontological investigations". On a traditional "existence-based" understanding of the theory, truthmaking involves something in reality in virtue of which a particular truth is true. Armstrong (1997, 2004) concurs with this understanding of truth-maker theory, arguing that we cannot explain the generally agreed upon aspect of this theory, viz., a dependency relation between true propositions and reality, without countenancing truth-maker *entities*. As noted above, truth-maker

---

[45] See Bliss and Trogdon (2024).

theory often posits special categories of entities to play this role, such as facts or states of affairs. However, in "sanitizing" truth-maker theory to fit with deflationism, Horwich (2008) argues against any truthmaking role for those kinds of ontological posits. Similarly, Simpson (2021, p. 3179) maintains that "[d]eflationism does block certain elements of traditional truthmaker theory", where these include the truth-maker principle and the principle that truth-makers must always be objects. This might seem to conflict with the sort of ontological understanding that Asay insists on for truth-maker theory. If truth-maker theory requires the positing of entities like facts or states of affairs as what makes any truth true, then it would seem to be incompatible, or at least in tension, with deflationism.

Even so, Asay (2022, pp. 118–19) argues that "a deflationist can find the notion of a truthmaker perfectly innocuous: it's just another tool for talking about what exists, as revealed by attending to the ontological grounds of what is true", and he contends that truth-maker theory actually offers a way for deflationists to accommodate the correspondence intuition. He (2022) further argues that truth-maker theory is something that deflationists *must* embrace, since denying it would amount to denying that truths have ontological grounds and thus subscribing to "the indefensible claim that truth and ontology are completely independent of one another". But, Asay (2022) notes, just as deflationists consider what is true to be fragmented or, as he puts it, "piecemeal", they should take an equally piecemeal approach to truth-makers. Asay (2022, pp. 126, 128) makes the point that a deflationist can see the term 'truth-maker' just as playing the kind of generalizing role that deflationists emphasize for 'true'. To this end, he (2022, p. 118) suggests that deflationists retain the idea of "truth-makers" but, in cases such as the truth of 'Kripke exists' or of 'There are penguins', they should replace the alethic label with separate instances of "there-being-Kripke-makers" or "there-being-penguin-makers". Since making there be something is more a matter of making the world be somehow than one of making some truth-bearer true,[46] this last point seems to align Asay with Simpson's contention that nontrivial truthmaking pertains to grounding "bearerless" truths, i.e., to determining how the world is.[47] Asay's deflating of the idea of truthmaking also connects with Simpson's (2021, p. 3158) claim that "the apparent conflict between deflationism and truthmaking rests on the fact that both sides have built more into the notion of truthmaking than is necessary", and "[w]ithout these optional extras, deflationism and truthmaking are entirely compatible."

While Horwich, Simpson, and Asay all defend the view that deflationism is compatible with truth-maker theory, their respective defenses are made in slightly different ways. However, it turns out that these different ways of fitting deflationism with truth-maker theory are not that far apart. Beyond the points of agreement just mentioned, between Asay's view and Simpson's, note that both Simpson and Horwich include the metaphysical element of "attending to the ontological grounds of what is true" that Asay takes to be the point of truth-maker theory. For Simpson, this is a matter of specifying what amounts to the ontological grounds of his non-entity "bearerless" truths, which are then, via the relevant instance of (TS), the grounds for the truth of truth-bearers. Horwich's understanding of sanitized truth-maker theory also still has an "attending to ontological grounds" aspect, in that he takes the "core" claims of truth-maker theory to specify orders of fundamentality and the relation of constitutive grounding. The

---

[46] Asay's examples focus on "truthmaking" for existential claims, but presumably this thought extends beyond these, e.g., to typical predicative examples, where the "truth-maker" for the truth of a claim like 'grass is green' will amount to a 'grass-being-green-maker'. Since Asay (2022, p. 120) also points out that there are versions of truth-maker theory that do not posit entities like facts or states of affairs, a deflationist embracing such a version can take a "grass-being-green-maker" just to involve more basic entities, such as grass and perhaps greenness.

[47] Simpson (2021, p. 3181) claims that the idea of "explaining a truth" is ambiguous. Sometimes it is read as explaining a "bearerless truth", e.g., grass being green, whereas other times it is read in the more typical way, as explaining what it is for a given truth-bearer, e.g., the proposition *that grass is green*, to be true. But he maintains that, given the former and the relevant instance of (ES), the latter is a trivial matter.

difference between the two camps seems to be that Asay insists that truthmaking can be done only by entities, so that claims specifying truthmaking, that is, specifying the ontological grounds for the world being somehow, must be formulated in terms of existential claims regarding objects. By contrast, Horwich and Simpson have a less restricted view about how truthmaking claims can be formulated. Both of the latter allow that objects can be truthmakers, so that some truthmaking claims can involve existence claims for those objects, but they reject the thesis that truthmaking can be specified *only* with existential claims.[48] However, whether one accepts Asay's restriction or not, it appears that deflationists can avail themselves of truth-maker theory, recognized as something separate from an understanding of truth (or truth-talk), and, following Horwich, they can use that framework as a means for capturing the correspondence intuition.

5.3.2 The Truth-Property Thesis

In keeping with what he takes to be common-sense considerations, Horwich (1990/1998, p. 16) maintains that there is a property of truth, in virtue of the fact that 'is true' is a perfectly good predicate, which he takes to be a "conclusive criterion" for standing for a property of some sort.[49] He (1990/1998, p. 142) denies that 'is true'

---

[48] Horwich (2008, p. 273) claims that it is a fallacy to suppose "that the world is the totality of 'things,' captured by means of singular terms rather than sentences", while others (e.g., Strawson (1950)) maintain precisely the opposite. But this is a metaphysical dispute that is independent of one's approach to the topic of truth, so, on this point and others, endorsing deflationism about truth-talk does not automatically dissolve metaphysical disputes. (Cf. Simpson (2021, p. 3177).)

[49] This view is rejected by *prosententialists*, who deny that 'is true' functions logically as a predicate at all. That said, see Grover (1981a/1992, pp. 155–58), where she explains how prosententialists can allow for something like properties of truth and falsity. As she explains there, the prosentences 'it is true' and 'it is false' could be used to partition possible sentence-tokenings into two sets that we could then stipulate to be the extensions of new linguistic *predicates* we introduce, 'True' and 'False'. These predicates would then attribute properties identified with those extensions. But Grover argues that such

attributes a "substantive property" but allows that, given a "liberal conception" of properties, according to which "every term that functions logically as a predicate stands for a property", the truth predicate can be said to attribute a property, since, as he (1990/1998, p. 142) contends, 'is true' must be treated as a predicate in logic. What deflationists deny with their Metaphysical Deflationism is that 'is true' attributes a complex or a naturalistic property with a substantive underlying nature. Field (1992, p. 322) suggests the idea that what 'is true' attributes is merely a "logical property", though he does not provide any insight into what a *logical* property is. Nevertheless, this raises a question for those deflationists who wish to maintain that 'is true' attributes a property, viz., how exactly one can distinguish that view from the inflationary view of the truth predicate as attributing a substantive property.

As Horwich (1990/1998) analyzes the idea of a "substantive property", a predicate attributes a property of this sort iff there is no a priori obstacle to the property's being reducible to non-semantic terms. Since, he contends, deflationists will maintain, on the basis of a priori considerations, that no putative truth property is so reducible, they will hold that 'is true' does not attribute a substantive property, though, as we have seen, they might grant that it nevertheless attributes a non-substantive (or "logical") property.

While Horwich is right that deflationists, in virtue of their adherence to Metaphysical Deflationism, will deny both that 'is true' attributes a substantive property and that any truth property is reducible to non-semantic terms, the analysis that he offers of what it takes for a predicate to attribute a substantive property is problematic, for it renders *primitivism* about truth, such as the view espoused by G. E. Moore (1901/1993), as one on which 'is true' attributes a non-substantive property, and that seems clearly wrong. But this raises a question: What is the difference between

predicates would be useless, since the so-called properties would be, as we sometimes put it, "fragmented". (Cf. Leeds (1995).)

a primitivist view about the truth property and a deflationary view about the truth property?

One way we might address this question is via Lewis's (1983, 1986) distinction between *sparse*, or *natural*, properties and *abundant* properties. According to Lewis, natural properties are those that are relevant to the causal powers of things and that "carve nature at the joints", marking objective resemblances among the objects that possess them. By contrast, Lewis (1983, p. 12) claims that

> any class of things, be it ever so gerrymandered and miscellaneous and indescribable in thought and language, and be it ever so superfluous in characterising the world, is nevertheless a property. So there are properties in immense abundance.

He claims that these "gerrymandered and miscellaneous" abundant properties do not capture the causal powers of things and do not indicate facts of objective resemblances. As Lewis sees matters, then, there are natural (or sparse) properties and there are abundant properties, where these categories are mutually exclusive. Among the natural properties, some are "perfectly natural". These are the most fundamental properties. (Naturalness applies to relations as well: The perfectly natural relations are the most fundamental relations.) Lewis (1983) contended that 'perfectly natural' is a primitive notion and that the naturalness of certain other properties can be defined in terms of those that are perfectly natural.

This distinction, between natural and abundant properties, is useful for marking out certain differences between deflationary and inflationary views on the truth property. Douglas Edwards (2013) and Asay (2014) separately propose that, for those deflationists who grant that 'is true' attributes a property, we should take it that, on their respective views, the truth property is an abundant property. By contrast, we should take inflationists to maintain that 'is true' attributes a natural property. Regarding inflationary primitivism, we might distinguish the sort of view that Moore espouses from other inflationary views, such as the correspondence theory of truth, by appealing to the distinction between perfectly natural and natural properties and maintaining that an inflationary primitivist like Moore should take 'is true' to attribute a perfectly natural property, in contrast, say, to a correspondence theorist, who would maintain that 'is true' attributes a natural property that is not perfectly natural, since they take truth to be reducible to non-semantic terms.

The view that 'is true' attributes an abundant property comports with what deflationists have wanted to say about any putative truth property, viz., that it has no causal-explanatory role and that it does not indicate genuine similarities, so that the true statements—sentences or propositions—do not resemble each other in any significant way. In addition, the view that 'is true' attributes a natural property comports with what inflationists have wanted to say about the truth property, viz., that it has a causal-explanatory role and that it indicates genuine similarities, so that the true statements do all resemble each other in some significant way.

Leeds (1995, p. 11) makes a related point about the idea of a reference relation, what he calls the "R-relation". In contrast to a causal theory of reference, of the sort originally developed by Kripke (1980), which would amount to an inflationary theory of the R-relation and yield an inflationary account of a truth property (in a Tarskian way à la Field (1972), Leeds notes that a deflationist about the R-relation would concede that "there are all sorts of causal relations that hold between our use of words, and the R-referents of these words", but the deflationist will go on to contend that these myriad and disparate relations do not amount to a unified substantive reference relation that could be characterized by an inflationary of the reference relation. This is the case, according to Leeds (1995, p. 12), because deflationists "will deny that the class of causal connections between words and their R-referents is a natural class in a way that requires a uniform explanation".[50]

So, on one understanding, the thesis that a truth predicate attributes a property violates Metaphysical Deflationism, but on a different understanding that view is compatible with Metaphysical Deflationism. This distinction lines up with the expanding sequence of presuppositions attributed above to inflationary theories of truth and employed in Chapter 3 to distinguish the main versions or species of deflationism both from inflationary views and from one another, namely:

(i) The alethic locutions (centrally, 'true') function logically as predicates.
(ii) These predicates express "attributive" concepts and thereby serve to describe or characterize putative truth-bearers.
(iii) These attributive concepts determine alethic properties the possession (or lack) of which is attributed in the descriptions that the uses of the alethic locutions provide.
(iv) The alethic properties attributed via the alethic locutions have robust (or substantive) natures.

Moore, an inflationary primitivist, accepts (i)–(iv), as do all other inflationists of which we are aware; he simply adds that the substantial nature of the truth property is unanalyzable and, as a result, the truth predicate is indefinable. As noted in Section 3.3, Horwich accepts (i)–(iii) but rejects (iv). Since Field (1992) suggests taking the truth predicate to attribute a "logical property", he might agree with Horwich on these assumptions, or, given his espousal of nominalism (cf. Field (1980/2016)), he might agree with his fellow disquotationalist, Quine, who accepts (i) but rejects (ii)–(iv). Some

---

[50] Leeds's (1995) discussion of the R-relation is reminiscent of our discussion above of what is true as being fragmented and of Asay's (2022) discussion of truth-makers as "piecemeal".

redundancy theorists reject all of (i)–(iv), for they take 'is true' to be part of a sentential-operator prefix, 'it is true that', but, as noted in Section 2.2, Ramsey still considers his account to be a kind of correspondence theory of truth, which suggests the idea of truth being a correspondence *relation*. In Section 3.1 we also noted that prosententialists reject all of (i)–(iv), since they either take 'is true' to be a prosentence-forming operator, or, more extremely, hold that the alethic locutions are non-detachable components of the atomic prosentences 'it-is-true' and 'that-is-true'. But, as mentioned above, arch-prosententialist Grover (1981a/1992) also allows that there could be a property of truth in a weak sense, one that is compatible with the Lewisian notion of an abundant property, which seems similar to Horwich's position. While this might amount to a kind of metaphysical parallel with minimalism, it would not indicate agreement with minimalism's acceptance of inflationary presuppositions (i)–(iii), since, on Grover's view, any such property would still not be attributed by the ordinary alethic locutions, which function non-predicatively in prosentences.

5.4 The Challenge from Normativity

A separate sort of challenge to Metaphysical Deflationism bypasses the issue of whether there is any causal-explanatory role requiring that the truth predicate attribute a substantive property and instead focuses on putative normative roles that supposedly require such a property. This line of criticism against deflationism traces back to Michael Dummett's (1959/1978) objection to the thesis that a redundancy theory of truth-talk—for Dummett (1978, p. xx), any account claiming that stipulating or providing a procedure for generating the instances of the (TS), so any version of deflationism—tells us everything there is to know about the notion of truth. Drawing an analogy between the concept of truth and the concept of winning a game, Dummett notes that trying to explain the latter simply by listing all of the winning moves for each particular game would still leave out what is common to all the cases, viz., that the point of playing a game is to try to win (1978, p. 8). A deflationary account of the functioning or role of the truth predicate seems similarly to leave out that speaking the truth is the point of statement-making (that by making a statement a speaker "commits himself to its being true") (1978, p. 11). As Dummett notes, "The roots of the notions of truth and falsity lie in the distinction between a speaker's being, objectively, *right* or *wrong* in what he says when he makes an assertion" (1978, p. xvii). Thus, "What has to be added to a [deflationary Tarskian] truth-definition for a language, if the notion of truth is to be explained, is a description of the linguistic activity of making assertions; and ... any such account of what assertion is must introduce a distinction between correct and incorrect assertions, and ... it is in terms of that distinction that the notion of truth has first to be explained" (1978, p. 20).

According to Horwich (1990/1998, pp. 23–25), this last point gets things backward. While there may be interesting connections between truth and assertion, in his view the theories of them should be kept separate. He considers the autonomy of his version of deflationism—that it "*provides a theory of truth that is a theory of nothing else*" (italics original)—to be a merit of the approach, since he also holds his view is "*sufficient, in combination with theories of other phenomena, to explain all the facts about truth*" (italics original). Thus, while a theory of assertion need not be part of an account of truth, an adequate understanding of assertion will still need to show how truth is connected to it. As a challenge to deflationism, this point has been developed as the thesis that truth plays a distinctive normative role, marking a kind of correctness for assertion, requiring the recognition that truth-talk attributes a substantive property of the sort needed to underwrite the norm.

Wright (1992, pp. 15–23) also mounts a challenge to deflationism along these lines. He claims that deflationism is inherently unstable because there is a distinctive norm for assertoric practice that goes beyond the norms for warranted assertibility, a norm that is already implicit in acceptance of the instances of the truth schema, (TS), themselves. The norm marked by the truth predicate is coincident with warranted assertibility, since, for any sentence, reason for thinking that the sentence is true transfers, via the instance of (TS) for it, to reason for assertorically uttering that sentence—that is, to reason for considering it warrantedly assertible. Conversely, reason for thinking a sentence is warrantedly assertible is reason for assertorically uttering it, which will transfer, via the instance of (TS) for it, to reason for regarding the sentence as true. This much is compatible with deflationism. But, Wright argues, the norms of truth and warranted assertibility are potentially extensionally divergent: Not having warrant to assert some sentence does not yield having warrant to assert its negation (i.e., there can be neutral information states). However, from any instance of (TS), we can infer its contrapositive, which takes us (going right to left) from it not being the case that the sentence in question is true to the negation of the sentence. But the instance of (TS) for the negation of any sentence takes us (going from right to left) from that negated sentence to an ascription of truth to that negated sentence. Thus, it not being the case that some sentence is true does yield the negation of the sentence being true, in contrast with warranted assertibility. This difference, Wright claims, shows that, by deflationism's own lights, the truth predicate expresses a distinct norm governing assertion, which, he claims (1992, p. 18), is incompatible with the deflationist contention "that 'true' is only grammatically a predicate, whose role is not to attribute a substantial characteristic" (i.e., incompatible with the Metaphysical Deflationism that follows from Linguistic Deflationism).

Rejecting Wright's argument for the instability of deflationism, Ian Rumfitt (1995, p. 103) notes that if we make the plausible additions of the ideas of denying something and of having warrant for doing so ("anti-warrant") to Wright's characterization of deflationism, this would make 'is not true' a device of rejection governed by the norm that "[t]he predicate 'is not true' may be applied to any sentence for which one has an anti-warrant". But then truth-talk's behavior with negation would not indicate that it marks a distinct norm beyond justified assertibility *and justifiable deniability*, which would be perfectly compatible with Metaphysical Deflationism. Field (1994a, pp. 264–65) responds to Wright's challenge (along with a similar objection regarding normativity from Putnam (1983/1985, pp. 279–80)) by citing the logical role of the truth predicate in specifications of such normative desires as to utter only true sentences or to have only true beliefs. Assuming his (1978) sententialist view of intentional attitudes, Field explains these desires in terms of desiring the infinite conjunction of all claims of the forms "I utter 'p' only if p" or "I believe 'p' only if p". Field agrees with Wright that truth-talk expresses a norm beyond warranted assertibility, but he (1994a, p. 265) maintains that "there is no difficulty in desiring that all one's beliefs be disquotationally true; and not only can each of us desire such things, there can be a general practice of badgering others into having such desires". Similarly, Horwich (1996, pp. 879–80) argues that Wright's denial of Metaphysical Deflationism does not follow from showing that the truth predicate expresses a norm beyond warranted assertibility. He claims that Wright misses the point that in the expression of such a norm the truth predicate just plays its logical role of generalizing from a particular normative principle like 'If you believe that snow is white, then you have reason for asserting that snow is white', to arrive at the general normative principle 'You have reason for asserting any proposition you believe to be true'.

Huw Price (1998) develops a different version of the challenge from normativity. Although he also objects to Wright's argument, Price (1998, p. 241) agrees with him that "truth is normative, in a way not explained by [deflationism]". He holds that Horwich's (1996) reply to Wright misses the real normative challenge because it only considers a "first norm" of subjective correctness for assertion (that one believe what one asserts, i.e., sincerity). But this, even combined with a "second norm" of objective correctness (that one have justification or warrant for what one asserts), can only underwrite "merely opinionated assertion" (Price (1998, pp. 245–47)). Adding a deflationary truth predicate, Price claims, would not turn this anemic practice into full-blooded assertion, since it would only express agreement with others' (potentially justified) opinions (1998, p. 248). Full-blooded assertion requires a "third norm" of further objective correctness.[51] For the actual sort of language-users that we are, the notion of truth is what actually provides this further norm, by giving us a way to express a commitment to something best formulated in the negative, via the schema 'if not-p, then it is incorrect to assert p'. This distinctive third norm of assertoric practice, Price (2003, pp. 186–87) claims, is supplied by "a notion of truth that differs from justification, even of a Peircean ideal variety". Without this third norm, he argues, disagreement would be frictionless—a difference of mere opinion—and thus genuine assertoric dialogue would not be possible. Echoing Dummett, Price concludes "we have not understood truth until we understand its role in the [assertion] game we currently play". (2003, p. 190). In response to Price, Matthew McGrath (2003, pp. 58–61) argues against his conclusion regarding deflationism, claiming that both Horwich and disquotationalists could account for the needed third norm of assertion by claiming that this kind of correctness at most presupposes the notion of truth, but even that is compatible with maintaining that its explanation belongs to a theory of something other than truth. In any case, an interesting aspect of Price's position is that while he believes that a deflationary account of truth-talk (i.e., Linguistic Deflationism)

---

[51] This is an important normative issue is also indicated by the fact that Horwich's example of a statement expressing a general norm could be made without employing truth-talk at all, simply as 'You have reason to assert any proposition you believe'. In fact, Horwich would be better served by considering a specific case like 'If snow is white, then you have reason for asserting that snow is white' and the general principle 'You have reason for asserting any proposition that is true'. Also note that Price's focus on "objective correctness" fits better with Wright's (1992) and Field's (1994a) discussions of the sorts of norms expressed by using truth-talk.

could not underwrite the third norm of assertion, he does not take this to undermine Metaphysical Deflationism. Instead, Price (2003, pp. 187–90) thinks that the norm is "made up" by us, and it is merely a "convenient fiction" that there is a property of truth.[52] Still, Price maintains that his "fictionalism" about truth should not be equated with deflationism, since a deflationary attitude, he claims, "tends to undermine the fictional-nonfictional distinction". By contrast, in Armour-Garb and Woodbridge (2014b) and (2015, pp. 119–26), we argue that deflationism as a genus should be understood as a kind of fictionalism about truth-talk, in part by arguing that truth-talk does not play anything more than an expressive role in distinguishing fiction-involving discourse from non-fiction-involving discourse. (Cf. (2015, pp. 5–7, 249–51).) We will say more about the relationship between the truth concept and certain philosophical "isms" and distinctions in the next chapter.

---

[52] Thus, since Price subscribes just to Metaphysical Deflationism, he is, by both his lights and ours, not a deflationist. See Section 1.2.

6

Challenges to Conceptual Deflationism

The second sort of challenge to deflationism that attempts to undermine the approach's primary linguistic thesis indirectly involves attacks on the second necessary condition of this thesis: Conceptual Deflationism. What is challenged here is the thesis that there is nothing more to the concepts expressed by the alethic locutions (most centrally, the truth concept) than what comes with deflationary accounts of the operation of these expressions. "We will thus be left with a deflated concept of truth—a 'thin' concept ... that is isolated from all other concepts of interest to us and can play no substantive explanatory role with respect to them" (Bar-On and Simmons (2007, p. 62); cf. O'Leary-Hawthorne and Oppy (1997, p. 174); see Horwich (1990/1998, p. 24) for an endorsement of this "explanatory isolation" thesis by a deflationist). The challenge to Conceptual Deflationism, however, maintains that the truth concept must be "thick" or substantial, rather than the "thin" concept that deflationism requires. This is supposedly indicated by the truth concept's putatively substantive explanatory role in accounts of other concepts—a role it could not play if the truth predicate operated in the way that deflationists claim it operates.

This type of explanatory challenge is different from the one discussed in Chapter 5, involving attempts to identify a substantive causal-explanatory role for a truth property. That challenge to Metaphysical Deflationism focuses on a putative role for truth in answering certain "why-questions" (typically, why some sort of success occurs). The challenge to Conceptual Deflationism attributes a role to the truth concept in a different sort of explanatory context: that of answering certain "what-questions" (for example, what some concept involves). This challenge focuses on the role of the truth concept in accounts of what something else is, or of what it involves, for example, the truth concept's role in the traditional account of knowledge as justified true belief. Sometimes (as in the account of the concept of knowledge) the challenge appears to move directly from a proposed counterexample to Conceptual Deflationism to the purported inadequacy of deflationism's linguistic thesis; sometimes (as seems to be the case in the challenge to deflationism based on the purported role of the truth concept in an adequate account of meaning (Devitt (2001, p. 603))), the challenge seems to run from an attack on Conceptual Deflationism to a proposed undermining of Metaphysical Deflationism, and from there to threaten the adequacy of Linguistic Deflationism. In either case, to deal with the challenge, a deflationist must address the purported role of the truth concept in the relevant what-explanation.

From a deflationist's perspective, there are two categories of challenges to Conceptual Deflationism that are distinguished by the ways that the putative challenge is to be addressed. The first category includes cases where truth-talk, and thus the truth concept, appears in what-explanations of various concepts in a way that deflationists can consider acceptable. About these, deflationists will typically claim that the truth predicate is just playing its familiar special logical role, as doing something like implementing the generalizing role of sentential variables and quantifiers. The second category of challenges involves cases where truth-talk has been used in an account of something, but where deflationists take that use of truth-talk, and thus that account, to be unacceptable. They claim that the concept of truth has been misapplied there, and some different concept or concepts should be applied in its stead in a different what-explanation.

6.1 "Truth-Involving" Accounts That Deflationists Can Accept

Starting with the first category of challenges to Conceptual Deflationism, given the traditional centrality of the notion of truth in philosophy, the list of widely accepted what-explanations that are "truth-involving" is quite long. Beyond explaining knowledge as justified true belief, or (after Gettier (1963)) as "true-justified-belief (+ . . .)" (Alston (1985, p. 57)), it includes explaining epistemic justification in terms of being "truth conductive" (Dickie (2016, p. 102)), explaining the verification of a hypothesis via making "observations . . . relevant to the determination of its truth" (Ayer (1936/1952, p. 38)), and explaining epistemic reliability in term of being "produced by a process (or series of processes) that has a high truth-ratio" (Goldman and Beddor (2021)). Communicative reliability has been explained in terms of "a certain tendency to tell the truth" (Casalegno (2005, p. 296)). A traditional view on the concept of assertion is that to assert is "to present as true" (Wright (1992, p. 34)), and, relatedly, there are Gottlob Frege's (1979, p. 139) view of judgment as "inwardly recognizing that a thought is true" and the view of belief as "regarding a proposition as true, with the intention of doing so only if it is true" (Velleman (2000, p. 250)). Within logic, the orthodox account of logical validity or entailment is that "it must be the case that that when the premises are true, the conclusion is true" (Caret and Hjortland (2015, p. 3)), with the soundness of an argument amounting to logical validity plus the truth of the premises. Standard truth-functional accounts of the logical connectives also mention truth, as in an account of '∧' as expressing the truth-function that outputs the value 'true' only when both conjuncts are true, as can be found in any introductory logic book. These examples (and more) all seem like cases of substantive concepts whose what-explanations involve the truth concept. As Bar-On and Simmons (2007, p. 68) pose the challenge, "We need to see how to deflate the explanatory role apparently played by truth in elucidations of various concepts that interest us", but their conclusion is that this "requires more than the 'thin' concept of truth afforded by deflationary accounts".

Deflationists will attempt to respond to the challenges posed by most of these cases in the same way: via the by now familiar claim that the truth predicate operates just as a device for formulating a special kind of generalization, here in the various what-explanations. The relevant what-explanations are "truth-involving" only in the sense that they employ the truth predicate, that is, they are 'true'-employing. But these uses of truth-talk are compatible with deflationism. To see how this would go in the case of assertion, consider Bar-On and Simmons's (2007, p. 78) claim that an account of what the illocutionary force of assertion is that distinguishes it from other illocutionary forces involves ineliminable use of the idea of "presenting as true". They claim that the problem is that there is no other way to express the distinguishing mark of assertoric force (in contrast with, e.g., interrogative or imperative force, or even the force of hypothesizing or of wishing). A deflationist might of course reject this supposedly Frege-inspired 'true'-employing account of assertoric force, but if they do not, then they can accept that truth-talk provides a way to express *in natural language* what is distinctive about assertion, but they can go on to note that in doing so the truth predicate serves only to express a special kind of generalization. To follow through on this reply, a deflationist could claim that if the language being used to explain assertion contained sentential variables and quantifiers, there would be a means for expressing the relevant content without bringing in the truth concept. But, as Bar-On and Simmons (2007, pp. 71–72) note, what seems tricky about following through with this line of thought is that the use of the phrase 'present *as* true' in the account of assertion is different from the use of 'is true' typically explained by deflationists. In a case of the latter sort of use, such as 'What Olivia said is true', the recasting in terms of sentential variables and quantifiers yields 'For some p, p and Olivia said that p'. However, since one can assert something that is false, despite presenting it *as* true, this sort of formulation must be adjusted.

To achieve the right sort of "*as* factual" element in explaining a particular mode of presenting, but without recreating truth-talk, a deflationist can recast the claim 'When one asserts, one presents what is asserted as true' using sentential variables and quantifiers along the lines of 'When one asserts, one presents the world as being such that, in it, for some p, p'. This recasting involves both the deflationary notion of "descent" from talk of "what is asserted" to talk of the world, and the use of higher-order logical devices to implement directly the special logical role that truth-talk is taken to implement in a language. Similarly, a deflationist can take the explanation, 'To believe something is to regard it as true, with the intention of doing so only if it is true' and recast it in terms of sentential variables and quantifiers as 'To believe something is to take the world as being such that, in it, for some p, p, with the intention of doing so only if p.' Along the same lines, the traditional claim that to know something is to have a justified true belief can be recast (reversing the order) in terms of sentential variables and quantifiers as 'To know is to take the world as being such that in it, for some p, p, only when p, and only when there are reasons for taking the world to be such that, in it, p, where those reasons are such that, for all q, those reasons are conducive for taking the world to be such that in it, q, only if q'. In all these accounts, truth-talk just provides a more concise and flexible means for implementing what these quasi-formal quantified-sentential-variable strings indicate about what it is to assert, believe, and know. But the use of truth-talk in these sorts of what-explanations does not indicate any substantive explanatory role for the truth concept in connection with these other concepts.

Turning to the role of the truth concept in accounts of various logical notions, we can see that, with respect to the concepts of the validity and soundness of arguments, a similar maneuver is available to deflationists. Consider what is it for a particular argument to be valid, say, the argument from it is raining and it is cloudy to the conclusion that it is cloudy. We can say, without bringing in the truth predicate at all, that what it is for this particular argument to be valid is for things to be such that, whenever it is both raining and cloudy, it must be the case that it is cloudy, or that it is impossible for it to be raining and cloudy without it being cloudy. A deflationist can understand the role of the truth predicate in an account of logical validity in general to be, again, just that of generalizing on the embedded sentences. As Scott Soames (2003, pp. 381–82) says, describing such cases,

> ascent to truth is a way of generalizing and systematizing our understanding of commitments we already have. The utility of the truth predicate in studying the basic forms of argumentative commitment lies in the role it plays in allowing us to abstract away from particular predications and particular argument forms, and to bring them under a small set of general headings: *logical consequence*, *logical inconsistency*, and so on. If this is right, then the deflationist insight about truth is part and parcel of our understanding of the relationship between logic and argument.

While the notion of truth gets used to state what logical validity in general is, a deflationist can say that what is actually expressed by 'An argument is logically valid just in case, if all of its premises were true, then the conclusion would have to be true' is just a generalization that employs sentential variables and quantifiers of the form "An argument is logically valid just in case, for all p and for all q, if the world were such that, in it, for every premise 'p' of the argument, p, then, for any conclusion 'q' of the argument, the world would also have to be such that, in it, q". An argument is sound just in case it is valid and, for all p, if 'p' is a premise of the argument, p. Logical entailment is the relationship that holds between the premises and conclusion of a valid argument.[1]

---

[1] In addition, Field (1994a, pp. 257–59) provides a deflationary interpretation of the standard truth-functional accounts of the logical connectives as they contribute to the (disquotational) truth conditions of the sentences that employ them.

The deflationary strategy applied in this subsection appeals to sentential variables and quantifiers in recasting the 'true'-employing what-explanations of certain concepts. This again raises the question of how we are to understand these formal devices. As mentioned in several places above, the standard approach to these formal devices is to read them as substitutional quantifiers, which some theorists find problematic. (Cf. van Inwagen (1981) and Horwich (1990/1998).) Attempting to avoid some of the putative problems by reading them as devices for encoding potentially infinite conjunctions or disjunctions (David (1994, pp. 98–99)), and embracing the related deflationist thought that is descended from Quine (1970/1986) and Leeds (1978), that the central function of truth-talk is to provide a means for expressing infinite conjunctions or disjunctions, generates the "fragmentation" concern mentioned above. More specifically, when the role of truth-talk in putatively acceptable 'true'-employing what-explanations is explained in terms of sentential variables and quantifiers understood as devices for encoding potentially infinite conjunctions and disjunctions, this threatens to fragment all the concepts with acceptable 'true'-employing what-explanations—concepts that strike us as unified and substantive. That would amount to a reductio ad absurdum of this approach to explaining the role of the appeal to the truth concept in an what-explanation of any other concept. Hence, as in the case of applying the strategy of appealing to sentential variables and quantifiers in response to challenges to Metaphysical Deflationism, applying it in a deflationary response to challenges to Conceptual Deflationism posed by 'true'-employing what-explanations that seem acceptable also requires a different, non-substitutional account of sentential variables and quantifiers.[2]

---

[2] Partly as an attempt to avoid the fragmentation concern, in Armour-Garb and Woodbridge (2023a, 2023b, and forthcoming), and in the appendix, below, we develop an alternative, non-substitutional way of understanding sentential variables and quantifiers.

6.2 "Truth-Involving" Accounts That Deflationists Must Replace

The second category of challenges to Conceptual Deflationism involves cases where deflationists see the use of the truth concept in some what-explanation as unacceptable. This assessment typically invokes the response that the relevant what-explanation needs to be given in different, entirely "truth-free" terms.[3] These challenge cases often involve the use of truth-talk in explaining some philosophical "ism" and in marking the distinction with its dual. These include the realism/anti-realism distinction, understood in terms of what notion of truth is appropriate for a class of statements (Dummett (1978, p. 146)); the cognitivism/non-cognitivism distinction, understood in terms of whether certain declarative sentences are apt for truth or falsity (Jackson et al. (1994, p. 287)) or, relatedly, the factualism/nonfactualism distinction, understood in terms of whether certain sentences express truth conditions (Boghossian (1990, p. 161)); and the fictionalism/non-fictionalism distinction, understood in terms of whether certain sentences require a "story-prefix" to be true (Rosen (1990, p. 331)).

Certain deflationists (e.g., Horwich (1993, p. 74)) might seem to have argued for the rejection or the elimination of some of these "isms" or distinctions (e.g., emotivism or expressivism in ethics, or the cognitive/non-cognitive distinction), and other theorists (e.g., O'Leary-Hawthorne and Price (1996, p. 275)) certainly have taken these deflationists to have argued for such eliminations, but, for the most part, the real proposals that have been made

---

[3] "Unacceptable" might be overly strong, since Horwich (1996b, pp. 194–96) explains how in some cases truth-talk can be understood as performing its generalizing role, e.g., from 'If there are infinitely many stars, then it is verifiable that there are' to the general anti-realist thesis 'Truth is not evidence-transcendent'. Still, the underlying what-explanation for anti-realism must first be reformulated in "truth-free" terms, unlike in the previous category of cases, where the 'true'-employing what-explanations are themselves fine and simply need to be understood properly.

involve a revision of the what-explanation of the "ism" or distinction in question, rather than an elimination or a dissolution of it. (But see Horwich (2006), for a slightly more eliminativist attitude.) Some critics of deflationism have maintained that the elimination of some of these distinctions is *forced* on some versions of a given species and have tried to use their favored thesis to argue that deflationism is incoherent or self-undermining. Paul Boghossian (1990, pp. 164-66) argues that nonfactualism, understood as grounded in the thesis that the central predicates that the target sentences employ do not attribute properties, only makes sense on the presupposition of a robust conception of truth (inflationism). So deflationary views seem to rule out nonfactualism. But, Boghossian (1990, pp. 180-81) claims, since deflationists are committed to the thesis that the truth predicate does not attribute a property, their view amounts to a nonfactualism about truth-talk, which presupposes an inflationary conception of truth, thereby rendering deflationism incoherent. While this argument appears quite powerful, it has been criticized by both friends and foes of deflationism. Paul Horwich (2006, pp. 142-43) argues that at least his version of deflationism is untouched by Boghossian's argument, since he accepts that the truth predicate attributes a property of a weak but perfectly legitimate sort. So, applied to his view, Boghossian's argument equivocates on the notion of "thin" property and the notion of "substantive" property. Robert Brandom (1994, pp. 326-27) also maintains that Boghossian's argument does not apply to his version of deflationism (leaving his view, he suggests, the only viable version). On his prosententialist account, after all, the alethic locutions are not, logically speaking, even predicates in the first place, so there is no conflict in denying that they do not attribute properties.

Michael Devitt (1990, pp. 252-55, 258-59) claims that Boghossian's argument is actually question-begging, since it assumes that the notion of truth must be used to characterize nonfactualism, while deflationary views (via their form of Conceptual Deflationism) deny that the concept of truth can be used to account for the semantic properties of sentences. As he (1990, p. 253) notes, "Any notion of truth used to describe or explain sentences must be a robust one in a truth-conditional semantics". So, according to Devitt, a deflationist would reject Boghossian's characterization of nonfactualism as "truth-involving" from the start, thereby blocking the latter's argument. Frank Jackson, Graham Oppy, and Michael Smith (1994, pp. 293–94) object that Boghossian's argument requires assuming that any version of deflationism would automatically include a "thin", mainly syntactic, notion of truth-*aptness*, but, they (1994, pp. 290–91) claim, deflationism is compatible with a substantive notion of truth-aptness connected with the notions of belief and assertion. The latter concepts might provide the basis of the kind of alternative account of nonfactualism that a deflationary view could endorse without undermining itself. While Price (2003, p. 171) also rejects Boghossian's conclusion that we have "a transcendental argument for semantic realism [and inflationism]", his reason for doing so is that he takes anti-realism about semantic notions (e.g., truth) to more or less undermine the whole realism/anti-realism distinction. He (2003, p. 188) considers "the issue of the status of truth [to be] enmeshed with the terms of the problem," so that "it may be impossible to formulate a meaningful antirealism ... about the semantic terms themselves [e.g., a deflationary view]". So, again, we find the thought that deflationism is forced to eliminate a distinction that it also seems to need to make, in order to locate itself on one side (anti-realism about truth) as opposed to the other. Price (2003, p. 189) also claims that deflationism "tends to undermine the fictional-nonfictional distinction", which motivates him to resist identifying his "fictionalism" about truth with deflationism. However, he does not take this to render deflationism either incoherent or incorrect; rather, he suggests instead that "we should be sensitive to the possibility that our existing categories—fictionalism, realism ... —may need to be reconfigured". On this view, if it turns out that the elimination of certain "isms" or distinctions were forced on deflationism, that might not be a bad result.

In responding to challenges to Conceptual Deflationism about truth based on 'true'-employing what-explanations that deflationists maintain need to be replaced with "truth-free" alternatives, deflationists have sometimes been aided by unallied theorists who have developed the needed alternative accounts of the relevant "isms" or distinctions. For example, Devitt (1997, pp. 39–43) argues against Michael Dummett's truth-centered anti-realism, claiming that realism is a metaphysical doctrine about mind-independent existence, so whether some position is realist or anti-realist is independent of any notion of truth. Horwich (1982, pp. 182, 200) claims that the kind of realism ("metaphysical realism") defined in terms of a non-epistemic, more-than-deflationary notion of truth should be rejected, leaving just more modest kinds of realism, understood in terms of facts existing independently of our minds. He later (1982, pp. 55–56) identifies three different strategies that generate anti-realist views in "truth-free" terms in response to the "tension in ordinary thinking between the metaphysical autonomy of the world (its independence from us) and its epistemological accessibility (our capacity to find out about it)". In both cases, the putatively better account of the realism/anti-realism distinction does not involve the truth concept, so it does not challenge a deflationist's commitment to Conceptual Deflationism.

In the case of the cognitive/non-cognitive distinction, Jackson et al. (1994, pp. 290–91) argue that deflationism itself does not rule out non-cognitivism, unless it is coupled with an independent minimal theory of truth-aptness (which, as mentioned above, they claim it need not be). They go on to argue (contra Horwich (1982, p. 84) and (2006, p. 189)) that the latter is actually best understood as a substantive notion, analytically tied to belief and assertion (Jackson et al. (1994, p. 294)). On this view, the difference between a cognitivist and a non-cognitivist amounts to the former holding and the latter denying that certain sentences can "be used to give the content of a belief, specifically, the belief of someone who asserts the truth-apt sentence" (Jackson et al. (1994, p. 294)). It is certainly open to a deflationist to understand the distinction in these "truth-free" terms, although it does have as a consequence that truth-talk does not apply to any sentences one is a non-cognitivist about. In a less restrictive deflationist response to the challenge from distinguishing cognitivism from non-cognitivism (or factualism from nonfactualism), Hartry Field (1994b, p. 433) claims that "a nonfactualist needn't say that such utterances can't legitimately be called true or false: a nonfactualist could just as well say that it is perfectly legitimate to call the claims true—it's just that the attributions of truth have the same not-fully-factual status as do the claims themselves". The trick for the deflationist, then, is how to convey the not-fully-factual status of the claim. To accomplish this, Field applies the method of relativizing the truth predicate to a parameter, with the idea that when the parameter is not a factual one (e.g., as an ethical expressivist claims about norms one applies when using evaluative terms), the relevant claim is not "fully factual" and thereby not "straightforwardly true (or false)", but only true or false relative to the non-factual parameter (e.g., complete or incomplete norms) (1994b, p. 436). A factualist position on the relevant claims is one that either rejects the relativization to the parameter in question or claims that the parameter is actually a factual matter (1994b, p. 441). In any case, Field claims that a deflationist can draw the distinction, since it gets explained in terms of the relevant parameter that gets added to the deflationary truth predicate, not in terms of the applicability of truth-talk.

Contra Price (2003), deflationists can also explain fictionalism about some fragment of discourse, since this "ism", and the distinction with its dual, can also be explained in "truth-free" terms. The "error-theoretic" view of fictionalism claims that, without some "story-prefix", the sentences of the target fragment of discourse are (mostly) false. (Cf. Sainsbury (2010, p. 173).) A different what-explanation can be formulated in terms of what we (Armour-Garb and Woodbridge (2015)) have called "semantic redirection". On this view, a fictionalist account of some fragment of discourse can be understood as one according to which what the relevant sentences actually say is not what they appear to say on a face-value reading; instead what they say is redirected, via some mechanism involving an appeal to some kind of fiction, to something else ((Armour-Garb and Woodbridge (2015, pp. 18–19)). This is accomplished either by means of a prefix that cites something as a fiction, such as "in the fiction of standard mathematics" (Field (1989)) or "in the fiction of modal realism" (Rosen (1990)), or via the claim's invocation of certain pretenses about locutions employed in the sentences and certain rules about when the pretenses put on display in the sentences' uses of those locutions are appropriate (Armour-Garb and Woodbridge (2015, pp. 40–42); cf. Walton (1990, Ch. 10)). The question of whether this account of fictionalism is "truth-free" then amounts to the question of (i) whether the fiction/non-fiction distinction can be explained in "truth-free" terms (for prefix-fictionalist views), or (ii) whether pretense can be explained in "truth-free" terms (for pretense-fictionalist views). The most prominent accounts of fiction (Searle (1975), Currie (1990), and Walton (1990)) explain it in terms of pretense, so (i) plausibly reduces to (ii). In Armour-Garb and Woodbridge (2015, pp. 249–51), we provide a "truth-free" what-explanation of pretense; if that account is correct, then deflationists can make sense of fictionalism without violating Conceptual Deflationism.

6.3 Deflationism and Theories of Meaning/Content

The most significant challenge to Conceptual Deflationism is based on considerations regarding the role that the truth concept plays in the orthodox approach to explaining linguistic meaning (and the contents of certain mental states) in terms of truth conditions. This approach to meaning traces back at least to Frege's (1892/1997) thesis that the meaning (sense) of a sentence amounts to a specification of the conditions under which it is true ("refers to the True"). Field (1994a, p. 249) attributes the view that "a theory of meaning or content is at least in large part a theory of truth conditions" to Bertrand Russell, (early) Ludwig Wittgenstein, and Frank Ramsey, along with Frege. The truth-conditional approach to explaining meaning has been most strongly associated with Donald Davidson's (1967/1984) thesis that the (T)-sentences generated by a (properly constructed) Tarski-truth-definition for a language give the meanings of the sentences mentioned (by specifying their truth conditions). In contemporary linguistics, a prominent account of sentence meaning explains it in terms of propositions, understood (following Lewis (1970) and Stalnaker (1970)) as sets of possible worlds, which are considered encapsulations of truth conditions (Elbourne (2011, pp. 50–51)).

The dominant view on the challenge that stems from the prominence of truth-conditional accounts of meaning comes from Dummett's (1959/1978, p. 7) claim that a deflationary view is incompatible with the thesis that one gives a sentence's meaning by specifying its truth conditions: The instances of (TS) cannot both tell us what the sentences they mention mean and give us an account of 'true' at the same time. As Horwich (1982, p. 68) puts it, "we would be faced with something like a single equation and two unknowns". If the only adequate what-explanation of meaning is in terms of truth conditions, then Conceptual Deflationism fails and, with it, deflationism does, too, as explained in Chapter 1. As a result, most theorists maintain that endorsing deflationism requires rejecting truth-conditional semantics in favor of a "truth-free" alternative.

The main alternatives available include Brandom's (1994) inferentialism, developed following Wilfrid Sellars (1974, 1979), Horwich's (1998) Wittgenstein (1953)-inspired use-based theory of meaning, and the computational-role + indication-relations account that Field (1994a, 2001e) adopts. However, given the orthodoxy of truth-conditional semantics, the mere availability of these alternatives is not enough to defang the challenge it poses for deflationism. Devitt (2001, p. 604) claims that truth-conditional semantics is the only adequate approach to meaning, since most of the afore-noted non-truth-conditional accounts are more "hand-waving" than theories, and the main one that is not (that developed by Brandom (1994)) is explicitly non-naturalistic. But this is criticism enough, Devitt (2001, p. 605) maintains, since naturalism is "worth dying for". On his (2001, p. 603) view, since meanings play a causal role (e.g., in behavior), and meaning is truth-conditional, truth conditions play a causal-explanatory role. Hence, according to Devitt, there is a causal-explanatory role being filled by a (compositional correspondence) property of truth, showing deflationism's understanding of truth-talk to be inadequate. While the prominence of truth-conditional approaches to meaning adds weight to this challenge to deflationism, it is still, contra Devitt, an open question whether any non-truth-conditional account of meaning will turn out to be adequate. Moreover, even if there is no viable "truth-free" account of meaning, Alexis Burgess (2011, pp. 407–10) argues that mainstream model-theoretic semantics in linguistics, understood as providing explanations of truth conditions, and the recognition of "the manifest power and progress of truth-conditional semantics are completely compatible with deflationary theories of the nature and notion of truth".

This last claim is an example of a more recent kind of response to the putative challenge to Conceptual Deflationism posed by the prominence of truth-conditional accounts of meaning. Theorists have begun to question Dummett's thesis about the incompatibility of deflationism and truth-conditional semantics. Claire Horisk (2008) argues that the kind of "circularity" arguments for "immiscibility" following Dummett actually fail, since the only circularity involved is a harmless kind so long as one is (like Davidson) offering a reciprocal rather than a reductive analysis of meaning (2008, pp. 293–94). Mark Lance (1997, pp. 186–87) claims that deflationism (specifically the anaphoric Linguistic Deflationism of prosententialism) is independent of, and thus compatible with, any underlying account of meaning, including a truth-conditional one. However, Douglas Patterson (2005, pp. 279–84) points out that it is crucial to distinguish between (i) giving a deflationary account in a metalanguage of truth-ascriptions within an object-language and (ii) giving a deflationary account of metalanguage truth-ascriptions to object-language sentences, using the truth predicate that applies to the latter but belongs to the former. When we keep this distinction clear, Patterson claims, we see that Lance's view holds only for the first sort of account, but these are trivially correct and uninteresting. Only in the latter case is the account of truth-talk nontrivial, but here Dummett's immiscibility thesis still holds.

Michael Williams (1999) rejects the immiscibility thesis and promotes combining deflationism with Davidson-style truth-conditional semantics, which Horisk (2007, p. 535) dubs "skim semantics". Williams (1999, p. 547) emphasizes the deflationary thesis that "the function of truth talk is *wholly* expressive, thus *never* explanatory". He (1999, p. 554) claims that the role of truth-talk in Davidsonian meaning theories for particular languages is just the expressive role that deflationists claim exhausts the truth predicate's function. Thus, virtually *any* version of deflationism is compatible with truth-conditional semantics, so long as it gives truth-talk the right expressive functions (1999, p. 564). Davidson (1990, pp. 271, 295–96) himself, however, argues that deflationism (exemplified by taking Tarskian truth-definitions as complete accounts of truth) is explanatorily inadequate for the purposes of giving a theory of meaning. At the same time, he (1996, p. 274) claims that we cannot understand what meaning is without the concept of truth. Deflationism fails, on his view, because what it takes to explain this, providing meaning theories for particular languages and extracting an understanding of what meaning is from these, requires more of the concept of truth than what deflationists provide—it takes a substantive and explanatory, albeit indefinable and primitive, concept (and property) (Davidson (1990, pp. 309–14; 1996, p. 278). Against Williams, Horisk (2007, p. 536) argues that a skim semantics employing any of the specific versions of deflationism that he has considered (viz., those of Quine, Horwich, and Brandom) will fail on the grounds that none of these versions of deflationism satisfy two criteria a view must meet if it is to play the sort of expressive role it would need to play in a meaning-theory for a language. The Quinean view, she (2007, p. 542) claims, does not satisfy the criterion of the metalanguage truth-ascriptions actually referring to the sentences of the object-language; the Horwichian and Brandomian views, she (2007, pp. 544, 547) argues, do not satisfy the criterion of picking out the object-language sentences in entirely non-semantic terms. Horisk (2007, p. 556) acknowledges, however, that it "remains to be seen" whether there could be versions of deflationism that do meet the criteria she identifies and any others required to permit a successful skim semantics.

These two different types of response to the putative challenge to Conceptual Deflationism that emerges from the apparent role played by the truth concept in providing an orthodox truth-conditional account of meaning shows that this specific challenge crosses the two categories initially laid out in this chapter. Some theorists see it as belonging to the first category of challenges, where the account in terms of truth-talk is acceptable because the talk plays a merely expressive role, but most theorists see it as belonging to the second category, where the use of the concept of truth must be replaced with a "truth-free" alternative. One of the biggest outstanding questions regarding the viability of any deflationary view is whether that view can be squared with an adequate account of linguistic meaning (and mental content).

7
Formal Challenges and Paradox Treatment Deflationism

One of the most significant challenges for any truth theorist, and thus for any would-be deflationist about truth, is how to deal with the semantic paradoxes, in particular, the Liar Paradox, which, as explained in Chapter 1, takes off from a self-referential sentence like

(L) Sentence (L) is not true.

Given the equivalence schema and classical logic, together with the resources for a language that has the ability to talk about itself, a contradiction seems imminent. After all, from (L) and a sentential version of the truth schema, (TS), we get

(TS_L) 'Sentence (L) is not true' is true iff sentence (L) is not true.

But sentence (L) = 'Sentence (L) is not true'. Hence, by substitution, given Leibniz's Law, we get

(TS_L*) Sentence (L) is true iff sentence (L) is not true,

which, given classical logic, yields the result that sentence (L) is true and is not true. Contradiction.

In this chapter, after identifying certain conditions or constraints on adequate resolutions of the semantic paradoxes, both generally and from the perspective of deflationary theories in particular, we turn to a number of different approaches to the paradoxes to determine how they fare with respect to these constraints. As will become apparent, it is harder to satisfy these conditions than one might originally have thought. To show this, we start by examining two of the most influential approaches to the Liar Paradox, those offered by Alfred Tarski and Saul Kripke, and assessing both how they fare with respect to the conditions of adequacy and how they fit with deflationism. We then consider other approaches to the semantic paradoxes that have been developed and defended by a number of theorists who explicitly identify as deflationists with an eye toward determining how well they succeed relative to the constraints that we have identified for an adequate deflationary solution.[1]

7.1 Constraints on an Adequate Resolution of the Liar Paradox

Within Charles Chihara's (1979) distinction regarding the Liar Paradox, introduced in Chapter 1, between the diagnostic problem of the paradox, the preventative problem of the paradox, and the treatment problem of the paradox, his description of the treatment problem as involving altering natural language "in order to remove the causes of the paradox" seems reminiscent of the "revolutionary" side of the revolutionary/hermeneutic distinction for approaches to philosophical theorizing.[2] In a *revolutionary* approach, a theorist

---

[1] In the appendix, after presenting our favored species of deflationism, we return to the semantic paradoxes and offer a consistent solution to the Liar Paradox and all of its putatively semantically pathological kin, showing how our approach satisfies the constraints that we have identified in this chapter.

[2] The distinction between revolutionary and hermeneutic approaches is introduced by Burgess and Rosen (1997) in their discussion of nominalistic positions in metaphysics, and the distinction has been applied to various fictionalist approaches. For discussion, see Stanley (2001) and Armour-Garb and Woodbridge (2015).

offers a replacement account of some fragment of discourse so that it no longer commits users of that fragment to anything they would not have antecedently accepted. This is in contrast with *hermeneutic* approaches, according to which no replacement theory is necessary, since the relevant fragment of discourse is already unproblematic when it is properly understood. While we appreciate Chihara's investigation into the nature of responses to the Liar Paradoxes, it is important to note that many attempted resolutions of this and the other semantic paradoxes are hermeneutic, rather than revolutionary. As mentioned in Chapter 1, all truth theorists must offer some form of "treatment" if they are going to resolve the semantic paradoxes in an adequate fashion. This is normally done by proposing moves in the service of solving the preventative problem. It is only a subset of truth theorists (e.g., Jody Azzouni (2006), as briefly discussed in Chapter 1, and Tarski on the paradoxes, as we explain below) who propose altering natural language in the way that Chihara describes as part of treatment programs as he describes them.

Having introduced the Liar Paradox and explained it in a bit more detail, we now consider two types of constraints—conditions that must be satisfied—that proposed resolutions of the paradox must meet to count as adequate. The first type includes constraints that apply in general, and the second type includes constraints that must be met for the response to fit specifically with deflationary accounts of truth-talk.

7.1.1 General Constraints on Adequate Paradox Treatment

NT (nontrivialism): The approach must explain how a language, despite having a truth predicate, which seems to engender the possibility of formulating liar sentences and thereby to manifest inconsistency in the language, still manages to avoid trivialism, the view that every sentence is true.

Gloss: Classical logic has an *explosive* consequence relation, given *ex falso quodlibet*, "from falsehood, anything follows". Since classically contradictions are logically false, if a contradiction is "correct" or is accepted as true, then so is every sentence, which gives rise to a form of *trivialism*. Dialetheists, who accept some contradictions, employ a paraconsistent logic that denies the validity of *ex falso quodlibet*. Since no truth theorist of any stripe endorses trivialism, all truth theorists subscribe to NT as a constraint on an adequate solution to the Liar Paradox. For a discussion of trivialism, see Priest (1987/2006).

ESC (exhaustive semantic characterization): The approach must provide resources for exhaustively characterizing the "semantic status" of the sentences of a language so that every sentence of L gets ascribed some sort of semantic characterization.

Gloss: ESC requires a response to the Liar Paradox to provide a semantic characterization of every sentence of L. But note that this might be different from providing a logical value for every sentence of the language. For example, one might require a semantic characterization of Noam Chomsky's sentence 'Curious green ideas sleep furiously', or P. F. Strawson's empty-demonstrative sentence, 'This is a fine red one', without requiring that either is assigned a logical value. Like NT, this is a constraint that any truth theorists should accept. In short, if truth theorists cannot state or convey the attitudes they take toward putatively paradoxical sentences, then they lack an adequate response to the Liar Paradox.

ELV (exhaustive logical valuation): Every meaningful sentence of the language must receive a logical value, for example, 1, 0, ½ or i, etc.

Gloss: ESC and ELV are separate constraints, since a semantic status is not necessarily to be equated with a logical value (cf. Field (2008, pp. 68–70)) and since, as we have seen above, one might have to provide a semantic status for a sentence that itself lacks any logical value. ELV highlights the importance of assigning a logical evaluation to sentences that are deemed meaningful as a means for determining their *inferential status,* viz., as designated (and thus acceptable or to be accepted) or undesignated (and thus unacceptable or to be rejected).[3]

RI (revenge immunity): Any solution offered must extend to all variants of the Liar Paradox; specifically, it must be immune to the generation of any *revenge problems.*

Gloss: A *revenge problem* undermines a proposed solution to the semantic paradoxes by making use of certain concepts that are identified by a theorist as important aspects of their response to a given paradox. An objector to the theorist's proposed treatment or prevention will include these very concepts in a recipe for committing the theorist to a new contradiction thereby demonstrating the inadequacy of the theorist's original solution to the paradox that they purported to solve.

To see this clearly, consider a naive response to the "simple" liar sentence introduced in Chapter 1,

(SL) Sentence (SL) is false.

The response maintains that (SL) falls into a "gap" between the standard truth-values, so that (SL) is deemed neither true nor false. This maneuver denies Bivalence but upholds the Law of Excluded Middle ("LEM"), thereby appearing to avoid generating a contradiction from (SL).

Having proposed this treatment of (SL), one is then confronted with a revenge case for proponents of this naive solution in the form of a "strengthened" liar sentence, such as

(L) Sentence (L) is not true,

---

[3] Even a condition of meaningfulness for sentences that admit of logical evaluations can be questioned, since Kripke (1975) insists on an assignment of a logical value to ungrounded sentences, which he takes not to express propositions as we discuss below in 7.3.

which incorporates the materials deployed in the proposed treatment of (SL). Applying the solution proposed for (SL) to (L) yields contradiction, since if (L), like (SL), is evaluated as neither true nor false, then it follows that it is not true, from which, given what (L) says, it follows that (L) is true after all—so paradox returns.[4] Most of the familiar proposed resolutions of the Liar Paradox face prima facie revenge problems, and it is generally accepted that unless these revenge problems can be deflected or resolved, they render the proposed resolutions inadequate.[5]

Graham Priest (2007, pp. 226) highlights the seeming inevitability of revenge for proposed resolutions of the semantic paradoxes. He also claims that theorists must show that their proposal does not lead to the reemergence of contradiction (or, in the case of dialetheism, trivialism, the view that every sentence is true). Priest further requires that none of the semantic notions that the theorist employs in a proposed solution leads to contradiction. Given these constraints on resolutions of the semantic paradoxes, theorists are then confronted with the question as to whether the semantic notions that they employ are expressible in the language they use in their proposed solution to the paradox. Priest (2007, pp. 226–27) considers three types of responses to this question, viz., (1) *Incompleteness*, (2) *Inconsistency,* and (3) *Inexistence.*

Response (1) answers the question negatively and maintains that not all of the notions are expressible in the theorist's language.

---

[4] In response to this concern, many advocates reject the LEM and advocate a *paracomplete* solution to the Liar Paradox. The term 'paracomplete' was introduced in Loparić and da Costa (1984), but it is now most applicable to Field (2008) and his followers, who argue against the LEM in the incorporation of their proposed resolutions of the semantic paradoxes and to the problem of vagueness.

[5] An exception to this condition of adequacy is Kripke's (1975) approach to the Liar Paradox, discussed below. Kripke is well aware of the revenge problem that his "outline" faces, but his approach has still been lauded in virtue of his introduction of a number of logical tools that have been instrumental in the development of many more recent proposed resolutions of the Liar Paradox. For discussion, see Field (2008).

The question then arises as to whether the relevant notions are expressible in some other language. If they are, then the theorist's language is *expressively incomplete,* since, on this view, there are some expressible notions that cannot be expressed in the theorist's language. Response (2) answers the question affirmatively and maintains that the relevant notions are expressible in the theorist's language. In that case, it always seems possible to construct a new revenge problem that makes use of these very notions. This response seems effectively to cede that the paradox is genuine. We discuss a response like this in Section 7.2 when considering Tarski's proposed solution to the Liar Paradox. Response (3) answers the question negatively and maintains that certain semantic notions are not expressible in any language. Unless the theorist gives up on *ineffability,* the thesis that certain meaningful notions cannot be expressed in a language, then they will maintain that, appearances to the contrary notwithstanding, the relevant notions are meaningless and, so, do not exist. This option may be traced back to work by Ludwig Wittgenstein (1921/1961). If Priest is right, anyone attempting to resolve the semantic paradoxes will fall into one of these three camps.

7.1.2 Constraints for Paradox Treatment Deflationism

The following constraints must be satisfied by a proposed resolution to the semantic paradoxes that a theorist offers if that theorist's overall approach to the topic of truth is to be deflationary in nature. Paradox Treatment Deflationism is important because a failure to satisfy this fourth dimension of deflationism would lead to a violation of Linguistic Deflationism.

Intersub (intersubstitutability): All non-opaque contexts sanction a substitution of a sentence, S, for 'S is true', and vice versa.

Gloss: Intersub requires the *intersubstitutability* of a sentence and an ascription of truth to that sentence and vice versa, in all non-opaque (or purely extensional) contexts. Intersub licenses a theorist to make this substitution even in embedded positions within complex sentences (e.g., in the antecedent or consequent of a conditional, or in a conjunction or disjunction). This makes it different from the application of the inference rules True-In and True-Out, explained above,[6] since these rules apply only to freestanding sentences and truth-ascriptions to them, but not to embedded cases. These two inference rules might be thought to underwrite a weaker form of Intersub, one that we might call "derived Intersub". A weaker rule of this sort might also be based on the procedure of explicitly bringing specific instances of some version of (TS) into derivations to enable a theorist to infer S from 'S is true' and vice versa. Many deflationary accounts sanction the stronger, "direct" version of Intersub as a consequence of their take on the status of the kind of equivalence that holds between a sentence, S, and a truth-ascription to that sentence, 'S is true'. For example, Intersub seems to follow from something that W. V. O. Quine (1970/1986, p. 12) emphasizes in explaining his version of deflationism, viz., that "by calling the sentence ['Snow is white'] true, we call snow white." On his view, asserting a sentence and ascribing truth to it amount to the same thing. Similar backing for Intersub appears to follow from prosententialism's thesis that 'S is true' is a prosentence that inherits its content from S. This result is an even more explicit consequence of Hartry Field's (1994a) contention that S and 'S is true' are *cognitively equivalent*, an equivalence that he explains in terms of precisely what Intersub aims to capture.

The sort of strong equivalence embraced by the foregoing theorists is denied by all inflationists and has even been

---

[6] A number of deflationists have insisted upon endorsement of True-In and True-Out. But see Maudlin (2004) for certain limitations on these inference rules, given his proposed treatment of the Liar Paradox.

questioned by some deflationists. Paul Horwich (1990/1998), as an outlier to deflationists generally, rejects a strong equivalence of this sort in virtue of maintaining that the truth predicate still functions to express an attributive truth concept, though he still accepts a stronger than material equivalence relation in every instance of (ES) (his propositional version of (TS)), *pace* his response to the Liar Paradox, which we discuss below in Section 7.6. The equivalence that Horwich endorses does not support direct Intersub, but he does embrace the weaker derived Intersub elsewhere in his minimalist account (cf. his (1990/1998, pp. 22–23) explanation of the contribution of true beliefs to successful behavior).[7]

Deflationists must endorse some version of Intersub because of the role that it plays in providing an explanation of the special generalizing function of truth-talk deflationists emphasize that comports with Linguistic Deflationism. As discussed in Section 1.2, according to deflationists, the role of the truth predicate is to enable us to express what one might indicate quasi-formally via appeal to sentential variables bound by sentential quantifiers. Thus, a claim like 'Everything the Oracle says is true' or, in its logically more perspicuous form,

(5) Everything is such that, if the Oracle says it, then it is true,

is said just to function to express in a natural language what we can indicate with the quasi-formal string

(3) For all p, if the Oracle says that p, then p.

But now consider what is involved in taking (5) to express what (3) indicates. Allowing that the "sayables" are indicated by sentence

---

[7] As we discuss below, Solomon Feferman also does not satisfy direct Intersub with his approach to the Liar Paradox, and we think that this makes his view non-deflationary.

nominalizations that we symbolize in general with '[p]', we can understand (5) as expressing

(5') For all [p], if the Oracle says [p], then [p] is true.

Since '[p]' is a nominal expression, (5') can still be understood to involve nominal, and even objectual, quantification, as in first-order logic. Understanding (5') as expressing what (3) indicates will involve reconceiving the quantification as a kind of "higher-order" quantification into sentence-in-use position, but for present purposes the transition that matters is between the embedded sentential string '[p] is true' in (5') and the embedded sentential string 'p' in (3). This requires that one substitute the latter for the former when they are embedded in more complex quantificational conditional sentences. A license for that substitution in that extensional context is thus required to understand (5) as functioning to express what is indicated by (3).

Similarly, going in the other direction, if one wants to understand (5) as a generalization on the embedded sentence-positions in a claim like

(1) If the Oracle says that birds are dinosaurs, then birds are dinosaurs,

then one will want to replace those positions with variables, as in

(2) If the Oracle says [p], then p,

and then bind that variable with a quantifier, as in (3). But to express this in a natural language like English, it seems that one must employ an ordinary nominal, objectual quantifier, so all of the variables must be nominal/objectual. To achieve this one needs a license to substitute '[p] is true' for the 'p' in the extensional context of the consequent position of the quantificational conditional.

That allows one to formulate (5) as a generalization on (1).[8] But the combination of the two licenses just described constitutes Intersub. Thus, without Intersub, it would seem that an advocate of deflationism cannot provide an account of how truth-talk can serve as a means for expressing something equivalent to what would otherwise take sentential variables and quantifiers to express.[9] This would violate Linguistic Deflationism, since the thesis of that dimension of deflationism relies on the idea that this generalizing role is the central, direct function of truth-talk, meaning that it must be explained directly. Note that an inflationist about truth-talk could capture this function of the discourse via an indirect explanation based on an account of the nature of the truth property underwriting all the instances of (TS). Since the alethic locutions are taken to be descriptive predicates that attribute properties to truth-bearers, inflationists can take the generalization (5) to quantify over those bearers and predicate truth of them in the conditional manner indicated. Anytime this allows one to infer an instance of '[p] is true', the relevant instance of (TS) allows an inference to the relevant instance of 'p', and this is what makes (5) cover what (3) would cover if our language had the resources to express directly what that string indicates. So, there is no need for an inflationary account to satisfy direct Intersub, since providing for a kind of derived Intersub is sufficient to explain what inflationists take to be truth-talk's *derivative* expressive role.

---

[8] Similarly, one could make a particular (or "existential") generalization on the embedded sentence-positions in 'The Oracle says that birds are dinosaurs, and birds are dinosaurs' to 'For some p, the Oracle says that p, and p'. Allowing for the substitution just described into a quantificational conjunction would allow one to take this to be expressed in ordinary language via 'Something is such that the Oracle says it, and it is true' or 'The Oracle says something true'. A license for substitution in the other direction would allow one to explain how the latter expresses what is indicated by the former quasi-formal string employing particular quantification into sentence-position.

[9] Field (2008, p. 210) argues for something similar. He argues that Intersub is needed for the truth predicate to serve its expressive function of enabling a thinker to affirm a string of conjunctions from an affirmation of 'Everything Field said is true'.

Notice that Horwich attempts to underwrite his claim to satisfy Linguistic Deflationism by explaining the generalizing role of truth-talk in a similar (i.e., indirect) way, viz., via the instances of his version of (TS) and their connection to the truth property. It is just that the way his minimalism satisfies Metaphysical Deflationism is by understanding the truth property directly in terms of the instances of (E*) (the propositional function from each proposition to the proposition expressed by the instance of (ES) for that proposition). This is supposed to provide his account with the version of derived Intersub that he relies on. The problem for Horwich, however, is that, unlike an inflationist, who has a unified understanding of the truth property which would underwrite all of the instances of (E*) and allow for a unified understanding of (5) as a real generalization, his specific understanding of the truth property cannot do this work. He is left with the kind of "fragmented" understanding of claims like (5) discussed with respect to the Formulation Problem in Section 4.2.1. Thus, Horwich's attempt to satisfy Linguistic Deflationism is thwarted by this problem (and the related Generalization Problem), in part because his view does not have direct Intersub and tries to make do just with derived Intersub.

SCT (Strong Convention T): Following Tarski's "condition of material adequacy" (see Section 2.6, above), which is colloquially known as "Convention T" (henceforth, *CT*), an adequate resolution of the Liar Paradox must yield that all *legitimate* instances of the relevant version of the truth schema, (TS), are correct. The deflationist's SCT constraint adds that the equivalence in the instances of the schema must be stronger than mere material equivalence. This is in virtue of the fundamental or immediate status that any deflationary view gives to the instances of some version of (TS).

Gloss: As noted above, given Intersub and the validity of the law of identity, viz., 'p → p' as a logical truth, SCT follows directly, for it licenses treating the equivalence in the instances of (TS) as having the same status that 'p → p' possesses. Hence, as we will see, there are responses to the semantic paradoxes that validate Intersub but do not satisfy the law of identity and thereby fail to satisfy SCT.

There is a strong connection between Intersub and the equivalence between the assertoric use of a sentence and a truth-ascription to that sentence, viz., between S and 'S is true', being a strong equivalence. After all, one cannot deny Intersub in extensional contexts while maintaining that there is a strong equivalence between a truth-apt sentence and an ascription of truth to it. For, *by definition*, if two sentences are extensionally equivalent, then they should support Intersub in all extensional contexts, and if they have a stronger equivalence, then they at least are extensionally equivalent. So, possessing a strong equivalence between S and 'S is true' appears to yield Intersub. From the other direction, Intersub appears to spell out what the strength of at least some notion of strong equivalence amounts to, in a clearer way than appeals to necessity or synonymy do. Despite the strong connection between Intersub and SCT, we still need the latter in addition to the former because while Intersub underwrites the "strength part" of SCT, it does not automatically yield the "CT part". But this too is required in order for truth-talk to play the special generalizing role that Linguistic Deflationism claims is its exhaustive (or at least central) function.[10] This is because if one does not always have an equivalence between a sentence, S, and an ascription of the truth predicate to it, then one will not be able to reason from an alethic generalization like 'Everything the Oracle says is true' to the relevant instance 'If the Oracle says that S, then S is true' and then disquote to 'If the Oracle says that S, then S'.

Intersub, in conjunction with SCT, can lead to inconsistency, given a liar sentence. This is especially so if a theorist relies on an unrestricted, or "naive", version of SCT that includes

---

[10] Fujimoto (2022, p. 859) also notes that a number of theorists maintain that a necessary condition for a truth theory to be deflationary is that it satisfies at least a version of CT.

liar-sentence instances of (TS). For example, if the biconditional in (TS) is material, and we have an instance of (TS) for the simple liar sentence, (SL), then we can deduce that (SL) is both true and false. As a result, one possible response is to weaken Intersub (cf. Feferman (1984)—see n. 20 below), and another is to alter the status of the instances of (TS) in some way. One way of doing the latter is to declare some instances false (cf. Horwich (1990/1998)), while another is to alter the biconditional by employing a nonclassical operator (cf. Field (2008)). We discuss Field's proposal in Section 7.4, and we examine Horwich's proposal in Section 7.6.

Before considering the various approaches that have been put forward in response to the semantic paradoxes, it is important to be clear on the two different types of constraints that we have imposed for adequate solutions. For deflationists to offer an adequate solution to the paradoxes in such a way that their overall approach to the topic of truth remains acceptable from a deflationary perspective, they must satisfy both the general constraints and those required for the satisfaction of Paradox Treatment Deflationism. It might be possible for a theorist to offer an acceptable solution to the paradoxes by satisfying the general constraints without satisfying the constraints for satisfying Paradox Treatment Deflationism. Such a theorist would not be a deflationist (whatever their aspirations), but they would offer an adequate solution to the paradoxes. Similarly, one can satisfy Paradox Treatment Deflationism without offering an adequate solution to the paradoxes, for example, by failing to satisfy some of the general constraints on an adequate solution. Such a theorist would be a deflationist who lacks an adequate solution to the paradoxes. As we go through the approaches considered here, it is important to keep in mind which of the two sets of criteria a given proposal satisfies or fails to satisfy.

7.2 Tarski's Replacement Theory and the Liar Paradox

Quine (1966/1976, pp. 7–8) attempts to resolve the Liar Paradox and its kin within his deflationary account of truth-talk by simply adopting Tarski's proposed solution, but it is not clear that this combination is as felicitous as Quine assumes. Tarski (1935b/1983) proves what is known as *Tarski's Undefinability Theorem* according to which no language of sufficient complexity can consistently contain its own truth predicate, i.e., a truth predicate that applies to all of the true sentences of that language.[11] Tarski remarks that English and indeed many natural languages seem to contain their own truth predicate. Hence, he concludes that such natural languages result in a form of inconsistency. As a result, Tarski offers a *replacement theory* of truth for use in the context of formal theorizing. We might extend this to a *revolutionary* account for natural language based on the thought that, come the revolution, when people recognize the problems with their own natural languages, they will adopt Tarski's theory, which covers most of what a natural language truth predicate was meant to accomplish. Given Tarski's theorem, his replacement theory involves distinguishing an *object language*, which contains sentences that are in some sense "about" the world, from a *metalanguage,* which enables its expressions to talk "about" a lower-level language.

While there are many good accounts of Tarski's replacement theory (cf. Soames (1998) and Field (2008)), to get a sense for how

---

[11] More specifically, Tarski's Undefinability Theorem applies to any formal language, L, that contains a negation operator and a device (e.g., Quine's (1940/2003) corner quotes) which, when applied to well-formed expressions of L, yields a singular term that designates that expression. It is generally assumed that the syntax of L can prove the diagonal lemma, which establishes the existence of a self-referential sentence in L, viz., a sentence, S, that says of itself that it has some property P.
Where S is a liar sentence, contradiction results, which establishes his Undefinability Theorem, viz., that no truth predicate for a language L can be a predicate of L itself, so that no sufficiently rich language can represent its own semantics (Tarski (1935a/1983, pp. 249–51)).

his theory works, in very broad strokes, let the first level of the language, L_0, contain all of the sentences (focusing on just the declarative ones) of a language save for those sentences that include semantic predicates, for example, 'true', 'false', 'true of', etc. Hence, L_0 functions as an object language. At the "next" level, L_1, which is the metalanguage for L_0, we let that language contain all of the sentences of L_0 together with the truth and falsity predicates, which are applied to all and only the sentences of L_0. (Tarski abided by classical logic, which requires Bivalence, so *every sentence of L_0* is either true or false (e.g., true or with a true negation).) At the next level, L_2, we allow the truth and falsity predicates to apply to all of the sentences of L_1, etc. For each language, L_n, there will be a language L_{n+1} that has the capacity to characterize the sentences of L_n, ad infinitum.

As is clear, at no level can we formulate a liar sentence, viz., a sentence that ascribes untruth to itself, so that paradox appears to be avoided. Hence, *for purely syntactic reasons*, no such sentence can be formulated. As a result, the Liar Paradox is solved (or avoided), albeit by introducing a syntactically driven hierarchy of languages. This is so because Tarski proposed separating sentences into *levels*. At the first level, we have sentences that do not include the truth or falsity predicates; at the second level, we have sentences that ascribe truth but only to the sentences of the first level; at the third level, we have sentences that ascribe truth to any sentence of the first two levels; etc. He then proposed going through the levels and assigning truth-values first to those sentences on the first level and proceeding, in a sense, upward. In this way, it is impossible to construct or formulate any sentence within the hierarchy that self-ascribes a truth-value, nor any pair, triple, etc. of sentences that assess or ascribe the truth-value of the others at the same or a higher level, given the *syntactic* restrictions Tarski imposes on the formulation of sentences in the hierarchy. Since no such sentences can legitimately be formulated, Liar Paradoxes and other cases that appear to manifest semantic pathology are completely blocked.

It is essential to see that Tarski's hierarchy is syntactically driven, for Kripke distinguishes his own hierarchical approach from Tarski's at exactly that point. One problem with Tarski's approach, which Kripke (1975) notes, is that the use of a truth predicate often does not come with an antecedent level-assignment but instead must "find its own level". Tarski's replacement theory has some known deficits. Below we shall review one such deficit related to the point of Kripke's just noted. Prior to doing so, we first address a potential worry for Tarski's theory to show that it is not really a challenge for his view.

As we have seen, Tarski's solution to the Liar Paradox takes off from the construction of an infinite hierarchy of languages. Hence, one might think that a revenge problem for Tarski would arise from a sentence like

(H) Sentence (H) is not true at any level of the hierarchy.

It is easy to see that (H) cannot be true at any level of the hierarchy, which thereby suggests that sentence (H) should be true, from which a contradiction again appears imminent. Or so, anyway, it would seem. In fact, (H) poses no genuine revenge problem for Tarski. This is because of the point noted earlier, that his proposed solution to the Liar is syntactically driven. As a result, a sentence like (H) cannot even be legitimately formulated, and what is not a well-formed formula cannot and thus need not be semantically characterized. As we would describe it, Tarski would characterize (H) as a "garbage sentence". Hence, although (H) appears to defy a consistent characterization, it poses no problem for Tarski since the putatively problematic sentence is not syntactically kosher. As a result, it seems that Tarski's theory satisfies RI. For Tarski, no language can contain a liar sentence. But this is to regiment languages in a way that contrasts with a natural language like English, which contains devices for self-reference and contains the "universal" predicates 'is true' and 'is not true'. Hence, certain non-Tarskian

CHALLENGES TO PARADOX TREATMENT DEFLATIONISM 241

resolutions try to avoid inconsistency without employing the tactic of ruling out the existence of liar sentences on revisionary syntactic grounds.

Some philosophers (e.g., Priest (2007) and Scott Soames (1998)) do not recognize Tarski's solution to the Liar Paradox as a *replacement theory* and offer criticisms that seem misdirected if you keep in mind that Tarski is not attempting to "discover" a solution for the paradoxes from within natural language and logic. By all accounts, Tarski accepts that natural languages are inconsistent and proposes a regimented replacement theory that includes a "Tarskian" language, an artificial language whose features may be stipulated for purposes of resolving the paradoxes.

To see the upshot of this, return to Priest's discussion of the three responses to the apparent inevitability of revenge problems discussed in Section 7.1. As an illustration, Priest (2007, 228–29) discusses Tarski's response to the Liar Paradox, and he highlights a revenge problem along the lines of the one considered above involving (H). He examines how each of his three responses (inconsistency, incompleteness, and inexistence) to this putative case of revenge would look when applied from within Tarski's theory. With respect to the incompleteness option, which Priest describes as maintaining that the revenge-related notion (in the case of (H), 'not true at any level of the hierarchy') is meaningful but cannot be expressed in the hierarchy of languages that Tarski describes, he (2007) notes that "there are [thus] semantic concepts with the potential to generate contradiction, and which are not dealt with in the theory. This is the incompleteness case." But what Priest misses is that Tarski offers a *revolutionary* approach, and so does not have to accommodate (H) from within the hierarchical structure that his theory involves. The theory is designed specifically to block any contradiction that would emerge from any attempted evaluation of (H) by excluding (H) from consideration. Thus, Priest is asking the wrong question about how to treat (H), viz., which of his three options is *correct* for the revenge problem. All that Tarski needs to explain is why (H) does not generate a revenge problem that needs to be resolved as part of his proposed treatment of the Liar Paradox.

Soames (1998, p. 155) contends that Tarski's constraints on the hierarchy are overly restrictive and that they "are not an accurate account of English". We agree with Soames on these assessments of Tarski's hierarchy, but we take issue with Soames's use of them in a criticism of Tarski's proposed solution of the Liar Paradox. While Soames is right that Tarski's theory is not an accurate account of English, Tarski should reply that this is no criticism, since he is offering a *replacement* theory, rather than a *descriptive* account of the truth predicate as it functions in a natural language. Qua replacement theory, the question is whether Tarski's theory is adequate for capturing or modeling the operation of a truth predicate for a language (on a specific regimentation); whether it accurately captures the truth predicate in English is therefore irrelevant.[12]

It also bears noting that Soames (1998) maintains that Tarski takes satisfying Convention T ("CT") to be both necessary and sufficient for the adequacy of one's theory of truth. But it seems that Soames is wrong about this, since Tarski (1935b/1983) rejects certain axiomatic theories of truth that consist of all instances of the (T)-schema (his version of (TS)), which thus satisfy CT. Hence, for Tarski, satisfying CT is at most a *necessary* condition for an adequate theory of truth.[13] Moreover, if an adequate theory of truth must come equipped with a solution to the paradoxes, then no one would take

---

[12] It is worth noting that a "contextualist" solution to the Liar Paradox, which appeals to "contexts", where different stages of reasoning occur in different contexts as a means for dispelling any contradiction that follows from an evaluation of a liar sentence, seems to involve a descriptive, rather than a replacement, account of 'is true'. As a result, a proposed revenge problem similar to the one based on (H) but modified for contextualism, starting with a sentence putatively claiming of itself that it is not true in any context, might be problematic in a way that (H) is unproblematic for a Tarskian. For contextualist resolutions of the Liar Paradox, see Parsons (1974), Glanzberg (2001), and Simmons (2008). For concerns about contextualism, see Gauker (2006).

[13] It is interesting to note that Tarski (1935b/1983) rejects certain axiomatic theories of truth on grounds that they do not allow for the proof of certain truth-involving generalizations. We have discussed this issue above in Section 4.2.2.

the satisfaction of CT to be necessary *and sufficient* for an adequate truth theory. Be that as it may, for deflationists there is an assumption in favor of the view that an approach to the Liar must vindicate the instances of (TS). This is because, if any instances of the schema were false (or, more generally, *undesignated*),[14] then there would not be an equivalence between some sentences and ascriptions of truth to them, which would violate Paradox Treatment Deflationism, as this requires a strong equivalence for the instances of (TS).

Though Soames's criticisms and his characterization of Tarski's insistence on CT miss the mark, there are legitimate worries about the Tarskian theory, some of which were identified by Kripke (1975) as a motivation for moving to the position he develops. Kripke highlights the fact that it may be easier than we think to enter the fray of paradoxes without even knowing it, and he contends that, as a consequence, Tarski's replacement theory is inadequate to capture some of our needs. Perhaps more worrisome is the example Kripke puts forward in criticism of Tarski's theory.

As we have seen, on Tarski's replacement theory, each use of the truth predicate is subscripted to indicate the appropriate level of the hierarchy. What Kripke notices is that there are some 'true'-employing sentences for which no subscripts can consistently be assigned. Kripke imagines Richard Nixon and John Dean, respectively, assertorically uttering the following sentences around the time of the Watergate scandal:

(A) Most things said by Dean about Watergate are true.
(B) Most things said by Nixon about Watergate are not true.

There seems to be no way to assign subscripts to the truth predicates in (A) and (B) given Tarski's method, for the subscript

---

[14] Being designated means having a logical status that is to be preserved in inference and argument. In classical logic, 1 is the designated value as truth is to be preserved in all inferences and arguments. In the case of a paraconsistent logic like the dialetheist's "LP" (short for the *logic of paradox*), $\{1, \frac{1}{2}\}$ are designated values where 1 lines up with truth and, informally, $\frac{1}{2}$ applies to sentences that are deemed both true and false. For more on this, see Priest (1987/2006).

in (A) would have to be at a higher level than that in any of Dean's utterances about Watergate, which includes (B), and the subscript for (B) would have to be at a higher level than those in any of Nixon's statements about Watergate, which includes (A). But this is impossible. What is worse, it seems clear that both (A) and (B) could well be true. This would be so if 75% of what Dean said about Watergate was true and 75% of what Nixon said about Watergate was not true. In addition, as Kripke notes, there is a risk of paradox arising from sentence pairs like (A) and (B). Suppose, for example, that, in addition to asserting (A) and (B), each speaker said an even number of things about Watergate with half of them true and half of them false. In that case, paradox would seem to ensue. What all of this suggests to Kripke is that if one goes the Tarskian hierarchical route in order to block sentences of the sort that Tarski aims to exclude, then they will have to block other sentences for which there is a mere risk of paradox, in addition to ones for which absolutely no paradox actually arises. As a result, Tarski winds up classifying certain non-paradoxical sentences as "garbage sentences".

Taking stock of how Tarski's approach fits with the general and deflationary constraints that we have set out for resolutions of the Liar Paradox, it satisfies NT and, because it is specifically designed to satisfy "Convention T" (CT), a form of derived Intersub. It also seems to satisfy RI by being highly revisionary. However, since Tarski has only material equivalence for the instances of the version of (TS) that his account generates, his approach does not satisfy the stronger deflationary constraint, SCT. Moreover, the fact that Tarski classifies certain non-pathological sentences as "garbage sentences" seems somewhat antithetical to ESC and ELV. Overall, then, *pace* Quine, Tarski's approach to the semantic paradoxes seems not to be a good option for deflationists.[15]

---

[15] It bears noting again that this raises concerns for certain deflationary accounts in addition to Quine (1970/1986), e.g., Leeds (1978), which explicitly attempt to combine deflationism with a Tarskian approach.

7.3 Kripke and Ungroundedness

In response to certain problems with Tarski's replacement theory, Kripke (1975) contends that we should not start by adding subscripts based on syntactic grounds to sentences of the first level, L_0, which does not include the truth or falsity predicates. Instead, rather than only ascribing truth to sentences of level 0 (in level 1), we should ascribe truth to any sentence whose truth-value is determined once the truth-values of level zero sentences have already been provided. To clarify this, consider the situation where Dean utters

(C) Snow is white or most of what Nixon said about Watergate is not true.[16]

Since 'Snow is white' is true, (C) should be true, given the truth conditions for a disjunction. However, because this sentence cannot be assigned a level on the Tarskian approach, in light of (A) and (B), it follows that Tarski's approach cannot handle (C). By contrast, Kripke can handle this sentence straightforwardly. Since 'Snow is white' will have been evaluated as true at a level, (C) would be evaluated as true at the next level. To get a better understanding of this, we must delve further into Kripke's approach.

Like Tarski, Kripke adopts a hierarchical approach, but, unlike for Tarski, the levels of Kripke's hierarchy do not arise through syntactic criteria. Kripke's goal is to move to an internal hierarchy within a single language with each "level" or "stage" expanding on what is true at the previous level. Each stage provides a fuller account of what is true or false (at earlier levels) until we reach a level, called "a minimal fixed point", at which everything that is true in

---

[16] For discussion of this, see Burgess (2013).

the language is recorded as true at that level, so that the process need not go any further.

On Kripke's approach, we start with no sentence getting a truth-value, "true" or "false", and then, by employing certain rules, we declare certain sentences true, other sentences false (and no sentence both or neither). The process continues until, at the minimal fixed point, it stops, and any sentence that is true has been assigned truth (and any sentence that is false has been assigned falsity). This is what it is for a sentence to be *grounded*: The *ungrounded* sentences are those that do not receive a truth-value at the minimal fixed point. Other, non-minimal fixed points arise from placing certain sentences which do not get truth-values at the minimal fixed point into the extension or anti-extension of the truth predicate. For example, a truthteller sentence that predicates truth of itself, as in

(K) Sentence (K) is true,

can consistently be placed in the extension of the truth predicate or in its anti-extension, which would render it false. Following this procedure, we either get a non-minimal fixed point in which (K) is declared true, or one in which (K) is declared false. Similarly, the sentences that we call the "Open Pair",[17]

(OP1) Sentence (OP2) is not true
(OP2) Sentence (OP1) is not true,

can get assigned divergent truth-values in certain non-minimal fixed points (and different divergent assignments in different non-minimal fixed points), but they too are ungrounded and receive no truth-values at the minimal fixed point. Thus, some ungrounded

---

[17] For a discussion of the Open Pair, see Armour-Garb and Woodbridge (2006, 2010b, 2015). The original Open Pair includes two sentences each of which says of the other that it is false.

sentences could have truth-values and do have those truth-values in other fixed points. By contrast, liar sentences will not be assigned a truth-value in any of the fixed points.

As we have said, the minimal fixed point is the first level at which every sentence classified as true is already classified as true at some level of the hierarchy. So, there is no sentence that is classified as true for the first time at that level–every true sentence will already have been classified as true at a level below it. At the minimal fixed point, whenever a sentence, S, has been classified as true, so has 'S is true' (or, formally, 'T(S)') and vice versa.[18] Thus, at the minimal fixed point, there is closure under True-In and True-Out. In this way, Kripke's approach supports a form of Intersub: We can always substitute S for 'T(S)' and vice versa in all non-opaque contexts. Indeed, Field (2008, p. 69) notes that the raison d'être of fixed points is the equivalence between a sentence and an ascription of truth to it. So, 'T(S)' is in the fixed point whenever S is, and if Y results from X by substituting 'T(S)' for S or vice versa, then Y is in the fixed point iff X is. Thus, Kripke enjoys full Intersub—'T(S)' and S are completely intersubstitutable in all non-opaque contexts.

Kripke's construction provides a means for identifying ungrounded sentences and thus offers an account of what *ungroundedness* amounts to: The *ungrounded* sentences are those that never get a truth-value at the minimal fixed point.[19]

---

[18] To understand Kripke's "minimal fixed point", consider the set of sentences, X_α, for any ordinal number, α. Let $X_{\alpha+1}$ be the set of sentences that are determined true relative to X_α. Field (2008, p. 61) notes that, for any ordinal numbers such that $\beta > \alpha$, it is easy to show that if a sentence is in a set X_α, then it will also be in the set X_β. Given a limit ordinal number, λ, where $\beta < \lambda$, we let X_λ be the set of sentences determined true relative to some set X_β. Note that these sets cannot keep on growing forever. Kripke shows that there will be a fixed cardinality of sentences so that there must be an ordinal number β for which $X_{\beta+1} = X_\beta$. At this level, as John Burgess (2013, p. 168) notes, we cease getting anything that is new, and the set of sentences that are determined true at X_β constitute *the minimal fixed point*.

[19] This also provides us with an understanding of *groundedness*: The grounded sentences are those that get a truth-value at the minimal fixed point. From this understanding of "groundedness", we can establish from Kripke's construction that, for each grounded sentence, the instance of (TS) for it is true at the minimal fixed point. This can be established by noting that, since (i) grounded sentences have truth-values at the minimal fixed points and (ii) the sentences that result from ascribing truth to those

Importantly, while ungrounded sentences are neither true nor false, this claim cannot be made from within the language at the minimal fixed point. Rather, such ungrounded sentences simply do not appear in the minimal fixed point. So, the claim that ungrounded sentences such as a liar sentence are neither true nor false is not a claim that can be made from within Kripke's construction. For that matter, neither is the claim that such sentences are ungrounded. As we will see below, this leads to an expressive weakness for Kripke's construction, one of which he is fully aware.

It is also worth noting that Kripke takes a sentence like

(D) Either sentence (D) is true or sentence (D) is false

to be without a truth-value at the minimal fixed point. It can be made true at some non-minimal fixed point, but (D) cannot be false at any fixed point. Kripke calls examples like (D) "intrinsically true" and shows that there is a "maximum intrinsic fixed point" where all of the intrinsically true sentences are true.

In a fixed-point construction, the determinate extension and anti-extension of 'true' at the first level of the hierarchy is empty. But there are non-minimal fixed points in which the truthteller is arbitrarily placed in the extension or the anti-extension of 'true'. More generally, *intrinsic fixed points* are those that make arbitrary assignments of truth-values to certain ungrounded sentences. A fixed point is said to be *intrinsic* iff the relevant sentence never gets assigned a truth-value that conflicts with the truth-values assigned to that sentence at any other fixed point. A sentence has an intrinsic truth-value iff it has a truth-value at some intrinsic fixed point. The minimal fixed point captures the interpretation

---

sentences have whatever truth-value the grounded sentence possesses at the minimal fixed point, it follows that (iii) their biconditionals, which are instances of (TS), have the value 'true' at the minimal fixed point.

of 'true' arising from the instructions that govern the truth predicate. These instructions license the assertion of the claim that S is true (not true) whenever the assertion of S (neg-S, where 'neg-S' names the negation of the sentence named by 'S') is legitimate and vice versa.

One point that is sometimes discussed is whether Kripke's construction supports truth-value gaps. If we identify a "semantic-value gap" (the term comes from Field (2008, p. 71)) in the classical semantics for the theory with sentences that have neither logical value, 0 or 1, then, on Kripke's construction, there are semantic-value gaps. But there are reasons for thinking that there are no truth-value gaps, in the sense of sentences that can truly be said to be neither true nor false, given Kripke's construction, for neither 'T(S) ∨ T(neg-S)' nor '∼[T(S) ∨ T(neg-S)]' is in the minimal fixed point, for an ungrounded sentence, S, and, so, neither is part of Kripke's construction. Moreover, while liar sentences get assigned the logical value i, given Kripke's construction, he cannot assert that a liar sentence is untrue. This has an interesting consequence noticed by Field (2008): The logical value 1 (from the set of values {i,0,1}) does not correlate with truth. To see this, note that, on Kripke's construction, a liar sentence cannot have the logical values 0 or 1 and so must have the value i. But if 1 is taken to correlate with truth, then the liar sentence is not true, given Kripke's construction. But the claim, that the liar sentence is not true, does not appear in any of the fixed points that emerge from Kripke's construction. Hence, it is simply not true that a liar sentence is not true, from which it follows that 1 is not taken to correlate with truth.

For Kripke, a fixed-point language can evidently contain its own truth predicate, because the extension of the predicate constructed is correct, but it cannot contain its own *untruth* predicate because there is no formula of the language that is true of all sentences of L that are not true (i.e., that are untrue). There are thus no true sentences of L that say of themselves that they are not true. Indeed, sentences that possess the logical value i cannot be said to be not true or untrue. So, Kripke will not characterize sentences that are neither taken to be true nor taken to be false as neither true nor false, nor as not true, nor as untrue. For Kripke, Bivalence holds for all sentences that express propositions—they are either true or false. He (1975, p. 699) follows Strawson by contending that certain sentences fail to express propositions because certain conditions that are necessary for them to do so are not satisfied. For Kripke, ungrounded sentences are like sentences that Strawson would claim fail to express propositions because of failed presuppositions. (Cf. Kripke (1975).) So, for Kripke, the minimal fixed point contains what we might call a "truth predicate" that applies to those sentences that are or express truths and a formula '$\sim T(x)$' that is true of the sentences of the language that express propositions that are not true. Liar sentences and truthtellers fail to express propositions but cannot be characterized as untrue. Of course, Kripke is happy to say in a metalanguage that we can truly say that such ungrounded sentences do not express propositions in the minimal fixed point and, therefore, that they are not true in the object language, L. They are also not false in L. Thus, one can, in a metalanguage, characterize those sentences as neither true nor false, which seems to some (e.g., Soames (1998, p. 193)) to be little different from accepting the extra truth-value that Kripke (1975, p. 700, n. 18) rails against. More importantly, however, having characterized ungrounded sentences as not true in the object language, while refusing to accept that '$\sim T(x)$' is true of them in the object language, we get the unfortunate result that '$\sim T(x)$' of the object language does not express the same notion as the metalinguistic expression 'is not a true sentence of L.' So, L does not contain its own untruth predicate.

As a result, one question for Kripke pertains to what his approach is an account of. As we saw above, Tarski maintains that English and other natural languages are inconsistent because of the Liar Paradox; he therefore offers a replacement view. Kripke does not advocate for a replacement view, but neither does he take himself to be providing an account of how 'is true' functions in English. Rather, he offers an idealization of how to theorize about truth-talk, which is prior to a philosophical analysis of that fragment of discourse. As Kripke says (1975, p. 714),

> If we think of the minimal fixed point ... as giving a model of natural language, then the sense in which we can say, in natural language, that a Liar sentence is not true must be thought of as associated with some later stage in the development of natural language, one in which speakers reflect on the generation process leading to the minimal fixed point. It is not part of that process. ... The ghost of the Tarskian hierarchy is still with us.

Presumably, Kripke makes this last point because, while he maintains that no liar sentence is true, in the minimal fixed point, a liar sentence is neither in the extension nor in the anti-extension of the truth predicate, and, so, it does not get characterized as untrue by Kripke's construction.

As mentioned above, Kripke is aware of the fact that his fixed-point construction suffers from this *expressive incompleteness* (viz., that liar sentences come out as untrue on his approach but cannot be characterized as such within the fixed-point language) in violation of ESC, but, as is evidenced from the quotation above, he takes the fixed-point construction to be an early stage in the modeling of a natural language. In a more advanced stage of development, essentially in the metalanguage from which Kripke can make claims *about* the language of his fixed-point construction, one can truly express the status of a liar sentence. But this metalanguage is not the fixed-point language from whence we get his expressive incompleteness. It is also worth noting that, while the logic that is involved in Kripke's construction—what is sometimes called the "inner (or internal) logic"—is non-classical, as it is strong Kleene logic, the logic for Kripke's metalanguage, in which he can make contentions that are about the construction he models—what is sometimes called the "outer (or external) logic"—is fully classical. So, the logic for the language of Kripke's fixed-point construction is non-classical, but the logic for the language that is about Kripke's fixed-point construction is fully classical.

One important criticism of Kripke's theory comes from Solomon Feferman (1984), who says that nothing like sustained ordinary reasoning can be carried out with the strong Kleene logic that Kripke employs, since, for one thing, none of the classical theorems are also theorems in that non-classical logic. In fact, since strong Kleene logic lacks an adequate conditional, it also ends up that none of the following formulae always come out as true, though they do under classical logic: '$p \to p$', '$(p \wedge q) \to p$'. This has an interesting consequence: Under strong Kleene logic, it is not true that whenever a conjunction is true then some of its conjuncts are true, as '$(p \wedge p) \to p$' is not a theorem. In addition, one cannot truly claim that True-In and True-Out preserve truth. Although, as we have seen, Kripke sanctions Intersub, since '$p \to p$' is not a theorem, neither is '$T([p]) \to p$' or vice versa, in which case '$T([p]) \leftrightarrow p$' is not valid. We should conclude from this that, even with a form of Intersub, the truth schema, (TS), is not generally valid for Kripke's inner logic. So, while Kripke's account satisfies Intersub, given his three-valued logic, he does not satisfy SCT (or, indeed, even CT). These are significant problems for anyone who wishes to endorse a form of deflationism, and they serve to explain Feferman's (1984) criticism.[20]

Taking stock of Kripke's account, while his construction satisfies ELV, NT, and Intersub, it exhibits a number of weaknesses noted above that lead to violations of ESC, RI, and SCT.

---

[20] While Kripke's approach relies on strong Kleene logic, a classical reading proposed by Feferman (1984) is also available. The problem with the latter approach (known as the "Kripke-Feferman approach" or "(K-F)") from a deflationist's perspective is that it gives up Intersub, since (K-F) is committed to the truth of an instance of '$p \wedge \sim T([p])$', which would yield a contradiction if Intersub were sanctioned.

7.4 Field on the 'Determinately' Operator

Field (2008) attempts to improve on Kripke's construction by offering a novel account of the conditional, which we shall represent as '$\to_F$'. If the biconditional in the instances of the sentential version of the schema (TS) is interpreted as a material biconditional, then not all of those instances hold, which would be in violation of SCT. But if the biconditional is understood in terms of Field's conditional, then the instances of (TS) hold generally, thereby satisfying SCT. It bears noting, however, that not all classical theorems and inference rules end up as correct on Field's account, for example, '$[p \land (p \to_F q)] \to_F q$' is not generally valid, and the logical laws that govern Field's conditional reject *importation*, so that the inference from '$p \to_F (q \to_F r)$' to '$(p \land q) \to_F r$' fails. (For more on this, see Field (2008).)

One of the virtues of Field's conditional is that it enables him to introduce a particular notion of *determinacy*, which he then uses to characterize liar sentences. Specifically, since '$D(p)$', which is shorthand for 'it is determinately true that p', gets defined as '$p \land \sim(p \to_F \sim p)$' (or, equivalently, as '$p \land (T \to_F p)$', where 'T' represents a truth constant), he can show that, for a standard liar sentence, $L = $ '$\sim T(L)$', it can be semantically characterized *via* '$\sim D(\sim T(L))$'. In this way, Field seems to provide a means whereby liar sentences can be semantically characterized.

Field also provides a means for extending a classical, two-valued interpretation, I, of a base language, L, to an interpretation, I+, of an extended language, L+,[21] for which the following theses can be established:

(1) Although, as noted above, not all inference rules end up as correct on Field's account, his conditional '$\to_F$' can be shown to be an acceptable conditional;

---

[21] L contains classical connectives but lacks the truth predicate and both Field's special conditional, '$\to_F$', and its related biconditional. By contrast, L+ adds the truth predicate together with Field's special conditional and biconditional. It bears noting that both L and L+ have the capacity for self-reference.

(2) I+ is in agreement with I regarding the assignment of logical values to the sentences of L ⊂ L+;

(3) For any I+ and for any sentence S of L+, all instances of (TS) of L+ hold (i.e., have the designated logical value 1).

Now, given the nature of Field's extended language, L+, we can formulate a liar sentence, R, of L+ to the effect that R is not true, so that R = '∼T(R)'. From (3) we have that the instance of (TS) for this sentence, that is, 'T('∼T(R)') ↔ ∼T(R)', has the logical value 1. By substitution and Leibniz's Law, it follows that 'T(R) ↔ ∼T(R)' also has the logical value 1. In classical logic, inconsistency would result from these biconditionals possessing a designated value, in light of the validity of the Law of Excluded Middle (henceforth, *LEM*). This is because, given the biconditional, and the relevant instance of the LEM, viz., 'T(R) ∨ ∼T(R)', the contradiction 'T(R) ∧ ∼T(R)' follows classically. Field avoids this potential disaster, while still maintaining that the (TS) biconditional for '∼T(R)' is designated, by denying the LEM. Since 'T(R) ∨ ∼T(R)' is not designated, it does not figure as a premise in an argument and, as a result, the proof of 'T(R) ∧ ∼T(R)' is thereby blocked.

One of Field's insights, following Kripke's construction, regards how thoroughgoing this denial of the LEM is. To see this, consider again our liar sentence, L. Field can characterize that sentence by saying that L is not determinately true. But then what about a strengthened liar sentence U = '∼D(U)', which says of itself that it is not determinately true? One might think that, with this strengthened liar sentence, Field is back in paradox. Not so, however, for while the relevant instance of the LEM fails, there is a *stronger* notion of determinate truth, D*, that can accurately characterize this new liar sentence, as in '∼D*(∼D(U))'. Indeed, to treat such strengthened liar sentences, Field (2008) defines a hierarchy of determinately operators within which U can be characterized as not determinately true in the stronger sense indicated by 'D*', though not in the weaker sense of being determinately true that is indicated by 'D'. When another liar sentence, for example, W = '~D*(W)', emerges from this, we can move to an even stronger notion of determinate truth, 'D**', which enables Field to semantically characterize this new liar sentence. The pattern iterates infinitely, resulting in a hierarchy of 'determinately' operators.

Field (2008) upholds direct Intersub, for he endorses a thoroughgoing deflationary account of truth, and, as noted above, his non-classical account of the conditional supports SCT and avoids the problem that Curry's Paradox appears to present.[22] This makes it appear that Field's account does everything that a deflationist wants a response to the Liar Paradox to do, and this seems to be reinforced by his (2003, 2008) completeness proof. However, to see why Field's approach to the Liar Paradox does not seem to be fully adequate, notice that, while he has an infinite hierarchy of determinately operators, and so, for any particular liar sentence, he can semantically characterize it as not determinately true, for some level of that notion within the hierarchy, he lacks a determinately operator that captures a maximal sense of determinate truth in which all of the sentences at every stage in a sequence of progressively stronger and stronger liar sentences can be characterized as not determinately true. Call this a "global determinately operator" (henceforth, *GDO*). Leon Horsten (2011, p. 146) contends that Field's lack of a GDO is "unsatisfactory". After all, Field's proposal is intended to improve on existing resolutions of the Liar Paradox, by introducing a hierarchy of determinately operators. But if Field is forced to deny that there is a GDO that can provide a unified notion of determinate truth, this would lead to an unacceptable

---

[22] Curry's Paradox takes off from a conditional, (C) = 'If sentence (C) is true, then $\perp$', where '$\perp$' is an absurdity constant representing any logically false sentence. For more on Curry's Paradox, see Beall (2009) and Armour-Garb and Woodbridge (2015, Ch. 5).

form of fragmentation of the very notion that he brought in as a means for characterizing liar sentences. This seems related to the Formulation Problem (FP) introduced in Section 4.2, which we have argued plagues a number of purportedly deflationary accounts of truth. In response, we suspect that Field might deny the coherence of a GDO, but this would seem to generate other concerns.

The "FP-like" fragmentation worry that would emerge from Field's denial of a GDO, given his response to the Liar Paradox, extends to a further challenge for his view. If his account lacks a GDO, then, even though it can provide a semantic status for *each* individual formula, it could not establish a generalization like

(G) Every sentence is either true, false, not determinately true, or not determinately false, in some sense or other of 'determinately'.[23]

We take this to demonstrate that, without a GDO, his account suffers from a form of omega incompleteness.[24]

JC Beall (2009) adduces something like (G) as a means for identifying a different worry for Field's solution to the Liar Paradox. According to Beall (2009), if Field could establish something like (G), then this would result in inconsistency, since it follows from (G) that a sentence like

(J) Sentence (J) is false or determinately false, in some sense or other of 'determinately',

---

[23] It bears noting that Field (2008) intends his treatment of the Liar Paradox to extend to the Sorites, i.e., the Paradox of Vagueness. This provides further reasons for thinking that he needs to be able to establish something like (G), since he does seem to accept what (G) appears to convey.

[24] As a reminder, an account or a theory, Θ, is *omega incomplete* if there is a formula, 'F(x)', such that, for each natural number named by a numeral, n, Θ can prove 'F(n)', but Θ is unable to prove its universal generation, '$\forall x F(x)$'. So, Θ suffers from *omega incompleteness* when it can prove every instance of a generalization, but it cannot prove the generalization itself.

CHALLENGES TO PARADOX TREATMENT DEFLATIONISM 257

possesses one of the aforementioned semantic statuses. But that would result in inconsistency. If Beall is right about this, then the issue of whether Field's account includes a GDO poses a catch-22 for him. If his approach included such a notion, then it would avoid the charge of omega incompleteness by being able to establish (G), but this would result in inconsistency in light of the result of semantically characterizing (J). However, if his account lacked such a notion, while that would avoid any inconsistency pertaining to (J), it would leave him with the aforementioned omega incompleteness. So, what we seem to get from Field's account is a trade-off between inconsistency or incompleteness (a trade-off that Priest (1987/2006) has highlighted as a problematic situation for proposed consistent resolutions of the Liar Paradox), in addition to a violation of ESC.

In response to the challenges posed by (G) and (J), we suspect that Field, like Tarski on the putative revenge problems for his view, might maintain that (G), and, thus, (J) are garbage sentences and, thus, are not cases that he has to worry about establishing, in the case of (G), or semantically characterizing, in the case of (J). We shall leave it to others to determine whether this is an acceptable response to the challenges posed by these particular cases.[25]

Taking stock of how Field's account fits with the constraints we have laid out on deflationary resolutions of the Liar Paradox, he satisfies NT, Intersub, SCT, and, it seems, ELV, but it is doubtful that he can satisfy ESC, in light of the points that we made above. Field (2008) claims that his solution to the Liar Paradox (and its

---

[25] It bears noting that whether (G) creates a problem for Field's approach depends on certain issues regarding expressibility, that is, about what can or cannot be expressed. In particular, it seems that for (G) to create a problem for Field, this might require a form of unrestricted general quantification, which involves quantification over absolutely everything. But there are a number of concerns about unrestricted general quantification. (See, e.g., the papers collected in Rayo and Uzquiano (2006).) Hence, if it can be shown that the problem that (G) appears to present requires unrestricted general quantification, and if it can be shown that this should not be accepted, then this would effectively defuse the worry that (G), and thus (J), appear to raise for Field's approach to the Liar Paradox.

kin) is "revenge-immune", thereby satisfying RI, but for challenges to this claim see Priest (2007, p. 230). All of that said, even given the limitations that we have pointed out, it is clear that Field comes closer to satisfying the full range of both general and deflationary constraints on a solution to the semantic paradoxes than does either Tarski or Kripke.

7.5 Grover and Semantic Inheritors

Dorothy Grover (1977) develops an approach to the Liar Paradox from within her prosentential deflationary account of truth-talk. Prior to explaining Grover's diagnosis of liar sentences, we need to clarify some of her terminology. According to Grover (1977, p. 593), an expression, for example, a pronoun or a prosentence, which inherits its content anaphorically from another expression, is to be called its "inheritor". Terms, such as proper names, etc., that get their referents in ways that are independent of other expressions having referents will be said to acquire their referents "independently". As discussed in Chapter 3, a prosentence such as 'That is true', which inherits its content from another sentence that it indicates, is called a "prosentence of laziness". A prosentence of laziness is said to be "grounded" if it is (ultimately) connected to a sentence that acquires its content independently. Similarly, a definite description inheritor is grounded if it is connected to an antecedent that can acquire a referent independently. With this terminology in mind, consider the following triple of sentences.

(A) Snow is white.
(B) (A) is true.
(C) 'Snow is white' is true.

In (C) the anaphoric antecedent is a proper part of the inheritor, and Grover contends that the antecedent of (B) is "on display" in (C). As inheritors with 'Snow is white' as antecedent, (B) and (C) are about whatever 'Snow is white' is about. In both of these cases, a sentential inheritor is *grounded* in virtue of being connected via an "inheritance chain" to an antecedent that acquires its content independently.

To see a case of an ungrounded inheritor, consider the following pair of sentences.

(D) (E) is true.
(E) That is true,

where (E) tries to inherit its content from (D), and (D) tries to inherit its content from (E). As Grover notes (1977, p. 597), these inheritors are ungrounded and, as a consequence, they both lack any content. Now consider liar sentences. As inheritors, liar sentences depend on their antecedents for content, but because they try to take themselves as their antecedents, these inheritors are ungrounded, as they are not connected to antecedents that acquire content independently. As a result, such sentences lack content. The same goes for a truthteller sentence, such as

(K) Sentence (K) is true.

Like any liar sentence, (K) is an ungrounded inheritor, and, as a consequence, (K) lacks any content. Indeed, on Grover's view, the grounded/ungrounded distinction separates those occurrences of inheritors that have content from those that lack content. Moreover, Grover reports (1977, p. 599) that the set of sentences that are grounded according to the way that she explains this notion roughly corresponds with the set of sentences that get truth-values at the minimal fixed point in Kripke's (1975) construction.

Grover's diagnosis of liar sentences is that they are all ungrounded and, as a consequence, lack content. If the predicate 'ungrounded' were added to her object language, then Grover's approach would satisfy ESC, since she could then characterize grounded sentences either as true or as false, and could characterize putatively pathological sentences as ungrounded. But now consider a potential revenge problem arising from the sentence

(F) (F) is false or (F) is ungrounded.

Such a sentence might foil a theorist who treats liar sentences by characterizing them as ungrounded. To see the problem, note that the first disjunct of (F) amounts to an inheritor that attempts to inherit content from (F) as a whole, and thus (at least in part) from itself. This makes that disjunct ungrounded. If *being ungrounded* constitutes a semantic status, then the second disjunct of (F) amounts to a semantic characterization of (F), one that can be correct or incorrect, that is, true or false. The question that arises is how we should understand the disjoining of an ungrounded disjunct with a disjunct that is true and with a disjunct that is false. In particular, the issue is whether (F) constitutes a genuine form of revenge for Grover's response to the Liar Paradox, revealing a failure to satisfy RI.

Grover (1977) considers a sentence like (F) and maintains that paradox can be avoided by moving to a three-valued logic. Given weak Kleene logic, if any part of (F) has the value i, then (F) itself has that value. Hence, if Grover goes this route, then (F) will have the logical value i, since the first disjunct has that value. Thus, (F) will be assigned the value i, and, correlating ungroundedness with this logical value, the claim that (F) is ungrounded will be true and will thus have the logical value 1. But in weak Kleene logic, disjoining a sentence with value i and a sentence with value 1 yields a sentence with value i, which is what (F) has been assigned.

As we have seen in Section 7.3, given strong Kleene logic, the first disjunct being ungrounded and thereby having the logical value i does not determine the logical value of (F). If the second disjunct has the logical value 1, then (F) as a whole has the logical value 1 and is thus true. But if the second disjunct has the logical value 1, then it is true, meaning that (F) is ungrounded. That would make (F) true and ungrounded, which is a seemingly impossible result. If the second disjunct has the logical value 0, then on strong Kleene the whole sentence has the logical value i. But if the second disjunct has the logical value 0 and is thus false, that means the sentence as a whole is grounded, despite having the logical value i, which seems to be another impossible result.

Given the foregoing, either Grover cannot avail herself of strong Kleene logic or she needs a different account of being "grounded" that renders (F) grounded despite having the logical value i. Grover (1977) pursues this second option. We think that this is a strange strategy to adopt, since it seems very difficult to understand how a grounded sentence could have the logical value i, just as it is difficult to understand how a sentence with value 1 could legitimately be evaluated as ungrounded. In fact, we think that this makes Grover's concept of being *grounded* somewhat incoherent, especially since she seems to want to latch onto Kripke's (1975) notion of groundedness. But allowing a grounded sentence to have the logical value i seems somewhat antithetical to Kripke's construction. As a result, we think that one should dismiss this option and also think that Grover should go with weak Kleene and contend that (F) has the logical value i with (F) itself being ungrounded. Whether this option would allow her account to satisfy RI then becomes an open question.

It bears noting that, by moving to a three-valued logic, Grover, like Kripke, does not offer an adequate conditional and that, for her, SCT is not satisfied, since liar sentences have a logical value i and, hence, their instances of (TS) do not have a designated value. In addition, she seems to suffer from the same expressibility worries that plague Kripke's construction, since, for her, a liar sentence that self-ascribes untruth is not true, though she cannot truly express that fact. In the end, applying Chihara's terminology, Grover (1977) offers a *diagnosis* of liar sentences but not an explicit *treatment* of them. This is not to say that she could not propose a treatment. Perhaps she could use 'ungrounded' or even 'meaningless' as a means of semantically characterizing liar sentences, but she does not develop this line of thought. We elaborate a method along this track in the appendix, one that preserves SCT while offering a revenge-immune approach to the semantic paradoxes.

Taking stock, we have seen that Grover satisfies NT and a version of ELV, by maintaining that meaningless sentences are assigned the logical value i. Given her prosententialism, it seems that Grover's view also satisfies a version of Intersub. However, we have seen that her view violates SCT, despite the content equivalence that her prosententialism posits between a sentence, S, and 'S is true'. Moreover, in failing to provide a semantic characterization for liar sentences, her approach leaves ESC unsatisfied as well. It also remains an open question whether her approach satisfies RI.

In assessing Grover's approach to the semantic paradoxes, what has emerged is that it is an inadequate deflationary response in more than one way. Since Grover's approach does not satisfy SCT, it does not satisfy a deflationary account's fourth dimension of Paradox Treatment Deflationism, and since she violates ESC by failing to provide a semantic characterization of liar sentences, her approach does not satisfy the general conditions for an approach to be adequate.

7.6 Horwich's Semantic Epistemicism

Horwich (1990/1998, 2005, 2010b) has offered what he claims is a consistent resolution of the Liar Paradox that fits with his minimalism and derives from his (1997, 1998) approaches to the problem of vagueness. Let 'L' name the proposition expressed by 'L is not true', so that $L = <L$ is not true$>$. Abiding by

CHALLENGES TO PARADOX TREATMENT DEFLATIONISM 263

classical logic, the *L*-instance of (ES), Horwich's version of (TS), yields a contradiction. Hence, Horwich (1990/1998, pp. 41–42) considers four possible responses to the paradoxicality that *L* appears to yield:

(1) Reject classical logic.
(2) Reject that 'true' coherently applies to truth-involving propositions.
(3) Reject that putatively paradoxical sentences express propositions.
(4) Restrict (E*) so that only certain instances are correct and part of the minimal theory of truth (henceforth, *MT*).

Horwich rejects (1) as being too radical and rejects (2) and (3) as being too costly. Hence, he endorses (4), that the instances of (E*) included in MT must be "restricted in some way so as to avoid paradoxical results" (1990/1998, p. 40), where, as noted in Chapter 3, (E*) stands for a function that yields a proposition of a particular form when applied to any proposition, viz.,

(E*) <<p> is true iff p>.

He (1990/1998, p. 42) notes that further theorizing is required to flesh this out, but, after specifying some constraints on such theorizing (presented and discussed below as conditions C1) and C2)), but he leaves the details for another occasion.

Horwich maintains that the only acceptable approach to dealing with the Liar Paradox is to apply strategy (4), that is, to somehow restrict which instances of (E*) are members of MT. We shall see precisely how Horwich (2005, 2010b) proposes restricting (E*), below. But it is worth noting that, given the "riskiness" of truth-talk with respect to liar sentences (Cf. Kripke (1975)), there seems to be no algorithm for winnowing out and, so, excluding all and only the paradoxical instances of (E*) as such.[26] That said, stealing a page from Horwich's particular *epistemicist* solution to the problem of vagueness, Bradley Armour-Garb and JC Beall (2005b) attribute to him what they call "semantic epistemicism" according to which, while a liar sentence express a liar proposition, L, and while that proposition is either true or false, we cannot know which truth-value it has.[27] More specifically, they (2005b, p. 90) attribute to him the following two theses:

(T1) L is either true or false.

(T2) It is conceptually impossible to know that L is true, and it is conceptually impossible to know that L is false.

As a result of Horwich's semantic epistemicism, in his response to the Liar Paradox,[28] he manages to hold onto both classical logic and classical semantics—propositional versions of the LEM and the principle of Bivalence are accepted, for example—while also aiming to avoid paradox, since the instances of (E*) for liar propositions will be "illegitimate" and thus are not members of MT.[29]

---

[26] Cf. Kripke (1975, p. 692), which says, "an adequate theory must allow our statements involving the notion of truth to be risky: they risk being paradoxical if the empirical facts are extremely (and unexpectedly) unfavorable."

[27] Horwich (2005, p. 82, n. 10) endorses the characterization of semantic epistemicism sketched by Armour-Garb and Beall. It is now widely recognized that Horwich's solution to the Liar Paradox takes off from his epistemicism regarding the problem of vagueness. See Asay (2015) and Marques (2018).

[28] One might deny our claim that Horwich's solution to the Liar Paradox is related to his epistemicist solution to the sorities. But we think that this may be too quick. After all, Horwich's epistemicist solution to the problem of vagueness is to deny some instances of the induction step—viz., the ones that involve a borderline case—without knowing which particular instances are falsified. Similarly, his epistemicist solution to the problem that liar propositions pose is to deny the instances of (E*) for them without knowing which particular side of any such equivalence is true and which is false. In both cases, rather than restricting or revising classical logic or classical semantics, his solution to these paradoxes involves falsifying some instances of rather entrenched principles coupled with the claim that we cannot know *which* (part) of them is falsified.

[29] For approaches to the Liar Paradox that likewise reject liar-sentence instances of the truth schema, (TS), see work on alethic nihilism by David Liggins (2014) and Will Gamester (2023). For a response to Liggins, see Armour-Garb and Woodbridge (2017); for a response to Gamester, see Armour-Garb and Woodbridge (2024).

One potential objection to Horwich's semantic epistemicism that we can dismiss quickly is the charge that it is ad hoc because it involves restricting (E*).[30] This is a consequence of the fact that Horwich's position on *indeterminacy*, in addition to his response to the problem of vagueness, is motivated, and this is what drives his response to the Liar Paradox. On his view, a proposition is *indeterminate* iff, though either true or false, there is a semantically induced impossibility of knowing which. Since he maintains that the *L*-instance of (E*) is false in virtue of the left and right sides not agreeing in truth-value, while also maintaining that there is no way to know which side is true and which is false, Horwich's approach to the Liar is motivated and is not in the least ad hoc.[31]

As noted above, on Horwich's epistemicist response to the Liar Paradox, a liar proposition will be either true or false though we cannot know which truth-value it possesses. In this way, Horwich proposes to hold onto classical logic and classical semantics—the LEM and the principle of Bivalence are maintained, for example—while also aiming to avoid paradox, since the instances of (E*) for liar propositions will be "illegitimate" and thus are not part of MT. But it is unclear how he can exclude those instances of (E*), that is, how he can satisfy (4), above.

Horwich (1990/1998, p. 42) proposes some conditions that must be met for restricting (E*) in support of (4):

(C1) MT should constitute a maximal consistent collection of instances of (E*),[32] where a set of formulae—sentences or

---

[30] See also Scharp (2013) on what he calls "monster barring" strategies.
[31] Asay (2015, pp. 687–88), and Marques (2018, pp. 1046–47) following him, deny that these considerations are sufficient to deflect the charge of ad hockery against Horwich's view because the analogy between vague sentences and liar sentences fails. They claim that the indeterminacies involved in the different kinds of cases are too different to support extending the idea from vagueness over to the Liar. However, even if they are right about the extension not being adequately supported by the analogy, Horwich could claim that the analogy is no longer needed to support the restriction of (E*), since his new groundedness criterion (see below) will do the job in a motivated way without any appeal to an analogy with vagueness.
[32] This presentation from McGee (1992) amounts to a combination of the first two conditions that Horwich specifies.

propositions—S is a "maximal consistent" set provided S is consistent and has only inconsistent proper extensions, which is to say that S is consistent and contains as many members as it can hold without becoming inconsistent; and

(C2) There must be a constructive means by which we identify which instances of (E*) are excluded from MT.

Unfortunately for Horwich, it has proven to be very difficult to restrict (E*) in the way he (1990/1998) imagines, and his idea for how to restrict the admissible instances of (E*) faces real problems. Vann McGee (1992), responding to the 1990 first edition of Horwich (1990/1998), shows that (C1) cannot succeed for Horwich's purposes; it is inadequate for determining which instances of (E*) should be included in MT.[33] More specifically, McGee (1992) shows that Horwich's proposal for restricting the instances to a maximal consistent set that nevertheless excludes all paradox-yielding instances cannot work.[34] McGee (1992) notes that, for the maximally consistent set of instances of (E*) that Horwich envisages, (i) there are actually infinitely many maximally consistent sets of instances of (ES), (ii) none of them is recursively axiomatizable,[35] (iii) each of them decides all sentences of the truth-free fragment of the language, as every 'true'-free sentence is provably equivalent to an instance of (E*), and (iv) there seems to be no principled reason for identifying one of them as *the* theory of truth. As a result, (C1) will not deliver a unique theory of truth.

---

[33] McGee shows this for the sentential version of schema (TS), but it can be applied to Horwich's MT (viz., the legitimate instances of (E*)), which employs propositions, rather than sentences.

[34] As a reminder, a "maximal consistent set" is a set of formulae (e.g., sentences) from a given language that satisfies the conditions for being maximal and for being consistent where the latter involves being free of contradictions and the former requires that, for every well-formed sentence of the language, either it or its negation is a member of that set.

[35] A theory is recursively axiomatizable iff it possesses a recursive set of axioms. If Horwich's theory had been recursively axiomatizable, then there would have been a way of enumerating all of the theorems of his theory without enumerating any instances that are not theorems.

After showing that Horwich's suggestion seems intractable, McGee (1992, p. 237) notes that

> the mere desire to preserve as many instances of [(E*)] as possible will give us too little to go on in constructing a consistent alternative to [unrestricted (E*)] ... we would not know where to begin our search for a consistent alternative to [[unrestricted (E*)]. relinquished. What the results here show is that, without some such inegalitarian attitude toward instances of [(E*)], we would not know where to begin our search for a consistent alternative to the naïve theory of truth. In particular, this gives us a reason for dissatisfaction with minimalism; acknowledging no basis for discriminating among the instances of [(E*)], the minimalist conception is completely dumbfounded by the Liar Paradox.[36]

Given the problem that McGee raises for (C1), Horwich (2010b) attempts to provide a means whereby, while non-maximal, (C2) can be satisfied, which would seem to satisfy (4). To this end, Horwich (2010b, p. 90) tries to restrict the instances of (E*) that belong to MT to a certain privileged subset of "grounded" propositions in something like Kripke's (1975) model. On this approach, our language, L, "is the limit of the expanding sub-languages L_0, L_1, L_2,... —where L_0 lacks the truth predicate; L_1 (which contains L_0) applies it, via the equivalence schema, to the grounded propositions of L_0; similarly, L_2 applies it to the grounded propositions of L_1; L_3 applies it to the grounded propositions of L_2; and so on" (Horwich (2010b, p. 90).[37] What this yields is that, according to Horwich's

---

[36] It bears noting that, while McGee shows this for the truth schema formulated for sentences, it can be applied to Horwich's MT (viz., the legitimate instances of (E*)), which employs propositions, rather than sentences.

[37] We should note that this quote from Horwich is a little bit sloppy. To be more precise, Horwich should say that L_1 applies the truth predicate to the grounded propositions *expressed by the sentences* of L_0, and L_2 applies the truth predicate to the grounded propositions *expressed by the sentences* of L_1. And so on. We will gloss over this detail in the discussion that follows.

(2010b) proposal, an instance of (E*) will be "acceptable" and, thus, will be a part of MT, even if it governs a proposition that includes truth, so long as that proposition is *grounded*, and the propositions of the L_is that will be grounded are those that are rooted in the non-truth-involving facts.

To clarify this, note that, within L_1, a proposition is grounded provided it or its negation is entailed by a combination of L_0-grounded facts and the facts of L_1 that are entailed by them via the legitimate instances of (E*), which are its applications to the grounded propositions of L_0. As a result of this process, a liar proposition, *L*, will not be a grounded proposition of L_1 because there are no facts of L_0 that, given the instance of (E*) for *L*, entail either it or its negation. In addition, it will not be a grounded proposition of any other higher-level sub-languages, which yields the result that the instance of (E*) for any liar proposition is not part of MT. Assuming that Horwich's notion of being grounded can be supported,[38] then, since a proposition failing to be grounded constitutes a sufficient condition for its (E*)-instance not being a member of MT, the charge that there is no non-ad hoc way to restrict which instances of (E*) are the members of MT must be rethought. If successful, Horwich's proposal will satisfy (C2) and, as a result, will underwrite strategy (4). Moreover, since generating a contradiction from a liar proposition requires reasoning with an (ES)-instance for it, and since the instances of (ES) expressing the instances of (E*) for ungrounded propositions cannot be applied

---

[38] Related to the point made in the previous footnote, Marques (2018, p. 1039) raises doubts about this on the basis of noting that Horwich appeals to *languages* in his explanation of grounded *propositions*, even though the latter are supposed to be independent of the former. We acknowledge that explaining groundedness as a property of propositions, instead of the usual understanding of it as a property of sentences, may be nonstandard. Kripke (1975) provides an account of the latter and goes on to claim that ungrounded sentences, such as liar sentences, do not express propositions. By contrast, Horwich does not deny that liar sentences express propositions. Rather, according to Horwich, liar sentences express propositions that are true or false; it is just that we cannot know which truth-value they possess. We maintain that, even if Horwich's notion of groundedness strikes one as odd, the insertions made into Horwich's explanation of it quoted above are enough to clarify the notion he introduces. Even so, below we consider reasons for thinking that it does not end up being a stable position.

in any reasoning, it follows that the instances of (ES) for any liar propositions cannot be used in inferences, and contradiction is thus avoided. In this way, Horwich aims to avoid paradox by providing principled reasons for restricting the instances of (E*) that count as the axioms of MT.

One consequence of Horwich's approach to the Liar Paradox that is still worth worrying about derives from his self-avowed commitment to establishing certain general principles, such as the principle of Bivalence. According to Horwich (1990/1998, 76–83), Bivalence follows from the instances of (ES), (FS)—the falsity schema explained in Section 3.3.1—and the LEM.[39] Given his (2010b) changes to MT, and his commitment to MT being sufficient for explaining all the facts about truth, Horwich must be able to derive Bivalence from the LEM, logic, and MT, where the latter is now understood to capture all and only the legitimate—that is, the grounded—instances of (E*) (and (F*), which has as its instances the propositions generated by the propositional function schema, <<p> is false iff ~p>). The problem for Horwich is that the way that the new restrictions on MT now limit which instances of (ES) and (FS) can be used in reasoning conflicts with his claim to be able to derive Bivalence.

Recall that Horwich maintains that Bivalence also holds for liar propositions, such as L. Hence, if he is to derive Bivalence from (E*), (F*) and the LEM, then he must be able to derive the L-instance of Bivalence (thesis (T1) of semantic epistemicism, above) from those principles as well. (This is because if there is an instance of a generalization that cannot be derived, and it is known that it cannot be derived, then one cannot derive the generalization itself.) Since the L-instances of (E*) and (F*) are illegitimate and, thus, are not included in MT, it follows that it is impossible to derive the L-instance of Bivalence from the relevant instances of (ES) and (FS). To see this,

---

[39] Armour-Garb and Beall (2005b, p. 93) contend that Horwich will accept the LEM on a priori grounds. If they are right, then he does not need to prove this logical principle, in contrast with the *semantic* principle of Bivalence.

note that, while L is true or L is not true, by the LEM, since the L-instance of (F*) is illegitimate, we cannot reason with the relevant instance of (FS) to derive that L is true or that L false.[40] Hence, it follows that Horwich cannot derive the general principle of Bivalence from (E*), (F*), and the LEM. Contrary to what he maintains, this generalization will be beyond his reach, given the restrictions on (E*) (and (F*)) that he (2010b) imposes. This conflicts with Horwich's claim that all facts about truth can be explained by MT.[41]

Setting aside the concern just raised, when we take stock of how Horwich's semantic epistemicism fares relative to the constraints that we have set out for an adequate deflationary solution to the Liar Paradox, we see that for *grounded* propositions he does quite well, satisfying NT, ESC, ELV, and SCT when dealing only with propositions of this sort. In addition, for these propositions, he satisfies a form of derived Intersub. As is not surprising, Horwich does not fare as well with respect to these constraints for *ungrounded* propositions. Since he accepts Bivalence for both grounded and ungrounded propositions, his approach satisfies ELV for ungrounded propositions as well. However, since derived Intersub requires a theorist to reason *from* an instance of the equivalence schema, and since ungrounded liar propositions have false instances of (ES), according to Horwich, it follows that he does not have derived Intersub for ungrounded propositions. This also explains why he does not satisfy SCT for ungrounded propositions, since he takes their (ES)-instances to be false. In addition, while ungrounded propositions satisfy the metaphysical analog of ESC,

---

[40] This seems to undermine Horwich's semantic epistemicism, or at least to render it unjustified. To block this, Horwich might declare that, like the LEM, the principle of Bivalence is also known a priori. Implausible though this may be, since, in contrast to logical principles, one might balk at declaring that *semantic* principles are known a priori, this would succeed in circumventing our argument. But declaring semantic principles to be known a priori in this context seems ad hoc—a desperate move that should be counseled against. Thus, Horwich needs some other way of justifying thesis (T1) of semantic epistemicism. For present purposes, we shall set this aside, since there are other problems with his approach to the Liar, even if he can adequately answer the present worry.

[41] We are presenting an updated variant of an argument that was originally put forward by Armour-Garb and Beall (2005b). Their argument was directed at Horwich (1990/1998 and 2005). By contrast, our updated argument takes into account Horwich (2010b). A still different version of this argument has been endorsed by Schindler (2020).

since every ungrounded proposition possesses a semantic *status*, given his semantic epistemicism, we cannot know what semantic status such propositions possess. Hence, in a sense, he does not satisfy an aspect of ESC. Of course, Horwich would likely maintain that just satisfying the metaphysical analog of ESC is enough for satisfying ESC, since it is built into his approach—in a non-ad hoc way—that we cannot know the semantic status of such propositions. We leave it to readers to decide whether that is an adequate reply. Even if it is, trouble is still brewing for Horwich with respect to satisfying condition RI, as there is a revenge problem for his semantic epistemicism that challenges whether his approach even adequately satisfies NT, the nontrivialism constraint.

Recall that Horwich's approach depends on the thesis that a liar sentence (or proposition) is either true or false, though we cannot know which truth-value it possesses. A potential revenge problem for his semantic epistemicism exploits this thesis and provides a sentence that seems to undermine his consistent approach. To get to the potential problem, consider the Principle of Unified Solution ("PUS"), which many theorists see as a constraint on any adequate solution to the semantic paradoxes:[42]

(PUS) Structurally similar paradoxes require the same solution.

Assuming that any concerns regarding (PUS) can be resolved, it seems that Horwich should accept this principle. To see this, note that, given Horwich's (1998, pp. 118–20) deflationary account of reference-talk, which parallels his account of truth-talk, it would be odd if he did not extend his approach to the Liar Paradox in a solution to Berry's Paradox about reference, which is structurally similar to the Liar.[43] If his approach to the Liar Paradox did not extend in

---

[42] For justification for this constraint, see Priest (1995/2002, 2000) and Armour-Garb and Beall (2005b, p. 94). For objections to this constraint Smith (2000), Badici (2008), and Beall (2009).

[43] For an explanation of Berry's Paradox, see Armour-Garb and Woodbridge (2015, pp. 205–9).

this way, then Horwich should admit that his solution to that paradox is unacceptable.

Assuming (PUS), a case of revenge for Horwich's semantic epistemicism about the Liar Paradox emerges from the following sentence (which is a version of what is standardly called "Montague's Paradox"),

> Nobody knows the proposition expressed by the only displayed sentence that begins with the word 'Nobody' in this book,

where the above displayed sentence is the only displayed sentence in this book that begins with 'Nobody'. Let 'N' name the proposition expressed by that sentence, making N the proposition that nobody knows N.[44] As we would describe the ensuing problem, it emerges from a particular reading of the "factivity" of knowledge, where the emphasis is on the *factual* side of 'factivity', captured by the schema,

(KF) K<p> → p.[45]

We shall employ an inference rule, IR, that captures a different form of factivity for knowledge, viz., that, from any instance of 'K<p>' (as an assumption, premise, etc.), we are entitled to infer the relevant instance of 'p', which is to say that one can always infer 'p' from 'K<p>'[46]. IR, together with classical logic, rules out any instance of the following conjunction schema:

---

[44] Armour-Garb and Beall (2005b) introduce N in offering a putative revenge problem for Horwich. While they are correct that N poses a problem for Horwich's semantic epistemicism, the details of their argument misfire by reasoning with an instance of (ES) that Horwich rejects in applying his new groundedness criterion. By contrast, the argument employing N that we present here avoids relying on any instance of (ES), and so applies to Horwich's newer position.

[45] While there have been challenges to the claim that 'knows' is a factive verb, we will not address these challenges here. (Cf. Hazlett (2010) for arguments against the factivity of knowledge and Goh and Choo (2022) for a response to Hazlett.)

[46] Given conditional proof, the veridicality principle–that if a proposition is known, it is true–follows from IR, but even though Horwich assumes classical logic, which sanctions conditional proof, we shall not rely on it for what follows.

'K<p> ∧ ~p'. Now, by relying on Horwich's commitment to classical logic, together with IR, we can demonstrate a problem for his semantic epistemicism as follows.

Given the LEM, we are committed to any instance of 'p ∨ ~p'. Now suppose that someone, S, knows some proposition, so we have some instance of 'K_s<p>'. From this supposition and our acceptance of any instance of the LEM, we can classically prove the relevant instance of the disjunctive form '(K_s<p> ∧ p) ∨ (K_s<p> ∧ ~p)'. But the latter, right-hand disjunct has been ruled out above. So, given our supposition, we have the relevant instance of the conjunctive form 'K_s<p> ∧ p'. But the proposition for our instance of 'K_s<p>' was picked at random from among the propositions. Thus, we conclude that, from our current supposition, IR, and classical logic, the relevant instance of 'K_s<p> ∧ p' follows from the assumption of any instance of 'K_s<p>', where, again, the proposition involved could be any proposition.

Now consider the proposition, N, which is expressed by the sentence 'Nobody knows N', viz., N = <Nobody knows N>. The LEM gives us that either N is known or it is not the case that N is known (i.e., N is not known). Assuming that N is not known trivially yields that N is not known, given classical logic. Now consider the assumption that N is known, that is, that, for some S, S knows N. Given IR, it follows from this assumption and classical logic that S knows N and nobody knows N. Hence, S knows N and S does not know N (since nobody does). Contradiction. So, by reductio ad absurdum, it is not the case that, for some S, S knows N, which yields the result that N is not known. Since it thus follows from an instance of LEM that N is not known, this amounts to a *proof* that N is not known. Thus, we have a proof that nobody knows N. Given that N just is the proposition that nobody knows N, a proof that nobody knows N thereby proves N. Since possessing a proof of some proposition yields knowledge of that very proposition, the above considerations result in our now having knowledge of N. So, N is known, meaning that someone knows N. But we have already seen that this yields a contradiction. Thus, the paradox that N presents cannot be resolved just by appealing to Horwich's semantic epistemicism, even given that N is not a grounded proposition and, thus, that the N-instance of (E^*) is not a member of MT.

One move that Horwich might make in response to the problem we have presented is to argue that, just as there are false instances of (ES) that involve liar sentences, on his approach, there are exceptions to IR, and N is one of them. Since our argument relies on the general validity of IR, if it can be denied for the N-instance, perhaps the revenge problem is avoided. While this might seem like a possible move, one that seems to be in line with Horwich's response to the Liar Paradox, it is important to understand its implications. The N-instance of IR being an exception to the rule requires that N be known while N is untrue, since, if N is true, this does not constitute an exception to IR. It thus follows that if one endorses this move, one is committed to accepting that it is possible to know untrue claims. While some might see this as a counterexample to IR, we think that allowing for knowledge of untrue claims is too high a cost to bear.

While Horwich takes putatively "paradox-yielding" sentences to express propositions, as we have seen, he (2005, 2010b) also brings in the distinction between grounded propositions and propositions that are not grounded, and he takes liar sentences to express propositions that are not grounded. If he were to claim that, unlike liar sentences, the "Nobody sentence" does not express a proposition, the onus would then be on him to distinguish a sentence that fails to express a proposition from one that expresses a proposition that is not grounded. We think that this is a large task and that ultimately there is no way for him to do this. After all, even leaving aside (PUS), there seem to be no non–ad hoc reasons for maintaining that liar sentences express propositions that are not grounded, whereas the "Nobody sentence" fails to express any proposition at all. We think that Horwich has no means for drawing this distinction, and, for this reason, as well as for the others that we have adduced above, we maintain that he fails to satisfy RI and so the prospects for his semantic epistemicist approach to the Liar Paradox are bleak.

7.7 Deflationary Dialetheism

Dialetheism is the view that some sentences are equivalent to their own negations, so that such sentences are both true and false.[47] Given standard views of negation and conjunction—that a negation is true (false) iff its negatum is false (true) and that a conjunction is true iff both of its conjuncts are true and false iff at least one of its conjuncts are false—it follows that if 'p' is both true and false, so is its negation and their conjunction, 'p ∧ ~p'. As a result, dialetheism is sometimes described as the view that there are true contradictions. In order to avoid *trivialism*, that is, to satisfy NT, dialetheists endorse a paraconsistent logic, which has a "non-explosive" consequence relation, so that from a contradiction, not everything follows. Thus, for the dialetheist, *ex falso quodlibet* (henceforth, *EFQ*) is invalid.

While certain deflationists (e.g., Armour-Garb (2001), Beall and Armour-Garb (2003), and Beall (2009)) have been attracted to dialetheism as a means for dealing with the Liar Paradox, it bears noting that the primary source of dialetheism is the work of Priest (1987/2006), who himself is no deflationist. In addition to rejecting Intersub,[48] Priest maintains that *truth* has a substantive normative role, which, as discussed in Chapter 5, is antithetical to any

---

[47] For an excellent survey of dialetheism, see Priest (1987/2006).

[48] Priest (1987/2006) does not support Intersub, since it would turn truth-value *gluts*, sentences that are both true and false (or true with true negations), into truth-value gaps, and vice versa. For consider a dialetheia, a sentence that is both true and false. Since falsity is truth of negation, from the claim that 'p' is both truth and false, we get 'T([p]) ∧ T([~p])', and Intersub together with DeMorgan's laws enables us to conclude '~[T([p]) v F([p])]', which expresses a truth-value gap.

deflationary approach to truth-talk. In a pair of papers, Armour-Garb and Beall (their (2001) and (2003)) argue that, in light of the semantic paradoxes, and, in particular, the Liar Paradox, deflationists about truth-talk should be dialetheists. The crux of their argument for "deflationary dialetheism" is that nothing in deflationism yields a principled reason as to why ungrounded and paradoxical sentences should not yield legitimate instances of (TS). Thus, they maintain that there are no good reasons for banning these types of statements from the domain of their truth theories. But if liar sentences and the like generate legitimate instances of (TS)—if they constitute legitimate targets of truth-ascriptions, by the lights of deflationary theories—then, without further constraints, a contradiction seems imminent. At base, their argument, to the effect that deflationists should be dialetheists, turns on a negative argument, that deflationists have no way of solving the *delimitation problem*, viz., the problem of specifying the proper targets of truth-ascriptions, that is, of specifying the domain of a given theory of truth. More specifically, they argue that deflationists have no non–ad hoc way of excluding liar sentences from the collection of instances of (TS). If they are right about this, then deflationists should accept and contain the resultant inconsistency that appears to follow. They contend that this contrasts with other truth theorists, such as correspondence theorists, who can exclude liar sentences on principled grounds.

Before briefly turning to responses to the delimitation problem, it is worth noting another consideration that one might offer in favor of the thought that deflationists should consider being dialetheists. This consideration turns on the thought that advocates of Metaphysical Deflationism deny that there is a truth property in any substantive sense. Hence, if truth ends up being an inconsistent property, as dialetheists maintain that it does, this does not have significant implications for the nature of our world. Even if this is right and deflationists have nothing to fear about truth being inconsistent, one might worry about embracing inconsistency from the perspective of Conceptual Deflationism, as this would render the truth concept inconsistent, too. But this worry might be assuaged, as there are a number of philosophers—some of whom are not even deflationists—who have defended the idea that the truth concept is actually inconsistent (cf. Azzouni (2007), Eklund (2002), Patterson (2012), Scharp (2013), and Burgess and Burgess (2011), for good examples of what Armour-Garb (2007) calls "consistent inconsistency theories"). If deflationists find those arguments compelling, they might have a positive reason for concluding that they should embrace dialetheism.

Even if the considerations of the last paragraph make it seem like dialetheic deflationism is an attractive option, it bears noting that very few truth theorists from any camp are actually dialetheists. Hence, most advocates of deflationism will seek responses to the delimitation problem. There seem to be at least two options for a deflationary reply to the delimitation problem: solve the delimitation problem, or admit that there is no way to solve this problem but avoid contradictions by strengthening the conditionals that feature in the instances of (TS). Whereas Kripke, as we have seen, fails to satisfy SCT in virtue of the conditional and biconditional he adopts with the move to strong Kleene logic, Soames (1998) puts forward a novel account of the biconditional according to which where 'A' and 'B' are both ungrounded sentences, their biconditional is determinately true, thereby appearing to satisfy a version of CT.[49] Soames calls this binary connective the "just in case biconditional" (1998, p. 177). Hence, for Soames, where (L) is a liar sentence, '(L) is true just in case (L) is not true' is true. This would satisfy CT, but it comes at a cost, since, for Soames, Intersub fails. Hence, this is not something that deflationists would want to endorse. Another possible move is to follow Field (2008), who, as we have seen, offers a strong conditional

---

[49] Whether this satisfies SCT turns on the modal status Soames affords to the instances of that schema. So far as we know, he is silent on that status.

that supports SCT and direct Intersub. A final option would be to come up with criteria that restrict the proper targets of truth-ascriptions in a way that does not compromise SCT. We develop this last tactic in the appendix.

With respect to taking stock of the extent to which a dialetheic approach satisfies the deflationary constraints on a resolution of the Liar Paradox that we have set out in this chapter, this is somewhat complicated because, as explained above, dialetheism was originally developed by Priest within an explicitly inflationary framework. Armour-Garb and Beall (2001, 2003) argue that deflationists both can and should be dialetheists, but Priest (1987/2006) combines a teleological view of truth with his conception of dialetheism. Armour-Garb and Beall present deflationary dialetheism as supposedly satisfying whatever constraints there are on a resolution of the Liar Paradox counting as deflationary, but there are challenges to their stance on this.

It seems as if deflationary dialetheism can satisfy conditions Intersub, SCT, and ELV. Priest (1987/2006) rejects Intersub on grounds that it would turn expressions of truth-value gluts, which he accepts, into expressions of truth-value gaps, which he does not.[50] But Armour-Garb and Beall (2001, 2003) and Beall (2009) incorporate Intersub into their versions of deflationary dialetheism. Relatedly, deflationary dialetheists can accept SCT, since there is nothing about dialetheism that would prevent them from doing so. Regarding ELV, it appears open to any dialetheist to employ a three-valued logic and assign all semantically pathological cases the value i, satisfying that condition.

---

[50] To see this, suppose that a truth-value glut, viz., that p is true and p is not true, is represented as 'T([p]) ∧ ~T([p])'. If one were to sanction Intersub for both the truth and falsity predicates and, contra intuitionism, also sanction double negation elimination, then, from our "glut" sentence, they could derive '~(T([p]) ∨ F([p]))'. Since this is the statement that it is not the case that p is either true or false, it would thus express a truth-value gap. Since Priest rejects gaps, this reasoning leads him to reject Intersub.

The main worries about whether a deflationist should adopt dialetheism as a means for resolving the Liar Paradox pertains to whether dialetheism can truly be said to satisfy constraints ESC and RI, with a failure of the latter potentially threatening the combination's satisfaction of NT. The concern with respect to the first of these constraints emerges from consideration of how dialetheists can deal with the other side of semantic pathology, the kind of indeterminacy apparently manifested by the truthteller, as in (K) above. In Armour-Garb and Woodbridge (2006), we argue that dialetheism does not seem to have the resources for resolving the related case that we above have called the "Open Pair":

(OP1) Sentence (OP2) is not true.
(OP2) Sentence (OP1) is not true.

If, as we argue (2006), a dialetheist cannot deal with all variants of the Open Pair and the other cases that appear to manifest the relevant kind of indeterminacy, then this approach to the Liar Paradox will fail to resolve all cases of semantic pathology, in which case there would be certain sentences that should be semantically characterizable that elude such characterization, in violation of ESC. This remains an open challenge to Priest's form of dialetheism, and Armour-Garb and Beall (2001, 2003) and Beall (2009) fail to address this issue as well. Hence, it remains an open question as to whether their deflationary dialetheism can resolve the semantic pathology that is revealed by cases of the Open Pair and thereby genuinely satisfy ESC.

It is an even more complicated question as to how dialetheists fare with respect to RI. This is because they are not offering a *treatment* of the semantic paradoxes so much as offering a *response* to them that attempts to avoid trivialism, while accepting some contradictions. However, there is a question about how dialetheists will treat Curry's Paradox and whether it amounts to a revenge problem for dialetheism's goal of satisfying NT.

As mentioned in a footnote above, Curry's Paradox takes off from a sentence like

(C) If sentence (C) is true, then everything is true.

To see the paradoxical that (C) presents, let us represent (C) formally as

(C*) $T((C^*)) \to \bot$,

where 'T' is a truth predicate and '$\bot$' is an explosive sentence, viz., one that implies all sentences.[51] Now consider the instance of the truth schema for (C*),

(TS$_{C^*}$) $T((C^*)) \leftrightarrow (T((C^*)) \to \bot)$

Before making evident the reasoning that takes off from (C*), we need one logical principle, *Contraction*, according to which whatever follows from two assumptions of the same formulae also follows from just one assumption of that formula. We can now reason as follows from (C*) and logic:

1. $T((C^*)) \leftrightarrow (T((C^*)) \to \bot)$ Premise
2. $T((C^*)) \to (T((C^*)) \to \bot)$ 1, Df. $\leftrightarrow$
3. $T((C^*)) \to \bot$ 2 Contraction
4. $(T((C^*)) \to \bot) \to T((C^*))$ 1, Df. $\leftrightarrow$
5. $T((C^*))$ 3,4 *modus ponens*
6. $\bot$ 3,5 *modus ponens*

In this way, we have proved that every statement is true from our reasoning with (C*).

---

[51] It is standard to read '$\bot$' as something like 'Every statement is true', which captures the thesis of trivialism.

The concern that Curry's Paradox presents for dialetheists is that their standard move for blocking trivialism seems ineffective for resolving the unacceptable conclusion that the reasoning with (C*) yields. Recall that dialetheists avoid trivialism by rejecting EFQ, the principle that from a contradiction, anything follows, and accepting and employing a paraconsistent logic. (Cf. Priest (1987/2006).) That is, they accept the contradiction that the Liar Paradox reveals but block the seemingly resultant trivialism by rejecting EFQ. The problem that (C*) (and thus, (C)) presents is that the reasoning from the truth conditions for (C*) to trivialism does not go by way of a contradiction. Hence, (C) does appear to present a kind of revenge problem for dialetheists.[52]

Priest (1987/2006) proposes avoiding the disastrous conclusion that Curry sentences appear to present by rejecting Contraction at premise 3. It is of course possible to reject Contraction, but if the primary reason for doing so is that it avoids Curry's Paradox, then the move seems to be unacceptably ad hoc. A further concern, raised by Beall (2015), is that invalidating Contraction from the perspective of a dialetheist seems to undermine one of Priest's primary reasons for opting for dialetheism in the first place, viz., because it offers a "semantically complete" theory, where such a theory consists of a set of sentences that is closed under logical implication, and that theory is taken to have the capacity to express all of the truths about English within that very language. While many non-dialetheists sacrifice semantic completeness in their solution to the Liar Paradox, since Priest touts not compromising completeness as one of the virtues of dialetheism, giving it up is a high cost for him to pay. Even so, Beall (2015, p. 580) thinks that dialetheists must give up on semantic completeness, as a way of avoiding trivialism. (See Priest (2015) for a reply to Beall.)

---

[52] The thought that Curry's Paradox poses a revenge problem for a dialetheist's approach to the Liar Paradox is amplified by the fact that one can construct a "Curry-Liar sentence", viz., (CL) If sentence (CL) is true, then sentence (CL) is false.

There is one last point about the concern that Curry's Paradox presents for Priest's form of dialetheism that bears noting. As we have said, Priest maintains that all of the paradoxes of self-reference are the same kind of paradox and, hence, that they admit of the same kind of solution. That is, he is a firm supporter of (PUS). He does this by setting out the "Inclosure Schema" (henceforth, *IS*) that he claims identifies the form of such paradoxes. Now, if Curry's Paradox satisfies the IS as the Liar Paradox does, then, by Priest's lights, it must be solved in the same way as the Liar. If it does not satisfy the IS, then the question is why it does not. Priest (2000) argues that whether Curry's Paradox fits the IS depends on how the conditional involved in the Curry sentence is interpreted, leaving space for a dialetheist to treat Curry's Paradox differently.

That said, Priest's favored response to Curry's Paradox is to deny that it is an IS paradox. (Cf. Priest (1987/2006).) This enables Priest to treat that paradox differently from how he treats the IS paradoxes, such as the Liar. But this seems to come at a cost. As Ben Burgis and Otávio Bueno (2019, p. 11) note, "Given that Curry and the Liar share precisely the same paradoxical traits, if one of them falls under the IS and the other does not, this seriously undermines the plausibility of the IS as a delineator of which paradoxes fall into the same type and thus require the same solution." This is serious because one of Priest's chief considerations in favor dialetheism is the promise of offering a unified treatment of all paradoxical cases. As Priest (1987/2006, p. 169) notes, "the only satisfactory uniform approach to all these [self-reference] paradoxes is the dialetheic one". If Curry's and the Liar are to be treated differently, it would seem that Priest's consideration would be significantly undermined. If, as Priest maintains, the IS semantic paradoxes present a compelling argument for dialetheism, then, if Curry's is an IS paradox, it would constitute a compelling argument for trivialism, in violation of NT. Hence, it appears that Priest faces a dilemma: deny that Curry's is an IS paradox, which seems to undermine or at least weaken his primary case for dialetheism, or maintain the force of IS by taking

Curry's Paradox to be an IS paradox and risk falling victim to a violation of NT.

Taking stock on whether deflationists can adequately deal with the semantic paradoxes by embracing dialetheism, there remain questions about how this combination fares with respect to NT, ESC, and RI. Whether it can satisfy NT and RI turns crucially on how a dialetheist resolves Curry's Paradox. As just discussed, Priest's approach to Curry's faces a dilemma: Since neither horn of the dilemma looks attractive, there seems to be a problem regarding satisfying NT and RI for Priest. Whether deflationists should endorse dialetheism thus remains an open question, one that cannot be answered until the dialetheic response to Curry's is resolved.[53]

7.8 Deflationism, the Paradoxes, and Concluding Remarks

In examining the formal challenges that arise from the semantic paradoxes, i.e., the Liar Paradox and its kin, this chapter has explained the fourth dimension, Paradox Treatment Deflationism, that must be included in the broad four-dimensional understanding of the deflationary approach to truth-talk explained in this book. Developing a deflationary resolution of the semantic paradoxes is something that most early deflationists (e.g., Ramsey, Leeds, Brandom, and even early Horwich and Field) often "set aside for later". However, just as a threat to Metaphysical or Conceptual Deflationism poses a threat for Linguistic Deflationism, a would-be deflationary account that offers no adequate resolution of the semantic paradoxes also opens the door to an undermining of Linguistic Deflationism. With a better understanding of the

---

[53] Beall (2009) offers a different response than Priest's to Curry's Paradox, but for space considerations, we cannot set out his approach here. That said, for some concerns about Beall's response to Curry's, see Burgis and Bueno (2019).

requirements that a deflationary resolution to the semantic paradoxes must satisfy in order to adhere to Linguistic Deflationism (e.g., Intersub and SCT, along with NT, ESC, ELV, and RI), most deflationists now recognize the importance of resolving those paradoxes in a way that comports with the constraints imposed by a deflationary framework.

We have surveyed several responses to the semantic paradoxes with an eye toward assessing whether certain proposed resolutions fit with deflationism and whether they succeed in satisfying the desiderata that we have set out for adequate resolutions to those paradoxes. Not surprisingly, each of the responses that we have surveyed faces certain limitations with respect to the desiderata we have identified. Some approaches fail to satisfy the general conditions for an adequate account, while others do fairly well on that front but fail to satisfy the conditions that are required for a proposed resolution to be deflationary. This is perhaps not surprising given the resilience of revenge problems for approaches to the paradoxes.

Nevertheless, we think that there is an approach that satisfies both sets of conditions, and, in the appendix, below, we present our favored deflationary account of truth-talk and explain how it resolves the Liar Paradox and its kin while satisfying Paradox Treatment Deflationism. After setting out its key elements, we first explain how our view responds to certain challenges that have been raised for the other three dimensions of Linguistic, Metaphysical, and Conceptual Deflationism. We then demonstrate the ways in which our approach provides an adequate, revenge-immune, deflationary resolution of the full range of semantic pathology that any truth theorist must address.

If inflationists about truth are right, then *truth* is the important property (or concept) that philosophers since antiquity have believed it to be. If deflationists are right, then 'true' plays an important expressive role in our language, but there is no genuine explanatory role for either the truth concept or any truth property.

In laying out their approach, deflationists often talk about the "expressive indispensability" of truth-talk. While the version of deflationism we offer in the appendix rejects this thesis and recognizes truth-talk as dispensable, we do not wish to downplay the importance of having a truth predicate in a natural language. Our goal in writing this book is for readers to come to understand and appreciate the importance of truth-talk, while also acquiring a thorough understanding of the details involved in, and both the reasons for and the challenges to, the deflationary approach to truth.

APPENDIX

New Directions via Sentential-Variable Deflationism and Alethic Fictionalism

The generalizing role discussed in Chapter 1 is something that many deflationists, inspired by W. V. O. Quine (1970/1986), emphasize as a central purpose for truth-talk, viz., its role of providing something equivalent to a means for generalizing on embedded sentence-in-use positions. (Cf. Horwich (1990/1998, pp. 2–5)). Theorists who attempt further, less "impressionistic" explanations of this function typically proceed by relating it to the operation of sentential variables and quantifiers. To return to the examples considered in Chapter 1, the idea is that the purpose of an instance of truth-talk like 'Everything the Oracle says is true' or its less colloquial logical expansion,

(5) Everything is such that, if the Oracle says it, then it is true,

is to capture the kind of generalizing over sentence-positions that is quasi-formally indicated in the quantified-sentential-variable (henceforth, *QSV*) string,

(3) For all p, if the Oracle says that p, then p.

Many deflationists thus see truth-talk as providing a first-order surrogate for the nonstandard, higher-order logical devices indicated in (3) by 'For all p' and 'p'. However, as noted in Chapter 1, the question that remains is exactly how we should understand these logical devices, that is, the issue of precisely what their operation amounts to or involves. A comprehensive deflationary account, then, must provide an interpretation of this logical machinery, explaining what it is that truth-talk serves to express and making good on Linguistic Deflationism's claim about the central purpose of the alethic locutions.

The issue of providing an account of these sentential logical devices is especially pressing for what we consider to be the most promising starting point for developing a deflationary account of truth-talk, what we call "sentential-variable deflationism" (*SVD*). As noted in Chapter 2, this path for developing a version of deflationism traces back to Frank Ramsey (1927/1990, 1929/1991) and his appeal to sentential variables and quantifiers as the *basis* of his *explanation* of the operation and purpose of the truth predicate, as well as what the quantificational instances of truth-talk express, making his more extensive view (beyond just the simple redundancy theory he is typically associated with) the first example of SVD. This track within the deflationary approach to truth starts with sentential variables and quantifiers and uses these logical devices to explain, not just what truth-talk functions as a surrogate for, but also the logical role and the purpose of the discourse and what its quantificational instances express.[1]

Since SVD makes sentential variables and quantifiers the explanatory basis of an account of truth-talk, for an adherent of SVD to provide an adequate explanation, they must provide an independent account of sentential variables and quantifiers, that is, they must provide an adequate account of what the operation of 'p' and 'For all p' in (3) involves. This is something that Ramsey fails to do, since he simply draws an inadequate analogy with Russell's influential account of first-order quantification, and that account analyzes quantification in terms of predication, identity, and *truth*, making Ramsey's appeal to Russell's account circular in the context of SVD. As mentioned in Chapter 1, many theorists have assumed that the sentential devices employed in (3) should be understood as substitutional quantifiers and variables, but, as mentioned several times, above, there are serious concerns about this assumption, concerns that are particularly worrisome for SVD. Depending on how these substitutional devices are explained, this approach would either raise circularity concerns, by explaining substitutional quantification in terms of the *truth* of the substitution results (cf. Parsons (1971), Kripke (1976), David (1994, pp. 85–90), Horwich (1990/1998, pp. 25–26)), or it would generate "fragmentation" concerns that are connected to the Formulation Problem and the Generalization Problem (see Chapter 4, above), by explaining substitutional quantification as a means for encoding infinite conjunctions or infinite disjunctions of the substitution instances (cf. David (1994, pp. 98–99)). Either way, the substitutional approach will not work as the basis of SVD.

As also noted in Chapters 1 and 5, Jody Azzouni (2001, 2006) and Lavinia Picollo and Thomas Schindler (2018, 2022) avoid the problems that arise for the substitutional approach in their different attempts to explain truth-talk's generalizing role—that is, their accounts of how we should understand the

---

[1] Deflationists who clearly do not pursue SVD projects include Quine and Horwich, since neither takes truth-talk to be explainable in terms of logical machinery beyond the logical connectives that figure in the instances of the relevant version of the truth schema. In addition, while Leeds and Field appeal to logical machinery beyond that of first-order logic to explain the purpose of truth-talk, they both (Field at least in (1994a), though see below for a qualification) should also not be considered *sentential-variable* deflationists, since they propose to explain truth-talk in terms of other logical machinery, viz., infinite conjunctions and infinite disjunctions, rather than sentential variables and quantifiers. (But see Field (1999) and (2006), where he seems to move closer to being an SVD-ist.)

'For all p' and 'p' employed in (3) and its ilk. They do this by stipulating alternative, technical accounts of these sentential logical devices that are non-substitutional. They advocate this "stipulated formalism" approach because of certain linguistic limitations that they claim exist. In their views, there is no "truth-free" way to explain the special generalizing role that truth-talk implements using natural language, so that task requires introducing the new formal machinery that they posit. The question then for an adherent of SVD is whether such a theorist could and should co-opt any of their proposals (or some other "stipulated formalism" proposal akin to theirs) as the prior basis for an account of truth-talk. If Azzouni and Picollo and Schindler are right about what is required to explain the generalizing role indicated by the 'For all p' in (3) as well as what a sentence like (3) expresses, then SVD-ists would need to go this route. However, while theorists are, of course, free to propose whatever technical formalism they choose in the process of doing formal theorizing, when the aim is to explain some aspect of ordinary discourse (e.g., truth-talk), a stipulated technical proposal will be successful only if there is a way of understanding that formalism. Moreover, if it is possible to capture the special kind of sentential generalizing indicated in (3) by 'For all p' directly in a natural language, then, this would obviate any need for going this "stipulated formalism" route and might provide a sufficient reason for not taking this approach at all.

Moreover, Picollo and Schindler (2021, p. 41) themselves note "an important but often overlooked distinction between theories that are intended for a *descriptive* purpose (roughly, a theory that provides a faithful account of the basic usage of 'true') and those that are intended for a *logical* purpose (roughly, a theory that characterises the correctness of inferences involving 'true')." (Italics original.) With respect to this distinction, we take SVD to aim at satisfying descriptive purposes as well as logical purposes. In other words, SVD seeks to account for both what the quantificational instances of truth-talk express in ordinary language and the special generalizing role that truth-talk implements in ordinary language. As we see it, the "stipulated formalism" approach might suffice to capture or model the latter, but it falls short on explaining the former.

One way of expanding on this last point is by drawing an analogy with the "revolutionary vs. hermeneutic" distinction introduced by John Burgess and Gideon Rosen (1997) in their discussion of nominalism.[2] A revolutionary approach to theorizing involves a stipulated introduction of a new way of understanding some fragment or aspect of discourse as a means for resolving

---

[2] The revolutionary/hermeneutic distinction has also been refined and extended to discussions of *fictionalism* as an approach to theorizing, by both advocates and critics of that approach. See Stanley (2001) for an application of the distinction by a critic of fictionalism (specifically of the hermeneutic kind), and Armour-Garb and Woodbridge (2015) for an example of an application of it by advocates of (hermeneutic) fictionalism.

certain alleged problems or limitations that a theorist claims exist there. In this sense, we can think of Azzouni's and Picollo and Schindler's different "stipulated formalism" approaches as analogous to revolutionary theorizing introduced for logical purposes: They maintain that there is a limitation to the quantificational capacities of ordinary language, making it insufficient for explaining the special generalizing role that truth-talk implements in a language. To address this limitation, they introduce new, technical logical machinery designed for explaining truth-talk's logical inferential role.[3]

By contrast with a revolutionary approach, a hermeneutic approach to theorizing maintains that there is no need to offer any new, stipulated way of understanding the fragment or aspect of discourse that one is theorizing about. A hermeneutic approach maintains that what we really need is an account aimed at satisfying descriptive purposes, that is, one providing a proper understanding both of how the relevant fragment or aspect of discourse has always already functioned. Applied to truth-talk, this approach to theorizing aims to explain how the truth predicate implements its generalizing role and what the quantificational instances of truth-talk express. Once this is attained, the putative problems or limitations with the discourse that a revolutionary theorist might claim as a motivation for offering their approach are revealed to be illusory. Thus, a hermeneutic counter to the revolutionary aspect of the "stipulated formalism" approach that Azzouni and Picollo and Schindler adopt would maintain that the quantificational capacity of ordinary language is not limited in a way that prevents it from being able to explain both the special generalizing role that truth-talk implements in a language and what its quantificational instances express. In the next section, we develop a hermeneutic approach that explains the generalizing role that truth-talk implements directly in English, as the basis for underwriting SVD. This is not to say that this role can be formulated in the framework of first-order logic; rather, we maintain that, while the quantificational capacity of English and other ordinary languages includes first-order quantification over objects, it also extends beyond that mode of quantification.

We have brought in the revolutionary/hermeneutic distinction, as applied to the aforementioned different types of approaches to explaining what exactly the special generalizing role that truth-talk implements in a language is, in order to make the following points. If a proposed hermeneutic account of some fragment or aspect of discourse is adequate, then the alleged problems that purport to motivate a revolutionary account dissolve. Hence, methodologically, if there are "equally good" competing accounts, one revolutionary and the other hermeneutic, one should endorse the hermeneutic account. Moreover, a hermeneutic account is better suited to satisfying both logical

---

[3] Similarly, our suggestion in Section 7.2, that one read Tarski's approach as a "replacement theory" of truth, would make his view count as revolutionary in this sense. The "revolutionary" label would also apply to Kevin Scharp's (2013) approach to truth, given his contention that the ordinary notion of truth is an inconsistent concept that needs to be replaced in the way he proposes.

and descriptive purposes for theorizing. In light of this, since the hermeneutic proposal that we offer below is adequate to account for the generalizing role that truth-talk plays and what its quantificational instances express in a natural language like English, and, moreover, since it accomplishes this in ordinary English, we have a reason for favoring that approach over Azzouni's and Picollo and Schindler's revolutionary approaches. After all, if truth-talk really is a means for implementing a logico-linguistic role that we can already explain in ordinary English, then there is no need to introduce the special sorts of formal devices that these theorists posit.

Given all of these considerations, we maintain that the best way to fulfill SVD aspirations is by adapting an approach that emerges from A. N. Prior's work. As mentioned in Section 3.1.1, Prior (1956, 1971) understands sentential variables and quantifiers as sui generis formal devices that function as non-nominal, *adverbial* sentential variables and quantifiers.[4] Accordingly, we call this type of deflationary account of truth-talk "adverbial sentential-variable deflationism" (henceforth, *ASVD*).

A.1 ASVD and the "How-Talk" NLI Approach

In developing ASVD, one need not follow Prior and embrace his informal adverbial quantifier and variable neologisms of 'anywhether', 'somewhether', and 'thether' described in Chapter 3.[5] These ("revolutionary") neologisms do maintain a "structural" clarity in tracking the form of a QSV string, such as

(3) For all p, if the Oracle says that p, then p,

by rendering it informally as

(3*) For anywhether, if the Oracle says that thether, then thether.

However, Prior's neologisms, as stipulated devices, provide only an impressionistic grasp of his adverbial reading of sentential variables and quantifiers.[6]

---

[4] It is not clear whether Prior's account of sentential variables and quantifiers is revolutionary or hermeneutic, since it seems to involve elements of each, as the discussions in Chapter 3 and in the next section illustrate.

[5] Cf. Armour-Garb and Woodbridge (2023a), where we introduce and motivate this version of SVD as a means for accounting for the so-called "alethic platitudes", which relate to some of the conceptual explanations discussed above in Chapter 6. Armour-Garb and Woodbridge (2023b) applies this "how-talk" approach to the full range of 'true'-employing what-explanations considered in Chapter 6. What follows (cf. Armour-Garb and Woodbridge (forthcoming)) updates and expands on those discussions of what we now call "ASVD".

[6] The same holds for the hyphenated expression 'things-are-thus' that Künne (forthcoming) employs in his newer, adverbial account of sentential variables and quantifiers. While this is not quite a neologism, it is still a stipulated technical term, rather than a natural language expression.

For a more adequate account of the formal devices that we can use to *explain* (rather than merely *model*) the generalizing role of truth-talk and what its quantificational instances express, we prefer the hermeneutic approach of interpreting them in language that we already understand, and for this we need to go beyond these stipulated expressions. Prior himself suggests how to do this as well, when he briefly notes that one can understand 'For some p, p' in terms of 'Things are somehow' and can understand 'For all p, if she says that p, then p' in terms of 'However she says things are, thus they are (or, that's how they are)'. (Cf. Prior (1967, p. 229; 1971, p. 38).)

We maintain that there are ways of extending Prior's ("hermeneutic") "how-talk" suggestions to provide an adverbial reading of sentential quantification in general in grammatical English. If, following Prior's aforementioned appeal to Ludwig Wittgenstein, we take 'this is how things are', or, more typically, 'that is how things are', along with 'things are thus', as English adverbial sentential-variable expressions, then we can interpret the QSV strings employing sentential quantifiers and variables via English how-talk, using the ordinary English expressions 'somehow' to interpret 'For some p' or 'there is some p such that', and 'however' to interpret 'For all p'. For example, we can understand a particular QSV string, for example,

(6) For some p, p and the Oracle said that p,

in terms of

(7) For somehow things are, that is how things are, and the Oracle said that that is how things are.[7]

Sentence (7) is intentionally formulated in a way that tracks the structure of the QSV string (6), which is what Prior's neologisms are specifically designed to do. It bears noting that quantifying with respect to "how things are" should not require that there always *are* such things that are thus, as (7) suggests. Agustín Rayo and Stephen Yablo (2001) handle this by reading the how-talk quantifiers (governing predicate-positions for relational predicates) *disjunctively*, in terms of somehow and however some things are *or are not* related. We can modify this move to apply to quantifiers governing sentential variables by expanding the how-talk quantifier interpretations of them to make their full forms 'For however things are or are not' and 'For somehow things are or are not.[8] Applying this to (7) then yields

---

[7] It is important to recognize that the use of the expression 'things' in the English phrases 'that is how things are' and 'things are thus' is, like the German 'es' in 'es verhält sich so', not ontologically committing. One way to see this is in the inappropriateness of the questions 'Which things?' or 'Which ones?' in response to those English phrases.

[8] The disjunctive element of how-talk quantification is missing from the discussion in Armour-Garb and Woodbridge (2023a).

(7+) For somehow things are or are not, that is how things are, and the Oracle said that that is how things are.

With the disjunctive element of how-talk quantification thus made explicit, we can provide a natural-language interpretation (henceforth, *NLI*) of a universal generalization like (3) as follows.

(8) For however things are or are not, if the Oracle says that that is how things are, then that is how things are.

It is possible to generate a condensed form of (8)—what we describe as *absorption*—in which the quantifier and the sentential-variable-employing antecedent of the conditional formula it governs in the QSV string get combined. We can already see this in Prior's suggestion for capturing a universal QSV string with how-talk, where the universal generalizing and the "filtering" performed by a separate antecedent are combined. Thus, the condensed how-talk rendering of (3) is

(8*) However the Oracle says that things are, that is how things are.[9]

A similar sort of "absorption" might also be applied to (7+) to produce what we call an "absorption-variant" how-talk NLI of (6). This yields a rendering that is not internally redundant and is closer to Prior's original, more colloquial, suggestion, namely,

(7*) The Oracle said that things are somehow, and that is how they are.[10]

The type of absorption that (8*) and (7*) illustrate is similar to how the object-variable 'it', along with the antecedent of a conditional that employs that variable, sometimes gets absorbed into the English quantifiers 'something' or 'everything' in more colloquial interpretations, for example, in providing the English-language sentence

(U*) Rufus enjoyed everything he ate.

as an interpretation of

(U) $\forall x(A(r,x) \to E(r,x))$.

---

[9] Note that how the Oracle says that things are might involve things not being somehow in particular, so the disjunctive aspect of the explicit how-talk quantification expression also gets absorbed.

[10] Some have balked at the grammaticality of the construction 'things are somehow'. To mitigate such concerns, one could replace that phrase with 'things are situated somehow', modifying the sentential-variable expression to 'that is how things are situated'. Similarly, in sentence (8), above, the word 'situated' can be added after both instances of 'are'. Alternatively, one could embrace Sellars's use of 'how things hang together' and replace the relevant uses of 'how things are' and the "how-talk" quantifiers with versions incorporating that turn of phrase.

To understand the operation of how-talk quantification in a bit more detail, and in the interest of seeing how the method of using it to give the NLIs of QSV strings works more generally, consider a case like

(9) For all p, p.[11]

While obviously no one should accept (9), it bears noting that, in giving the NLI for this universal generalization, one must take care not to jump to the more colloquial absorption-variant, 'However things are, that is how things are'. This is because this how-talk sentence already involves the variable/antecedent-absorption explained above and is really the NLI of 'For all p, if p, then p'. Instead, the NLI for (9) should apply the full disjunctive form of the how-talk quantifier expression to the QSV string. This yields

(10) For however things are or are not, that is how things are.

A potentially more condensed variant involving variable-absorption might be 'Everyhow is how things are', or, following Prior's rendering of 'For some p, p' as 'Things are somehow',

(10*) Things are everyhow.[12]

Both (10) and its absorption-variant (10*) can be understood by English speakers (the latter employs an archaic expression rather than a neologism), even if speakers recognize that the claims are false because they entail contradictions.

To see the details of the interaction of the how-talk quantifiers with negation (including the parallels with how objectual quantifiers and negation interact), consider the following QSV string:

(11) For some p, ~p.

Applying the NLI procedure to (11), as we did in generating (10) from (9), yields

(12) For somehow things are or are not, that is not how things are.

Just as (10) has (10*) as an absorption-variant, (12) can be similarly condensed to

(12*) Things are not somehow.

As a result of the variable-absorption in (12*), the negation it employs attaches to the how-talk quantifier expression directly.

---

[11] Rumfitt (2014, p. 28) acknowledges this sort of extension of the how-talk interpretations that Prior suggests, in noting that the approach can be applied to express logical laws, such as the classical law of double negation. Following our particular way of doing this, 'For all p, p iff ~~p' ($\forall p(p \leftrightarrow \sim\sim p)$) would be interpreted in terms of 'For however things are or are not, they are thus if, and only if, it is not the case that it is not the case that they are thus.

[12] If one prefers to avoid our revival of the expression 'everyhow', the expression 'anyhow whatsoever' can serve in its stead, resulting in the NLI 'Things are anyhow whatsoever'.

The line of reasoning analogous to that regarding (11) also applies to interpreting the use of negation with a universal adverbial quantifier, as found in the QSV string,

(13) For all p, ~p.

The NLI procedure here yields

(14) For however things are or are not, that is not how things are.

As in the previous two examples, this official NLI can be condensed into an absorption-variant, in this case using a standard variant of the universal quantifier 'however', to yield the seemingly meaningful (albeit unacceptable) English sentence,

(14*) Things are not anyhow.

The how-talk NLI procedure also extends to multiple adverbial quantifiers. For example, applying the foregoing points about variable/antecedent-absorption and negation, the QSV string

(15) For all p, there is some q such that $((p \wedge ([q] = [\sim p])) \to \sim q)$[13]

gets a how-talk NLI along the lines of

(16) For however things are or are not, there is somehow things are or are not, such that if the former is how things are, and the latter being how things are amounts to the former not being how things are, then the latter is not how things are.

We maintain that this how-talk NLI approach provides an adequate account of sentential variables and quantifiers: It explains the logical devices in independent terms and ultimately in ordinary language that we already understand. The most striking aspect of this how-talk NLI approach that we develop from Prior's suggestions is that it deploys a form of non-nominal quantification, which does not involve a domain of entities that serve as the values of the variables (no "hows"), or even a class of linguistic items that serve as the substituends of the sentential variables. That is, these quantifiers are not *objectual*, as they do not range over a domain of things, and they are not *substitutional*, since, as Ian Rumfitt (2014, p. 27) notes, while considering Prior's use of such quantifiers, "things might be said or thought to be somehow, even though no sentence in a given substitution class says that things are thus. From a formal point of view, these

---

[13] This is the QSV re-rendering of a sentence that Wright (1992, p. 34) claims is an alethic platitude, 'For every true proposition, there is a negation of it that is a false proposition.' The use of nominalized sentential variables, '[q]' and '[~p]', in (15) is to be understood as employed in (TS) from Chapter 1. Here it provides a QSV "non-entity-implicating" rendering of Wright's (1992) talk of propositions and their negations.

'non-nominal' quantifiers are a species of higher-order quantifier". There are no things of any sort that get associated with the sentential variables; the quantifiers that govern them implement an entirely sui generis non-nominal type of generalizing.

A.2 The Merits of ASVD

An interesting consequence of the ASVD how-talk NLI approach is that it reveals that truth-talk is *not* expressively indispensable, contrary to what most contemporary deflationists maintain. On our understanding, any generalization that other deflationists would claim we must use truth-talk to express could also be expressed, albeit a bit more awkwardly, with a how-talk generalization.[14] As we will show, this approach to explaining the functioning of truth-talk will help avoid several problems that confront different species of the deflationary approach to truth. At the same time, we should also note that ASVD is not a cure-all that makes all of the problems with truth-talk that deflationists must address simply disappear. However, even where it does not directly eliminate problems, we think that it opens the door to ways of resolving them that comport with the deflationary approach to truth.

A.2.1 Avoiding the Formulation and Generalization Problems

One type of problem that our approach eliminates includes the issues surrounding both the Formulation Problem (FP) and the Generalization Problem (GP) discussed in Chapter 4. This elimination results from a central element of our proposal: that it deploys the non-nominal generalizing operation implemented via the quantification that we find in how-talk. A potential concern about this understanding of how-talk quantification arises from a standard view about quantification stemming from Quine, namely, that all quantification or generalization is nominal and objectual. Even non-Quineans who embrace substitutional quantification still consider the substitutional variables to be associated with a class of *things* (in their case, linguistic items). These understandings of quantification might raise a suspicion that our proposal fails to provide an

---

[14] The issue of how to treat *transparent* instances of truth-talk, such as 'It is true that birds are dinosaurs' or '"Birds are dinosaurs' is true", seems to be a challenge for SVD. There are two ways that SVDists have approached it: i) by assuming a separate "redundancy" account for transparent instances (as Ramsey and Prior seem to do), or ii) by treating transparent instances as implicitly quantificational (similar to opaque instances, as C. J. F. Williams seems to do). We leave this issue aside here, since our focus is on how the truth predicate operates in the more interesting, explicitly or at least plausibly quantificational instances, and what such instances of truth-talk express.

adequate account of sentential variables and quantifiers, since our adverbial understanding of these logical devices rejects both of these dicta. One who endorses Quine's view of quantification might even declare our view incoherent, unless we analyze how-talk quantification in terms of nominal and objectual quantification over something like *ways*. This objector would insist that the most accurate NLI for (3) is not (8)/(8*) but rather

(8**) Whatever way the Oracle says that things are, that is the way things are.

We maintain that non-nominal quantification is legitimate, since it can be interpreted in terms of natural language that we already understand. In fact, for a deflationist who is accounting for sentential variables, our approach is to be preferred. On the legitimacy issue, while one *can* understand sentential variables and the quantifiers that govern them in terms of nominal quantification over ways, one is not *required* to do so. Siding with Prior (1971), and more recently with Rayo and Yablo (2001), we maintain that non-nominal quantification is a completely legitimate sui generis form of generalizing. After all, how-talk is perfectly legitimate English, and only one in the grips of a contentious theory would demand that English how-talk is to be explained or explicated in terms of English ways-talk. In fact, a claim like 'I'll manage it somehow' is no less clear, if not clearer than, the claim 'I'll manage it in some way' or the claim 'There is some way that I'll manage it'.[15]

We should also note that our non-nominal understanding of how-talk quantification, as employed to interpret sentential variables and quantifiers, avoids a potential internal conflict within a would-be SVD account of truth-talk. We have acknowledged that one *can* understand sentential quantification in terms of nominal quantification over *ways*, if one wants to do so. (Cf. Künne (2003).) But consider that, if there were ways, then a natural understanding of the "global" level of ways that this approach would need, to fit with an interpretation of the bound sentential variable 'p' as 'that is the way things are', is as possible worlds, however one understands such things. (Cf. Lewis (1986) and Stalnaker (1976).) But then there would be sets of possible worlds, which would amount to propositions (at least of a coarse-grained, unstructured sort). If there were propositions of this sort, then, as Hartry Field (1992, pp. 322–23) notes, it would follow directly that, for any proposition, there is a basic set-theoretic property—having the actual world as a member—that amounts to the property of being true. So, quantifying over ways would lead to the conclusion that the truth predicate serves to attribute a property to propositions. In the context of pursuing SVD, this conclusion conflicts with that approach's thesis that the truth predicate is just a linguistic device of convenience that allows us to express what would otherwise require the use of sentential variables and quantifiers. So,

---

[15] For other possible objections to the non-nominal adverbial approach and our replies to them, see Armour-Garb and Woodbridge (2023a and forthcoming).

an advocate of SVD cannot explain these logical devices in terms of objectual quantification over ways. By contrast, the non-nominal, adverbial quantification approach fits with the truth predicate just being a linguistic device of convenience that does not attribute any genuine property.

The non-nominal aspect of how-talk quantification is the element of our approach that allows it to avoid both the FP and the GP. On the one hand, since the quantifier 'however' does not simply encode infinite conjunctions or infinite disjunctions of the instances of the "formulae" it prefixes, the generalizations it expresses are not fragmented ersatz generalizations. On the other hand, since our procedure thereby avoids a central challenge facing deflationary accounts of alethic generalizations, and since it clearly involves a genuine form of generalizing, it is not obvious what argument could be made that it falls afoul of the FP. Regarding the GP, since our ASVD account of truth-talk is not an infinitely axiomatized or otherwise fragmented account the way that those of Horwich and potentially Field and Brandom are, we are not plagued by the Tarski-inspired concerns that originally motivated the GP. As a result, there seems to be nothing preventing us from applying whatever methods that truth theorists like Halbach, Horsten, Picollo and Schindler, and others employ to avoid the GP.

Our non-nominal approach also avoids any fragmentation concerns that arise from the uses of sentential variables and quantifiers discussed in Chapters 5 and 6, as a means for QSV recastings of certain 'true'-employing explanations that have been offered as challenges to Metaphysical and Conceptual Deflationism. According to our account, sentential variables and quantifiers are to be interpreted in terms of natural-language how-talk and the non-nominal, adverbial quantification over *how things are*, that is, *how the world is* that this involves. On this understanding, there is something that provides unity and substantiality in the QSV recastings of the relevant explanations. Consider, for example, the recasting of the 'true'-employing account of assertion provided in Section 6.1, viz., 'When one asserts, one presents the world as being such that, in it, for some p, p'. While reading the formal devices 'for some p' and 'p' in term of "how-talk" might fragment how *in particular* each different assertion presents the world as being, making this a case-by-case matter, they all always involve the same substantive thing—the world—being presented in the same manner—as being such that, in it, things are somehow.[16] This avoids the fragmentation concerns that an appeal to sentential variables and quantifiers might generate. It prevents the "fragmenting" aspect of deflationism itself (i.e., the fact that the members of the "set of truths" have nothing substantive in common) from spreading to other concepts, when deflationists find the use of truth-talk in certain what-explanations of those concepts acceptable.

---

[16] Armour-Garb and Woodbridge (2023b) provides similar "how-talk" renderings of the other sentential-variable recastings of 'true'-employing accounts of belief, knowledge, and validity.

A.2.2 Emergence and Resolution of the Liar Paradox

One challenge to deflationism about truth (and, plausibly, to every approach to theorizing about truth or truth-talk) that does not simply disappear on our ASVD how-talk NLI approach is the putative challenge of semantic pathology that is posed by the Liar Paradox and its kin. The reason for this is because, even if one "eliminates" truth-talk in favor of antecedently and independently explained sentential variables and quantifiers, liar sentences still emerge given this formal machinery. Consider, for example, the QSV string

(C) For all p, if ⌜p⌝ = (C), then ~p.[17]

Sentence (C) yields paradox, if, as it seems, it entails its own negation, and the negation of (C) entails (C). This particular quasi-formal example employs quotation, which, since these "brackets" function as corner quotes, might suggest a possible resolution in terms of a gap between the mention of the sentence in the antecedent and the (negated) use of it in the consequent.

No such gap is present, however, for the liar sentence that emerges when the sentential variables employed in (C) are given a how-talk NLI. This yields what we shall call the "How-Talk Liar":

(HL) For however things are or are not, if (HL) presents things as being thus, then that is not how things are.

The aforementioned potential gap in (C) disappears in (HL) because the latter replaces (C)'s mentioned occurrence of the sentential variable with a nominalized but still used (natural-language) sentential variable by bringing in the notion of "how a sentence presents things as being", which can be universally generalized over to yield the quantificational clause of (HL). Though perfectly grammatical, one might view (HL) as somewhat artificial, so we might also consider an absorption-variant like 'However (HL) presents things as being, that is not how things are', or, to use the Priorian form employed in the examples above,

(HL*) Things are not however (HL*) presents them as being.

To see how this case yields apparent paradox, consider the following line of reasoning as applied to (HL*): Either things are however (HL*) presents them as being, or things are not however (HL*) presents them as being. Suppose that things are however (HL*) presents them as being. In that case, given how (HL*) presents things as being, things are not however (HL*)

---

[17] See Simmons (1999, p. 460), where recognition of this putatively paradox-yielding sentence is attributed to Tarski. Cf. Hill (2002, pp. 116–18, 121–26) on how paradox follows directly from logical machinery that quantifies into sentence-position (which he attempts to view as "substitutional quantification for propositions") without appealing to a truth predicate.

presents them as being. So, if things are however (HL*) presents them as being, then things are not however (HL*) presents them as being. Suppose, then, that things are not however (HL*) presents them as being. But, in that case, given that this is how (HL*) presents things as being, things are however (HL*) presents them as being. So, if things are not however (HL*) presents them as being, then things are however (HL*) presents them as being. Thus, the familiar, putatively paradox-yielding looping that occurs in reasoning with the Liar Paradox also arises for reasoning with (HL*) and its kin.[18] The takeaway point here is that, in virtue of being a way of implementing sentential variables and quantifiers in natural language, how-talk, just like truth-talk, appears to yield paradox.

We maintain that ASVD opens the door to a resolution, or rather a dissolution, of the paradoxicality that (C) and (HL)/(HL*) appear to present. The interpretation of these formal devices in terms of how-talk, and the anaphoric functioning of this adverbial way of talking, allows for the application of our (2013, 2014a, 2015) dissolution of semantic pathology in terms of semantic defectiveness (what we sometimes call "s-defectiveness").

The anaphoric functioning of sentential variables interpreted via adverbial NLIs arises in virtue of the demonstratives involved in the how-talk expressions '*that* is how things are' and '*this* is how things are'. These adverbial expressions seek to inherit a presenting of things as being somehow from some demonstrated presenting of things as being somehow. To see this, consider the following sequence of claims:

(17) Birds are dinosaurs.

(18) However (17) presents things as being, that is how things are.

(19) However (18) presents things as being, that is not how things are.

The second clauses in (18) and (19) both point back to how the sentences mentioned in their quantificational clauses present things as being, indicating this presenting with the demonstrative 'that'. The adverbial locution 'is how things are' serves to denominalize the demonstrated presenting of things as being somehow, with the result that the sentence anaphorically inherits that presenting and makes it indirectly (negated, in the case of (19)). We can see from this sequence of sentences that sometimes sentences inherit a presenting of things as being somehow from sentences that themselves present things as being somehow only indirectly via *anaphoric inheritance*: (19) inherits a presenting of things being somehow from (18), which itself presents things as being somehow only indirectly, via its own anaphoric inheritance of this from

---

[18] This reasoning, of course, assumes that (HL*) succeeds in presenting things as being somehow, but, as with standard liar sentences, rejecting that assumption is part of a *response* to the paradoxicality that the sentence appears to yield.

(17). Since (17) presents things as being somehow directly, the inheritance operations of both (18) and (19) "ground out", resulting in all three sentences presenting things as being somehow: in (18) as their being how (17) presents them as being, and in (19), via two stages of inheritance and negation, as their not being how (17) presents them as being.

Unlike in the case of (17)–(19), however, sometimes the content-inheritance operation of the adverbial sentential-variable expressions fails to ground out. This occurs, for example, in (HL) and (HL*). To see this, consider how in (HL) the combined generalizing and filtering of how things are attempts to hone in on however (HL) itself presents things to be. But since (HL) involves anaphoric how-talk sentential-variable expressions, it only presents things as being somehow indirectly, via an inheritance of such a presenting. The specific presenting it seeks to inherit is the one that its filtering hones in on, which, again, is however (HL) presents things as being. In other words, (HL) attempts to inherit a presenting of things as being somehow from itself, with the result that it loops endlessly back onto itself and thus never manages to land on any actual direct presenting of things being somehow. The same diagnosis holds for its variant, (HL*), as an interested reader can confirm.

In our (2013, 2014a, 2015), we explain how the quasi-anaphoric aspect of our accounts of truth-talk, reference-talk, and predicate-satisfaction-talk enables us to provide both diagnoses of, and treatment for, the full range of cases of putative semantic pathology. In addition to the Liar Paradox, this includes Curry's, Yablo's, Grelling's, and Berry's, along with the truthteller and all of the indeterminate analogs we identify for the rest of these putative semantic paradoxes. (It also covers all of the dual-symptom variants of the Open Pair.) We (2015) provide a principled, unified solution for the putative semantic pathology manifested in certain sentences employing these traditional semantic notions, by showing that none of them has any of what we call "real-world content". This is because these putatively pathological sentences do not specify any "M-conditions" ('M' for "meaning", although we now think that 'W' for "worldly" might have been better), which is to say that they do not end up indicating anything about the world. They, therefore, all turn out to be s-defective in our specified sense. These sentences have this status in virtue of a content-seeking type of looping that arises in their quasi-anaphoric semantic functioning.[19] This looping keeps the semantic reach of these sentences from

---

[19] Our diagnosis of semantic pathology in terms of the sort of looping (and thus not "grounding out") that we have described here and in our (2013, 2014a, 2015) is similar to (and inspired by) the diagnosis that Grover (1977) offers that is discussed in Section 7.5. But, as explained there, in marked contrast with our approach to the *treatment* of such cases, Grover's treatment of the semantic paradoxes suffers from a number of problems (related to those that plague Kripke's (1975) proposed treatment of the Liar Paradox) that our treatment avoids.

making contact with the world, thereby yielding a defect in their semantic operation.[20] Since the problematic sentences are all thereby s-defective, they cannot serve as premises or conclusions in any arguments, nor, we argue, can they be embedded in truth-functional constructions without rendering the whole s-defective as well. As a result, the putative instances of (TS) one might syntactically construct for s-defective sentences will be s-defective as well. This "infectious" aspect of s-defectiveness factors into the immunity that we (2015, Ch. 5) argue our dissolution of semantic pathology has to the sorts of revenge problems that plague other responses to versions of the Liar Paradox and its kin. In this way, our view satisfies condition RI, which is required for the adequacy of any proposed resolution of the semantic paradoxes. Moreover, given the diagnosis that we provided above, viz., of (HL)'s and (HL*)'s semantic looping in virtue of the anaphoric operation of their how-talk sentential-variable expressions, the same treatment can be applied to resolve the apparent pathology presented by the sentential-variable analogs of the apparently pathological cases of truth-talk.

While the above provides only a brief sketch of how we resolve the semantic paradoxes, it bears noting that our approach fares well with respect to the general constraints on an adequate resolution of the paradoxes and the details of Paradox Treatment Deflationism that we set out and articulated in Chapter 7. We have just explained how our view satisfies the general condition of revenge immunity (RI). Since our approach explains the putatively paradox-yielding sentences as lacking worldly content and, so, as being, in a certain sense, meaningless, neither they nor the putative instances of (TS) syntactically constructed from them are the sorts of things with which we can or should reason. This blocks any reasoning thought to yield trivialism and, thus, enables us to uphold the general condition of nontrivialism (NT).

Armed with the notion of s-defectiveness, we (2015, Ch. 5) explain how to characterize the putatively pathological sentences semantically, both those that appear to exhibit inconsistency and those that appear to exhibit indeterminacy (along with the various "dual-symptom" cases as well). This enables us to satisfy exhaustive semantic characterization (ESC). Moreover, we can also explain how our approach satisfies exhaustive logical valuation (ELV), by arguing that, while those sentences with *determinable* (classical) logical values are assigned those logical values, s-defective sentences do not admit of any logical values, since they are not even *apt* for such values at all. This is because these sentences

---

[20] In the larger context of the pretense-based accounts that we develop in our (2015) and that we briefly return to below, we explain the quasi-anaphoric operation of all of the traditional semantic locutions, which yields the looping that results in s-defectiveness, as a product of the principles of generation that govern the use of the semantic locutions according to the games of make-believe that we claim underlie the traditional semantic fragments of discourse.

do not meet the standard semantic requirement for receiving a logical value, in a way similar to how Noam Chomsky's sentence, 'Colorless green ideas sleep furiously', fails to receive a logical value on semantic grounds.[21] Thus, on our view, every sentence that *can* have a logical value does.

With respect to the further conditions required to satisfy Paradox Treatment Deflationism, our approach to putative semantic pathology sanctions direct intersubstitution between any sentence, S, and a truth-ascription to it, 'S is true', for all non-opaque contexts (thereby satisfying Intersub). As discussed in Chapter 7, this has consequences for the satisfaction of Strong Convention T (SCT). If we uphold classical logic and refrain from assigning any logical value to s-defective sentences (declaring them in effect to constitute "garbage sentences"), then, given Intersub, we get all of the non-s-defective instances of the truth schema, (TS), with an equivalence based on sameness of content, which satisfies SCT.

A.2.3 ASVD and the Conservativeness Argument

Understanding truth-talk in terms of sentential variables and quantifiers, which are themselves interpreted in terms of how-talk may have consequences for one of the central concerns that appear to threaten Metaphysical Deflationism, viz., the Conservativeness Argument. As discussed in Section 5.2.3, when responding to this challenge, Picollo and Schindler (2018) contend that, for deflationary truth theories, the truth predicate serves as a tool for mimicking higher-order quantification from within a first-order framework. In particular, they maintain that truth-talk enables users to implement quantification into sentence- and predicate-positions, where they explain these types of higher-order quantification in terms of stipulated technical formalisms. We maintain that our interpretation of higher-order quantification in terms of how-talk can capture certain results that Picollo and Schindler demonstrate regarding the function of truth-talk, using their stipulated formalisms. If we are right about this, it has important consequences for ASVD's ability to respond to the Conservativeness Argument. As a reminder from our discussion in Section 5.2 and directly above, Picollo and Schindler (2018, p. 345) argue that the original conservativeness constraint imposed by Stuart Shapiro (1998), Jeffrey Ketland (1999), and others should not be required for the adequacy of deflationary truth theories. They (Picollo and Schindler (2021, p. 62)) claim that "[t]he conservativeness requirement should be given up." Their argument for this is as follows. First, they demonstrate that truth-talk mimics second-order quantification within a first-order framework. Second, they observe that

---

[21] For a defense of the decision not to assign a logical value to semantically defective claims, see Warren (2023).

adopting second-order resources, which include those of second-order quantification into predicate-position, sometimes results in a non-conservative extension of a first-order theory. From these considerations they infer that, since, for a deflationist, the truth predicate simulates these second-order resources, it follows that adding a deflationary truth theory to a first-order theory will occasionally result in a non-conservative extension of the latter. Thus, given the apparent inevitability of non-conservativeness for a deflationary truth theory, they conclude (2021, p. 68) that deflationists should be "untied to the conservativity requirement", thereby rejecting the presupposition of the Conservativeness Argument, viz., that conservativeness must be preserved for the adequacy of any deflationary truth theory.

To demonstrate the way in which truth-talk mimics second-order quantification, Picollo and Schindler (2018, p. 333) consider an instance of truth-talk of the form

(20) There is a predicate x, such that the concatenation of x with 'Tom' is true.

This, they maintain, captures the second-order quantification found in

(21) $\exists X\, X(\text{Tom})$.

To demonstrate how our ASVD account of truth-talk also captures second-order quantification, we start with an analysis of (20) in terms of sentential variables and quantifiers, as presented by the quasi-formal string

(20^{SV}) There is a predicate x, such that, for all p, if the concatenation of x with 'Tom' = $\ulcorner p \urcorner$, then p.

Applying our how-talk NLI approach, as developed in Section A.1, above, to (20^{SV}) would yield something along the lines of

(22) There is a predicate x, such that, however things are presented as being in the concatenation of x with 'Tom', that is how things are.

It bears noting that how-talk quantification also operates in a more "specifying" form, where the "global" or "non-specific" expression 'things' that occurs in the *sentential* variable and quantifier how-talk locutions gets replaced by a subject expression, for example, names or definite descriptions, as well as existential and universal objectual quantifiers. (Cf. Rayo and Yablo (2001).) This allows us to reformulate what (22) expresses more concisely with

(23) There is a predicate x, such that, however Tom is, the concatenation of x with 'Tom' presents how Tom is.

Recall how Picollo and Schindler illustrate the way that a disquotational truth predicate can capture second-order quantification by suggesting that (20) can be taken to express what we might call a "semantically ascended implementation" of the quantification found in (21). Similarly, we suggest that (23) can be taken as a semantically ascended implementation of the how-talk quantification found in

(23*) Tom is somehow.

What (23*) reveals, even more explicitly than (23) does, is that the more "specifying" form of how-talk quantification implements quantification into *predicate*-position, rather than into *sentence*-position. As a result, (23*) captures how we would apply the non-nominal quantification available in another form of how-talk to interpret (21). Showing that one can express the generalizing implemented in (23*) in terms of (22) reveals that how-talk's *sentential* quantifier and variable role can also capture a *second-order* quantification role that how-talk also plays.[22] So, adding a truth predicate understood in terms of our ASVD account of truth-talk to a first-order theory includes adding the resources of second-order quantification to that theory, along with the resources of sentential variables and quantifiers.

Suppose, then, that Picollo and Schindler are right about the two premises in their argument for rejecting the conservativeness constraint on deflationary truth theories, and suppose as well that we are right that truth-talk's being a means for expressing the non-nominal adverbial quantification found in how-talk covers both sentential quantification and quantification into predicate-position. In that case, it would seem that understanding truth-talk in terms of how-talk would enable the truth predicate to function in ways that parallel how Picollo and Schindler describe it as functioning in their account, viz., as mimicking their stipulated technical interpretations of higher-order quantification. Now consider an extension of first-order Peano Arithmetic (PA) that involves just the addition of higher-order logical resources that allow for the expression of certain arithmetical principles that entail sentences that are not provable from within PA. If the higher-order quantification implemented in the formulations of those arithmetical principles can be interpreted in terms of how-talk, then the addition to this first-order theory of the non-nominal adverbial quantification implemented by how-talk would also result in a non-conservative extension of that theory. Thus, if adding a truth predicate to a first-order theory amounts to adding the logical resources of how-talk quantification to that theory, and we claim that it does, then adding a truth predicate understood in terms of our

---

[22] We should also note that, when how-talk functions to capture quantification into predicate-position, the how-talk implements *adjectival* quantification, rather than the adverbial quantification it implements when it captures *sentential* quantification. But this is not surprising, since some linguistic theories recognize adverbs and adjectives as subcategories of a broader "supercategory" of modifier, labeled 'A'. For more on this, see Carnie (2013, p. 51).

ASVD account of truth-talk would inevitably yield a non-conservative extension of the relevant first-order theory. This would seem to render the conservativeness constraint on deflationism otiose. In other words, if, by employing a how-talk interpretation of higher-order quantification, we can do, or at least can *mimic*, whatever Picollo and Schindler claim to be able to do with their "stipulated formalism" accounts of higher-order quantification, the mimicking of which they argue is the function of a disquotational truth predicate, then we can follow their lead and draw a similar conclusion against the requirement of a conservativeness constraint. In that case, like them, and like Volker Halbach (2011) and others, who likewise reject this constraint, we would respond to the Conservativeness Argument by denying its presupposition that conservativeness is a requirement for an adequate version of deflationism.

A.2.4 Why Have a Truth Predicate?

We have advocated for an account of truth-talk in terms of sentential variables and quantifiers that have been given a prior, independent account, specifically one that interprets these formal devices via natural-language how-talk. One consequence of our ASVD how-talk NLI approach is an acknowledgment that these devices of generalization already exist in English. As we have seen, this even emerges from our response to the Conservativeness Argument. Hence, contrary to what contemporary deflationists have claimed going all the way back to Quine's (1970/1986) original observations of the role and function of truth-talk, we take truth-talk actually to be expressively *dispensable*. If our dispensability thesis is correct, then natural languages like English do not need a truth predicate to capture all of the expressive purposes for which it was introduced. This seems significant, since these are the only purposes a deflationist acknowledges for truth-talk, but it raises the question of why English has, or should have, a truth predicate at all.

Since we have argued that our favored ASVD understanding of truth-talk renders the truth predicate technically dispensable in ordinary, natural languages that contain the adverbial, sui generis, non-nominal quantification expressed by how-talk, it is important to separate the question as to why such natural languages have a truth predicate from the question as to why, given the availability of how-talk, it might still be advantageous for deflationists not to jettison a truth predicate. We shall first answer the question as to why it is advantageous for ASVD-ists to retain truth-talk, and this will spill over to the answer to the former question as to why natural languages should retain a truth predicate.

It is advantageous for a natural language like English to retain truth-talk, even though it is technically dispensable in terms of how-talk, because English how-talk involves a rougher and less flexible mode of generalization. Again, how-talk quantification is neither objectual nor nominal. This makes this type of quantification less fine-grained and thus less flexible than the kind of generalizing one gets with either objectual or substitutional quantification. How-talk quantification is also inherently disjunctive, which might make it more complicated to process.

To improve on the evident "clunkiness" of how-talk, one might want to cover what it expresses via a more standard framework for formalization, one that is more easily integrated with other formal theorizing. The most direct way to do this is by positing *objects* for objectual quantification. With this in mind, one might countenance propositions as objects denoted by 'that'-clauses and other expressions substitutable for them. But since 'that'-clauses nominalize presentings of things as being somehow, we need a way to denominalize that result, to return to the presentings, as it were. This answers the question as to why deflationists might want to retain truth-talk, even though it is unnecessary in virtue of the logical role that how-talk is able to implement: Having a truth predicate in a natural language like English enables its users to reap the benefits of replacing the rough non-nominal quantification of how-talk with a "faux-nominal" objectual quantification that can be regimented in first-order logic. So, the main reason for employing or retaining truth-talk, along with proposition-talk, to cover what how-talk quantificational claims express, is that the object-and-property combination of those discourses provides certain expressive advantages over how-talk. (Cf. Yablo (1996, pp. 267-70) for more on this.)

One such expressive advantage is that by using truth- and proposition-talk we can regiment genuine entailments that seem difficult to understand formally in terms of how-talk. This would allow us to capture general, logical entailments in inference and argument in a more tractable way.

This idea of positing object-and-property discourses to cover what adverbial non-nominal quantificational discourse expresses is where a deflationist's talk of the truth predicate being "merely a formal device" that plays "only an expressive role" has bearing, and where it answers the question as to why English has a truth predicate. Deflationists can view the framework of propositions as just implementing a form of semantic ascent, from talk about the world being somehow to talk of these supposed objects. And deflationists can claim that the reason for introducing truth-talk is just what Quine says it is, viz., to provide a device of semantic descent that returns our focus to how the world is. Since such theorists maintain that semantic ascent and descent are the central functions of proposition-talk and truth-talk, they should take these fragments of discourse as formal devices that provide certain theoretical advantages in expressing things that one could express without them, but only in a rougher and less flexible (and so less advantageous) way.

A.3 From ASVD to Alethic Fictionalism

We have noted that a deflationist can think of bringing in the framework of propositions as just implementing a form of semantic ascent, from talk about the world and how it is to talk of these supposed objects that are posited as entities that specify the world as being somehow. And they can claim that the point of introducing truth-talk here is to implement a kind of semantic descent, to undo the semantic ascent implemented by introducing objects over which we can quantify, returning our focus to how the world is. We can see a suggestion of this understanding in some of what Prior says. In his adverbial sentential-variable account of truth-talk, he follows Ramsey in maintaining generally that no instance of truth-talk is really about any proposition (being instead "about whatever the proposition is about" (Prior (1971, p. 21)). However, Prior still allows that one might engage in proposition-talk (as we just quoted him doing), including talking "about them" being true or being false. But he considers this kind of talk just to involve a figure of speech about logical constructs, or talk of "quasi-properties of quasi-objects", rather than being some genuinely ontologically committing form of discourse (1971, pp. 29–30, 98; cf. Prior (1967, p. 229)). This is how a deflationist should think of the introduction of the framework of propositions, with one central role of truth-talk being to "logically unconstruct" applications of that framework. But notice that Prior's comments regarding figures of speech about "logical constructs" and "quasi-properties of quasi-objects" fit especially well with alethic fictionalism, that is, fictionalism about truth-talk.

In previous work (centrally, Armour-Garb and Woodbridge (2015, Chs. 3 and 4), but also Armour-Garb and Woodbridge (2010a, 2012, 2014, 2018a, 2018b) and Woodbridge (2005, 2006)), we have developed fictionalist accounts of truth-talk and proposition-talk in terms of *semantic pretense*. A semantic pretense-involving fictionalist account (henceforth, a *SPIF* account) applied to a fragment of discourse explains that way of talking as invoking something akin to games of make-believe, where these are understood along the lines introduced by Kendall Walton (1990, 1993). Such games involve the use of various linguistic items as props, the deployments of which in the game are governed by two different sorts of rules: stipulated pretenses regarding the props and principles of generation that make some of what is to be pretended in the game depend systematically on real-world conditions outside of the game. The latter in particular are what allow speakers to exploit the pretenses that a pretense-involving discourse invokes, in order to make serious assertions about the world indirectly. In our (2015), we provide detailed explanations of the sorts of rules we take to govern the games of make-believe that we claim truth-talk and proposition-talk invoke. However, in the templates that those earlier accounts employ, we rely on substitutional quantification in formulating the rules. With our endorsement of ASVD and the version of it that explains the "nonstandard" formal devices via how-talk NLIs, we now provide templates for the rules that avoid substitutional quantification and the problems that it can generate.[23] So, for example, in place of the rules for truth-talk provided in our (2015, pp. 130–31), we would now begin by providing the following quasi-formal presentations of the rules for the game of make-believe that truth-talk invokes, employing a "neutral" version of sentential variables and quantifiers.

Truth-Talk Make-Believe

(T-I) The central props for the game are the linguistic expressions 'is true', 'is false', 'is not true', and their cognates (e.g., 'is correct', 'is right', 'is so', etc.), as well as the expressions 'truth' and 'falsity'. Other props include 'that'-clauses and linguistic (and cognitive-state) items that can be related to them, as per our (2012, 2015) pretense account of proposition-talk. The following pretenses are stipulated about these props:

(i) The adjectival expressions 'is true', 'is false', etc. function predicatively to describe objects as having or lacking certain properties.

(ii) The nominal expression 'truth' picks out the property attributed with the expression 'is true' (and 'falsity' picks out the property attributed with the expression 'is false').

(iii) The most basic objects that directly have or lack the properties that 'is true', etc. attribute are abstract, mind-, and language-independent entities called "propositions". (These are also a pretense. Cf. Armour-Garb and Woodbridge (2012, 2015).) Other kinds of objects (e.g., linguistic items) can have the properties that 'is true', etc. attribute only derivatively, in virtue of "expressing a proposition" that has the relevant property.

(T-II) For all p, the pretenses displayed in an utterance of ⌜(The proposition) that p is true⌝ are prescribed iff p[24]

(T-III) For all p, the pretenses displayed in an utterance of ⌜(The proposition) that p is false⌝ are prescribed iff ~p

(T-IV) $\forall x \forall y$(if x is a sentence and y is a sentence and x ≠ y, but x and y are alike except that $\exists z$(z is a sentence and x has (in some transparent context)

---

[23] Nota bene: The updating below of the formulations of rules (T-IV) and (T-V) from our (2015) to eliminate the use of substitutional quantification turns out not to require anything more than first-order objectual quantification. This is because they are essentially metalinguistic rules for intersubstitution, so they employ only mentions of sentences and not any uses of them.

[24] As we have indicated above, we are here treating '⌜' and '⌝' as semi-permeable "corner quotes", allowing for the embedded variable to be governed by the quantifier that prefixes the quoted schema, while the rest of the schema remains constant.

z as a subsentence where y has an ascription of the truth predicate to z as a subsentence), then one can directly infer x from y and y from x)

(T-V) $\forall x \forall y$(if x is a sentence and y is a sentence and $x \neq y$, but x and y are alike except that $\exists z$(z is a sentence and x has (in some transparent context) the negation of z as a subsentence where y has an ascription of the falsity predicate to z as a subsentence), then one can directly infer x from y and y from x)

As we (2015) explain, the first rule, (T-I), states the stipulated, *expressly* made-believe, background pretenses for the make-believe, while Rules (T-II) and (T-III) are the central principles of generation for the game. Rules (T-IV) and (T-V) (reformulated here in a slightly more perspicuous manner) are further principles that explicitly codify certain consequences of Rules (T-II) and (T-III) that are crucially important for the truth and falsity predicates playing their more important expressive roles, specifically the intersubstitutability rules that apply to uses of the truth and falsity predicates. The key maneuver now is to explain (T-II) and (T-III) in terms of how-talk NLIs.

Having endorsed ASVD, we understand the sentential variables and quantifiers employed in the rules just presented as implementing non-nominal, adverbial quantification. This then leads to our re-rendering the above quasi-formal QSV versions of these rules with the following how-talk NLIs:

(T-II*) For however things are or are not, if that is how things are presented as being in the 'that'-clause displayed in the pretense-invoking claim that (the proposition that) that is how things are is true, then the pretenses displayed in that claim[25] are prescribed iff that is how things are.

(T-III*) For however things are or are not, if that is how things are presented as being in the 'that'-clause displayed in the pretense-invoking claim that (the proposition that) that is how things are is false, then the pretenses displayed in that claim are prescribed iff that is not how things are.

A deflationary understanding of truth-talk provided by a SPIF account based on the foregoing rules for a game of make-believe provides the link between the surface form of truth-talk and what ASVD explains truth-talk as expressing. It also explains how a fragment of discourse with first-order predicative logical form manages to implement logical devices it appears completely unsuited to implement, rather than leaving this as a brute fact. The link to ASVD yields the result that this SPIF account inherits the former's ability to avoid both the FP

---

[25] The relevant pretenses here pertain to some of those stipulated in (T-I), including that (the nominalized presenting of things as being somehow provided by) the embedded 'that'-clause functions as a referring expression that picks out a proposition, and that the locution 'is true' functions as a descriptive predicate that attributes some (substantive) property of truth to the proposition picked out. It is for the prescription of these pretenses that (T-II*), and analogously (T-III*), provides a rule.

and the GP, and the SPIF account also explains the intuition one might have that alethic generalizations are more than just (potentially infinite) conjunctions or disjunctions of their instances. This is in part because the how-talk quantifiers employed in direct specifications of the serious content put forward indirectly by 'true'-employing generalizations express genuine, albeit non-nominal, generalizations. But it is also in part because the make-believe invoked includes the pretense of there being propositions to quantify over (objectually), and specifically more propositions than those that are currently expressible in a given language. (See Armour-Garb and Woodbridge (2015, pp. 141–42).) Additionally, our SPIF account neatly explains a number of truth-involving intuitions that, as we have seen above, have been thought to challenge deflationary views. We think, for example, of the correspondence intuition, the accompanying, more theoretical truth-maker intuition, and the truth-property thesis. All of these stem from the pretense that is invoked in and that underwrites all uses of truth-talk.

The present account can still apply the approach we have presented previously (in our (2013), (2014a), and (2015)) for dealing with the Liar Paradox and other putative cases of semantic pathology, and thereby still satisfy Paradox Treatment Deflationism. This is because the quasi-anaphoric aspect of truth-talk, which tracks the anaphoric operation of adverbial sentential variables, is still indicated by the fact that, in the making of a 'true'-employing assertoric utterance, the pretenses put on display in doing so are put forward as appropriate, that is, as prescribed or "to be pretended". Since these pretenses are to be pretended iff the real-world conditions that the principles of generation determine as required for the appropriateness of the pretenses obtain, it follows that, when one makes an assertoric utterance, one indirectly expresses a commitment to those conditions obtaining. In other words, such an utterance expresses that things in the real world are however the rules require them to be, in order for the pretenses put on display in the making of the utterance to be prescribed in the game of make-believe that the discourse invokes.[26]

Since our account of truth-talk explains it as having a quasi-anaphoric operation, our (2013, 2014a, 2015) diagnosis of the Liar Paradox and its kin as s-defective, in virtue of a looping generated by the operations of the relevant locutions yielding a semantic misfiring, still applies. In fact, the fictionalist or pretense element of our account makes it a particularly good fit for this sort of diagnosis. It also enables us to distinguish between "pretend" content pertaining to how things are in the relevant make-believe and "serious" content about the world outside of the game. As a result, even s-defective sentences are not necessarily entirely meaningless—they can still have pretend content despite lacking any serious content, that is, despite not saying anything about the

---

[26] We should note that the quasi-anaphoric operation that our account attributes to truth-talk means that it is not restricted by immanence. Moreover, our ASVD analysis of 'true'-employing generalizations also yields the result that our deflationary account of truth-talk is not restricted to what is expressible in a natural language.

world. While we maintain that all instances of truth-talk invoke pretense, the non-defective instances might be said to make "partially pretend" claims by putting forward serious content about the world indirectly, via the pretenses that they involve. The semantic reach of the s-defective instances of truth-talk, such as sentences that supposedly yield the Liar Paradox, loops entirely within the make-believe that truth-talk belongs to, with the result that these sentences make "purely pretend" claims, putting forward only pretend content. This is another way of diagnosing what is going on with these problematic sentences and of understanding the reasons for their s-defectiveness.

A.4 Conclusions: Accommodating Broad Four-Dimensional Deflationism

As explained in Chapter 1, any adequate deflationary account of truth-talk must be part of an extended and comprehensive approach that we call "broad four-dimensional deflationism". There we first identified and explained the dimensions of any deflationary account: Linguistic Deflationism, Metaphysical Deflationism, Conceptual Deflationism, and Paradox Treatment Deflationism. One thing that this "dimensional" specification requires is that a deflationary account of truth-talk must satisfy all four of these dimensions. Moreover, given the dependencies among the dimensions, it follows that a "partial deflationism", which accords with some but not all of the four dimensions, is unstable and is not sufficient for an account to qualify as deflationary.

Our SPIF account of truth-talk maintains that the various functions of the talk that involve the truth predicate performing its logico-linguistic expressive roles should be understood centrally in terms of principles that are formulated using how-talk quantification. Since this application of this non-nominal adverbial mode of quantification just implements sentential variables and quantifiers (and by extension, quantification into predicate position), all that truth-talk adds to a language on our account is another, more flexible way of capturing the logically expressive capacity of these higher-order logical devices. Since the thesis that truth-talk just implements certain special logical roles is precisely what Linguistic Deflationism maintains about truth-talk, our SPIF account clearly satisfies Linguistic Deflationism.

Our SPIF account of truth-talk also satisfies Metaphysical Deflationism. This is because it is part of our view that, really, in the world outside of the make-believe that underlies the use of truth-talk, there is no property of truth (certainly no "substantive" truth property). Within the make-believe, there is a truth property attributed by uses of the truth predicate,[27] but the property is

---

[27] We note that our SPIF approach to analyzing truth-talk can also accommodate alethic pluralism by developing a make-believe according to which there is a plurality of different substantive properties attributed by the truth predicate relative to different subject matters.

just a denizen of a fiction. Since we reject fictional realism (cf. Armour-Garb and Woodbridge (2015, Ch. 1)), while one might say that the property of truth is a sort of "fictional entity", this does not imply that it exists in any sense.

Our SPIF account satisfies Conceptual Deflationism as well because it renders the truth concept insubstantial, which this dimension of deflationism demands. While the make-believe that underwrites truth-talk does include a concept of a substantive truth property and might, as a result, seem to involve a substantial truth concept, the pretense employs only a concept *of* something substantive. This is not the same thing as being a *substantive concept*, in the sense that a substantive concept would be indicated by that concept playing a genuine explanatory role in a what-explanation of something substantive, whereas the concept of something substantive might not play such a role.[28] In fact, in our (2023b) and in Chapter 6, above, we consider a strategy for recasting various 'true'-employing what-explanations of other philosophically interesting concepts in terms of sentential variables and quantifiers. Since our SPIF account of truth-talk tracks ASVD and explains the use of the truth predicate in terms of these higher-order logical devices, which are then understood in terms of how-talk quantification, our account provides a understanding of the role of the truth predicate in these conceptual explanations in keeping with Conceptual Deflationism.

Our SPIF account of truth-talk also satisfies Paradox Treatment Deflationism in virtue of its incorporation of ASVD, shown in Section A.2.2 to satisfy this dimension of a fully adequate deflationary account. This should not be too surprising, since our rules for the pretense that truth-talk invokes are specifically designed to satisfy the requirements for being a deflationary account. That the rules for pretense are formulated to satisfy four-dimensional deflationism has further consequences. For example, rules (T-II) and (T-III) ensure the preservation of Intersub, while rules (T-IV) and (T-V) codify this important consequence of including (T-II) and (T-III) in the rules for the pretense. These rules also ensure the strong equivalence required to satisfy Strong Convention T (SCT), as that is built into the pretense as well. There is a kind of meaning (or "cognitive") equivalence that holds with respect to the "serious" or "worldly" content of an instance of truth-talk and that to which the instance of truth-talk ascribes the truth predicate. So the equivalence in the instances of (TS) that our account yields is a more-than-material equivalence.

There is a further important point about the meaning of truth-ascriptions that is not evident from the rules of the pretense that we have set out. This point emerges from our treatment of the semantic paradoxes. Given our

---

[28] Consider the concept *being magical*. This certainly seems to be a concept of something substantive (at least in the context of works of fiction), but it is just an empty concept made up by us and thus is not a concept that plays any genuine explanatory role in an account of anything substantive (beyond its own use). Our SPIF account maintains that the truth concept is also an empty concept just made up by us, so it is similarly insubstantial.

understanding of s-defective sentences, they are in a certain sense meaningless in virtue of having no serious or worldly content. Since, on our account, s-defective sentences yield only s-defective logical compounds, such sentences cannot factor into legitimate instances of (TS). These illegitimate "instances" of (TS) are also unable to factor into inferences, thereby blocking the reasoning that appears to yield contradiction, satisfying NT. In addition, by identifying 's-defective' as a semantic characterization along with 'true' and 'false', our view satisfies ESC. Since we maintain that only non-defective sentences are apt for logical evaluation, we take our resolution to satisfy ELV with respect to all genuinely logically evaluable sentences. By excluding putative instances of (TS) involving s-defective sentences as illegitimate, our view ensures SCT for all of the *legitimate* instances, while treating (by dissolving) the apparent pathology that s-defective sentences seem to manifest. For more on how our approach to the semantic paradoxes satisfies the conditions of an adequate resolution (in particular, how it also satisfies RI), see Armour-Garb and Woodbridge (2013 and 2015, Ch. 5).

As just explained, our SPIF account of truth-talk satisfies all four dimensions of broad four-dimensional deflationism. The other criterion that this framework requires, as noted in Chapter 1, is that a deflationary account of truth-talk must be part of a "broader" deflationary approach that extends to fragments of discourse that involve the other traditional semantic notions, viz., reference-talk and predicate-satisfaction-talk. The question for our SPIF account of truth-talk, then, is whether it fits with deflationary accounts of these other fragments of discourse that explain them as performing merely "expressive" logico-linguistic functions. Broad four-dimensional deflationism takes these other semantic fragments of discourse also to effect something like a collapse of the use/mention distinction, providing a way of using linguistic items through mentioning them via some sort of nominalization. Our SPIF account of truth-talk explains this collapse at the sentential level via an ASVD how-talk NLI analysis of the discourse as implementing a new level of variables and quantifiers, that of sentential quantification. On a similar analysis of predicate-satisfaction-talk, it, like truth-talk, also functions to implement a new level of variables and quantifiers—specifically, the level of quantifying into predicate-position. The how-talk NLI approach featured in our SPIF account of truth-talk is easily extendable as a means for explaining this logically expressive function of predicate-satisfaction-talk. This is indicated in our discussion in Section A.2.3 of the predicate-position quantification that a more "specifying" form of how-talk implements.[29] Thus, our SPIF account

---

[29] We maintain that this also extends to a deflationary account of talk seemingly of properties that are thought to be implicated by what we might call "property-talk". Although we do not have the space here to explain such an account fully, we have already

of truth-talk fits quite naturally with a similar deflationary SPIF account of predicate-satisfaction-talk.

The remaining component of the "broadness" aspect of broad four-dimensional deflationism—reference-talk—is different from the other semantic fragments of discourse in that it does not involve effecting the implementation of quantification into any position other than the "subject position" in any sentence. Thus, there is no need to bring in how-talk to account for the logically expressive functions of this fragment of discourse. Reference-talk is an "explicitly metalinguistic" version of language deployment involving a use/mention collapse for nominal expressions. But since such a use/mention collapse for nominal expressions still results in expressions we can generalize on with first-order quantification, the only variables and quantifiers needed in a sentence like 'Every name on the list refers to an ally' or 'Someone the list refers to is a collaborator' will be objectual (with the objects in the relevant domain being either names or persons). So, there is no need to bring in how-talk with its "higher-level" non-nominal mode of generalizing in a deflationary account of reference-talk. While reference-talk thus does not fit with the logical tools of the ASVD how-talk NLI approach that we currently employ in explaining our SPIF account of truth-talk, in Armour-Garb and Woodbridge (2015, Ch. 6) we offer a SPIF account of reference-talk that provides a deflationary understanding of this fragment of discourse. Our SPIF account of reference-talk parallels and thus fits with a SPIF account of truth-talk. Hence, our SPIF account of truth-talk fully satisfies the "broadness" aspect of broad four-dimensional deflationism.

In virtue of the many merits, discussed above, that the ASVD how-talk NLI approach offers for addressing the most significant challenges to deflationism, we maintain that this version of the new (or perhaps *renewed*) direction for deflationism provided by sentential-variable deflationism offers the best strategy for developing a deflationary account of truth-talk. In virtue of the additional benefits of endorsing alethic fictionalism (specifically, by applying our SPIF approach) to explain how first-order truth-talk manages to implement a non-nominal adverbial mode of quantification, benefits that include accommodating many common intuitions about truth and bolstering a response to the Liar Paradox and to the rest of apparent semantic pathology, we

---

indicated how how-talk implements quantification into predicate-position. On this approach, cases that involve quantificational property-talk would get re-rendered in terms of sentences employing predicate-variables and quantifiers, which in turn would be interpreted via *adjectival* how-talk quantification. This would support resisting a commitment to properties on the basis of talk apparently about them. For example, a sentence like 'Whatever property Isabel has, Zev has it, too' can be understood in terms of the sentence, 'However Isabel is, that is how Zev is, too' (or, more colloquially, 'Zev is however Isabel is'). We leave development of this approach for future work. We mention it here to make evident how thoroughgoing or "broad" our deflationism is.

hold that pursuing this new direction for deflationism via developing a SPIF account of truth-talk provides the best way of formulating an ASVD analysis of the discourse. As a further mark in its favor, our SPIF account of truth-talk also satisfies all of the requirements of broad four-dimensional deflationism, in addition to satisfying a further aspect of "broadness" in virtue of providing deflationary resolutions of the apparent semantic paradoxes that involve the notions of reference and predicate-satisfaction. (Cf. Armour-Garb and Woodbridge (2015, Ch. 6).) Hence, we maintain that combining these two new directions for deflationism in developing the kind of SPIF account we have sketched here is the most promising strategy for pursuing the deflationary approach to truth.

Bibliography

Alston, W. (1985). "Concepts of Epistemic Justification." *Monist* 68(1): 57–89.
Alston, W. (1996). *A Realist Conception of Truth*. Ithaca: Cornell University Press.
Armour-Garb, B. (2001). "Deflationism and the Meaningless Strategy." *Analysis* 61(4): 280–89.
Armour-Garb, B. (2004). "Minimalism, The Generalization Problem and the Liar." *Synthese* 139(3): 1–22.
Armour-Garb, B. (2007). "Consistent Inconsistency Theories." *Inquiry* 50(6): 639–54.
Armour-Garb, B. (2010). "Horwichian Minimalism and the Generalization Problem." *Analysis* 70(4): 693–703.
Armour-Garb, B. (2011a). "Challenges to Deflationary Theories of Truth." *Philosophy Compass* 7(4): 256–66.
Armour-Garb, B. (2011b). "Deflationism (about Theories of Truth)." *Philosophy Compass* 7(4): 267–77.
Armour-Garb, B. and Beall, JC (2001). "Can Deflationists Be Dialetheists?" *Journal of Philosophical Logic* 30(6): 593–608.
Armour-Garb, B. and Beall, JC (Eds.) (2005a). *Deflationary Truth*. Chicago: Open Court Press.
Armour-Garb, B. and Beall, JC (2005b). "Minimalism, Epistemicism, and Paradox." In Beall and Armour-Garb (Eds.) (2005), pp. 85–96.
Armour-Garb, B. and Woodbridge, J. (2006). "Dialetheism, Semantic Pathology, and the Open Pair." *Australasian Journal of Philosophy* 84(3): 395–416.
Armour-Garb, B. and Woodbridge, J. (2010a). "Why Deflationists Should Be Pretense Theorists (and Perhaps Already Are)." In *New Waves in Truth*, pp. 59–77. Edited by C. Wright and N. Pedersen. New York: Palgrave Macmillan.
Armour-Garb, B. and Woodbridge, J. (2010b). "Truth, Paradox and Plausibility." *Analysis* 70(1): 11–23.
Armour-Garb, B. and Woodbridge, J. (2012). "The Story about Propositions." *Noûs* 46(4): 635–74.
Armour-Garb, B. and Woodbridge, J. (2013). "Semantic Defectiveness and the Liar." *Philosophical Studies* 164(3): 845–63.
Armour-Garb, B. and Woodbridge, J. (2014a). "Semantic Defectiveness: A Dissolution of Semantic Pathology." In *Recent Trends in Philosophical Logic*, pp. 1–12. Edited by R. Ciuni, H. Wansing, and C. Willkommen. Cham: Springer International Publishing.

Armour-Garb, B. and Woodbridge, J. (2014b). "From Mathematical Fictionalism to Truth-Theoretic Fictionalism." *Philosophy and Phenomenological Research* 88(1): 93–118.

Armour-Garb, B. and Woodbridge, J. (2015). *Pretense and Pathology: Philosophical Fictionalism and Its Applications*. Cambridge: Cambridge University Press.

Armour-Garb, B. and Woodbridge, J. (2017). "Alethic Fictionalism, Alethic Nihilism, and the Liar Paradox." *Philosophical Studies* 174(12): 3083–96.

Armour-Garb, B. and Woodbridge, J. (2018a). "Summary: *Pretense and Pathology: Philosophical Fictionalism and Its Applications*." *Analysis* 78(4): 687–92.

Armour-Garb, B. and Woodbridge, J. (2018b). "Replies." *Analysis* 78(4): 718–36.

Armour-Garb, B. and Woodbridge, J. (2023a). "The Alethic Platitudes, Deflationism and Adverbial Quantification." *Philosophical Quarterly* 73(2): 323–45.

Armour-Garb, B. and Woodbridge, J. (2023b). "Answering the Conceptual Challenge: Three Strategies for Deflationists." *Synthese* 201(3): Article 98. Online at https://doi.org/10.1007/s11229-023-04071-z.

Armour-Garb, B. and Woodbridge, J. (2024). "Revenge for Alethic Nihilism." *Journal of Philosophy* 121(12): 686–697

Armour-Garb, B. and Woodbridge, J. (forthcoming). "Sentential-Variable Deflationism and Adverbial Quantification." *Inquiry*. Online at https://doi.org/10.1080/0020174X.2025.2499112.

Armstrong, D. (1989). *Universals: An Opinionated Introduction*. Boulder: Westview Press.

Armstrong, D. (1997). *A World of States of Affairs*. Cambridge: Cambridge University Press.

Armstrong, D. (2004). *Truth and Truth-Makers*. Cambridge: Cambridge University Press.

Asay, J. (2014). "Against Truth." *Erkenntnis* 79(1): 147–64.

Asay, J. (2015). "Epistemicism and the Liar." *Synthese* 192(3): 679–99.

Asay, J. (2021). "TRUTH: A Concept Unlike Any Other." *Synthese* 198 (Supplement Issue 2): 605–30.

Asay, J. (2022). "The Best Thing about the Deflationary Theory of Truth." *Philosophical Studies* 179(1): 109–31.

Ayer, A. (1936/1952). *Language, Truth and Logic*. 2nd ed. New York: Dover.

Azzouni, J. (1999). "Comments on Shapiro." *Journal of Philosophy* 96(10): 541–4.

Azzouni, J. (2001). "Truth via Anaphorically Unrestricted Quantifiers." *Journal of Philosophical Logic* 30(4): 329–54.

Azzouni, J. (2004). *Deflating Existential Consequence: A Case for Nominalism*. Oxford: Oxford University Press.

Azzouni, J. (2006). *Tracking Reason: Proof, Consequence and Truth*. Oxford: Oxford University Press.

Azzouni, J. (2007). "The Inconsistency of Natural Languages: How We Live with It." *Inquiry* 50(6): 590–605.

Azzouni, J. (2010). *Talking About Nothing: Numbers, Hallucinations, and Fictions*. Oxford: Oxford University Press.
Azzouni, J. (2017). *Ontology Without Borders*. Oxford: Oxford University Press.
Azzouni, J. (2018). "Deflationist Truth." In *The Oxford Handbook of Truth*, pp. 477–502. Edited by M. Glanzberg. Oxford: Oxford University Press.
Badici, E. (2008). "The Liar Paradox and the Inclosure Schema." *Australasian Journal of Philosophy* 86(4): 583–96.
Baker, G. and Hacker, P. (1980). *Wittgenstein, Meaning and Understanding: Essays on the "Philosophical Investigations"*. Oxford: Basil Blackwell.
Bar-On, D. and Simmons, K. (2007). "The Use of Force Against Deflationism." In *Truth and Speech Acts: Studies in the Philosophy of Language*, pp. 61–89. Edited by D. Greimann and G. Siegwart. London: Routledge.
Bartunek, N. (2019). "Truth in the *Investigations*." *Synthese* 196(10): 4091–111.
Båve, A. (2009a). "A Deflationary Theory of Reference." *Synthese* 169(1): 51–73.
Båve, A. (2009b). "Why Is a Truth Predicate Like a Pronoun?" *Philosophical Studies* 145(2): 297–310.
Beall, JC (2004). "True and False—As If." In *The Law of Non-Contradiction: New Philosophical Essays*, pp. 197–216. Edited by G. Priest, JC Beall, and B. Armour-Garb. New York: Oxford University Press.
Beall, JC (Ed.) (2007). *Revenge of the Liar: New Essays on Paradox*. Oxford University Press.
Beall, JC (2009). *Spandrels of Truth*. Oxford: Oxford University Press.
Beall, JC and Armour-Garb, B. (2003). "Should Deflationists Be Dialetheists?" *Noûs* 3737(2): 303–24.
Beall, JC and Armour-Garb, B. (Eds.) (2005). *Deflationism and Paradox*. Oxford: Oxford University Press.
Beaney, M. (Ed.) (1997). *The Frege Reader*. Oxford: Blackwell Publishing.
Belnap, N., Jr. (1962). "Tonk, Plonk, and Plink." *Analysis* 22(6): 130–34.
Bigelow, J. (1988). *The Reality of Numbers: A Physicalist's Philosophy of Mathematics*. Oxford: Oxford University Press.
Blackburn, S. (1984). *Spreading the Word*. Oxford: Clarendon Press.
Bliss, R. and Trogdon, K. "Metaphysical Grounding." In *The Stanford Encyclopedia of Philosophy* (Summer 2024 edition). Edited by E. Zalta and U. Nodelman. https://plato.stanford.edu/archives/sum2024/entries/grounding/.
Boghossian, P. (1990). "The Status of Content." *Philosophical Review* 99(2): 157–84.
Boyd, R. (1983). "On the Current Status of the Issue of Scientific Realism." *Erkenntnis* 19(1–3): 45–90.
Bradley, D. (2023). "The Explanatory Power of Deflationary Truth." *Erkenntnis* 88(8): 3439–56.
Brandom, R. (1983). "Asserting." *Noûs* 17(4): 637–50.
Brandom, R. (1984). "Reference Explained Away." *Journal of Philosophy* 81(9): 469–92.

Brandom, R. (1988). "Pragmatism, Phenomenalism, and Truth Talk." *Realism and Anti-Realism: Midwest Studies in Philosophy* 12(1): 75–93.

Brandom, R. (1994). *Making It Explicit: Reasoning, Representing, and Discursive Commitment.* Cambridge, MA: Harvard University Press.

Brentano, F. (1904/1966). *The True and the Evident.* Edited and translated by R. M. Chisholm. London: Routledge & Kegan Paul.

Burgess, A. (2011). "Mainstream Semantics + Deflationary Truth." *Linguistics and Philosophy* 34: 397–410.

Burgess, A. and Burgess, J. (2011). *Truth.* Princeton: Princeton University Press.

Burgess, J. (2013). *Saul Kripke: Puzzles and Mysteries.* Cambridge: Polity Press.

Burgess, J. and Rosen, G. (1997). *A Subject with No Object: Strategies for Nominalistic Interpretation of Mathematics.* Oxford: Clarendon Press.

Burgis, B. and Bueno, O. (2019). "Liars with Curry: Dialetheism and the Prospects for a Uniform Solution." In *Dialetheism and its Applications*, pp. 1–20. Edited by A. Rieger and G. Young. Cham: Springer Nature.

Button, T. (2014). "The Weight of Truth: Lessons for Minimalists from Russell's Gray's Elegy Argument." *Proceedings of the Aristotelian Society* 114(3): 261–89.

Caret, C. and Hjortland, O. (2015). "Logical Consequence: Its Nature, Structure, and Application." In *Foundations of Logical Consequence*, pp. 3–29. Edited by C. Caret and O. Hjortland. Oxford: Oxford University Press.

Carnap, R. (1934/1937). *The Logical Syntax of Language.* Translated by A. Smeaton (Countess von Zeppelin). London: Routledge, Trench, Tubner.

Carnap, R. (1942). *Introduction to Semantics.* Cambridge, MA: Harvard University Press.

Carnie, A. (2013). *Syntax: A Generative Introduction.* 3rd ed. Oxford: Wiley-Blackwell.

Casalegno, P. (2005). "Truth and Truthfulness Attributions." *Proceedings of the Aristotelian Society* 105(3): 279–304.

Chihara, C. (1979). "The Semantic Paradoxes: A Diagnostic Investigation." *Philosophical Review* 88(4): 590–618.

Cieśliński, C. (2015). "The Innocence of Truth." *Dialectica* 69(1): 61–85.

Cieśliński, C. (2018). "Minimalism and the Generalisation Problem: On Horwich's Second Solution." *Synthese* 195(3): 1077–101.

Collins, J. (2002). "Truth or Meaning? A Question of Priority." *Philosophy and Phenomenological Research* 65(3): 497–536.

Corcoran, J. (Ed.) (1983). *Logic, Semantics, Metamathematics.* 2nd ed. Indianapolis: Hackett.

Crimmins, M. (1998). "Hesperus and Phosphorus: Sense, Pretense, and Reference." *Philosophical Review* 107(1): 1–47.

Currie, G. (1990). *The Nature of Fiction.* Cambridge: Cambridge University Press.

Damnjanovic, N. (2005). "Deflationism and the Success Argument." *Philosophical Quarterly* 55(218): 53–67.

David, M. (1994). *Correspondence and Disquotation: An Essay on the Nature of Truth*. Oxford: Oxford University Press.

David, M. (2006). "A Substitutional Theory of Truth?" *Philosophy and Phenomenological Research* 72(1): 182–89.

Davidson, D. (1967/1984). "Truth and Meaning." In *Inquiries into Truth and Interpretation*, pp. 17–36. Oxford: Clarendon Press.

Davidson, D. (1969/2001). "The Individuation of Events." In *Essays on Actions and Events*, 2nd ed., pp. 163–80. Oxford: Clarendon Press.

Davidson, D. (1990). "The Structure and Content of Truth." *Journal of Philosophy* 87(6): 279–328.

Davidson, D. (1996). "The Folly of Trying to Define Truth." *Journal of Philosophy* 93(6): 263–78.

Davidson, D. (1999). "The Centrality of Truth." In *Truth and Its Nature (If Any)*, pp. 105–15. Edited by J. Peregrin. Dordrecht: Kluwer Academic Publishers.

Devitt, M. (1990). "Transcendentalism about Content." *Pacific Philosophical Quarterly* 71(4): 247–63.

Devitt, M. (1997). *Realism and Truth*. 2nd ed. Princeton: Princeton University Press.

Devitt, M. (2001). "The Metaphysics of Truth." In *The Nature of Truth: Classic and Contemporary Readings*, pp. 579–611. Edited by M. Lynch. Cambridge, MA: MIT Press.

Dickie, I. (2016). "The Essential Connection Between Epistemology and the Theory of Reference." *Knowledge and Mind: Philosophical Issues* 26: 99–129.

Dodd, J. (2008). *The Identity Theory of Truth*. Oxford: Oxford University Press.

Douven, I. and Hindriks, F. (2005). "Deflating the Correspondence Intuition." *Dialectica* 59(3): 315–29.

Dummett, M. (1959/1978). "Truth." In Dummett (1978), pp. 1–24.

Dummett, M. (1963/1978). "The Philosophical Significance of Gödel's Theorem." In Dummett (1978), pp. 186–201.

Dummett, M. (1978). *Truth and Other Enigmas*. Cambridge, MA: Harvard University Press.

Dummett, M. (1991). *The Logical Basis of Metaphysics*. Cambridge, MA: Harvard University Press.

Edwards, D. (2013). "Truth as a Substantive Property." *Australasian Journal of Philosophy* 91(2): 279–94.

Edwards, D. (2018). *The Metaphysics of Truth*. Oxford: Oxford University Press.

Eklund, M. (2002). "Deep Inconsistency." *Australasian Journal of Philosophy* 80(3): 321–31.

Elbourne, P. (2011). *Meaning: A Slim Guide to Semantics*. Oxford: Oxford University Press.

Feferman, S. (1984). "Toward Useful Type-Free Theories—I." *Journal of Symbolic Logic* 49(1): 75–111.

Field, H. (1972). "Tarski's Theory of Truth." *Journal of Philosophy* 69(7): 347–75. Reprinted in Field (2001a), pp. 3–26.

Field, H. (1978). "Mental Representation." *Erkenntnis* 13(1): 9–61. Reprinted in Field (2001a), pp. 30–67.

Field, H. (1980/2016). *Science Without Numbers*. 2nd ed. Oxford: Oxford University Press.

Field, H. (1987). "The Deflationary Conception of Truth." In *Fact, Science and Morality: Essays on A.J. Ayer's "Language, Truth, and Logic"*, pp. 55–117. Edited by C. Wright and G. McDonald. New York: Blackwell Publishing.

Field, H. (1989). *Realism, Mathematics and Modality*. Oxford: Basil Blackwell.

Field, H. (1992). "Critical Notice: Paul Horwich's *Truth*." *Philosophy of Science* 59(1): 321–30.

Field, H. (1994a). "Deflationist Views of Meaning and Content." *Mind* 103(411): 249–85.

Field, H. (1994b). "Disquotational Truth and Factually Defective Discourse." *Philosophical Review* 103(3): 405–52.

Field, H. (1999). "Deflating the Conservativeness Argument." *Journal of Philosophy* 96(10): 533–40.

Field, H. (2001a). *Truth and the Absence of Fact*. Oxford: Oxford University Press.

Field, H. (2001b). "Postscript to 'Tarski's Theory of Truth.'" In Field (2001a), pp. 27–29.

Field, H. (2001c). "Postscript to 'Mental Representation.'" In Field (2001a), pp. 68–82.

Field, H. (2001d). "Postscript to 'Deflationist Views of Meaning and Content.'" In Field (2001a), pp. 141–56.

Field, H. (2001e). "Attributions of Meaning and Belief." In Field (2001a), pp. 157–74.

Field, H. (2006). "Compositional Principles vs. Schematic Reasoning." *Monist* 89(1): 9–27.

Field, H. (2008). *Saving Truth from Paradox*. Oxford: Oxford University Press.

Forster, M. (2004). *Wittgenstein on the Arbitrariness of Grammar*. Princeton: Princeton University Press.

Frege, G. (1892/1997). "Über Sinn und Bedeutung [On Sense and Reference]." In Beaney (Ed.) (1997), pp. 151–71.

Frege, G. (1897/1997). "Logic: Extract." In Beaney (Ed.) (1997), pp. 227–50.

Frege, G. (1915/1997). "My Basic Logical Insights." In Beaney (Ed.) (1997), pp. 322–4.

Frege, G. (1918/1977). "Thoughts." In *Logical Investigations*, pp. 1–30. Edited by P. Geach. New Haven: Yale University Press.

Frege, G. (1979). *Posthumous Writings*. Edited by H. Hermes, F. Kambartel, and F. Kaulback. Translated by P. Long and R. White. Oxford: Basil Blackwell.

Friedman, M. (1974). "Explanation and Scientific Understanding." *Journal of Philosophy* 71(1): 5–19.

Fujimoto, K. (2022). "On the Logicality of Truth." *Philosophical Quarterly* 72(4): 853–74.

Galinon, H. (2015). "Deflationary Truth: Conservativity or Logicality?" *Philosophical Quarterly* 65(259): 268–74.
Gamester, W. (2018). "Truth: Explanation, Success, and Coincidence." *Philosophical Studies* 175(5): 1243–65.
Gamester, W. (2023). "Nothing Is True." *Journal of Philosophy* 120(6): 314–38.
Gauker, C. (1999). "Logic and Deflationism." *Facta Philosophica* 1(1): 167–96.
Gauker, C. (2006). "Against Stepping Back: A Critique of Contextualist Approaches to the Semantic Paradoxes." *Journal of Philosophical Logic* 35(4): 393–422.
Gentzen, G. (1935/1969). "Investigations into Logical Inference." PhD dissertation, Universität Göttingen. In *The Collected Papers of Gerhard Gentzen*, pp. 68–131. Edited by M. Szabo. Amsterdam: North-Holland.
Gettier, E. (1963). "Is Justified True Belief Knowledge?" *Analysis* 23(6): 121–23.
Glanzberg, M. (2001). "The Liar in Context." *Philosophical Studies* 103(3): 217–51.
Goh, E. and Choo, F. (2022). "Addressing Two Recent Challenges to the Factive Account of Knowledge." *Synthese* 200, Article 435 (https://doi.org/10.1007/s11229-022-03916-3).
Goldman, A. and Beddor, B. (2021). "Reliabilist Epistemology." In *The Stanford Encyclopedia of Philosophy* (Summer 2021 edition). Edited by E. Zalta. https://plato.stanford.edu/archives/sum2021/entries/reliabilism/.
Gross, S. (2015). "Does the Expressive Role of 'True' Preclude Deflationary Davidsonian Semantics?" In *Meaning Without Representation: Essays on Truth, Expression, Normativity, and Naturalism*, pp. 47–63. Edited by S. Gross, N. Tebben, and M. Williams. Oxford: Oxford University Press.
Grover, D. (1977). "Inheritors and Paradox." *Journal of Philosophy* 74(10): 590–604.
Grover, D. (1981a/1992). "Truth." In Grover (1992), pp. 146–72.
Grover, D. (1981b/1992). "Truth: Do We Need It?" In Grover (1992), pp. 173–206.
Grover, D. (1990/1992). "On Two Deflationary Truth Theories." In Grover (1992), pp. 215–33.
Grover, D. (1992). *A Prosentential Theory of Truth*. Princeton: Princeton University Press.
Grover, D., Camp, J., and Belnap, N. (1975). "A Prosentential Theory of Truth." *Philosophical Studies* 27(2): 73–125. Reprinted in Grover (1992), pp. 70–120.
Gupta, A. (1993a). "Minimalism." *Language and Logic: Philosophical Perspectives* 7: 359–69.
Gupta, A. (1993b). "A Critique of Deflationism." *Philosophical Topics* 21(2): 57–81.
Gupta, A. (2006). "Remarks on Christopher Hill's *Thought and World*." *Philosophy and Phenomenological Research* 72(1): 190–5.
Halbach, V. (2001). "How Innocent Is Deflationism?" *Synthese* 126(1): 167–94.
Halbach, V. (2011). *Axiomatic Theories of Truth*. Cambridge: Cambridge University Press.

Halbach, V. and Leigh, G. (2022). "Axiomatic Theories of Truth." In *The Stanford Encyclopedia of Philosophy* (Spring 2022 edition). Edited by E. Zalta. https://plato.stanford.edu/archives/spr2022/entries/truth-axiomatic/.

Heck, R. (2005). "Truth and Disquotation." *Synthese* 142(3): 317–52.

Heck, R. (2021). "Disquotationalism and the Compositional Principles." In *Modes of Truth: The Unified Approach to Modality, Truth, and Paradox*, pp. 115–50. Edited by C. Nicolai and J. Stern. New York: Routledge.

Heck, R. (2023). "Disquotation, Translation, and Context-Dependence." In *Oxford Studies in Philosophy of Language*, vol. 3, pp. 104–30. Edited by E. Lepore and D. Sosa. Oxford: Oxford University Press.

Heck, R. and May, R. (2020). "The Birth of Semantics." *Journal for the History of Analytical Philosophy* 8(6): 1–32.

Hazlett, A. (2010). "The Myth of Factive Verbs." *Philosophy and Phenomenological Research* 80(3): 497–522.

Hersch, R. (1997). "Prove—Once More and Again." *Philosophia Mathematica* 5(2): 153–65.

Hill, C. (2002). *Thought and World: An Austere Portrayal of Truth, Reference, and Semantic Correspondence*. Cambridge: Cambridge University Press.

Hill, C. (2006a). "Précis of *Thought and World: An Austere Portrayal of Truth, Reference, and Semantic Correspondence*." *Philosophy and Phenomenological Research* 72(1): 174–81.

Hill, C. (2006b). "Replies to Marian David, Anil Gupta, and Keith Simmons." *Philosophy and Phenomenological Research* 72(1): 205–22.

Horisk, C. (2007). "The Expressive Role of Truth in Truth-Conditional Semantics." *Philosophical Quarterly* 57(229): 535–57.

Horisk, C. (2008). "Truth, Meaning, and Circularity." *Philosophical Studies* 137(2): 269–300.

Horsten, L. (1995). "The Semantical Paradoxes, the Neutrality of Truth, and the Neutrality of the Minimalist Theory of Truth." In *The Many Problems of Realism*, pp. 173–87. Edited by P. Cortois. Tilburg: Tilburg University Press.

Horsten, L. (2011). *The Tarskian Turn: Deflationism and Axiomatic Theories of Truth*. Cambridge, MA: MIT Press.

Horwich, P. (1982). "Three Forms of Realism." *Synthese* 51(2): 181–201.

Horwich, P. (1990/1998). *Truth*. 2nd ed. Oxford: Clarendon Press.

Horwich, P. (1993). "Gibbard's Theory of Norms." *Philosophy and Public Affairs* 22(1): 67–78.

Horwich, P. (1996a). "Realism Minus Truth." *Philosophy and Phenomenological Research* 56(4): 877–81.

Horwich, P. (1996b). "Realism and Truth." *Metaphysics: Philosophical Perspectives* 10: 187–97.

Horwich, P. (1998). *Meaning*. Oxford: Clarendon Press.

Horwich, P. (2001). "A Defense of Minimalism." *Synthese* 126(1–2): 149–65.

Horwich, P. (2005). "A Minimalist Critique of Tarski on Truth." In Beall and Armour-Garb (Eds.) (2005), pp. 75–84.

Horwich, P. (2006). "A World Without Isms: Life after Realism, Fictionalism, Non-Cognitivism, Relativism, Reductionism, Revisionism, and So On." In *Truth and Realism*, pp. 188–202. Edited by P. Greenough and M. Lynch. Oxford: Oxford University Press.

Horwich, P. (2008). "Being and Truth." *Truth and Its Deformities: Midwest Studies in Philosophy* 32(1): 258–73.

Horwich, P. (2010a). *Truth—Meaning—Reality*. Oxford: Clarendon Press.

Horwich, P. (2010b). "A Minimalist Critique of Tarski." In Horwich (2010a), pp. 79–97.

Horwich, P. (2016). "Wittgenstein on Truth." *Argumenta* 2(1): 95–105.

Howat, A. (2018). "Constituting Assertion: A Pragmatist Critique of Horwich's 'Truth.'" *Synthese* 195(3): 935–54.

Incurvati, L. and Murzi, J. (2017). "Maximally Consistent Sets of Instances of Naive Comprehension." *Mind* 126(502): 371–84.

Jackson, F., Oppy, G., and Smith, M. (1994). "Minimalism and Truth Aptness." *Mind* 103(411): 287–301.

Jackson, F. and Pettit, P. (1990). "Program Explanation: A General Perspective." *Analysis* 50(2): 107–17.

Kalderon, M. (1997). "The Transparency of Truth." *Mind* 106(423): 475–97.

Kaye, R. (1991). *The Mathematics of Logic: A Guide to Completeness Theorems and Their Applications*. Cambridge: Cambridge University Press.

Ketland, J. (1999). "Deflationism and Tarski's Paradise." *Mind* 108(429): 69–94.

Ketland, J. (2005). "Deflationism and the Gödel Phenomena: Reply to Tennant." *Mind* 114(453): 75–88.

Kiparsky, P. and Kiparsky, C. (1970). "Fact." In *Progress in Linguistics: A Collection of Papers*, pp. 143–73. Edited by M. Bierwisch and K. Heidolph. The Hague: Mouton.

Kirkham, R. (1992). *Theories of Truth: A Critical Introduction*. Cambridge, MA: MIT Press.

Kitcher, P. (1989). "Explanatory Unification and the Causal Structure of the World." *Scientific Explanation: MSPS* 13: 410–505.

Kitcher, P. (2002). "On the Explanatory Role of Correspondence Truth." *Philosophy and Phenomenological Research* 64(2): 346–64.

Kölbel, M. (2001). "Two Dogmas of Davidsonian Semantics." *Journal of Philosophy* 98(12): 613–35.

Kölbel, M. and Weiss, B. (Eds.) (2004). *Wittgenstein's Lasting Significance*. New York: Routledge.

Kripke, S. (1975). "Outline of a Theory of Truth." *Journal of Philosophy* 72(19): 690–716.

Kripke, S. (1976). "Is There a Problem About Substitutional Quantification?" In *Truth and Meaning*, pp. 324–419. Edited by G. Evans and J. McDowell. Oxford: Clarendon Press.

Kripke, S. (1980). *Naming and Necessity*. Cambridge, MA: Harvard University Press.

BIBLIOGRAPHY

Kripke, S. (1982). *Wittgenstein on Rules and Private Language: An Elementary Exposition.* Cambridge, MA: Harvard University Press.

Künne, W. (2003). *Conceptions of Truth.* Oxford: Oxford University Press.

Künne, W. (forthcoming). "Spelling Out a Truism about Truth." *Inquiry.*

Lance, M. (1997). "The Significance of Anaphoric Theories of Truth and Reference." *Truth: Philosophical Issues* 8: 181–98.

Laudan, L. (1981). "A Confutation of Convergent Realism." *Philosophy of Science* 48(1): 19–49.

Leeds, S. (1978). "Theories of Reference and Truth." *Erkenntnis* 13(1): 111–29.

Leeds, S. (1995). "Truth, Correspondence, and Success." *Philosophical Studies* 79: 1–36.

Lewis, D. (1970). "General Semantics." *Synthese* 22(1–2): 18–67.

Lewis, D. (1983). "New Work for a Theory of Universals." *Australasian Journal of Philosophy* 61(4): 343–77.

Lewis, D. (1986). *On the Plurality of Worlds.* Oxford: Blackwell Publishers.

Lewis, D. (1999). *Papers in Metaphysics and Epistemology.* Cambridge: Cambridge University Press.

Lewis, D. (2001). "Truthmaking and Difference-Making." *Noûs* 35(4): 602–15.

Liggins, D. (2012). "Truth-Makers and Dependence." In *Metaphysical Grounding*, pp. 254–71. Edited by F. Correia and B. Schnieder. Cambridge: Cambridge University Press.

Liggins, D. (2014). "Constructive Methodological Deflationism, Dialetheism and the Liar." *Analysis* 74(4): 566–74.

Liggins, D. (2016). "Deflationism, Conceptual Explanation, and the Truth Asymmetry." *Philosophical Quarterly* 66(262): 84–101.

Loparić, A. and da Costa, N. (1984). "Paraconsistency, Paracompleteness, and Valuations." *Logique et Analyse*, n.s. 27(106): 119–31.

Lynch, M. (2001). "Deflationary Views and Their Critics: Introduction." In *The Nature of Truth: Classic and Contemporary Perspectives*, pp. 421–31. Edited by M. Lynch. Cambridge, MA: MIT Press.

Lynch, M. (2009). *Truth as One and Many.* Oxford: Oxford University Press.

MacBride, F. (2022). "Truthmakers." In *The Stanford Encyclopedia of Philosophy* (Fall 2022 edition). Edited by E. Zalta and U. Nodelman. https://plato.stanford.edu/archives/fall2022/entries/truthmakers/.

Mancosu, P. (2001). "Mathematical Explanation: Problems and Prospects." *Topoi* 20(1): 97–117.

Marques, T. (2018). "This Is Not an Instance of (E)." *Synthese* 195(3): 1035–63.

Maudlin, T. (2004). *Truth and Paradox: Solving the Riddles.* New York: Oxford University Press.

McGee, V. (1992). "Maximal Consistent Sets of Instances of Tarski's Schema (T)." *Journal of Philosophical Logic* 21(3): 235–41.

McGee, V. (2016). "Thought, Thoughts, and Deflationism." *Philosophical Studies* 173(12): 3153–68.

McGrath, M. (2003). "Deflationism and the Normativity of Truth." *Philosophical Studies* 112(1): 47–67.
Moore, G. (1901/1993). "Truth and Falsity." In *Selected Writings*, pp. 20–22. Edited by T. Baldwin. London: Routledge.
Moore, G. (1953). *Some Main Problems of Philosophy*. London: George, Allen and Unwin.
Mount, B. and Waxman, D. (2021). "Stable and Unstable Theories of Truth and Syntax." *Mind* 130(518): 439–73.
Mulligan, K., Simons, P., and Smith, B. (1984). "Truth-Makers." *Philosophy and Phenomenological Research* 44(3): 287–321.
Murzi, J. and Rossi, L. (2018). "Conservative Deflationism." *Philosophical Studies* 177(10): 535–49.
Nicolai, C. (2021). "Fix, Express, Quantify: Disquotation After Its Logic." *Mind* 130(519): 727–57.
O'Leary-Hawthorne, J. and Oppy, G. (1997). "Minimalism and Truth." *Noûs* 31(2): 170–96.
O'Leary-Hawthorne, J. and Price, H. (1996). "How to Stand Up for Non-Cognitivists." *Australasian Journal of Philosophy* 74(2): 275–92.
Oms, S. (2019). "Conceivability, Minimalism and the Generalization Problem." *Dialogue* 58(2): 287–97.
Parsons, C. (1971). "A Plea for Substitutional Quantification." *Journal of Philosophy* 68(8): 231–37.
Parsons, C. (1974). "The Liar Paradox." *Journal of Philosophical Logic* 3(4): 381–412.
Parsons, T. (1990). "True Contradictions." *Canadian Journal of Philosophy* 20(3): 335–53.
Patterson, D. (2005). "Deflationism and the Truth-Conditional Theory of Meaning." *Philosophical Studies* 124(3): 271–94.
Patterson, D. (2012). *Alfred Tarski: Philosophy of Language and Logic*. New York: Palgrave-Macmillan.
Pedersen, N. and Wright, C. (2018). "Pluralist Theories of Truth." In *The Stanford Encyclopedia of Philosophy* (Winter 2018 edition). Edited by E. Zalta. https://plato.stanford.edu/archives/win2018/entries/truth-pluralist/.
Picollo, L. and Schindler, T. (2018). "Deflationism and the Function of Truth." *Philosophy of Language: Philosophical Perspectives* 32: 326–51.
Picollo, L. and Schindler, T. (2021). "Is Deflationism Compatible with Compositional and Tarskian Truth Theories?" In *Modes of Truth: The Unified Approach to Modality, Truth, and Paradox*, pp. 41–68. Edited by C. Nicolai and J. Stern. New York: Routledge.
Picollo, L. and Schindler, T. (2022). "Higher-Order Logic and Disquotational Truth." *Journal of Philosophical Logic* 51(4): 879–918.
Podlaskowski, A. (2022). "Methodological Deflationism and Semantic Theories." *Erkenntnis* 87(3): 1415–22.

Price, H. (1998). "Three Norms of Assertibility, or How the Moa Became Extinct." *Language, Mind, and Ontology: Philosophical Perspectives* 12: 241–54.

Price, H. (2003). "Truth as Convenient Friction." *Journal of Philosophy* 100(4): 167–90.

Priest, G. (1987/2006). *In Contradiction*. 2nd ed. Oxford: Oxford University Press.

Priest, G. (1995/2002). *Beyond the Limits of Thought*. 2nd ed. Oxford: Oxford University Press.

Priest, G. (2000). "On the Principle of Uniform Solution: A Reply to Smith." *Mind* 109(433): 123–26.

Priest, G. (2004). "Wittgenstein's Remarks on Gödel's Theorem." In Kölbel and Weiss (2004), pp. 207–28.

Priest, G. (2007). "Revenge, Field, and ZF." In Beall (Ed.) (2007), pp. 225–33.

Priest, G. (2015). "Fusion and Confusion." *Topoi* 34(1): 55–61.

Prior, A. (1956). "Definitions, Rules and Axioms." *Proceedings of the Aristotelian Society* 56: 199–216.

Prior, A. (1958). "Epimenides the Cretan." *Journal of Symbolic Logic* 23(3): 261–66.

Prior, A. (1960a). "The Runabout Inference-Ticket." *Analysis* 21(2): 38–9.

Prior, A. (1960b). "On a Family of Paradoxes." *Notre Dame Journal of Formal Logic* 2(1): 16–32.

Prior, A. (1967). "Correspondence Theory of Truth." In *The Encyclopedia of Philosophy*, vol. 2, pp. 223–32. Edited by P. Edwards. New York: The Macmillan Co. and The Free Press.

Prior, A. (1971). *Objects of Thought*. Edited by P. Geach and A. Kenny. Oxford: Clarendon Press.

Putnam, H. (1973). "Meaning and Reference." *Journal of Philosophy* 70(19): 699–711.

Putnam, H. (1978). *Meaning and the Moral Sciences*. London: Routledge and Kegan Paul.

Putnam, H. (1983/1985). "Vagueness and Alternative Logic." In *Realism and Reason: Philosophical Papers*, vol. 3, pp. 271–86. Cambridge: Cambridge University Press, 1985.

Putnam, H. (1983/1994). "On Truth." In Putnam (1994), pp. 315–29.

Putnam, H. (1985). "A Comparison of Something with Something Else." *New Literary History* 17: 61–79. Reprinted in Putnam (1994), pp. 330–50.

Putnam, H. (1991). "Does the Disquotational Theory Really Solve All Philosophical Problems?" *Metaphilosophy* 22(1–2): 1–13. Reprinted in Putnam (1994), pp. 264–78.

Putnam, H. (1994). *Words and Life*. Edited by J. Conant. Cambridge, MA: Harvard University Press.

Quine, W. (1940/2003). *Mathematical Logic*. Rev. ed. Cambridge, MA: Harvard University Press.

Quine, W. (1960). *Word and Object*. Cambridge, MA: MIT Press.
Quine, W. (1966/1976). *The Ways of Paradox and Other Essays*. 2nd ed. Cambridge: Harvard University Press.
Quine, W. (1970/1986). *Philosophy of Logic*. 2nd ed. Cambridge, MA: Harvard University Press.
Quine, W. (1981). *Theories and Things*. Cambridge, MA: Harvard University Press.
Quine, W. (1992). *Pursuit of Truth*. Rev. ed. Cambridge, MA: Harvard University Press.
Railton, P. (1981). "Probability, Explanation, and Information." *Synthese* 48(2): 233–56.
Ramsey, F. (1927/1990). "Facts and Propositions." In *Philosophical Papers*, pp. 34–51. Edited by D. Mellor. Cambridge: Cambridge University Press.
Ramsey, F. (1929/1991). *On Truth: Original Manuscript Materials (1927–1929)*. Edited by N. Rescher and U. Majer. Dordrecht: Kluwer Academic Publishers.
Rayo, A. and Uzquiano, G. (2006). *Absolute Generality*. New York: Oxford University Press.
Rayo, A. and Yablo, S. (2001). "Nominalism Through De-Nominalization." *Noûs* 35(1): 74–92.
Read, R. (2000). "What 'There Can be No Such Thing as Meaning Anything by Any Word' Could Possibly Mean." In *The New Wittgenstein*, pp. 74–83. Edited by A. Crary and R. Read. New York: Routledge.
Rendsvig, R. and Symons, J. (2019). "Epistemic Logic." In *The Stanford Encyclopedia of Philosophy* (Summer 2021 edition). Edited by E. Zalta. https://plato.stanford.edu/archives/sum2021/entries/logic-epistemic/.
Resnik, M. (1997). *Mathematics as a Science of Patterns*. Oxford: Oxford University Press.
Rosen, G. (1990). "Modal Fictionalism." *Mind* 99(395): 327–54.
Rumfitt, I. (1995). "Truth Wronged: Crispin Wright's *Truth and Objectivity*." *Ratio*, n.s. 8: 100–107.
Rumfitt, I. (2014). "Truth and Meaning." *Proceedings of the Aristotelian Society, Supplementary Volumes* 88: 21–55.
Russell, B. (1910). "On the Nature of Truth and Falsehood." In *Philosophical Essays*, pp. 147–59. New York: Simon and Schuster.
Sainsbury, R. (2010). *Fiction and Fictionalism*. New York: Routledge.
Scharp. K. (2013). *Replacing Truth*. Oxford: Oxford University Press.
Schiffer, S. (2003). *The Things We Mean*. Oxford: Oxford University Press.
Schiffer, S. (2017). "Deflationist Theories of Truth, Meaning, and Content." In *A Companion to the Philosophy of Language*, 2nd ed., vol. 1, pp. 463–90. Edited by B. Hale, C. Wright, and A. Miller. Oxford: John Wiley & Sons.
Schindler, T. (2020). "A Note on Horwich's Notion of Grounding." *Synthese* 197(5): 2029–38.

Schindler, T. and Schlöder, J. (2022). "The Proper Formulation of the Minimalist Theory of Truth." *Philosophical Quarterly* 72(3): 695–712.

Schnieder, B. (2006). "A Certain Kind of Trinity: Substance, Dependance, Explanation." *Philosophical Studies* 129(2): 393–419.

Schnieder, B. (2010). "A Puzzle About 'Because.'" *Logique & Analyse* 53(211): 317–43.

Searle, J. (1975). "The Logical Status of Fictional Discourse." *New Literary History* 6: 319–32.

Searle, J. (2006). "Insight and Error in Wittgenstein." *Philosophy of the Social Sciences* 46(6): 527–47.

Sellars, W. (1974). "Meaning as Functional Classification." *Synthese* 27(3): 417–37.

Sellars, W. (1979). *Naturalism and Ontology*. Atascadero: Ridgeview.

Shapiro, S. (1991). *Foundations Without Foundationalism: A Case for Second-Order Logic*. Oxford: Clarendon Press.

Shapiro, S. (1998). "Proof and Truth: Through Thick and Thin." *Journal of Philosophy* 95(10): 493–521.

Shapiro, S. (2005). "Gurus, Logical Consequence, and Truth Bearers: What Is It That Is True." In Armour-Garb and Beall (Eds.) (2005a), pp. 153–70.

Simmons, K. (1999). "Deflationary Truth and the Liar." *Journal of Philosophical Logic* 28(5): 455–88.

Simmons, K. (2006). "Deflationism and the Autonomy of Truth." *Philosophy and Phenomenological Research* 72(1): 196–204.

Simmons, K. (2008). *Universality and the Liar: An Essay on Truth and the Diagonal Argument*. Cambridge: Cambridge University Press.

Simmons, K. (2018). "Three Questions for Minimalism." *Synthese* 195(3): 1011–34.

Simpson, M. (2021). "Deflationism and Truthmaking." *Synthese* 198(4): 3157–81.

Smith, N. (2000). "The Principle of Uniform Solution (of the Paradoxes of Self-Reference)." *Mind* 109(433): 117–22.

Smith, N. (2009). "Frege's Judgement Stroke and the Conception of Logic as the Study of Inference Not Consequence." *Philosophy Compass* 4(4): 639–65.

Smorynski, C. (1977). "The Incompleteness Theorems." In *Handbook of Mathematical Logic*, pp. 821–65. Edited by J. Barwise. Amsterdam: North-Holland.

Soames, S. (1984). "What Is a Theory of Truth?" *Journal of Philosophy* 81(8): 411–29.

Soames, S. (1998). *Understanding Truth*. Oxford: Oxford University Press.

Soames, S. (2003). "Understanding Deflationism." *Language and Philosophical Linguistics: Philosophical Perspectives* 17: 369–83.

Stalnaker, R. (1970). "Pragmatics." *Synthese* 22(1–2): 272–89.

Stalnaker, R. (1976). "Possible Worlds." *Noûs* 10(1): 65–75.

Stanley, J. (2001). "Hermeneutic Fictionalism." *Figurative Language: Midwest Studies in Philosophy* 25(1): 36–71.
Steiner, M. (1978). "Mathematical Explanation." *Philosophical Studies* 34(2): 135–51.
Stern, J. (2023). "Methodological Deflationism and Metaphysical Grounding: From *Because* via *Truth* to *Ground*." *Inquiry*. Online first at https://doi.org/10.1080/0020174X.2022.2138964.
Strawson, P. (1949). "Truth." *Analysis* 9(6): 83–97.
Strawson, P. (1950). "Truth." *Proceeding of the Aristotelian Society* 24: 129–56.
Sullivan, P. and Johnston, C. (2018). "Judgments, Facts, and Propositions: Theories of Truth in Russell, Wittgenstein, and Ramsey." In *The Oxford Handbook of Truth*, pp. 150–92. Edited by M. Glanzberg. Oxford: Oxford University Press.
Tarski, A. (1935a/1983). "The Concept of Truth in Formalized Languages." Translated J. Woodger. In Corcoran (Ed.) (1983), pp. 152–278.
Tarski, A. (1935b/1983). "On the Concept of Logical Consequence." Reprinted in Corcoran (Ed.) (1983), pp. 409–20.
Tarski, A. (1944). "The Semantic Conception of Truth." *Philosophy and Phenomenological Research* 4(4): 341–75.
Tarski, A. (1969). "Truth and Proof." *Scientific American* 220: 63–77.
Taschek, W. (2008). "Truth, Assertion, and the Horizontal: Frege on 'The Essence of Logic.'" *Mind* 117(466): 375–401.
Tennant, N. (2002). "Deflationism and the Gödel Phenomena." *Mind* 111(443): 551–82.
Textor, M. (2010). "Frege on Judging as Acknowledging the Truth." *Mind* 119(475): 615–55.
Thomasson, A. (2015). *Ontology Made Easy*. New York: Oxford University Press.
Van Fraassen, B. (1980). *The Scientific Image*. Oxford: Clarendon Press.
Van Inwagen, P. (1981). "Why I Don't Understand Substitutional Quantification." *Philosophical Studies* 39(3): 281–85.
Velleman, D. (2000). "On the Aim of Belief." In *The Possibility of Practical Reason*, pp. 244–81. Oxford: Clarendon Press.
Walker, R. (1989/2001). "The Coherence Theory." In *The Nature of Truth: Classic and Contemporary Readings*, pp. 123–58. Edited by M. Lynch. Cambridge, MA: MIT Press, 2001.
Walton, K. (1990). *Mimesis as Make-Believe*. Cambridge, MA: Harvard University Press.
Walton, K. (1993). "Metaphor and Prop-Oriented Make-Believe." *European Journal of Philosophy* 1(1): 39–56.
Warren, J. (2023). "The Liar and 'Meaningless' Revenge." *Journal of Philosophical Logic* 53(1): 49–78.

Waxman, D. (2017). "Deflationism, Arithmetic, and the Argument from Conservativeness." *Mind* 126(502): 429–63.
Whyte, J. (1990). "Success Semantics." *Analysis* 50(3): 149–57.
Williams, C. (1976). *What Is Truth?* Cambridge: Cambridge University Press.
Williams, C. (1992). *Being, Identity, and Truth*. Oxford: Clarendon Press.
Williams, M. (1986). "Do We (Epistemologists) Need a Theory of Truth?" *Philosophical Topics* 14(1): 223–42.
Williams, M. (1999). "Meaning and Deflationary Truth." *Journal of Philosophy* 96(11): 545–64.
Williams, M. (2004). "Wittgenstein, Truth and Certainty." In Kölbel and Weiss (2004), pp. 249–85.
Wittgenstein, L. (1921/1961). *Tractatus Logico-Philosophicus*. Translated by D. Pears and B. McGuinness. London: Routledge & Kegan Paul.
Wittgenstein, L. (1934/1974). *Philosophical Grammar*. Edited by R. Rhees. Translated by A. Kenny. Oxford: Blackwell Publishing.
Wittgenstein, L. (1937/2005). *The Big Typescript: TS 213*. Edited and translated by C. Luckhardt and M. Aue. Oxford: Blackwell Publishing.
Wittgenstein, L. (1953). *Philosophical Investigations*. 4th ed. Translated by G. Anscombe, P. Hacker, and J. Schulte. Oxford: Blackwell Publishing, 2009.
Woodbridge, J. (2003). "Deflationism and the Generalization Problem." In *The Logica Yearbook 2003*, pp. 285–97. Edited by L. Behounek. Prague: Filosofia.
Woodbridge, J. (2004). "A Neglected Dimension of Semantic Pathology." In *The Logica Yearbook 2004*, pp. 277–92. Edited by L. Behounek. Prague: Filosofia.
Woodbridge, J. (2005). "Truth as a Pretense." In *Fictionalism in Metaphysics*, pp. 134–77. Edited by M. Kalderon. Oxford: Oxford University Press.
Woodbridge, J. (2006). "Propositions as Semantic Pretense." *Language & Communication* 26(3–4): 343–55.
Wrenn, C. (2011). "Practical Success and the Nature of Truth." *Synthese* 181(3): 451–70.
Wrenn, C. (2021). "Deflating the Success-Truth Connection." *Australasian Journal of Philosophy* 101(1): 96–110.
Wright, C. (1992). *Truth and Objectivity*. Cambridge, MA: Harvard University Press.
Yablo, S. (1996). "How in the World?" *Philosophical Topics* 24: 255–86.

Index

For the benefit of digital users, indexed terms that span two pages (e.g., 52–53) may, on occasion, appear on only one of those pages.

adverbial
    quantification, 61–62, 66, 105n.21, 291–92, 295, 297–98, 305–6, 310, 312, 315–16
    sentential-variable deflationism (ASVD), 105n.21, 291–316
alethic
    concepts/notions, 1–2, 4, 7–8, 13, 57, 65, 76–77, 79–80, 93, 200, 201–2 (*see also* truth concept)
    fictionalism, 204–6, 215–17, 296–97
    generalization, 11–12, 52, 92n.16, 103–4, 107–8, 120–34, 142–43, 148–49, 170–71, 213, 233, 235–36, 298, 310–11 (*see also* Formulation Problem (FP); Generalization Problem (GP))
    locutions, 3–4, 6–8, 13, 19, 23, 57–58, 59, 64–66, 68, 70–77, 79–80, 88–89, 91, 93–94, 107–8, 109, 120–21, 194–95, 200–1, 207, 214–15, 233–34, 287, 311–12, 314–15n.29
    nihilism, 265n.31
    platitudes, 179n.36, 291n.5, 298n.16
    pluralism, 3n.1, 312–13
    properties (*see* properties, alethic)
anaphora, 19–20, 59, 63–64, 67, 69–70, 72–74, 221–22, 258, 300–2, 311

arithmetic, 30–31, 116–17, 153–54, 156–59, 163–73, 305–6
    Peano (PA), 30–31, 116–17, 154–59, 162–69, 171–72, 174–75, 305–6
Asay, Jamin, 7, 182–83, 193–96, 198–200, 263–65
assertibility (warranted), 202–6
assertion, 18–20, 37, 42, 45, 49–50, 201–6, 209–11, 215–18, 298
Ayer, A. J., 37, 44–46, 76–77, 178, 209–10
Azzouni, Jody, 12–13, 20–24, 75, 78–79, 170–72, 174–75, 225–26, 276–77, 288–91

Bar-On, Dorit, 7, 15–20, 36–37, 207–11
Båve, Arvid, 16–17, 113
Beall, JC, 16–17, 25–26, 255–57, 263–64, 269–72, 275–83
belief, 4–5, 13, 38n.6, 39–40, 42–44, 46–47, 92–93, 95, 100–1, 119–20, 136–37, 140–43, 144–47, 149–51, 203–4, 205n.51, 209–11, 215–18, 231–32, 301n.19 (*see also* truth-bearers)
    ascription/specification, 38–41, 60, 140–43, 144–45
Belnap, Nuel, 68, 161–62

INDEX

Bivalence, 228, 238–39, 249–50, 264–65, 269–71
Boghossian, Paul, 214–17
Brandom, R., 6, 16–20, 45, 72–76, 113, 120–23, 187, 214–15, 220–21, 222–23, 284–85, 298
Bueno, Otávio, 282–83
Burgis, Ben, 282–83

Carnap, Rudolf, 39, 44, 54
categorical theory, 167–68, 172–73
Chihara, Charles, 15, 225–26, 261–62
Cieśliński, Cezary, 130, 168
cognitive equivalence (*see* content, equivalence/redundancy)
coherence
  conditions, 21–22
  theory, 3–4, 57
compositional
  principles, 22–23, 82–83, 86–87, 166–67
  truth-theory, 86–88, 156–58, 165–67, 220–21
concepts, 15, 17–18, 19–20, 36n.4, 48, 81, 95–96, 98–100, 102, 103–4, 107–8, 128, 133, 185–86, 189–90, 207–12, 213, 241–42, 298, 313
  attributive/substantive, 4, 8, 57, 65, 76–77, 79–80, 85–86, 93, 200, 207, 209–10, 213, 215–17, 313
  deflated/thin, 13–14, 58, 61–62, 95–96, 207, 209–10, 215–17
Conceptual Deflationism, 7–8, 13–14, 15–22, 23–24, 29–30, 34, 44, 48, 58, 61–62, 65–66, 68–69, 73–75, 79–81, 83–84, 85–86, 93–94, 95–96, 103–4, 107–8, 144n.2, 207–23, 276–77, 283–84, 298, 312–13
conservativeness, 152–77

content, 19–20, 24–30, 37, 42, 115–16n.3, 118–20, 138–39, 143–44, 147, 150–51, 160, 217–23, 258–60, 301–2, 313–14
  equivalence/redundancy, 4–5, 13–14, 35–36, 38–39, 45, 60–62, 63–64, 66–67, 71–72, 76–77, 79–81, 85–86, 110–11, 115–16n.3, 122–23, 131, 187, 231, 262, 303, 313–14
  inheritance, 59–60, 63–64, 231, 258–60, 300–1
  theory (*see* meaning, theory)
contradiction, 14–15, 63, 103–4, 224, 227–29, 240–42, 242n.12, 253n.21, 254, 262–63, 267n.36, 268–69, 273–78, 279, 281, 294, 313–14
Convention (T) (CT), 53–54, 79, 85, 219–20, 235–36, 242–44, 252, 277–78
  Strong (SCT), 235–37, 244, 252–53, 255–56, 261–62, 270–71, 277–78, 283–84, 303, 313–14
correspondence
  intuition, 55–56, 103–4, 135, 177–86, 187–90, 190n.42, 192–93, 194–96, 310–11
  relation, 21–24, 37–38, 44, 47–49, 55–56, 57, 103–4, 177–83, 183n.39, 200–1, 220–21, 310–11
  theory, 3–4, 35–36, 47–49, 50–51, 179–83, 183n.39, 198–99, 200–1

David, Marian, 12–13, 82–83, 91–93, 99–100, 103, 133–34, 288
Davidson, Donald, 219–23
denominalization, 22–23, 73–74, 98, 300–1, 307
determinately operator, 253–56
  global (GDO), 255–57
Devitt, Michael, 28, 33, 143–44, 207–8, 215–17, 220–21

diagnosis of paradox/pathology, 15, 21n.19, 63–64, 225–26, 258–60, 261–62, 301–2, 311–12
dialetheism, 227, 275–83
dimensions of deflationism, 7
discourse
  fictional vs non-fictional, 204–6, 215–17, 218–19
  fragment, 1–2, 3–4, 7–8, 16, 30–31, 79n.9, 218–19, 310–11, 315–16 (*see also* truth-talk)
  nonfactual (*see* nonfactualism)
  semantic (*see* semantic, discourse)
disquotation, 76–77, 121, 136–37
  device, 78–80
disquotational
  account/view, 52–53, 76–79, 81–83, 90, 92–93, 96–97, 98–99, 121–23, 156, 175–76
  schema (DS), 56, 79, 81, 83–87, 96–97, 99–100, 110–11, 115–16n.3, 131–32, 156n.12
disquotationalism, 1–2, 7n.6, 52–53, 69, 76–77, 98–99, 100–1, 109–10, 112, 135–36, 200–1, 203–4
  pure, 26–27, 85–93, 100–1, 109–10, 113–15, 131
  recursive, 82–83, 85–87, 135–36, 169
Douven, Igor, 187–90
Dummett, Michael, 42, 47–48, 161–64, 201–2, 204–6, 214, 217, 220–22

entailment, 209–10, 212, 307
epistemicism (*see* semantic, epistemicism)
equivalence, 5–6, 31–32, 79–80, 85–86, 98–99
  content/meaning/cognitive (*see* content, equivalence/redundancy)
  strong, 6, 63–64, 98–100, 187, 189–90, 193–94, 231–33, 235–36, 303, 313–14
equivalence schema (ES), 16–17, 56, 96–99, 100–1, 112, 119–20, 128–30, 184–86, 195n.47, 231–32, 235, 262–71, 274, 277n.49
ex falso quodlibet (EFQ), 227, 275
exhaustive logical valuation (ELV), 227, 244, 252, 257–58, 262, 270–71, 278, 283–84, 302–3, 313–14
exhaustive semantic characterization (ESC), 227–28, 244, 251–52, 257, 259–60, 262, 270–71, 279, 283–84, 302–3, 313–14
explanation, 90, 100–1, 135–36, 139–40, 143, 146–50, 166, 176–77, 183n.40, 185–86, 187–90, 192–94, 199–200, 298
  of behavior, 119–20, 143–45
  of behavioral success (*see* success argument)
  conceptual, 189–90
  of meaning/content (*see* meaning, theory)
  of other concepts (*see* explanatory, role (conceptual))
  of success of scientific theories/method (*see* success argument)
  truth free, 145–47, 208, 214, 218–23
  what- vs why-, 207–8
explanatory
  asymmetry, 185–93
  dependence/relationship/connection, 184–85, 187–90
  ineliminability/fundamentality, 19, 135–36, 138–39, 142–43
  role (causal), 83–84, 107–8, 135–53, 188–89, 199–202, 207–8, 220–21, 284–85

explanatory (*cont.*)
  role (conceptual), 13–14, 18–20, 24–25, 29–30, 34, 48, 74–75, 83–84, 107–8, 207–23, 284, 313
  role (mathematico-logical), 135, 284–85 (*see also* conservativeness)
expressive
  device/convenience/advantage, 51–52, 139–40, 141, 307
  dispensability, 127, 284–85, 306
  incompleteness/weakness, 229–30, 247–48, 251–52
  indispensability/ineliminability, 9n.8, 19, 284–85, 296, 306
  role/capacity/function, 7, 10–11, 19, 26–28, 54–55, 61–62, 68–69, 76–77, 80–84, 95–96, 120–21, 135–36, 138, 141, 143, 146–47, 150–51, 152–53, 159, 162n.25, 166, 174–75, 177–78, 192–93, 203–6, 207–8, 210–11, 214n.3, 222–23, 231–36, 284–85, 287–92, 306, 310, 312, 314–15
expressivism, 214–15, 217–18
extension, 116, 153–54, 161–62, 164–65, 167, 171, 174–76, 178, 185–86, 189–90, 195–96, 246, 248–50, 251, 265, 294, 303–6, 312
extensional context, 231, 233, 236

facts, 37–38, 55–56, 63, 102, 124, 129, 143, 177, 179–83, 184, 190–92, 193–95, 198, 202, 217, 264, 267–70
false, 1–2, 3–4, 14, 21–22, 36, 39–41, 45, 47–48, 52, 62–64, 70, 77–78, 81, 98–99, 101, 114, 149, 160, 163, 167, 171–72, 184, 196–97, 211, 227–29, 236–37, 238–39, 242–46, 247–50, 255–56, 259–61, 263–65, 268–71, 274–75, 278, 281, 294–95, 308–10, 313–14
falsity, 1–2, 4–5, 13–14, 47–48, 52, 70, 94, 101, 109–11, 149, 160, 196–97, 201–2, 214, 238–39, 245–46, 269, 275–76, 278, 309–10
falsity schema (FS), 101, 269–70
Feferman, Solomon, 231–32, 236–37, 252
fictionalism, 204–6, 215–17, 218–19, 228n.3
  alethic (*see* alethic, fictionalism)
  vs. non-fictionalism, 214, 215–17
  hermeneutic vs. revolutionary, 289n.2
Field, Hartry, 13–14, 24–28, 29–30, 54–55, 85–94, 99–100, 109–23, 131–33, 143–46, 166–67, 176–77, 203–4, 217–18, 231, 253–58, 288n.1, 297–98
foreign sentences, 77–78, 90–91, 109–10, 111–16, 118 (*see also* immanence)
formal
  challenges, 107–8, 224, 283–84
  correctness, 53–54
  devices/machinery, 11–12, 17n.14, 103–5, 151–52, 213, 288–92, 297–300, 303–4, 305–7, 308–9
  languages, 53–54, 78–79, 92–93, 242n.12
  theorizing, 52–53, 56, 65–66, 78–79, 152–53, 155–56, 162–63, 169, 238, 288–89, 295–96, 307
Formulation Problem (FP), 12–13, 74n.6, 88n.15, 100, 109, 120, 122–24, 126, 133–34, 140n.1, 151–52, 235, 255–56, 288, 296–97, 298, 310–11

fragmentation, 12–13, 23–24, 100, 122–23, 150–52, 190–92, 194–95, 196–97n.49, 199–200, 213, 235, 256, 288, 298
Frege, Gottlob, 17–20, 30–31, 32–33, 34–40, 61–62, 209–11, 219–20

Gamester, Will, 149–52, 264n.29
gap (truth-value), 122–23, 228, 249, 275–76, 278, 299
garbage sentence, 240–41, 243–44, 257, 303
Gauker, Christopher, 86, 242
generalization (generalizing), 8–9, 84n.10, 86–87, 92n.16, 99–100, 150, 156n.12, 157–58, 174n.32, 234n.9, 256, 269–70, 293–94, 296–99, 301, 305–7, 310–11, 315 (*see also* Formulation Problem (FP); Generalization Problem (GP))
　alethic (*see* alethic, generalization)
　role (*see* expressive, role/capacity/function)
Generalization Problem (GP), 120, 123–24, 126–27, 130–31, 133–34, 143, 151–52, 157, 296–97, 298, 310–11
genus, 1–2, 6–7, 59, 204–6
glut (truth-value), 275–76, 278
Gödel
　numbering, 153–56, 164n.26, 169
　sentences, 159, 163–66, 169, 171–72
groundedness, 245–51, 258–61, 267–71, 274–75
grounding (*see* truth-maker theory)
Grover, Dorothy, 21n.19, 60n.2, 68–76, 113n.2, 196–97n.49, 200–1, 258–62, 305n.22

Gupta, Anil, 76n.7, 100, 120–23, 128, 132n.13, 143
guru problem, 116–19

Halbach, Volker, 124, 153–54, 158–59, 161–63, 167–68, 298, 305–6
Heck, Richard Kimberly, 7–8, 25–26, 35–36, 91–92
hermeneutic theorizing, 225–26, 289–92
hierarchy, 4, 21–22, 25–26, 29–30, 239–46, 247–49, 251, 254–56
Hill, Christopher, 102–5, 133, 179–81
Hindriks, Frank, 73–75
Horisk, Claire, 221–23
Horsten, Leon, 3–4, 8, 52–53, 152–56, 158–59, 161–63, 166–68, 172, 174–75, 255–56, 298
Horwich, Paul, 6, 11–14, 16–17, 46–48, 52–53, 55–56, 93–105, 112, 118–23, 127–30, 140–41, 146–49, 176, 180–87, 189–90, 192–98, 200–2, 203–6, 207, 214n.3, 214–15, 217, 220, 231–32, 235, 262–75, 288, 298
how-talk, 62n.4, 291–316

identity theory, 38n.7, 180–81
idiolect, 77–78, 110–12, 114–15, 118–19
illocutionary
　act, 19
　device, 51–52
　force, 19, 210–11
immanence, 77–78, 109–20, 148, 311
immiscibility, 221–23
Inclosure, 282
incompleteness, 97, 149
　expressive, 229–30, 241–42, 251–52
　omega (ω-), 125–26, 256–57
　theorem, 159, 162–63

inconsistency, 21–22, 31–32, 53–54, 129, 212, 229, 236–37, 238, 240–42, 251–52, 254, 256–57, 265–66, 275–77, 289–90, 302–3
indeterminacy, 115, 265, 279, 301–3
inference-rule deflationism, 7–8, 86, 231
inflationism, 1–7, 10–11, 14–15, 21–22, 25, 26–29, 31–33, 44–46, 56, 57–59, 65–66, 68, 71, 72–73, 75–77, 85–86, 91, 93–96, 99, 116–17, 146–47, 149, 176, 177–78, 182–83, 185–86, 189–92, 196–202, 214–17, 231–35, 278, 284–85
  presuppositions, 1–2, 4, 6, 19, 28, 31–33, 57–59, 65–66, 71, 72–73, 74–76, 79–80, 176, 200–1
intentional/propositional attitude (*see* mental/intentional states)
intersubstitutability (Intersub), 230–37, 244, 247, 252, 255–56, 257–58, 262, 270–71, 275–76, 277–78, 283–84, 303, 313–14
  derived, 231–32, 233–35, 244, 270–71
intersubstitution, 86, 230–31, 234n.9, 247, 303, 308–10

judgment, 4–5, 18, 37–38, 42, 180–81, 209–10
justification, 33, 169, 186, 204–6, 209–10, 271

Ketland, Jeffrey, 52–53, 152–54, 160–61, 163–64, 169–70, 172, 174–75, 303–4
Kirkham, Richard, 29, 33, 179
Kitcher, Philip, 135–36, 139–40, 146–47, 150–51, 188–89
Kripke, Saul, 12–13, 47–48, 155–56, 194–95, 199–200, 224–25, 227–29, 240, 243–55, 257–59, 261, 263–64, 267–69, 277–78, 288, 301–2

Künne, Wolfgang, 41–42, 60–61, 189–92, 297–98

Lance, Mark, 221–22
language, 9–10, 15, 21–22, 53–54, 60–61, 77–79, 83–84, 90–93, 109–11, 113, 116, 118, 222–23, 238–42, 249–50, 267–69, 290, 293, 299, 306
Law of Excluded Middle (LEM), 228–29, 254, 264–65, 269–70, 273
Leeds, Stephen, 6, 9–10, 52–53, 54–55, 82–84, 86, 88–89, 92–93, 120–22, 135–37, 145–47, 184, 196–97, 199–200, 213, 244, 283–84, 287–88
Lewis, David, 177–78, 192–93, 198, 219–20, 297–98
Liar Paradox, 14–15, 19–20, 31, 34, 36–37, 53–54, 56, 58, 63–64, 67, 74–75, 82, 86–87, 98–99, 102, 103–4, 107–8, 155–56, 224–32, 235, 238–44, 250–51, 255–58, 260, 262–65, 267, 269–72, 274–76, 278–79, 281–84, 299–302, 311–12, 315–16
liar proposition (L), 262–65, 268–69, 270–71
liar sentence, 14–15, 31, 63, 100n.20, 226, 236–37, 239–41, 242n.12, 242n.13, 246–52, 253–64, 266n.33, 270n.41, 274, 275–78, 299–300
  simple (SL), 14–15, 31, 63, 228–29, 236–37
  strengthened (L), 224, 228–29, 253–54, 277–78
Liggins, David, 185–87, 189–92, 264
Linguistic Deflationism, 7–19, 21–24, 26–28, 30–31, 35–36, 38, 43–45, 48, 51–52, 58, 60–62, 65–66, 68–69, 73–75, 80–81, 83–84, 88–89, 94–96, 104, 107–8, 109–34, 152–53, 202–3,

204–6, 207–8, 213, 230, 232, 233–36, 283–84, 287, 312
linguistics, 25, 220–21
logic, 34–35, 40–41, 44, 116–17, 129–30, 161–62n.24, 196–97, 209–10, 212, 224, 233, 238–39, 241, 254, 269, 280
   classical, 21n.20, 79n.9, 161–62, 224, 227, 238–39, 244n.15, 252–54, 262–65, 272–74, 295n.13, 302–3
   first-order, 17n.14, 79n.9, 83–84, 125–26, 132n.13, 148, 157n.15, 158n.21, 161–63, 164, 167–68, 170–72, 174–76, 233, 288, 290, 303–7, 310–11, 315
   Kleene, 251–52, 260–61, 277–78
   paraconsistent, 227, 242–43, 275, 281
   second-order, 157n.15, 172–75
   three-valued, 252, 260–62, 278
   underlying, 71–74, 83–84, 88
logical
   connectives/devices/machinery, 41–42n.11, 61–62, 64–65, 70, 83–84, 103–4, 127–28, 150, 151–52, 157–58, 163, 174–75, 211, 212n.1, 213, 231n.6, 287, 288n.1, 288–99, 305–7, 310–11, 312–13
   form, 39–42, 45, 65–66, 71–72, 75, 81–82, 86–87, 96–97, 103, 120–26, 127, 132n.13, 154, 212, 232, 263, 273, 292–94, 299, 304, 310–11
   role/function, 4, 6n.4, 7–8, 10n.9, 17n.14, 27–28, 41–42, 54–55, 57, 59, 65, 68, 76–77, 80, 83–84, 88–89, 90, 93–96, 113–14, 135–36, 148, 150–52, 175–76, 196–97n.49, 197, 200, 203–4, 211–12, 287–91, 307, 312, 314–15
   value, 227, 229n.4, 244n.15, 249–50, 254, 260–62, 278, 302–3, 314–15

Lynch, Michael, 3n.1, 37, 147–48, 150–51

Marques, Teresa, 263–65, 268–69
mathematical, 153–54, 166–68, 188–89, 200–1
mathematics, 182–83, 218–19
Maudlin, Timothy, 231
maximal, 255–56, 265–68
maximalism, 182–84
McGee, Vann, 265–68
meaning, 20n.18, 24–25, 26–27, 29–32, 34n.2, 37, 42, 47–48, 91, 100–2, 118, 144n.2, 207–8, 219–23, 301–2 (*see also* content)
   entities, 77–78, 91, 102
   theory, 20n.18, 27–28, 31–32, 37, 42, 48, 98–99, 102, 118, 219–20
meaningful, 14–15, 110–11, 215–17, 227–28, 241–42, 295
meaningfulness, 44, 228
meaningless, 44, 110–11, 227–28, 261–62, 302, 311–12, 313–14
meaninglessness, 63–64
mental/intentional states, 37, 63, 86–87, 92–93, 95–96, 100–1, 140, 143–44, 203–4, 219–20, 309
metalanguage, 53–54, 131, 156, 221–23, 238–39, 250–52
Metaphysical Deflationism, 7–8, 13, 15–18, 21–22, 23–24, 27–28, 36, 38, 43, 46, 48, 50–51, 58, 62, 65, 71, 74–75, 81, 83–84, 88–89, 93–94, 95–96, 103–4, 107–8, 135–206, 207–8, 213, 235, 276–77, 283–84, 298, 303–4, 312
methodological deflationism, 24–33
minimal fixed point, 245–51, 259

minimalism, 1–2, 6–7, 16–17, 55–56, 93–94, 96–105, 112, 118, 127–30, 133, 148, 184–86, 187, 190–93, 200–1, 231–32, 235, 262–63, 267

Murzi, Julien, 157–58, 165, 168, 174

naturalism, 29, 54–55, 93–94, 135–36, 196–97, 220–21

natural-language interpretations (NLIs), 293, 300, 308–9

negation, 47–48, 70, 132, 155–56, 161–62, 202–4, 238–39, 242n.12, 248–49, 267n.36, 268–69, 275, 278, 294–95, 299, 300–1

nominal, 9–11, 12–13, 45, 152–53, 155–56, 233, 291, 294, 295–98, 305–7, 309–12

nominalization, 72–74, 232–33, 314–15

nominalized, 9–10, 295, 299, 310

nominalizing, 5–6, 41, 155–56, 164, 187

non-cognitivism, 214, 217–18

nonfactualism, 214–18

nontrivialism (NT), 226–27, 244, 252, 257–58, 262, 270–71, 275, 279, 282–84, 302, 313–14

norm, 202–6, 217–18, 233–34

normative role, 135, 201–6, 275–76

normativity (*see* normative role)

opacity (blind/opaque endorsement), 22–23, 35–36, 38–41, 49–52, 61–62, 73–74, 82–83, 109, 138, 166, 299n.17

operator
  determinately, 253–56
  intentional attitude, 65–66
  prosentence-forming, 72–73, 75, 200–1
  sentence-modification, 70, 73–74
  truth, 35–37, 38, 155n.9, 201–2

Oppy, Graham, 7–8, 207, 215–17

ordinary language/discourse, 10–11, 25–26, 43, 60n.2, 71, 79n.9, 90, 121, 234n.9, 289–92, 295–96, 306

Paradox Treatment Deflationism, 7, 15–18, 21n.19, 21n.20, 26n.23, 34n.1, 37n.5, 63–64, 67, 71, 74–75, 82, 84n.11, 89, 102, 103–4, 107–8, 224–85, 302–3, 311–14

paradox. *See* Liar Paradox; semantic, paradox/pathology

pathological sentences/cases, 225n.1, 244, 259–60, 278, 301–2

pathology, 15, 155–56, 239, 279, 284, 299–303, 311, 313–16

Patterson, Douglas, 52–53, 221–22, 276–77

performative theory, 49–52, 69–70

Picollo, Lavinia, 10, 12–13, 151–52, 161–62, 172, 174–77, 288–91, 298, 303–6

possible worlds, 99, 147, 219–20, 297–98

pragmatist theories, 3–4, 42, 57, 188–89

predicate-satisfaction, 16, 17n.15, 23, 54–55, 98–99, 133, 135–36, 301–2, 314–16

pretense, 123n.5, 218–19, 308–14, 309n.23

Price, Huw, 204–6, 215–17, 218–19

Priest, Graham, 47–48, 227, 229–30, 241, 242–43, 257–58, 271, 275–76, 278–79, 281–83

primitive,
  concept/notion, 18–19, 153–54, 198, 222–23
  denotation, 54–55
  formalism, 152n.5
  formulae, 168
  status, 182–83
  terms, 7–8

primitivism, 3–4, 57, 197–201
Principle of Unified Solution (PUS), 271–72, 274–75, 282
Prior, A. N., 34n.2, 61–72, 150, 151–52, 161–62n.24, 180–81, 291–96, 297, 299, 308
pronouns, 11–12, 40–41, 59, 66, 72–75, 258
proof, 120, 126–27, 129–30, 132, 156–66, 169–70, 174–77, 242–43, 254–56, 272–74
properties, 4, 6, 7–8, 10–11, 22–23, 35, 57–58, 65, 71, 81, 93–94, 95–96, 102, 176, 196–201, 203–4, 214–17, 233–34, 297–98, 307–9, 314–15
  abundant, 176, 198–99, 200–1
  alethic, 4, 57, 93, 200
  fragmented/disunified, 13, 23–24, 100, 150–51, 190–92, 194–95, 196–97n.49, 200n.50
  logical, 93–94, 95–96, 196–97, 200–1
  primitive/unanalyzable, 37–38, 200–1, 222–23
  sparse/natural, 176, 198–99
  substantive/robust, 6, 7–8, 12n.12, 13, 23, 33, 46, 93–94, 135, 152–53, 196–97, 200–2, 211–12, 214–15, 310, 312–13
  thin/insubstantial, 3–4, 13, 150–51, 160, 176, 197, 214–15
propositions (*see* truth-bearers)
prosentence, 59–61, 66, 68–70, 72–76, 122–23, 196–97, 200–1, 231, 258
  atomic, 68, 70, 72–73, 200–1
  forming operator, 72–73, 75, 200–1
prosententialism, 1–2, 6–7, 19–20, 43, 59–61, 63–65, 68–75, 79–80, 89–90, 98–99, 113, 122–23, 187, 196–97, 200–1, 214–15, 221–22, 231, 258, 262

psychological theory, 25, 140–49
Putnam, Hilary, 7n.6, 52–54, 82–83, 136–37, 141–44, 149, 203–4

quantification, 9–13, 40–42, 59–62, 64–69, 72–74, 79–80, 82–84, 86–89, 98–100, 102–5, 122–23, 132–34, 148, 150–52, 156–58, 161–62, 172–77, 180, 192–93, 208, 210–11, 232, 257, 287–316
  adverbial, 61–62, 66, 291–92, 295, 296–98, 305–6, 310, 312, 315–16
  first-order, 9–12, 84n.10, 162n.25, 174n.32, 174–75, 287–88, 290, 309–10, 315–16
  non-nominal, 61, 152n.6, 291, 295–98, 305–7, 310–12, 315
  objectual/nominal, 11–12, 40n.10, 84n.10, 98, 121, 180, 233, 296–98, 304, 306–7, 310–11, 311n.26, 315
  into predicate-position, 174n.32, 305
  second-order, 157n.15, 172–75, 303–5
  sentential, 11n.11, 13n.13, 17n.14, 40–42, 61–62, 64–66, 99, 122–23, 134n.14, 148, 150–52, 174–75, 192n.44, 208, 210–11, 232, 233–34, 287–89, 291–92, 295–99, 303–6, 310, 312–15
  substitutional, 12–13, 64–65, 87–89, 99–100, 102–5, 122–23, 132–34, 151–52, 180, 213, 288, 295–97, 299, 306–10
Quine, W. V. O., 6, 9–10, 11–12, 34, 52–53, 54–55, 69, 76–86, 88–89, 90–92, 109–15, 121–24, 125, 135–36, 143–44, 147, 174, 180–81, 200–1, 213, 222–23, 231, 238, 244, 287–88, 296–97, 306–7

INDEX

quotation, 21–22, 24–25, 40–41, 62, 66–67, 72, 73–74, 76–77, 78–80, 81, 86–87, 113–14, 131, 164, 169, 238, 251–52, 299, 309

Ramsey, Frank, 34n.2, 37–45, 47–49, 51–52, 60–62, 66, 68, 70, 80, 150, 178, 180–81, 200–1, 219–20, 283–84, 287–88, 299n.17, 308
Rayo, Augustín, 257, 292, 297, 304
realism, 28, 138–40, 146–47, 182–83, 214, 215–17, 218–19, 312–13
redundancy theory, 6–7, 35–38, 40–41, 44–48, 52–53, 61–62, 71–72, 109, 160–61, 200–1, 287–88
reference, 54–55, 98–99, 136–37, 149
 causal theory, 54–55, 136–37, 199–202
 deflationism, 16, 23, 75, 82–83, 135–36, 199–200, 271–72, 301–2, 314–15
 inflationism, 23
 self-, 155–56, 224, 240–41, 242n.12, 255n.22, 282
regimentation, 21–22, 78–79, 240–42, 307
replacement theory, 90, 225–26, 238, 240–43, 245, 250–51, 290n.3
Resnik, Michael, 111
resolution of the semantic paradoxes, 14–15, 58, 63–64, 67, 74–75, 82, 103–4, 107–8, 155–56, 224–30, 235–38, 240–42, 244, 255–58, 261–62, 265n.30, 270–72, 278, 281–84, 299–303, 314–16
revenge
 immunity (RI), 228, 240–41, 244, 252, 257–58, 260–62, 270–71, 274–75, 279, 283–84, 302, 313–14
 problem, 228–30, 240–42, 242n.13, 257, 259–60, 270–72, 274, 279, 281, 284, 301–2
revolutionary theorizing, 225–26, 238, 241–42, 289–91
Rosen, Gideon, 214, 218–19, 225–26, 289–90
Rossi, Lorenzo, 157–58, 165, 168, 174
Rumfitt, Ian, 37–38, 42, 203–4, 294–96
Russell, Bertrand, 4–5, 40n.10, 219–20
Russellian, 40–41, 65–66, 99

Scharp, Kevin, 265, 276–77, 289–90
Schiffer, Stephen, 114–15, 178
Schindler, Thomas, 10, 12–13, 97–98, 151–52, 161–62, 172, 174–77, 269–70, 288–91, 298, 303–6
Schnieder, Benjamin, 185–86, 189–92
semantic
 argument, 164–65, 169
 ascent, 69, 80–83, 125–26, 304–5, 307–8
 completeness, 281
 conception of truth, 49–50, 52–53, 158n.19
 concepts/notions, 76–77, 133, 180, 215–17, 229, 241–42, 301–2, 314–16
 consequence, 159, 165, 172–73
 content, 160
 defectiveness (s-defectiveness), 300, 301–2, 309n.24, 311–14
 descent, 22–23, 83, 174–75, 211, 307–8
 discourse/terms, 1–2, 16, 53–54, 86–87, 215–17, 238–39, 301–2, 309n.23, 314–15

epistemicism, 262–75
externalism, 143–44
inheritors, 59–60, 231, 258–60, 300–1
looping, 299–302, 311–12
paradoxes/pathology, 14–15, 18n.16, 21n.20, 37n.5, 58n.1, 63–64, 67, 71, 74–75, 85n.12, 89, 96–97, 103–4, 155n.10, 224–26, 228–30, 235–37, 239, 244, 257–58, 261–62, 271, 275–76, 278–79, 282–84, 299–303, 311, 313–16
pretense-involving fictionalism (SPIF), 122–23, 308–16
principles (*see* Bivalence)
redirection, 218–19
vs. syntactic conservativeness, 167–68
theory, 25–26, 29–30, 44, 77
value/status/characterization, 21n.20, 227, 228, 240–41, 249, 253, 254–57, 261–62, 270–71, 302–3, 313–14 (*see also* truth-value)
semantics, 28–29, 34, 172–73, 242n.12
classical, 14–15, 249, 253, 264–65
computational-role, 91–92, 220–21
conceptual role, 110–11
model-theoretic, 220–21
skim, 222–23
success, 42, 172–73
truth-conditional, 42, 215–17, 219–23
sentences (*see* truth-bearers)
sentential
quantification (*see* quantification, sentential)
variable (*see* variable, sentential)

variable deflationism (SVD), 41–42, 61–62, 104–5, 150–52, 287–91, 297–98
Shapiro, Stuart, 110–12, 116–19, 152–54, 160–61, 163–64, 170–75, 303–4
Simmons, Keith, 7–8, 12–13, 15–20, 36–37, 104–5, 207, 209–11, 242, 299
Soames, Scott, 35–36, 52, 54–55, 211–12, 241–43, 277–78
Sorites (*see* vagueness)
species, 1–2, 6–7, 16–17, 33, 57–61, 76–77, 91–94, 98–99, 107–8, 109, 120–21, 129, 141, 176, 179, 181–82, 187–88, 190–93, 200, 224–25, 295–96
Stalnaker, R., 219–20, 297–98
states of affairs, 95–96, 179–83, 193–95
Strawson, P. F., 48–52, 60–61, 66, 69–70, 91–93, 178, 180–81, 195–96, 227, 249–50
substantivism (*see* inflationism)
success argument, 119–20, 136–52

Tarski, Alfred, 15, 23, 31–32, 34, 52–56, 78–80, 82–85, 87, 91–92, 94, 99, 124–26, 130, 133, 135–36, 155–56, 157–58, 161–62, 169, 199–200, 201–2, 220, 222–23, 224–26, 229–30, 235, 238–44, 250–51, 257–58, 290–91, 298–99
Tennant, Neil, 159, 168–70
traditional theories of truth (*see* inflationism)
treatment of paradox/pathology, 15, 21n.19, 63–64, 225–26, 228–29, 232n.7, 242, 256n.24, 262, 279, 282, 301–2, 313–14
trivialism, 226–27, 275, 279–83, 302

344 INDEX

truth, 1–2, 3–33, 34–56, 57–101, 103–5, 109–31, 133, 135–52, 153–81, 204–6, 207–23, 225–28, 230–32, 233–40, 242–44, 245–56, 258–59, 263–72, 275–78, 280–81, 283–85, 287–92, 296–316
- ascriptions, 5–6, 6n.3, 7–8, 13–14, 28, 32–33, 47–48, 50–52, 55–56, 71, 78–79n.8, 80, 96, 97n.17, 110–13, 115–18, 179, 231, 236, 275–76, 277–78, 313–14
- conditions, 5–6, 9, 19–22, 24–25, 26–27, 29–30, 32–33, 37, 39, 42, 44, 47, 53–54, 58, 63–64, 67, 69, 90–91, 103–4, 107–8, 113–15, 124, 129, 143–46, 184, 212, 214, 219–22, 224–26, 245, 249–50, 262–63, 265–66, 278, 281, 284, 301–2, 303, 308–9, 311, 313–14
- definition, 7–8, 38n.6, 38n.7, 38–39, 40n.10, 41–42n.11, 53–56, 79, 82–83, 85, 87, 91, 98–99, 102–3, 124n.6, 133, 158n.19, 201–2, 219–20, 222–23
- theory, 13–14, 24–28, 30–33, 43, 47–48, 50–51, 55–56, 57–58, 68, 71, 93–94, 96–99, 100–1, 107–8, 110–11, 124, 125n.9, 129–30, 153–64, 166–71, 172–73, 174–75, 202, 204–6, 238n.11, 238–43, 263, 264n.27, 266–67, 275–76, 290n.3, 299 (*see also* inflationism)
- value, 20–23, 36, 77–78, 157–58, 209–10, 228, 239, 245–50, 259, 263–65, 270n.41, 271, 278, 283n.53, 302–3

truth-apt, 21–22, 214–18, 236, 302–3, 313–14

truth-bearers, 3–4, 7–8, 57, 76–77, 93, 95–96, 153–54, 176, 182–83, 194–96, 200, 233–34 (*see also* truth, ascriptions)

truth concept, 1–2, 4, 6, 13–14, 18–20, 25–26, 34, 44–45, 48, 52–54, 56, 57–58, 61–62, 83, 91, 93–96, 98–99, 103–4, 115, 122–23, 135–37, 146–47, 152–53, 164, 168, 190, 200–2, 204–6, 207–23, 231–32, 264n.27, 276–77, 284–85, 290n.3, 313

truth predicate, 5–6, 7–8, 16–17, 22–23, 25–27, 32–33, 33n.25, 36–37, 38–42, 45, 46–47, 49, 50–51, 71, 76–78, 79–81, 85, 89–92, 94, 95–96, 97n.17, 99–100, 101, 107–8, 110–18, 120–21, 122, 126–27, 137–38, 150–51, 152–56, 157–63, 164–67, 170–71, 174–77, 190–92, 196–97, 204–6, 210–11, 217–18, 222–23, 226, 236, 238–40, 242–44, 246, 248–51, 255n.22, 270n.40, 280, 284–85, 290, 302n.20, 305–7, 309–10, 312–14
- function/operation, 1–2, 4–5, 10–13, 22–23, 26–27, 31, 33, 35–36, 41, 43, 45, 49–51, 54–56, 57–58, 65–66, 71, 75–76, 78, 80–84, 84n.10, 85–90, 93–96, 98–99, 100, 107–8, 109–10, 120–23, 125–26, 129–30, 135–43, 145–49, 152–54, 159, 166, 174–78, 196–97, 200–6, 207–8, 210–12, 214–15, 222–23, 232, 236n.10, 238, 287–88, 290, 297–98, 299n.17, 303–5, 306–7, 312–14
- meaning/definition, 13–14, 30–31, 35, 38–39, 53–54, 57–58, 78–79, 82–83, 85, 86–87, 91, 94–96, 98–99, 101, 127–131, 158n.19, 200–1, 313

truth-maker theory, 21–22, 177–96, 200n.50, 310–11

truth property, 3–4, 7–8, 12n.12, 13, 23–24, 26–28, 31, 35–36, 38, 48, 50–51, 59, 71, 74–75, 93–94, 96, 98–99, 135, 159, 178, 190–93, 196–99, 204–6, 207–8, 220–21, 233–35, 276–77, 284–85, 297–98, 312–13
truth schema (TS), 5–6, 8–11, 13–14, 21–23, 30–33, 38n.8, 52–54, 59, 79, 94, 96–97, 124–26, 128, 130–31, 133, 153–56, 161–62, 164, 184, 187, 189–90, 192–93, 195–96, 201–3, 220, 224, 231–37, 242–44, 252n.20, 252–54, 261–62, 264, 265n.31, 266n.35, 275–78, 280, 288n.1, 293, 298n.16, 301–3
   explanation of instances, 5–6, 12n.12, 22–23, 31–32, 233–34
truth-talk, 3–4, 7–17, 26–33, 46–52, 57–78, 82–84, 100–1, 109, 112–14, 126–31, 135–36, 138, 141, 148, 150–52, 159, 174–76, 190–92, 203–6, 210–11, 213–15, 221–22, 233–36, 284–85, 287–91, 293–307
   descriptive role, 4–5, 8, 33, 49, 51–52, 57–58, 69–70, 78–79n.8, 176, 233–34, 314–15n.29
   expressive role (*see* expressive, role/capacity/function)
truthteller, 246, 248–50, 259, 279, 301–2
T-schema (*see* Convention (T))
T-sentences/T-biconditionals (*see* truth schema)

Undefinability Theorem, 31–32, 155–56, 238
ungroundedness, 227–28, 245–50, 259–62, 268–69, 270–71, 275–78

untruth, 239, 249–51, 261–62, 274
use
   independence vs dependence, 89–91
   /mention collapse, 314–15
   theory of meaning, 48, 98–99, 101–2, 118, 220–21 (*see also* meaning, theory)
utterances (*see* truth-bearers)

vagueness, 229, 256, 262–65
validity, 209–10, 211–12
van Fraassen, Bas, 135–36, 188–89
van Inwagen, Peter, 12–13, 213
variable
   absorption, 293–95, 299
   objectual/nominal, 9–10, 17n.14, 40n.10, 45, 84n.10, 98, 120–21, 233–34, 293–94
   predicate-position, 305, 314–15
   schematic, 84n.10, 86–89, 131–32
   sentential, 5–6, 8–13, 39–42, 45, 61–62, 64–66, 71–72, 73–74, 97, 100, 104–5, 122–23, 131, 133–34, 156n.12, 187–90, 192–93, 208, 210–11, 232, 287–88, 291–306, 308–13, 315–16
   substitutional, 12–13, 64–65, 86–89, 99–100, 103–5, 296–97

Waxman, Daniel, 154, 157–60, 165, 167–72
Williams, C. J. F., 64–70, 72–74, 299n.17
Williams, Michael, 139–40, 142–43, 146–50, 222–23
Wittgenstein, Ludwig, 46–48, 61–62, 219–21, 229–30, 292
Wrenn, Chase, 150–52, 186
Wright, Crispin, 3n.1, 184–86, 202–6

Yablo, Stephen, 151–52, 292, 297, 301–2, 304, 307